LYBEAUS DESCONUS

EARLY ENGLISH TEXT SOCIETY

No. 261

1969

PRICE 50s.

Lybeanus stode þan
And lay don þere a man
for nouȝyng nolde þey sayȝe
þ þorte seyde þan
þys ys fend sataā
þt mankende dyȝt for fayȝe
for wham Lybeanus aryȝste
After hys forste draȝȝte
he slep for euer mayȝe
But sone he das be sette
As þey þys yn a notte
þt symply wondes sayȝe

Deolf knyȝtes all tryȝst
he sade come yn þe foryst
yn armes cleȝr & bryȝt
Alday yey hadde y þost
And þonz yn þe foryst
to slo Lybeanus þe knyȝt
Of sute were all treȝlfe
þon das ye lord hym self
yn pyme to jade a wyȝt
þey þmyte to hym all at ones
And þorte to broke hys bones
And felle hym doun yn fyȝt

þe myȝte wen þey þruȝe
And þorȝes lode wyne
Among hem all yn fere
So harde yey gone yyuȝe
þe strokes gone out syyuȝe
fram schold & holmes cleȝr
Lybeanus stonz of hem þy
And ye founȝ gone to flo
And þoyst naȝt nyȝhe hym nere
ye lord stolede yn y schour
And hys sones four
So felle hay lynes yere

þ jonne ye payþes yyue
he aȝone hem fyue
fauȝt as he seyȝe þod
noȝȝ þoy gone hym doun
As watery yey doȝ of clyue
Of ham hym ran þe blode
As he das noȝ y styl
hys swerd brast yn þe hylt
ye das he mad of mode
ye lord a þrok hym sette
þonȝ helm & baruet
þ yn þe schold hyt stode

A swoȝt he fell a doun
An hys hynde a þoun
As man y das made
hys fomen wey swȝt betū
To porȝes hys rekcoun
þyroll mayl and plate
As he gan soȝe swuȝte
up he prllede hys hoȝte
And beþouȝt of hys state
An ox he houte all boun
At hys hynde a þoun
All most hym þouȝte to late

þan be storȝede he hy as at nyȝt
ye fades hewede doun wȝt
he smot at strokes þyo
ye lord seȝ y syȝt
And on hys conyþey lyȝt
A wey he ganto flo
Lybeanus eruo longey abode
But aftyr hym he þode
And onyey a þostoyn tyo
þ he hadde hym an hyo
But ye lord hym yeld
At hys dylle to be

The m[ess]age with grete honoure
went to kynge Arthoure
And saide kynde kynge
this childe to be werronge
And to do suche labo[ur]
go not worthe a sethynge
or that go thus . . . lady fre
he shall do batayllco thre
wyth oute eny lesynge
att poynte gilonge
Ayein syde the chapell of Mountpou[n]
shall be his begynnynge
Syr lybens than answoorde
yeth was gnon a ferde
for dred of wordys sore
to fyght with spere and swoorde
Saundell hane of . . . lerde
therefore many midid gathe to slowe
that man that floyth by way or strete
q wolde the doryll hed broke hur nekt
whor on go hym tale
also q wolde he were to drawe
And with the wynne to walwe
till the danse ta tale
the batayll q endn tale
and now none for say false
As git to londe lewo
the kynge saide anone ryght
than yettyt thare none of knyght

Lambeth Palace MS. 306, f. 76r

LYBEAUS DESCONUS

EDITED BY

M. MILLS

Published for
THE EARLY ENGLISH TEXT SOCIETY
by the
OXFORD UNIVERSITY PRESS
LONDON NEW YORK TORONTO
1969

PRINTED IN GREAT BRITAIN

TO
G. V. SMITHERS

FOREWORD

In this edition of *Lybeaus Desconus* the two best copies (those of MSS. Cotton Caligula A. ii. and Lambeth Palace 306) have been printed as parallel texts. The remaining four copies of the romance attest a very high degree of variation from these and from each other, and since it has not proved possible to set out any of them in full, I have tried to make their essential characteristics plain (together with those of such lost sources as are implied by the groupings of variants) by presenting these variant readings in sections. As might be expected, a much greater degree of diversity is offered by the continental versions of the story; so much greater, indeed, as to make it impossible to deal with these at all adequately within the limits of the present edition. I have therefore restricted myself, in the Introduction, to a brief discussion of the chief episodes of the story, indicating, where possible, the form which these seem likely to have assumed in the earliest developed version of it. In the Commentary I have made reference to the cognate romances only where they can throw light on detail contained in the ME. version, or where they can be used to support readings in one of the parallel texts against the variants offered by the other.

I wish to thank Professor G. V. Smithers for his most detailed and valuable supervision of the original form of this edition, from its beginnings to its submission for the degree of D.Phil.; Mrs. D. R. Sutherland, for constant friendly help in Old French matters; Professors J. A. W. Bennett and E. J. Dobson, for criticisms and suggestions made at the viva voce examination; members of the Council of the Early English Text Society and the Honorary Secretary, Mr. R. W. Burchfield, for advice given over the long period during which the edition has been reshaped for publication; and the librarians and staff of the libraries of the British Museum, Bodleian, Lincoln's Inn, Lambeth Palace, and of the Biblioteca Nazionale, Naples. And it is especially pleasant to record the debt that I owe to my wife; without her never-failing encouragement this work would never have been completed.

CONTENTS

INTRODUCTION

I. THE MANUSCRIPTS

C. British Museum MS. Cotton Caligula A. II: paper, ff. 1–141 and 144–210; parchment, ff. 142 and 143, with four fly-leaves at the front and two at the back. Binding and first and last fly-leaves modern (August 1957), as are the present gatherings. The size of the original page averages 21 × 14 cm. ff. 1, 2, 13ᵛ, 140ʳ–143ᵛ, 148ᵛ–156ʳ, 207ʳ–208ᵛ, and 209ᵛ–210ʳ were originally left blank. There are two systems of foliation; the earlier sequence begins at the first item and does not take ff. 141–3, 149–55, and 207–8 into consideration; the latter begins at the first contents list. This volume is made up of two distinct manuscripts bound together in the seventeenth century.[1] *Lybeaus* appears in the first of these, which contains thirty-nine items. Of these, eight are romances: *Eglamour of Artas* (ff. 5ᵛᵃ–13ʳᵇ), *Octouian imperator* (ff. 22ᵛᵃ–35ʳᵇ), *Launfal miles* (ff. 35ᵛᵃ–42ᵛᵃ), *Lybeaus Disconus* (ff. 42ᵛᵇ–57ʳᵇ), *Emare* (ff. 71ʳᵃ–76ᵛᵇ), *The Sege of ierusalem* (ff. 111ʳ–125ʳ), *Cheuelere Assigne* (ff. 125ᵛ–129ᵛ), and *Isumbras* (ff. 130ʳᵃ–134ʳᵇ). The texts of *Sussan* (ff. 3ʳ–5ʳ), *The Sege of ierusalem* and *Eustache* (ff. 137ᵛ–139ᵛ) are defective.

The present state of MS. Caligula A. II does not permit us to determine the original collation, nor can this be reconstructed from what can now be observed of the sequence of watermarks.[2] Of these last the *raisin* of ff. 3–13 stands fairly close to Briquet's no. 12999, the date of which (1451–6) agrees very comfortably with Rickert's suggestion that ff. 1–139 were written between 1446 and 1460.[3] All of these leaves appear to be the work of a single scribe. All prose items are in single columns; verse items may be in single or double columns. The number of lines to the page varies from 25 to 44. In the text of *Lybeaus* the dimensions of the area covered by writing are approximately

[1] See E. Rickert, *Emaré* (E.E.T.S., E.S. 99 (1906)), p. ix and note.

[2] There are no catchwords.

[3] Because they contain Lydgate's *Nightingale* (ff. 59ʳ–64ʳ) and a short Latin chronicle extending to the reign of Henry VI (ff. 109ʳ–110ᵛ). See also O. Glauning, *Lydgate's Minor Poems* (E.E.T.S., E.S. 80 (1900)), pp. xxxvii–xxxviii.

17 × 12 cm. Spaces have been left for capitals on ff. 17ʳ, 39ʳ, and 111ʳ; the initial letters of ff. 14ʳ–69ʳ and 134ᵛ–135ʳ are touched in with red, of ff. 3ʳ–13ʳ, 69ᵛ–134ʳ, and 135ᵛ–139ᵛ, with yellow.

L. Lambeth Palace MS. 306: paper, ff. 202 with one fly-leaf at the front and two at the end. The binding, which is of leather on wood and stamped with a roll design, is Tudor;[1] the backing is modern. The manuscript was secured by two clasps; these are now missing. The page averages 29·5 × 21·5 cm. and has been trimmed along its length (see, for example, ff. 7ᵛ, 9ʳ, and 10ʳ). The foliation is modern. *Lybeus dysconeus* (ff. 73ʳ–107ʳ) is the only romance; other items in the same hand are *Cronycullys of Englonde* (ff. 1ʳ–17ᵛ), *William Conquerour* (ff. 17ᵛ–18ᵛ), *The names of the kepers and Baylyffes of the Cite of london in the tyme of kynge Richarde the fyrst* (ff. 18ᵛ–46ʳ),[2] [*The Adulterous Falmouth Squire*] (ff. 107ʳ–110ʳ), *Sent gregoris Trentall* (ff. 110ʳ–113ᵛ), medical prescriptions and a tract on the humours (ff. 114ʳ–126ᵛ), *The lyve of Sent Evstas* (ff. 127ʳ–131ᵛ), and *This is the maner to kepe haukes* followed by two shorter items connected with hunting (ff. 166ʳ–176ʳ). With the exception of the pages covered with notes by the historian John Stowe (who names himself on f. 52ᵛ) and with medical prescriptions, the remainder of the manuscript is taken up almost exclusively with short love lyrics and historical and religious poems;[3] the longest items are Lydgate's *Horse, Goose and Sheep* (ff. 142ʳ–145ʳ, defective), Lychfelde's *Complaynt of Criste* (ff. 145ʳ–152ʳ), *The Stacyons of Rome* (ff. 152ᵛ–165ʳ), and *A Fable of a Wryght that was maryde to a pore wydows dowter* (ff. 178ʳ–187ʳ). ff. 188ʳ–201ᵛ contain a printed life of *Saynt Wenefryde*.[4] *Lybeus* and some

---

[1] The decoration on the binding consists of Oldham's roll AN. g. 1 and his ornament I. 2 which he records on bindings of books printed between 1504 and 1512 (J. B. Oldham, *English Blind-stamped Bindings*, Cambridge, 1952, p. 43).

[2] These and other historical items from this manuscript are printed in J. Gairdner's *Three Fifteenth Century Chronicles* (Camden Society, N.S. 28 (1880)).

[3] A number of these are included in F. J. Furnivall's *Political, Religious and Love Poems* (E.E.T.S. 15 (1866 and 1903)).

[4] For a complete list of the contents of this manuscript, see M. R. James

other items have been assigned numbers, but the sequence is fragmentary and is certainly a late addition to the manuscript. ff. 1–112 are made up of fourteen quires of eight leaves; after these the collation up to f. 187 is 15^1 (f. 113), 16^8 wants 1–3, 17^8 18^6 wants 6, blank, 19^{10} 20^{16} 21^8 22^{12} 23^{10}. The evidence of catchwords, signatures, and watermarks shows that quires 7–9 (ff. 49–72) were a late insertion. The majority of the leaves written in the principal hand[1] are marked with an *anneau* which although it cannot be certainly identified is very close in size to Briquet's no. 685 (1447), whereas ff. 49–72 carry a *main* surmounted by a five-leaved flower that closely resembles his no. 11166 (1505). The remaining quires offer a variety of marks of which the *tête de bœuf* of quires 16 and 22 (ff. 114–18 and 166–77) is surely Briquet's no. 14323 (1460 and 1467), and the *demi-bœuf* of quire 23 (ff. 178–87) his no. 2740 (1460–2). It seems very likely that the original manuscript was assembled *c.* 1460 and that it assumed its present form at the beginning of the sixteenth century. The first date is supported by the fact that the third of the items in the principal hand ranges as far as the fourth year of the reign of Edward IV (1464).

The pages in the principal hand normally contain 31–34 lines, and in *Lybeus* the area covered by writing averages 19·5 × 7 cm. Frames have usually been ruled on ff. 1–48 and 73–186, enclosing an area that averages 19 × 12·5 cm. Capitals in red are found throughout this part of the manuscript, and on ff. 73^r–113^v and 175^v–176^r the first letters of lines are generally touched in with the same colour. From ff. 132^r to 141^v the hand varies considerably in size but the letter forms are those of the principal hand; on ff. 142^r–165^v and 178^r–187^v, however, some differences are apparent. ff. 142^r–165^v carry large ornate capitals sometimes filled in with yellow or green. Throughout the manuscript we find traces of ruling, sometimes with ink but most often with a stylus.

H. Lincoln's Inn MS. Hale 150: parchment, ff. 125 plus one seriously damaged fly-leaf at the front and part of a deed[2] as

and C. Jenkins, *A Descriptive Catalogue of the Manuscripts in the Library of Lambeth Palace*, Cambridge, 1930–2, pp. 421–6.

[1] ff. 1–46, 73–113, and 119–31.
[2] See G. V. Smithers, *Kyng Alisaunder*, ii, pp. 3 f.

fly-leaf at the back; two paper fly-leaves at the beginning and end. The binding is of leather; the page size averages 31 × 13 cm. The contents are as follows:

   (i) *Libeus Desconus*, f. 1, ff. 4^r–12^v (defective).
   (ii) *The History of Merlin* [*Arthour and Merlin*], f. 13, ff. 2^r–3^v and 14^r–27^v (defective).
   (iii) [*Kyng Alisaunder*] ff. 28^r–90^r.
   (iv) *Bellum Troianum* [*The Seege of Troye*], ff. 90^v–108^v.
   (v) *Plowman Piers*, ff. 109^r–125^v (defective).

ff. 14–121 comprise nine regular quires of twelve leaves; no two leaves of ff. 122–5 are conjugate but ff. 1–13 are the remains of two further quires of twelve leaves. With the help of the Lambeth and Naples texts of *Lybeaus* we can establish that these were made up as follows (with the missing leaves indicated by Roman numerals):

   Q^i i, ii, 4, 5, iii, 6, / 7, iv, 8, 9, v, vi.
   Q^{ii} vii, 1, viii, 10, 11, ix, / x, 12, 13, 2, 3, xi.

This result is confirmed by the arrangement of the hair and flesh faces of the leaves. The foliation is modern.

Many of the leaves are damaged, and the condition of ff. 1^r and 125^v suggests that these must have formed the outer leaves of the manuscript for some considerable period before it was given its present binding. All the items are in single columns; the rectangular frame-ruling averages 26 × 9·5 cm. In *Libeus* the area covered by writing averages 25·5 × 5·5 cm. and the number of lines to the page varies from 52 to 60. The whole manuscript is written in a single hand of the late fourteenth or early fifteenth century. Spaces have been left for capitals throughout, but only on f. 13^r has one been provided. There are occasional rough sketches and scribbles; an example of the first occurs on f. 9^r of the text of *Libeus*.[1]

A. Bodleian Library MS. Ashmole 61: paper, ff. 162 plus two fly-leaves (ff. i and ii) at the beginning and one (now f. 162) at the end. The binding is leather with two brass clasps. ff. 1–162

---

[1] It is of the hindquarters of an animal and is found alongside the description of the hunt in the forest.

are numbered but since the foliator missed a leaf after f. 29 the numbers run from 1–161 instead of 1–162 (this leaf has now been numbered 30 and the leaf after it—originally 30— 30*). ff. 9–161 of this foliation also carry an earlier (but post-medieval) sequence of numbers, but this too is faulty as the number 91 is given to both the ninety-first and ninety-second leaves, and the numbers run 1–91, 91–150, 160–2. This suggests that ff. 1–8 of the manuscript as it stands today were put in their present position after ff. 9–161 had been assembled and given the numbers 1–150 as far as f. 158 of the later sequence. At this point the leaves must have been recounted from the beginning and found to number 159 and the numbers 160–2 were then assigned to ff. *151–3 of this sequence. All references made in the paragraph which follows are taken from the later sequence of numbers (1–30, 30*–161).

There are forty items besides *Lybeus Dysconius* (ff. 38ᵛ–59ᵛ); other romances are *Ysombras* (ff. 9ʳ–16ᵛ), [*The Erle of Tolous*] (ff. 27ᵛ–38ᵛ), [*Sir Clegys*] (ff. 67ᵛ–73ʳ), and *Kyng Orfew* (ff. 151ʳ–156ʳ). Otherwise moral and religious pieces predominate; these include a life of *Seynt ewstas* (ff. 1ʳ–5ʳ).[1] The manuscript is made up of fourteen quires, which vary from eight to sixteen leaves; two leaves are missing after f. 65 and one after f. 98. Catchwords are given between ff. 8ᵛ and 136ᵛ. In the last two gatherings (ff. 151–161) only ff. 159 and 160 are certainly conjugate. ff. 1–8, 9–18, and 92–104 carry no watermarks, but the third to fifth gatherings (ff. 19–57) are marked with an *anneau* very like Briquet's no. 694 (1479), the sixth to eighth (ff. 58–91) with a *main* that may be his no. 11164 (1493–5), and the tenth to fourteenth (ff. 105–61) with a *licorne* that is almost certainly his no. 10116 (1488).

The leaves had already been folded across their width at the time that they were made up into this volume; they have subsequently been trimmed along all exposed edges and their dimensions now average 42 × 13·5 cm. All items are written in single columns with about fifty-four lines to the page. A few

---

[1] A defective contents list is found on a fragment that has been pasted to f. ii; this also contains lines 1–19 and 21–32 of *Seynt ewstas*. For a complete list of items, see W. H. Black, *A Descriptive, Analytical, and Critical Catalogue of the Manuscripts Bequeathed unto the University of Oxford by Elias Ashmole*, Oxford, 1845, pp. 106–10.

spaces have been left for large capitals and occasionally the frame and lines have been carelessly ruled with a stylus: the area covered by this frame averages 33 × 10·5 cm. The whole manuscript appears to be the work of the scribe who names himself *Rate* (*Rathe*, f. 107^r) throughout, and who was particularly addicted to using a fish and a flower as decorative motifs at the end of individual items and, on occasion, at the bottom of pages.

N. Biblioteca Nazionale, Naples, MS. XIII B. 29: paper, ff. 73 plus three fly-leaves. The leaves have been trimmed and their size averages 28·5 × 19·5 cm. The binding is of vellum with *MS di Poesie Tedeschi* written on the spine; on the front fly-leaf is written *Hampton Henry* in a sixteenth-century hand. The manuscript contains:

(i) Medical prescriptions, pp. 1–19.[1]
(ii) *Sir beuys of hampton*, pp. 23–79.
(iii) *Of seint Alex[ius] of Rome*, pp. 80–86.
(iv) *Libious Disconious*, pp. 87–113.[2]
(v) [*Sir Ysumbras*], pp. 114–15 (defective).[3]
(vi) [Chaucer's *Clerkes Tale*], pp. 119–46 (defective).[4]

pp. 1–20 and 23–142 comprise six quires, originally of twelve leaves each. There are catchwords but no signatures. The first quire lacks its tenth and eleventh leaves, of the twelfth (pp. 19/20) only a strip *c.* 9 cm. deep remains. The condition of p. 18 suggests that it was exposed for some time before the first quire was placed in its present position in the manuscript; it is not, however, possible to determine whether the tenth and eleventh leaves were already missing when the medical prescriptions were written down or were removed afterwards. Of the re-

---

[1] See T. Vallese, *Un ignoto ricettario medico inglese del xiv secolo*, Naples, 1940. p. 20 is blank except for a large *HC* (for *JHC*) in the centre.
[2] See the facsimile of ll. 1–90 in F. Steffens, *Lateinische Paläographie*, Freiburg, 1903, pl. 44*a*.
[3] pp. 116–18 were originally blank; the top quarter of p. 117 is now covered with four lines of Italian verse relating to the Invention of the Cross, in a hand of the late fifteenth or sixteenth century. The *Clerkes Tale* lacks the first five stanzas.
[4] At the bottom of p. 146 are eight lines which form an envoy to Lydgate's *Beware of Doubleness* (H. N. MacCracken, *Minor Poems of John Lydgate*, ii (E.E.T.S. 192 (1934)), pp. 438–42).

maining leaves, the second fly-leaf (f. ii) and pp. 21/22 form
a bifolium, as do pp. 143/144 and 145/146. pp. 1–20 and 23–
146 are marked with a *tête de bœuf* that resembles Briquet's
nos. 15068 (1462) and 15096 (1455); the first of these must
be ruled out if we accept the scribe's own dating of the manuscript (1457) as exact. On the front fly-leaf is a very indistinct
specimen of an *arbalète* that does not correspond to any listed
by Briquet; equally impossible to identify is the *bouc* found on
the bifolium formed by f. ii and pp. 21/22.

The medical prescriptions are written across the page; with
the exception of item (vi) the verse items are all in double
columns. Spaces have been left for capitals throughout the
manuscript but never filled in. A frame-ruling in ink is usual,
but in the earlier pages of *Beuys* a plummet has occasionally
been used; in the medical prescriptions, a stylus. In *Libious*
the area enclosed by the frame averages 21·5 × 14·5 cm., and
the number of lines to the column, 44. This romance is written
in a fifteenth-century hand identical with that of *Alexius* and
the *Clerkes Tale* and the second half of *Beuys* (pp. 56–79). Like
Libious the first two of these terminate with the formula *hic
pennam fixi penitet me si male scripsi*. In *Libious* this is preceded
by four lines of doggerel verse[1] immediately followed by *q[uo]d
More*;[2] at the end of the *Clerkes Tale* the formula is followed by
q[uo]d mprf, the drawing of a long-eared animal, the date
(*A[nn]o d[omi]ni* 1457) and a series of Arabic numerals from
one to ten.

Nothing is known of the way in which the manuscript first
came to Italy, but some light is thrown upon its later history
there by the drawings on f. ii and p. 21. On the first is a large
bell to which is pointing a hand with the index finger extended;
above this is written *Q[u]esto manuscritto in lingua tedesca*[3] *l ho
hauuto da Diomede le[o]nardis e fu primieramente* . . .; on p. 21 a
book and the head and shoulders of a man in sixteenth-century

---

[1] See the Appendix, Section (*f*).
[2] For some interesting if inconclusive speculation about More's identity,
see J. M. Manly and E. Rickert, *The Text of the Canterbury Tales*, i. 378.
The doggerel may perhaps have been inspired by a medical prescription on
p. 5, which tells how to make hair grow on any part of the body.
[3] *tedesca* has been deleted and *inglese* written above it.

costume are depicted. **Professor T.** Vallese has demonstrated[1]
that the philosopher Tommaso Campanella—who in his trial
for treason was defended by a member of the Leonardis family
—had used a bell as his personal emblem, and suggested that
the manuscript might have been given by Campanella to his
advocate as a token of gratitude. The Diomede of the inscrip-
tion has not been identified but it seems at least possible that the
drawing on p. 21 could be of him (it is certainly not of Campanella). If so, both the donor and the recipient of the collection
would be depicted on the bifolium; the first emblematically,
the second in a more representational manner.

P. British Museum Additional MS. 27879 (MS. Percy): paper,
ff. 268 plus three fly-leaves. The binding is modern and the
original leaves have been gauzed on both sides and inset in
larger frames of modern paper. These new pages measure
44·5 × 23·5 cm., the originals average 39 × 14·5 cm., but many
are fragmentary. Full-length pages are found on ff. 1, 30–258,
and 266–8; ff. 2–28 contain only the top halves of the leaves
represented and on ff. 259–65 are fragments of irregular size
and shape. The original manuscript was paginated; of this,
pp. *1–4, 13–14, 250–3, and 488–9 are now missing. The two
halves of pp. 59–60 appear on two successive leaves of the
present manuscript (ff. 28–29), while two faces of a single
leaf (now f. 63) carry the page number 127 and another two
(now ff. 187ᵛ and 188ʳ) the page number 379. The page now
contained on f. 188ᵛ was not assigned a number. The contents
list is given on ff. 266ʳ–267ᵛ and comprises 191 items;[2] on f. 268ʳ
there is an alphabetical list of titles. Because of the present form
of the manuscript the original collation cannot be deduced.[3]

The entire manuscript is written in a single seventeenth-
century hand. The number of lines to the page varies con-

---

[1] In *La Novella del Chierico di Oxford di G. Chaucer*, Naples, 1939,
pp. 7–10.

[2] The index describes items 1–13 as imperfect, and the first complete
text is that of *Sir Lambewell*. The contents of this manuscript are printed in
full in J. W. Hales and F. J. Furnivall, *Bishop Percy's Folio Manuscript*,
3 vols., London, 1867–8.

[3] The catchwords give no help here, as these are found at the bottom of
each complete leaf.

siderably (56–94) as does the layout of individual items. *Libius* (ff. 156ᵛ–171ʳ) like some other long pieces is divided into sections numbered in the left-hand margin. The area covered by writing in this text averages 38·5 × 6·5 cm. There are many marginal notes, usually glosses but sometimes suggesting emendations to the text.

II. TEXTUAL HISTORY AND AFFILIATION OF THE MANUSCRIPTS

Of these six manuscripts C and L have been chosen as our parallel texts, and before justifying this choice by an account of their relationship to each other and to the four remaining copies, it will be helpful to outline their most significant features.

MS. Caligula is sharply distinguished from all other texts in that (1) it alone preserves 430–41[1] and 688–99,[2] and (2) it omits a number of equally authentic passages that have been preserved in the other texts. A few of these omissions may result from slips in copying: the stanza left out after 1734 (L 1797–1808) begins with the same word as the one immediately following, while the half-stanza omitted after 15 (L 16–21) begins with a line that closely resembles L 23 (16). But some, at least, of the remaining passages omitted from C had made statements that were at odds with other parts of the narrative, and could thus have been excluded quite deliberately in order to make better over-all sense. The most likely instances are:

1. L 190–201 and 849–60. These criticize the hero for his lack of experience and breeding, shortcomings which although important in other versions of the story were hardly insisted upon by Chestre.[3]

2. L 1245–68. This rounds off the encounter with Otes in a spirit of great friendliness, and so contrasts oddly with

---

[1] Throughout this edition line references to Caligula are given without a prefatory symbol; those to Lambeth are preceded by L.

[2] See the notes to these lines in the Commentary.

[3] The omission of L 16–21, already mentioned as a possible mechanical error, may in fact have been prompted by the unflattering picture which the lines give of the hero. For Chestre's authorship of LD and of the 'Southern' *Octavian* (SO), as well as of *Sir Launfal* (SL), see *MÆ* xxxi (1962), 88–109.

the wholesale slaughter that had gone before. Moreover, L 1269 follows on more neatly from L 1244 than from L 1268, since there is then no abrupt change of subject from Arthur to Otes.

3. L 1305-16. This describes Maugys as a typically uncouth Saracen giant although in much of the fight which follows he acts like the conventional knight of the romances.

More difficult to explain (either as mechanical errors or as deliberate revisions) are the omission in C of L 49-54, L 502-13, and L 538-43. The second and third of these exclusions are to some extent complementary since between them they reduce the number of single combats between Lybeaus and the nephews of Selebraunche from three to two. They could therefore be deliberate, but it is not easy to grasp the reviser's motives in making them. Possibly he felt that it would be straining credulity too far to make so young and untried a hero cope successfully with three seasoned opponents, but if this is so his new version of the scene leaves much to be desired, since it is not much more plausible, and a good deal less consistent, than the original account had been.[1]

These 'revisions' of *C also raise questions about the circumstances under which their author had worked: did he make use of a written exemplar, or did he rely upon his memories of such a text? In fact, evidence can be found to support either hypothesis. When compared with the version of the text that lies behind MSS. A, N, and P—which can hardly be anything but the work of a *disour* who knew this and other ME. romances by heart[2]—that of C seems at once rather half-hearted in its treatment of the archetypal text and very clumsy from a mechanical point of view. The author of *ANP eliminated some of the more serious contradictions of Chestre's story by writing in a considerable amount of new material, as well as by omitting some of the old, but was generally careful

---

[1] See the note to 508-10. Nor does the absence of L 1305-16 remove all the incongruities present in the characterization of Maugys, since he is alluded to as a giant at a number of later points (1246, *et passim*).

[2] See the material contained in the Appendix, Section (c), and *MÆ* xxxii (1963), 11-23.

to present this new material in stanzas which, although simpler in their internal organization than those of Chestre,[1] yet possessed their proper complement of tail-rhymes, and so did nothing to interrupt the necessary succession of twelve-line units. In C, however, this succession is upset at a number of points; as we have noted, half-stanzas corresponding to L 16–21, L 49–54, and L 538–43 are omitted, and further six-line stanzas are produced by alterations of the tail-rhymes in the sections which correspond to L 417–40, L 1005–40, L 1821–32, and L 2049–87 (as well as others of fifteen lines). Such irregularity hardly suggests the work of anyone who set down from memory a text intended for public performance, and is better explained as the product of (1) the miscopying of certain rhyme-words by one scribe working in the C-tradition, and (2) the rather short-sighted attempts of a later copyist to set things right. On the other hand it must also be recognized that some of the alterations of C imply a degree of familiarity with the text that would hardly have been possible to a scribe who did no more than copy his exemplar line by line; the omission of L 190–201, L 849–60, and L 1305–16, if deliberately made, would reflect an awareness of later events in the story, as might the odd corruptions of rhyme that are found in 1753–8.[2] Perhaps we should assume that an early form of *C was indeed written down from memory, but that the later stages in this line of transmission were completely scribal.

The second part of this conjecture is supported by the number and nature of the small-scale errors of copying that are found throughout C.[3] Of these a few have been allowed to stand without alteration (172 *spyng*, 260 *swyw*, 286 *wych*, 331 *ste*, 887 *he*, and 1125 *her*[4]), but the great majority were at once corrected (within the line) by the scribe himself. Sometimes he has substituted a single letter for another (*fa* for *fe* 1121),

[1] See below, p. 19 n. 2.
[2] See the note to 2044–9. It should be added, however, that there are no examples of purely verbal anticipation in C more significant than the variants which it offers at 1180 f. and 1597 (which could depend upon 1321 f. and 1639 respectively). For the importance of such corruptions to the question of memorial transmission, see L. F. Casson, *Sir Degrevant* (E.E.T.S. 221 (1949)), p. xx.
[3] As in other texts contained in this manuscript: see p. 12 n. 3.
[4] See the Frontispiece.

sometimes inserted an omitted letter (*squy* for *sqy* 1457) or rearranged transposed letters (*help* for *hepl* 916); in a very few cases he has substituted a whole word for another of roughly similar meaning or force (*auȝte* for *hadde* 1027, *glad* for *good* 2047). In most examples it seems certain that the initial error was made by the C-scribe himself, since, although a dogged worker, who transcribed word by word (and sometimes, letter by letter),[1] he frequently lapsed into carelessness. All these characteristics emerge clearly at 1036, where his first attempt at writing the line (*þey seyȝ an hounde come stryke*) was deleted and rewritten as *þey sawe an hynde com styke*. Since this line occurs in the middle of a description of a hunt it is hardly imaginable that he should have been able to correct a mistaken **hounde* in his exemplar back to the archetypal **hynde*, by the light of his unaided intelligence; it seems very much more probable that the *hounde* of his first attempt—like the *styke* of his second—was a blunder of his own making, and that it was set right by making reference to a written copy in front of him. Here again, however, the case is not ideally clear, since a very small minority of the corrections of C look less like the restoration of readings already present in his exemplar than the rewriting of certain forms of *C in terms of a less idiosyncratic system of spelling. Thus at 1163 the **poȝ* of *C is deleted and followed by *doþ*; at 1217, **þongede* by *þonkeþ*.[2] This type of correction is of some help in deciding the ultimate provenance of the distinctive orthography of C, and the contents of an earlier form of the Caligula manuscript.[3]

MS. Lambeth is quite free from the omissions of C, and since it likewise shows no trace of the spurious interpolations of *ANP and is not defective in the manner of H,[4] it is fundamentally the best text of those available to us. Unfortunately,

---

[1] A further indication that he could not have been responsible for the larger-scale alterations, already discussed.

[2] See the Frontispiece and compare SO 1084 where *toȝþ* (*a*) is blotted and is followed immediately by the more comprehensible form *toghe*.

[3] See below, pp. 38 f. That the C-scribe was not responsible for all the errors in his copy is also suggested by the greater density of these in *Lybeaus* (LD) and the immediately preceding copies of *Octavian* (SO) and *Launfal* (SL) than in any other text in the manuscript.

[4] H does, however, include three stanzas that appear to derive from a pre-archetypal copy of LD. See below, pp. 17 f.

however, its textual history has been complex and its surface is pitted with a large number of minor corruptions, some of which imply a connexion with an earlier form of MS. Ashmole.[1] A few of its errors seem auditory rather than scribal, notably L 1696 *shoved* for **sat*, under the influence of 1695 *shafte*, and L 1894 *dysseyved* for **betrayd* under the influence of 1893 *dismayed*, but these may result from a habit of pronouncing lines aloud as they were copied, and certainly do not allow us to suppose that the text was written down from memories of a public recitation of *Lybeaus*.[2] Other corruptions in L suggest that its immediate source (*L) was very difficult to read at some points: see, for example, L 932 *Off hir no loose make J* for **Of her noreserye*, or L 1035 *Hit blowis motis jolelye* for **Hit blowis Sir Otis de Lyle*.[3] There are also signs that this source-text was seriously damaged at L 43–48 and 88–93, since at both these points doggerel sequences have been substituted for half-stanzas of the original in a way that suggests that part of the bottom of the first leaf in *L was missing. If so this text would have contained approximately forty-eight lines to the page, and the manuscript in which it appeared would have been similar in appearance to MSS. Hale 150 and Ashmole 61, both long and narrow 'holster-books'. A third seriously corrupt passage, L 208–13, is, however, in a different category since here very few of the words of the original have been lost, although much fresh material has been added. L 208 *That man that fleyth by wey or strete* suggests that in *L two consecutive verses resembling those found at the same point in N (*The man that fleith for drede* / *Bi wey othir bi strete*) had been written as one and the sequence of tail-lines disrupted in consequence. But corrupt as it is this passage reveals a feeling for the tail-rhyme stanza that is quite absent from L 43–48 and 88–93.

Besides these corruptions lines corresponding to 209, 346–8, and 737 are lacking, and an extra line has been inserted after L 481. A large number of alterations to the text have been

---

[1] See the note to L 896.

[2] As opposed to the memories of a written text that resulted in the *ANP version of *Lybeaus*.

[3] Further examples are given by Kaluza in his edition of *Lybeaus* (*Altenglische Bibliothek*, v), Leipzig, 1890, p. xxix.

made by a corrector[1] between lines 1 and 658, and 2093 and 2146 (and sporadically elsewhere). Sometimes, as in L 19–20[2] these 'corrections' serve to eliminate incongruous detail or smooth over rhymes that were obviously imperfect,[3] but for most of them the scribe can have had no authority stronger than his own fancy. The great majority of them, indeed, merely tinker with the spelling of certain words, often by erasing or supplying final -e or by substituting one form of that letter for another.

The interrelationship of the six texts that we possess is complex but it is easy to discern three fundamental groupings: ANP, HANP, and LHANP. In Kaluza's stemma[4] (which provides a convenient starting-point for any discussion of the texts) these are represented as x, y, and z:[5]

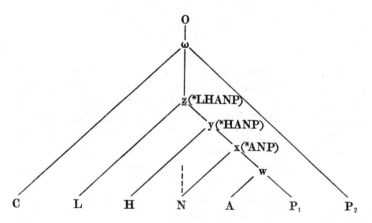

The first two of these groupings (ANP and HANP) are supported by a mass of very striking common readings, many of

---

[1] Who is probably distinct from the scribe of L in spite of a certain similarity of hand.

[2] Where the youthful savagery of Lybeaus is turned into a wise passiveness: see the footnotes to these lines.

[3] As in the substitution of *leerde* for *lerned* in L 206 and *dismaysed* for *dismayde* in L 226.

[4] Op. cit., p. xxxviii. I have replaced I as the symbol for the Lincoln's Inn text by H.

[5] The reality of his fourth 'lost source', w (*AP), is a good deal more doubtful. See below, p. 24.

which are obviously inferior to their counterparts in CLH or
CL: these are set out in detail in Sections (*b*) and (*c*) of the
Appendix. That of LHANP—which is of crucial importance
to the textual independence of C and L—rests upon a much
smaller weight of evidence but it is put beyond reasonable
doubt by the absence in these five texts of two perfectly
authentic stanzas that are found in Caligula: 430–41 and 688–99.
Also of importance, though not quite conclusive in itself, is the
absence of 460–2 in these texts[1] and their replacement by less
authentic-looking material. At some points, however, the case
for the textual independence of C and L seems undermined by
the fact that they coincide in readings that seem either corrupt
in themselves or are shown, by making reference to the analogues of LD, to be less 'authentic' than variants preserved in
HAN(P). Thus at 2058 both texts disrupt the sequence of tail-
rhymes by substituting *chaunterye* for the *charmure demanded
by the third line of its stanza, and at 859–61, 1710, and before
L 2193 they alter or omit motifs that seem to have formed a
genuine part of the story of the Fair Unknown. Strictly speaking, of course, any common error that cannot plausibly be explained by the workings of coincidence must imply descent
from a single corrupt antecedent, but when such 'errors' are
found in a romance as popular as *Lybeaus* they are capable of
being quite differently explained. We have only to assume a less
than perfect archetype (or even original) and free revision by
later copyists, for the 'errors' of CL to transform themselves
into survivals from the common source of all extant texts, and
for the 'authentic variants' of HAN(P) or AN(P)[2] to be seen as
moderately intelligent acts of rewriting, with or without the
support of a version of LD that was superior to the archetype.
This reversal of perspective seems justified by what we can
infer of Chestre's mode of composition and of the character

[1] See the note to these lines. There are also a number of points at which
LHANP agree against the reading of C, but since very few of these readings
are certainly common errors they could derive from the archetype (Kaluza's
ω) and have been first corrupted in *C.
[2] Many readings which P must originally have shared with HAN or AN
have been eliminated by the later influence of texts of LD belonging to
quite different manuscript traditions. See below, pp. 25-27.

of *HANP and *ANP,[1] since these intermediate copies were clearly the work of scribes who were thoroughly familiar with the romance, recognized some of its weaker points, and 'improved' it by substituting or interpolating fresh material. As might be expected, the primitive form of these revisions has been obscured by subsequent corruption of a more mechanical kind, but their essential nature is beyond doubt; their authors had differed from Chestre in degree rather than kind, and, like him, had relied to a large extent upon their memory in compiling their own versions of the story.

The most interesting of the apparent 'common errors' of CL are three which involve the rejection of material (preserved, of course, in the other texts) that seems to have formed part of the traditional story of the Fair Unknown:[2]

(1) BD 1711–13 give the following account of the equipment of Giflet li fius Do (Gyffroun le Flowdous LD):

> Ses escus a argent estoit,
> Roses vermelles i avoit,
> De sinople les roses sont.

With minor variations, the floral motif is clearly reproduced in HANP (*dyʒt al wiþ floures*), but the corresponding passage in CL (859–61) is much less close to the French:

> Of þe selue colours
> *And of non oþer flowres*[3]
> Was lyngell and trappure.

(2) Both BD 3309 and W 4172–4 describe the lady oppressed by the enchanters as being of royal birth. The same point is made in the Lincoln's Inn and Naples MSS. of *Lybeaus*,[4] where she is said to be *of kynges kynne*, but the CL variant (1710) makes her only *of knyʒtes kynne*. (3) W 9561 ff. describe

---

[1] The first of these topics is discussed in *MÆ* xxxi (1962), 88 ff., the second, in *MÆ* xxxii (1963), 11 ff.

[2] Since none of the surviving romances of the Fair Unknown will account for all the significant material in LD, we have to infer the pattern and contents of Chestre's source (or sources) from the most important of these cognates. The contents of these are outlined and their relationship discussed in Section IV of the Introduction.

[3] This line is discussed further in the Commentary.

[4] MS. A is independently corrupt at this point, and P has been influenced by a text in the C-tradition.

the reunion of the hero with his father, Gawain, and as such are reflected in the first of two stanzas which HAN place immediately before L 2193, but of which no trace remains in either C or L. At first sight this stanza could be held to point to borrowing into *HANP from some other version of the story of the Fair Unknown (a version derived from Wirnt or his source), especially since the motif is not clearly presented by any other extant version of the story but the late and composite *Giglan*. But we can hardly ignore the fact that, despite extensive corruption, these stanzas[1] suggest Chestre's manner more firmly than any later interpolations would seem likely to do; they are certainly much less idiosyncratic than the extra passages found only in ANP. Particularly striking is the way in which the first stanza exhibits two tendencies characteristic of Chestre's work as a whole: a rearrangement of source-motifs that produces an illogical sequence, and the sudden introduction of a fresh character into the tale. The account which W 9606–10 had given of the meeting between Gawain and Wigalois was orderly and natural: father and son are the first to embrace (*si sich underkusten*) and the son then tells his wife to greet Gawain and the knights accompanying him. In HAN, on the other hand, Gawain, quite without preamble, makes himself known to his daughter-in-law, and is embraced by her before his son has even recognized him.[2] Furthermore, no more abrupt introduction of a long-forgotten character into the narrative[3] can be imagined, than the mention of *Sir Gawayn knyȝt of renoun* immediately after the description of the way in which minstrels were honoured at the wedding feast (L 2190–2).[4] These facts combine to suggest that the three stanzas of HAN(P), like the variants which these texts offer of 860 and 1710, derive, not from any continental version used to supplement

---

[1] Together with a third found in HANP after L 216.
[2] See Section (b) of the Appendix.
[3] A tendency particularly marked in Chestre's *Octavian*.
[4] In W 9613–40 his sudden arrival is explained as the result of a letter sent to him by the hero. *ANP had tried to soften the impact of the insertion in *HANP by writing in an introductory stanza in which the mother of Lybeaus (who materializes even more unexpectedly than Gawain had done) introduces him to his father. No exact parallel to this scene can be found in any of the cognates, although Carduino's mother comes to Arthur's court, at the end of the story, after being sent for by her son (II. 69).

Chestre's romance, but from that romance itself. At first sight, this view would imply that there was, after all, a common (corrupt) source for C and L, in which such 'genuine' material was first omitted, but the total evidence of variants puts this out of the question. We must rather suppose that *HANP, far from being essentially superior to the source of C and L, was in fact a meeting-point of two distinct manuscript traditions. Of these, one was inferior to the general source of all six texts; the other (drawn upon to a much lesser extent) had contained genuine material that was left out of this archetype. This explanation may appear perversely complicated, but it is the only one that will explain all the facts, and the process of fusion that it implies was a reality in the transmission of ME. romance texts: for proof of this we need look no further than the Naples and Percy copies of *Lybeaus* itself.[1]

The variants peculiar to ANP are of less importance to the textual independence of C and L, since all those which offer readings that are in any way preferable to those of the other texts can be explained as the work of a redactor who possessed considerable knowledge of other vernacular romances, but who worked without the supporting authority of any second (and better) text of LD. The most striking example of such variants in ANP occurs at 232, where, as in 221, we learn the name of the fourth of the knights who help to arm Lybeaus. The significant feature here is that whereas ANP must derive from a source in which he was named Agravain at both points,[2] CLH refer to him as Agravain in 221 but Lancelot in 232. The obvious explanation—that the mistake first appeared in a common source of CLH—cannot hold, since there is virtually no other reason for suspecting that these texts were particularly closely related. It can only be assumed that the corruption was already present in the archetype,[3] and set right in *ANP on the scribe's own initiative. Such independent correction would have required no great powers of intelligence, since the two stanzas involved are consecutive, and there is other evidence

---

[1] See below, pp. 23–27.

[2] There has been much corruption in the Ashmole and Naples texts: see the Names of Persons and Places.

[3] In view of Chestre's own carelessness in such matters, it is even possible that the error goes back to the original.

to show that the redactor of *ANP was of a rationalizing dis-
position and familiar with a number of the characters and
motifs of Arthurian romance.[1]
It is clear from the above examples that the archetype was
already imperfect in some of the statements which it made;
there are also one or two suggestions that it was not always
perfectly regular in form. At one point, at least, the rather
demanding pattern of rhymes in the *Lybeaus*-stanza (*aabaab-
ccbddb*)[2] may have been simplified to the more common and less
exacting *aabccbddbeeb*: *fyghte* L 1389: *myght*:*laughte*:*vnsaught*.
Here and in the Ashmole text the spelling distinguishes
between the two couplets making up the *a*-rhymes in a way
that suggests they had no longer rhymed together;[3] only in
the variant sequence of C (*fyȝte* 1327: *myȝte*:*myȝte*:*vn-syȝt*) is
a full set of *a*-rhymes suggested, and this has all the marks
of being a late attempt to eliminate the distinction preserved
in L and A.[4] A second example of this type of distinction seems
at first to be provided by *rod* 2044: *abod*:*glad*:*hadde* (a sequence
offered by C and P alone). But it is far from certain that this
sequence had formed part of the archetype; it is much more
credible that it was created in *C to make good a gap in the
archetype, and subsequently taken over into the supremely
'mixed' text of *P.[5] It is, however, intimately bound up with
the one disturbance of rhyme that must have been present in
the archetype: the substitution at 2058 of *chaunterye* (further
corrupted to *sorcerye* in AN)[6] for the *charmure* required to
complete the sequence of tail-rhymes. This change initiates
a sequence of stanzas of which the first and second couplets do
not rhyme together (since they had stood as the second and
third couplets—*aa*, *cc*—in the stanzas of the original), and the

---

[1] See the note to L 474–6.
[2] For the main varieties of the tail-line stanza, see Kölbing, *Amis and
Amiloun*, pp. xiv f.
[3] N is still more confused (*fouȝt*:*myȝt*:*rauȝt*:*vnsauȝt*); P widens the gap
between the two couplets (*man*:*then*:*caught*:*ffought*); H is defective.
[4] The variant offered at 1330 is relatively weak, and the form *vn-syȝt* is
not attested elsewhere (see, however, the note to 1327–31). That the scribe
of *C was not familiar with *vnsauȝt* is perhaps suggested by its rendering
as *vp sawȝt* in 632.
[5] See below, pp. 26 f.
[6] H and P are both defective at this point.

correct definition by tail-rhymes is not restored until 2092–4.
It may be noted, in conclusion, that what we can infer of
Chestre's rhyme-technique makes it highly unlikely that the
first and third, at least,[1] of these sequences can derive from his
original. For in spite of the demands of his chosen stanza, and
his familiarity with texts in which the two schemes of *aabaab-
ccbddb* and *aabccbddbeeb* had alternated,[2] he seems much more
likely to have secured his quota of rhymes by sacrificing normal
contextual sense or extending the semantic range of words in
rhyme-position, than by ever reducing the number of words
rhyming on a single phonetic group.[3]

Once we have granted that the archetype could misrepresent
the pattern of rhymes of the original, it becomes likewise
plausible that it should have tampered with the metrical
regularity of that text. But although the manuscript evidence
suggests that some of its lines were less smooth than others,
it is dangerous to reject them as spurious simply because they
do not conform to a generalized notion of the metrical structure
of the line. The need for caution here is pointed by the totally
divergent views held by Luick and Kaluza on the metre of LD.
Luick, who gave the prosody of the work a cursory glance in
the course of a study of ME. alliterative poetry, decided that
the majority of the lines had contained two lifts, although he
conceded that some could be read more comfortably by giving
them three or even four stresses.[4] Kaluza, on the other hand,
after a very much more exhaustive study concluded that in
LD both couplet and tail-lines had contained three beats and
that the light and heavy stresses had alternated with complete
regularity.[5] In an appendix to his study of the prosody, he raised
some objections to Luick's recently stated position,[6] but his
own is in fact weakened by its tacit insistence upon the metrical
regularity of the text and the possibility of defining this in

---

[1] Although he might have passed the sequence* *rād:abād:glad:hadde*:
compare *j-māde* 85:*bad:glad:had*.

[2] In MS. Auchinleck: see especially the tail-line conclusion of *Guy of
Warwick*. For his knowledge of this collection (or of one very like it) see
Kaluza, op. cit., pp. cxlv–clviii.

[3] See the note to 952–3.   [4] *Anglia*, xii (1889), 442 f.

[5] Once allowance had been made for certain metrical licences: see
pp. lx–lxix of his edition.

[6] Op. cit., pp. lxix–lxxiv.

simple terms. Neither of these assumptions can pass un-
questioned. Chestre was a hack-writer who had a borrowing
acquaintance with a number of other ME. romances[1] and
since almost all of these were composed in a metre palpably
different from that of *Lybeaus* he might from time to time have
incorporated into his *gleichmetrische strophe* phrases that were
not easily digested by the 'three-beat' impulse. But even if we
grant that the movement of the line has its own kind of regularity,
this is hardly to be described in terms as simple as those of
Kaluza. One marked feature of Chestre's style in this romance
is its use of alliterative phrases (roughly one line in six is
affected) and these may bring complications of their own into
the verse. Where they are composed of three alliterating words
they naturally fit in very well with a 'three-beat' scansion
(L 424 *To fell his fone in fyght*) but where only two words are
involved there is a pull away from this norm, negligible when
the line contains a third word that is bound to be stressed to
some extent (L 504 *Had lorne bothe mayne and myght*) but more
serious when such a word is lacking (L 53 *With thi mery mouthe*).
For this reason I tend to regard *Lybeaus* less as a work in which
the same parts of the stanza must everywhere exhibit the same
metrical structure[2] than as one in which two distinct metrical
impulses existed side by side: one towards the regular alterna-
tion of light and heavy stresses, the other emphasizing certain
key (usually alliterating) words, and that now one, now the
other would predominate.[3]

Of greater importance to any attempt to distinguish between
original and archetype are a limited number of couplet lines
which appear to be hypermetric; some of these, indeed, by
containing one stress more than the tail-lines which follow
them are distinguished from the latter in the manner of the
great majority of tail-line romances in ME. Kaluza recognized
the existence of such lines in some or all of his texts, and with

[1] Proof of this is offered by most pages of the Commentary.

[2] A metrical principle which Bülbring regarded as fundamental (*Unter-
suchungen zur mittelenglischen Metrik*, Halle, 1913, pp. 5 and 7).

[3] This aspect of the three-beat tail-line was noted by Trounce (*MÆ* ii
(1933), 36 f.). Luick recognized that the metrical antecedents of LD were
mixed, and the two-lift and three- or four-beat lines 'keineswegs scharf von
einander geschieden, sondern bunt vermischt' (loc. cit. 443).

his characteristic instinct for tidiness chose to restrict them to two clearly defined groups of stanzas (L 1–42 and L 1677–1724)—a move which allowed him to explain them away as the work of a later redactor who, faced with two obvious gaps in the text from which he was working, filled them in to the best of his ability.[1] It is difficult to accept this theory. (1) In content and style the stanzas in question differ very little if at all from the rest of the work (as we might surely have expected them to do if written by someone other than Chestre).[2] (2) The rhymes of the first stanza (L 1–12) evidence a shift of EME. $\bar{e} > \bar{\imath}$ that is also found in Chestre's *Octavian*,[3] but in relatively few other texts; it is a rather odd coincidence that the unknown redactor should also have been familiar with it. (3) It is only in Kaluza's edited text that these stanzas contrast so sharply and consistently with the rest of the poem, and this can hardly carry much weight when we remember that his text was designed to reproduce the metrical perfection that he assumed to have been a feature of LD. In fact, a number of the 'spurious' couplets can be read more naturally with three stresses than with four (17 *For douute of wykkede loos*), while hypermetric lines are also found in parts of the text that, according to Kaluza's theory, should have reflected the original with fair accuracy (853 *Þan syȝ þey Gyffroun come ryde*).[4] Of course objections such as these do not affect the *general* plausibility of the view that LD was at first as regular in its metre as in its rhyme but that both were impaired at the archetypal stage; but they have the effect of making it almost impossible to use metrical regularity as an index of textual corruption at any specific point.

The above discussion, by throwing into relief the short-comings of the archetype, has done much to vindicate the textual independence of C and L, and makes it plain that a reasonably full idea of the archetype (though not necessarily

---

[1] The first of these blocks is not found in H (which is defective until L 216[d]) but otherwise both are to varying degrees 'irregular' in all surviving texts.

[2] Contrast the interpolations of *ANP.

[3] SO 1453 ff.

[4] It may also be noted that the 'four-beat' couplet lines of CL 1–2 are exactly reproduced at CL 2128–9 where they ought to conform to the regular 'three-beat' pattern.

Chestre's original) can be obtained from these two copies.[1]
There remains, however, the problem of choosing between
variants in these texts when neither is obviously corrupt or
clearly supported by material in the cognates. Such a choice—if
it is not to be wholly subjective—can only be made with the
support of the four remaining texts of LD, and (since L
belongs to the same manuscript tradition as these) this support
can only be given to C against L. But even where C is concerned, we cannot in practice accept the isolated support of
either N or P, since both of these texts have been contaminated
by copies in the C-tradition.

MS. Naples. Kaluza deserves the credit for pointing out that
N at times agrees with C in ways that should have been put
out of the question by its derivation (via *ANP) from *HANP.[2]
The following are the most striking of these agreements (minor
variations in spelling have not been recorded):

CN 128	*plex* (*fax* L, *haire* P)
CN 265	*Wylleam Celebronche* (~ *Dela[b]raunche* LHAP)
CN 322	*Wylleam* (*That he* LHA)
CLN 331 f.	*ago : also* (*away : say* H, *away : pray* AP)
CLN 369	*grace* (*space* HAP)
CLN 370 f.	*op : gop* (*anone : gon* AP, *anon : broun* H)
CLN 391	*susteres sones* (*emes sonis* HAP)
CN 664	*mornynge* (*evenynge* LHAP)
CLN 726	*He haþ do crye and grede* (*And worthyest in wede* HAP)
CN 961	*regge* (*backe* LHAP)
CN 1106	*fulfelde* (*full* LAP)
CN 1767	*ly3t* (*tente* LHA)

At first sight, the small scale of these alterations gives plausibility to the suggestion that they were deliberate improvements
made with the help of a better text of LD—presumably introduced into *N over deletions or erasures in that text and then
neatly incorporated into the body of the transcript that has
survived. By this view, *N would have had much in common

---

[1] Making reference to H(ANP) when both C and L are independently
corrupt: see the variants of L 1031 and L 1034 (Appendix, Section (*b*)) and
of L 892 (Appendix, Section (*d*)).

[2] Op. cit., pp. xxiv-xxvi.

with the surviving Lambeth text of *Lybeaus*: like L it would
have been scarred by 'corrections' in its earlier pages[1] but left
fairly clean in the remainder of the text as the zeal of the
corrector declined. But a closer look at the evidence raises
some serious objections to the theory. Our suspicions are at
once aroused by the small number of observable corrections
(which would not have been remarkable had their author—like
the corrector of L—worked without the support of any better
text), and are strengthened by the absence in N of some of the
most characteristic readings of C(L), and the obscurity of the
'corrector's' motives: none of the affected readings in (L)HA(P)
is obviously corrupt, and the words that replace them never
seriously alter the sense (most pointless of all is the reversal of
the order of lines or rhyme-words at 298 f. and 391 f.). Altogether it is hard to believe either that these alterations were
deliberate, or that the group listed above (together with a handful of more dubious examples) can really exhaust their number.
When it is also remembered that the part of the romance in
which N offers the greatest density of apparent 'corrections' is
that in which A and P present the greatest number of 'common
errors',[2] it becomes possible to argue that (1) a respectable
number of corruptions in *ANP were eliminated in *N under
the influence of a text in the C-tradition, and (2) their elimina-
tion made the relationship of A and P in the first half of the
romance seem much closer than it really was.[3] A necessary
corollary of this view would be that what took place in *N was
less the deliberate correction of isolated readings than the
accidental fusion of two texts which represented distinct
manuscript traditions, by a copyist who relied to a large extent
on his memories of one or both of them. In this connexion it is
illuminating to refer briefly to the Caligula and Naples texts
of *Sir Ysumbras*—the only other work that is common to both
manuscripts—since a comparison of these brings out three
points that are of special interest to the present discussion.
(1) Despite the brevity of the Naples copy here (only 122 lines
of it have survived) there is no doubt that it is more closely

---

[1] See above, pp. 13 f.
[2] See the first part of Section (*c*) of the Appendix.
[3] And led Kaluza to postulate the lost source *w* (*AP).

related to the Caligula text than to any other.[1] (2) Where Naples is inferior to Caligula, its variants are often so considerable as to suggest a stage of writing down from memory.[2] (3) The presence in Caligula of a few corruptions from which Naples is free implies that either the latter text or its source (*N) must be derived from *C rather than the surviving Caligula copy. All these facts are perfectly consistent with— and indeed, actively support—our earlier hypothesis: that the scribe of *N had carried in his memory some of the material contained in MS. *C.[3]

MS. Percy. This text also bears witness to the fusion of distinct manuscript traditions, most obviously in that the connexion with A(N) so fully attested in the first half of the romance, (corresponding to L 1–908), becomes hardly perceptible in the second.[4] Kaluza, indeed, convinced that this second half (P_2) was free from all the omissions and interpolations of the other five texts, concluded that after L 908 the redactor of *P had turned from *ANP to an exemplar which derived independently from the archetype.[5] If matters were as simple as this we could agree with him that P_2 represents a third textual tradition and therefore offers a valuable guide to the authenticity of variant readings in C and L, since whichever of these it supported would have to be preferred. Unfortunately, matters are not simple: P is a text with an antecedent history long enough to allow for several layers of partial or total rewriting,[6] both as the result of independent rationalization by one or more scribes, and through contamination by texts belonging to quite distinct traditions. A close study of P_2 shows unmistakable signs of both types of revision. Loose ends in the narrative are tidied up

[1] See G. Schleich, *Sir Ysumbras* (*Palaestra*, 15), pp. 69 f. and 87. It certainly seems quite unrelated to the text of this romance preserved in MS. Ashmole 61 (which is greatly superior to those of Caligula and Naples).

[2] Short as it is, the Naples text has substituted four whole couplets of its own for more authentic variants in Caligula (at ll. 40 f., 46 f., 76 f., and 109 f. of Schleich's text).

[3] The use of *C by *N is further discussed on pp. 38 f.

[4] See Sections (*b*) and (*c*) of the Appendix.

[5] Op. cit., pp. xxxv ff. In his discussion he derives P_2 directly from Chestre's original, in his *stammbaum*, from the archetype.

[6] See the note to L 192.

at L 2049–57 and 2038–40, while at L 1247 and L 1311–12 we find corrupt readings that can only be derived from *L.[1] Furthermore, the connexion with AN never quite disappears: Kaluza noted a number of points at which PA or PNA agree against CL in the second half of the story,[2] and there are others at which PN here agree against CL(H)A.[3] When all these facts are borne in mind, even the most impressive example of the 'authenticity' of P_2—its version of 2044–94—cannot unhesitatingly be accepted as proof of familiarity with a pre-archetypal text of *Lybeaus*. It is true that, once allowances have been made for subsequent corruption, this passage implies that *P_2, in marked contrast to any other text, here offered a sequence of stanzas of which the first two couplets rhymed together;[4] of these stanzas the most significant is that corresponding to 2044–55, since only in C and P does this offer a possible set of four *a*-rhymes (*rode:abode:glad:had* P), and only in P a full set of *b*-rhymes (*crye:tormentrye:barronye:Marye* against *wylle:vylanye:a-gye:Marie* in C). In themselves these two features could add up to reasonable proof of the textual independence of P_2, but we have also to take into account the corruption of *charmure* to *chaunterye* at 2058 in CL, and this suggests a quite different explanation of the 'good' stanzas in P_2. For the corruption at 2058, which clearly goes back to the archetype,[5] can only be understood on the assumption that in this text, as in the present copies of LAN, three lines had been missing after 2046; without this gap there would have been no reason for altering the rhyme-word so that it might be linked with those at L 2123, 2126, and 2129. And if this was so, the three lines that are now found only in C and P (at 2047–9) must first have appeared in a version of *C, probably as a reminiscence of 1756–8, which follow three that strikingly resemble 2044–6.[6] From this text they would have

---

[1] See the notes to these lines. An example of rationalization in P_1 is mentioned in the note to 397.   [2] Op. cit., p. xxxvii.

[3] At L 971 (*renoune* NP, *raundoun* CLHA), L 987 (*smote* NP, *sat* CLHA), L 1232 ((*him*) *home* NP, *hym* CLA), and L 1905 (*come ride* NP, *rod* CLA). The same opposition is found in P_1 at L 235, L 536, L 540, and L 726).

[4] The stanza corresponding to 2056–67 has been lost, and subsequent alteration of certain rhyme-words in 2068–91 has converted this section into four six-line stanzas.   [5] See above, p. 19.

[6] See the note to 2044–9. A clearer case of the insertion of lines in *C to fill out a defective set of tail-rhymes is found at 1002, 1004, and 1006.

been incorporated into an antecedent of P, and the redactor of this or some later copy must have then set right the archetypal distortions of tail-rhymes in the stanzas which followed. As always, we return to the view that the textual history of P has been so radically confused by eclecticism and rationalization[1] that, although some of its readings might have been derived from a pre-archetypal text, it is impossible to be dogmatic on this point, especially since (in contrast to some passages in HANP) none is supported by the evidence of any cognate romance. For this reason agreement with P can never be used as proof of the authenticity of any given reading in either C or L.

The variants listed in the Appendix are grouped under the following heads: (a) those which confirm the superiority of a reading in C over its counterpart in L; (b) those derived from the common source of HANP; (c) those derived from the common source of ANP; (d) those peculiar to H; (e) to A; (f) to N, and (g) to P. A division of this kind has a number of advantages: section (a) is of particular use to the reader who confines his attention to the two best texts of Lybeaus and wishes a guide to their relative authenticity; (b) and (c) give detailed support to views expressed about the affiliation of texts; all sections except (a) allow us to form some idea of the special characteristics of a number of texts of the romance, both extant and lost, that for reasons of space cannot be printed in full. But it must be remembered that the transmission of LD has been so complex that it is not possible to keep these categories completely watertight. In the first place, the fragmentary nature of H makes it impossible to be sure that some readings now listed as typical of *ANP were not also present in the full text of H, and so are really characteristic of *HANP. Second, since both the Naples and Percy texts betray extensive contamination of their common source with some version of *C it will often happen that one or both of them will no longer contain a reading that was in fact present in *ANP. Finally, any one of our texts is liable to have obscured its connexion with its closest relations by extensive corruptions of its own.

[1] See the note to 1295.

Of these complicating factors, the first is the most formidable, and we can only try to bear in mind which sections of H are now missing, when making use of material contained in (c). As far as the second and third difficulties are concerned, I have chosen to select the available reading which seems to stand closest to that of the common source (*HANP or *ANP), reproduce this with a minimum of emendation, and follow it, first by the symbol for the text in which it occurs, and then for those of the other texts, in descending order of fidelity. Where one or more of these texts offers significant variants of its own ('subvariants') these are normally given between round brackets at the appropriate point in the line; if, however, they are un-wieldy or seem especially typical of the text in which they occur, they are listed in the section ((d), (e), (f), or (g)) devoted to that text (where the line-number may be followed by a reference back to HANP or ANP), and the symbol for that text given between round brackets in the original reference in (b) or (c). If the common variant has been obscured in any of the members of the group as the result of contamination with *C, the symbol for the 'mixed' text (in practice, this always proves to be either N or P) will simply be omitted in the original reference. This means that there are a number of variants listed under (c) which are followed by the symbols AN or AP, instead of by the ANP that we should theoretically expect.

III. LANGUAGE AND PROVENANCE

The Language of the Archetype

The following are the significant or controversial features attested by the rhyme.

1. OE. $\check{æ}$ usually gives $\check{a}$; only in *was* 768, *wes* 946, and *pell* 1407 does it rhyme on $\check{e}$. However, these last three examples need not be SE. rhymes, since *wes* is a widely distributed form that must often have developed under conditions of reduced stress within the sentence (Luick § 363 A. 5, Jordan § 32 A. 3), and in OE. the form *pell* was not confined to the Kentish dialect area.

2. OE. $\breve{æ}+g+d$ gives $\bar{e}d$ in *sede* 980 and 1319, and *seid*
L 849; *aid* is found only in *sayd* 1823.

3. There are no sure indications of the quality of OE. $\breve{a}$ before
a nasal consonant. Even *lemman* 724:*woman*:*oon* [OE. $\bar{a}n$]:
swan is not conclusive, since in this text OE. $\bar{a}$ may have given
either $\bar{a}$ or $\bar{\varrho}$, and the rhyme here might thus be upon an unrounded no less than a rounded vowel. If the first, it would
be typical of the N. or N. Midlands; if the second, of the W. or
W. Midlands. Features of both dialects are attested in other
rhymes.

4. OE. $\breve{a}$ before lengthening consonant groups has probably
given $\bar{\varrho}$ but there are no conclusive rhymes. *strong* 1365:
wrong [OE. *wrungon*] need not imply the shift of *ong* > *ung*
which Jordan (rashly) characterized as W. Midland (§ 31),
since the vowel of the pt. sg. of *wringan* could well have been
levelled into the plural here.

5. The earlier diphthongization of OE. $\breve{e}$ after an initial
palatal consonant is suggested by pp. *for-ʒette* 591: *spyte* [OE.
spitu]: *wete* [OE. *witan*]: *sette* [OE. *sittan*]; compare SO 123
begete (pp) which rhymes on *wyte* (2 sg. pr. sb.): *spyte*:*ysmyte*.
The dialectal significance of such rhymes is not wholly clear,
since Jordan has claimed -*ʒiten* as a form typical of the 'E.
Saxon' dialect (§ 79), while in any case the phonetic environ-
ment of the stressed vowel might have caused raising in most
ME. dialects (Luick § 379).

6. OE. $\breve{e}+g$ has usually followed the normal ME. develop-
ment to *ai*, but gives $\bar{\imath}$ in *aweye* 1806: *jmagerye*:*eye*:*trye*. It is
customary to explain this special form of the adverb in terms of
descent from the *wig* of the OK. Glosses, but C. J. E. Ball has
recently suggested that the raising to $\bar{\imath}$ could have resulted
from a tendency to use the word in weakly-stressed position
(*RES*, N.S. 11 (1960), 52 f.).

7. OE. i may rhyme upon OE. or OF. $\bar{\imath}$: 3 sg. pr. *nys* 1247:
prys:*ryse* [OE. *hrīs*]:*Mauugys*. There are no clear examples of
$\breve{e}$:$\bar{\imath}$ rhymes. That the palatal spirant consonant was still sounded
in [içt] is suggested by the spellings of the best manuscripts
and confirmed by the fact that in 784 ff. the *a*-lines rhyme
upon [i:t] and the *b*-lines upon [içt].

8. In *pouʒt* 1978:*noʒt*:*be-cauʒt*:*a-bouʒt*, EME. [ouχt] has

shifted to [ɑuχt]. The same shift is implied by L 1389 ff.: see
the note to 1327–31.

9. Only self-rhymes of OE. *ŭ* are found, but lengthening of
the vowel before certain consonant groups is suggested by the
frequency of the spelling *ou* in this position. POE. **gung* (a.) is
everywhere represented by *ying* in rhyme.

10. OE. *ӯ* gives *ĕ* in some words and *ĭ* in others. *ĕ* is found in
dent 177, *bregge* 1252, and 3 sg. pt. *leste* 1736; *ē* in *schrede* 32
and *fyer* 571. *ĭ* occurs in *kynne* 1646 and *kyste* 2006; *ī* in *pryde*
L 182, *hyve* L 1313, and *kythe* L 1805.

11. Rhymes which involve OE. *ǣ*[1] and *ǣ*[2] do not point to
any consistent development of these sounds in Chestre's dialect.
Both may rhyme upon words which contain *ę̄* (*were* 119:*fere*;
y-mene 1666:*kene*), as on words with *ẹ̄* (*prede* 883:*red*:*heed*:
brede; *hete* 108:*mete*:*ete*:*y-sete*). Nor—as the last two sequences
demonstrate—can it be determined whether a following dental
consonant inevitably had the effect of raising *ę̄* from earlier *ǣ*[2]
(in *brede* and *hete*).

12. OE. *ā* gives *ǭ* in most cases. *so* 302:*þo* and *two* 305:*go*,
if exact rhymes, must be upon *ǭ*, and so imply that OE. *ā* was
not raised to *ǭ* when preceded by a consonant+*w* (Luick
§ 370). On the other hand, *ǭ* and *ǭ* are apparently linked in
rhyme in *op* 164:*sop* and *tolde* 1533:*bolde*:*gold*:*wolde*, and
if these are inexact, 302 ff. may be so too. Unrounded *ā* is
preserved in *hame* 52:*Jame*:*name*:*game* and *sare* 1134:*spare*:
for-fare:*euer-mare* and *sore* L 2051:*fare*:*care*:*bare*. *rod* 2044:
abod:*glad*:*hadde* is less certainly authentic: see p. 19.

13. In *chere* 576:*spere*:*per*:*brere*, *ẹ̄* appears to have been
lowered to *ę̄*, since not only is one of the rhyme-words OE.
speru, but the whole sequence provides the *b*-rhymes of a stanza
in which the *a*-rhymes must be upon *ę̄*. Such a lowering before
r is usually recognized as LME. (Luick § 431 and A. 2; Dobson
§ 126 and N. 4). Flasdieck distinguished the *a*- and *b*-rhymes
in this stanza by supposing the second to have been upon *ī* (and
thus further proof of the alleged SE. Midland shift of *ē* > *ī*
mentioned under (15) below), but in spite of the fact that one
of the rhyme-words is modern 'briar' (which must have contained *ī* before the Vowel Shift) the presence of *spere* in the
sequence makes a rhyme upon this vowel unlikely.

14. OE. *ē+g* regularly gives *ai* in *tway(ne)* 523, etc., and *ī* in *dye* 1103, etc. For these developments see Luick §§ 373 and A. 5, 378, 401, 407.1, and 408.1.

15. OE. *ī* rhymes with OE. *ǣ¹* and *ē* in *syde* 9:*nede*:*dede*: *rede*: compare the *wyde*:*ryde*:*chyde*:*stede* of SO. 1453 ff. Both sequences were used by Flasdieck in support of his theory of a SE. Midland shift of EME. *ē > ī* (*ES* lviii (1924), 11), but the LD rhyme, at least, is hardly to be explained in this way, since in the region he defined OE. *ǣ¹* would have produced *ā* rather than an *ē* that was subsequently raised to *ī*. It seems preferable to accept the rhyme as proof of a more general tendency to raise the vowel in ME. (Dobson § 136).

16. OE. *ū* appears to rhyme with [y] in *vs* (pro.) 1836: *aunterous*:*precyous*:*Jhesus*. But Central French [y] was often velarized to *u* in Anglo-Norman (Pope § 1142), and this development is reflected not only in N. and N. Midland texts in ME. but also in the London *Arthour and Merlin* (659 f. and 3437 f.); see p. 83 of A. Liedholm's study of the language of this romance.

17. POE. *ǎ+ld* gives *ēld* much more frequently than *ǭld* (9:1). However, the word involved is usually *teld(e)* (sg. and pl. pt. and pp.), quite often as part of a generally useful phrase like *as þe Frenssch tale teld* 2122. The phonological value of these rhymes is further undermined by the possibility that *teld(e)* is not the direct reflex of OE. *teald(e)*, but an analogical form based on the present: see *OED*. 'Tell' v. A. 2. δ and 3. δ (examples from N. and N. Midland texts are given).

18. *ǣ* before *hs* has given *ě* in *wax* 127:*plex*.

19. POE. *ǣ* before *ll+i, j* has given *ǐ* in *fell* 1847 and *fylle* 1950.

20. OE. *feolu* is represented only by the remodelled form *fale*, which Jordan claims as a SW. feature (§ 73 A. 2).

21. OE. *swī(o)ra* 'neck' gives *swyre* in L 253, 840, 1324, and 1896; only at 2007 does the word rhyme on *ē*.

22. The sequence *hewe* 1879:*schrewe*:*knew*:*fewe* is not quite clear, as the first word is a 3 pl. pt. in C and an infinitive in L. But the presence of *knew* suggests that we are in any case dealing with a rhyme involving both *ēu* and *iu* (for the shift of ME. *ēu > iu* see Luick §§ 399.2 and 407.3 and Dobson § 188

(*a*) and N. 1). Jordan suggested that these two diphthongs might genuinely have been rhymed together in popular poetry (§ 288), but the phonetic discrepancy is very great. If we could assume that *hewe* was indeed the infinitive form and that OE. *cnāwan* had been remodelled on the pattern of such verbs of Strong II as *hrēowan* or *brēowan* then the whole sequence could have rhymed upon *ęu*; on the other hand, a rhyme upon *iu* throughout might have been obtained if Chestre had known of variant (originally *ęu*-) forms of the words that should have contained *ęu*.

23. Three sequences involve vowels which are not under the main stress: *goules* 856: *oules*:*colours*:*flowres*; *tours* 1295: *Maugys*:*prys*:*ladyes*; and *leynthe* L 1305:*strenthe*:*be-thynke the*:*macched be*.

24. The rare plural form *bryn* [ON. *brýnn*] is implied by the *browyn*:*swyn* preserved in N at L 1311 f. See the note to L 1247.

25. No significant pronominal forms are found in rhyme but a survey of their spelling in the better texts of LD suggests that the forms used by Chestre were: 3 sg. fem. *sche* (*hy* 448, 449, *he* 1012); 3 pl. nom. *þey* (*hy* 338, *he* L 1126); gen. *har* or *her*; dative *ham* or *hem*.

26. The 1 pl. pr. ends in -*þ* in *goþ* 371: *oþ*, but the 3 pl. pr. in -*s* in *hewes* 1958: *Lybeauus*. The latter example is made less certain by the fact that the context demands a preterite form; since Chestre does not usually alternate present and past tenses in narrative passages, we may emend the noun to the oblique form *Lybeawe* found in 1913 (:*schrewe*) and the verb either to 3 pl. pt. *hewe* or *gan hewe*: see (22), above. As the hero's name rhymes on *ęu*(*s*) in 1669 and 1913, *gan hewe* is probably correct.

27. Syncopated present forms are *ryȝtte* 270 and *sytte* 276; within the line *ryȝt* 403, *stant* 737, and *halt* 1684 are almost certainly genuine. On two occasions Chestre seems to have taken over as part of a borrowed couplet a verb that is in form a syncopated present and to have used it with preterite force: see the note to 952–3.

28. The OE. ablaut pattern has been modified at a number of points: (*a*) the vowel of the singular has been levelled into the plural in certain verbs of Strong III: *to-braste* 320:*faste*;

faȝt 1031: *auȝte:kaȝte:saȝt*; *wrong* 1368: *strong:long:fonge*.
(*b*) Levelling of the plural vowel into the singular may have
taken place in the 3 sg. pt. *smyt* 497, 956, and 1350, but this
may equally well be a new weak preterite form on the analogy
of verbs such as OE. *cīdan* (Brunner, *Die Englische Sprache*, ii.
193). *set* 485: (*sket*) should represent OE. *sittan* but the *e* could
here have arisen through confusion with OE. *settan*. (*c*) In
vp-haf 247 and 637: *yaf* the 3 sg. pt. of OE. *hebban* seems to have
been attracted into Strong IV or V because of the similarity of
the vowel of the present stem to that of verbs such as *beran*
or *cwepan* (see Brunner, op. cit., ii. 216). This tendency is particularly common in texts of the S. and S. Midlands, but also
operates in Mannyng's *Chronicle* (11754).[1]

29. In the past participle OE. *ge-* was retained quite as often
as it was dropped. The final *-n* has disappeared everywhere
except in (*y*)-*s*(*c*)*layn* 1861, 1963, 2042, 2053, 2065, where it
was needed to provide a rhyme upon the name of the second
enchanter, *Yrayn*.

30. The vocabulary offers little that helps to localize the text.
A number of the words seem to have been of predominantly
Northern distribution: *awe* 183, *gryse* 597, *extente* 1195, *tyll*
1364 and 1846, *gate* [ON. *gata*] 1516, and *lende* L 1250, as well
as forms such as *wore* 404, 964, and 1275 and *slo* 533, 1929,
and 2019. As is usual, words that seem typical of the south are
rarer, but *molde* ('head') 841 and 877 and *wate* (adv.) 1548
deserve mention here, while *arsoun* in the sense of 'saddle'
(483, 623, 1614) seems to occur only in S. and London texts.

Much of the evidence contained in §§ 2, 10, 12, 17, 26, and
29 would be consistent with a SE. Midland place of origin, but
this localization seems at times to be called in doubt by a handful of rhymes that are typical either of the N. or N. Midlands
(see §§ 12, 21, and 30), or of the W. or W. Midlands (see
§§ 19, 20, and, perhaps, 5). Since these 'discrepant' rhymes
pull away from the basic linguistic type in two different
directions, they cannot be explained by assuming that LD was

[1] O. Boerner, *Die Sprache Roberd Mannyngs of Brunne*, Halle, 1904, pp.
229 f.

composed in some 'border region' between distinct dialectal types,[1] since none can be found that will account for all the significant features. Nor are we much advanced by a study of the rhymes of Chestre's other romances, the 'Southern' *Octavian* (SO) and *Sir Launfal* (SL).[2] We might, optimistically, expect that one or both of these works would offer a 'purer' type of ME. which we could regard as Chestre's own dialect, and which we could assume was later enriched as the result of his increasing familiarity with other parts of the country than his own. In fact, however, although SO and SL show no trace of the survival of OE. *ā* as does LD, almost all the other 'Northern' or 'Western' features are to be found in them: *wore* in SO 352, SL 99 and 174; *slo* in SO 1085, 1349, 1541, and SL 837; *tylle* in SL 537; *swyre* in SO 1121, and *fale* in SO 57, SL 480, and 496. On the other hand, it is something that the majority of the meaningful rhymes in SO and SL—whether they are of a type found in LD or not[3]—would agree well enough with localization in the SE. Midlands. In the last resort it seems that any peculiarities in Chestre's rhymes are to be explained not in strictly linguistic terms, but as an aspect of his eclectic mode of composition. Such rhymes, in fact, tell us less about his own dialect than about the dialects of some other writers of romances, from whose work he borrowed extensively. As several notes in the Commentary make plain, Chestre was very liable to combine with his primary source or sources— which were directly related to the story of the Fair Unknown— material drawn from romances of quite a different kind,[4] but which offered some local points of contact with his; and this

[1] For the dangers of this mode of interpreting evidence, see G. Wacker, *Über das Verhältnis von Dialekt und Schriftsprache im Altfranzösischen*, Halle, 1916.

[2] For a full consideration of the rhymes of all three works, see E. Fischer, *Der Lautbestand des südmittelenglischen Octavian*, Heidelberg, 1927.

[3] The most striking examples of the second group attest 'East Saxon' *ă* (in SO 553 [d]*an*, and SO 908 and 1479 *men*) and various Kentish features (*by* [OK *bīon*] SO 1260; *au* in *drawe* SL 609, and *hoth* ('heath') SL 250: see Fischer, op. cit., pp. 54–56, 134 f., and 154, and A. J. Bliss, *Sir Launfal*, pp. 9 f.).

[4] He was particularly attracted to the more 'heroic' romances (which gave prominence to encounters with large bodies of pagans); particularly important to LD are *Guy of Warwick*, *Bevis of Hamtoun*, and *Arthour and Merlin*.

material might include not only motifs and phrases, but whole rhymes, even when these last depended upon linguistic developments that had not taken place in his own dialect.[1] For this reason, although we must reject the idea that he was a native of a region lying between two clearly defined dialectal types of ME., he may yet be described as a product of a *literary* 'border-region' of some complexity, in that he had a wide, if erratic, acquaintance with other vernacular romances of widely-ranging provenance,[2] from which he—quite accidentally—seems to have devised his own private *Schriftsprache*.

Once it is granted that Chestre worked in this way, it becomes possible to clear up the problems posed by some of the less predictable rhymes of LD. The type represented by *spare* 1125: *for-fare*:*euer-mare*:*sare* is quite common in *Amis and Amiloun*, a work that was certainly known to him;[3] *iu* as the rhyme-value of OE. *hēaw* might have been suggested by the *sue* 9367: *hewe* of *Arthour and Merlin*,[4] while *wī* as the rhyme-value of 'way' appears in a number of other texts found in the Auchinleck manuscript.[5] It is also possible that Chestre was familiar with the (closely cognate) romance of *Sir Perceval*,[6] and this could have furnished him with the model for two of his most surprising sequences of rhymes: compare SP *hame* 324:*tame*: *name*:*dame* with LD 49 ff. and SP *betyde* 420:*stede*:*byde*:*ryde* with SO *wyde* 1453:*ryde*:*chyde*:*stede*. It is worth remembering that all the above sequences from SO or LD constitute the

[1] See especially the note to 952–3. An illuminating account of Chestre's use of the rhymes of the ME. *Landevale* in SL is given by Bliss, op. cit., pp. 5–8.

[2] It is possible that he was by profession a *disour* accustomed to give public performances of such works. Sarrazin, in his edition of SO, p. xxviii, suggested that by the time he came to compose LD he had acquired a familiarity with other (Northern) romances that he did not have when writing SO.

[3] See *MÆ* xxxi (1962), n. 84.

[4] Though this will not in itself clear up all the difficulties offered by LD 1879 ff.

[5] It occurs in *Sir Orfeo, Lai le Freine, Sir Degarre*, the tail-line portion of *Guy of Warwick* and, perhaps, *Arthour and Merlin*. Kaluza listed the most important borrowings from MS. Auchinleck (with the exception of those from *Arthour and Merlin*) on pp. cxlv–clviii of his edition; there is, however, some evidence of familiarity with other versions of several of the Auchinleck texts.

[6] See also p. 40, n 2.

a- or *b*-rhymes of their stanzas, where the need to provide four
words rhyming together would have made Chestre more than
usually prone to ease the burden of composition by drawing
upon his memories of other works in the same genre. This
acknowledgement of the 'literary' nature of some of the rhymes
proves of help in dealing with those couplings that appear
inexact: of ME. $\bar{e}$ with $\bar{e}$; $\bar{e}u$ with $\bar{e}u$; $\bar{o}$ with $\bar{o}$, and $\bar{\imath}$ with $\bar{\imath}$. The
classic explanation of such is that they are precisely what we
can expect in the work of a person of minimal literary taste,
writing for a 'popular' audience; but the logic of this may be
contested, both on the general ground that in a work orally
presented, weaknesses of rhyme would be made more than
usually obvious,[1] and on the more specific one that Chestre
again and again shows himself prepared to make almost any
sacrifices in order to secure a rhyme. He will endow words
with new or at least strained meanings, and introduce notions
that are either quite at odds with the immediate context of the
rhyme-word embodying them, or conflict with statements made
a very short period of time earlier.[2] That this versifier should
at the same time have been prepared to upset the smooth
succession of rhyme-words by introducing such palpably
clumsy couplings as the $\bar{e}u:iu$ suggested by 1879 ff. becomes
very difficult to credit. It seems much more likely that he would
rather have used variant forms of certain words (which contained a vowel distinct from that normally familiar to him),[3]
in order to achieve an over-all smoothness of effect.

The Language of MS. Caligula

More than any other surviving text of LD, Caligula reflects
in its spellings the dialectal type of ME. that is indicated by the
rhyme-evidence. What discrepancies there are can be explained
by the difference in date between the composition of the
original romance and the writing down of C, and by the fact
that within the line no mechanical considerations would have
impelled the scribe to introduce fresh 'discrepant' forms of the

---

[1] Thus Dobson § 108, n. 2.
[2] See particularly the notes to 344, 360, 643 f., 915, 952 f., 1547 f.,
1586, and 1844.
[3] For a detailed consideration of such forms, see Dobson §§ 106–8.

kind discussed above. The C-scribe's treatment of forms of this kind in his author's work is an interesting pointer to his own conservatism and to the fact that an unbroken tradition of texts set down in very much the same region must link C with Chestre's original. For he quite often spells words in rhyme-position in a way that accurately renders the sound demanded by the rhyme but which does not correspond with his spelling of the same words within the line. The following instances are particularly striking:

1. WS. *ǽ* is rendered by *e* only in the rhyme-words *wes* 946 and *pell* 1407.
2. 'Saxon' *ǽde* (Anglian *ǽgde*) is written *ede* only in 980 and 1319, where the rhyme demands it.
3. POE. **gung*, usually written *yong(e)* within the line, is given in rhyme as *ȝyng* at 94 and *ynge* at 1018.
4. OE. *ā*, usually written *o* within the line, is preserved as *a* in rhyme: *hame* 52, *euer-mare* 1131, *sare* 1134 and 1977.
5. POE. *ǽ+ld* normally gives *old* within the line, but in most of the examples in which it rhymes upon *ę̄ld* it is written *eld*.
6. POE. *ǽ+ll+i, j* in OE. *f(i)ellan* gives *ell* at all points except in rhyme at 1950 *fylle*.
7. Within the line OE. *fe(o)la* is represented only by *fele*, but *fale* occurs in rhyme at 1007 and 2110.[1]

At two points, however, the scribe's conservatism in rendering words in rhyme-position has broken down:

8. OE. *e* after an initial palatal consonant is written *e* in *for-ȝette* 591.
9. WS. and Anglian *weg* is written with *ey* in *aweye* 1806.[2]

To these differences between the archetype and the C-text may be added the following aspects of the orthography of the latter,

---

[1] The tautology of 1007 *fele yeres ferly fale* further suggests that *fale* was an unfamiliar form.

[2] Since neither C nor L presents the spelling demanded by the rhyme at these two points it may be that the substitution of *for-ȝette* for **for-ȝitte* and *aweye* for **awy* had already taken place in the archetype.

some of which imply developments unlikely to be clearly attested by rhyme:

10. OE. *a* before a nasal consonant is usually written *a* except in *ony* (90, etc.) and *þonkede* (650, etc.).[1]

11. OE. *i* in open syllable is written *e* in *wete* 70 and 585.

12. The palatal spirant consonant may have been effaced in *knytes* 1096 and 1827.

13. Shortening and monophthongization of EME. *au* and *ou* after the shift of [χ] > [f] appear in *doftyr* 689, *arafte* 1129 and *softe* 1972.[2]

14. Forms such as *þyngyþ* 196, *þyngeþ* 94 and 1479, the over-written *þangede* of 605 and the deleted *þongede* of 1217 suggest the voicing of intervocalic *nk* in either C or *C.

15. The symbols *d* and *þ* are frequently interchanged, as are *ȝ(t)* and *þ/th* (*clodeþ* 121, *wyth* 267), as the result of a series of related phonetic developments.[3]

This last feature, or group of features, is of particular interest to any study of the genesis of C, since some of the relevant spellings suggest a purely scribal extension[4] of what was originally a genuine—if rather sporadic—attempt to record some significant changes in the distribution of [θ], [ð], and [d], and that, therefore, such forms as *þay* ('day') or *de* ('the') were not first introduced by the C-scribe, but had an antecedent history perhaps going back to the original text of the romance. This suggestion is supported by two other points: (1) traces of the interchange of *d* and *þ/th* are also found in the Naples text of LD,[5] where they conflict with the predominantly

---

[1] The forms in *ng* noted under (14) suggest that the *o* may have developed because of lengthening of the original *a*.

[2] See Dobson §§ 240, 371.

[3] Which are defined by A. J. Bliss in *Anglia*, lxxv (1957) as 'the voicing of every initial [θ] to [ð]; the voicing of final [θ] in an unstressed syllable; and the change of every [ð], in whatever position, to [d]' (281). The article as a whole is most concerned with the relevant forms in SL, but a number of those in LD are also discussed.

[4] See in particular the note to 1139. The uncorrected *no deþ* of 1671 (*nothinge* L) may derive from an exemplar in which *d* had already replaced *þ* in *no d[yng]*.

[5] At a number of points the weak preterite ending is rendered by *-ith/-yth*, the dwarf's name is written *Deodelyne, Deodolyne*, and **mākid* (for L 1154 *mankynde*), *makith*.

Western colouring of the language and are probably derived
from the copy of *C that influenced *N in other ways;[1] (2) the
phenomenon is not attested to anything like the same extent
in the Caligula texts of *Eglamour* and *Ysumbras* (copied by the
same hand as LD), which stand near the beginning and end of
the manuscript respectively.[2] This unevenness of distribution
could suggest that the characteristic orthography of C had been
present in the three Chestre romances from the beginning,
and that subsequently other romances—not of SE. Midland
provenance—came to form part of the same manuscript
collection as these, and in being written down by scribes of the
region came to acquire their own, smaller, complement of
the typical spellings.

It is worth remembering that L. H. Loomis also suggested
the existence of a fourteenth-century ancestor of Caligula,
which already contained a number of the texts now forming
part of it. In this case the earlier form of the collection was
postulated to account for the full range of the familiarity with
popular romances that Chaucer displays in *Sir Thopas*; this
familiarity, Mrs. Loomis held, could most rapidly have been
acquired from personal contact with one or more manuscript
collections that contained a high proportion of romances. Of
the important romance collections that have survived, only MS.
Auchinleck could possibly have been known to Chaucer, but
since a number of romances—possibly or probably reflected in
Sir Thopas but not present in Auchinleck—are found together
in Caligula, she suggested that an earlier version of this collection may also have come into the poet's hands.[3] If this theory
is valid, the parody could offer a useful guide to part at least of
the contents of the Ur-Caligula, and the parallel passages
assembled by Mrs. Loomis in fact imply that it had contained
Lybeaus, *Launfal*, *Octavian*, *Eglamour*, and *Ysumbras* (as well
as the *Trental of St. Gregory*). This would push the appearance

[1] See above, pp. 23 f., and the note to 990–1008.

[2] That is, of the Vespasian D VIII part of the manuscript. We may also
note the curious coupling of *ope* 424: *rope*, which most probably entered the
text at some point intermediate between Chestre's original and C: see the
note to 424–5.

[3] See W. F. Bryan and G. Dempster, *Sources and Analogues of Chaucer's
Canterbury Tales*, London, 1958, pp. 488–90.

of *Eglamour* and *Ysumbras* in the same collection as LD rather further back than the evidence of the spellings might have suggested,[1] but in fact, as Mrs. Loomis recognized, the parallels with *Octavian* and *Ysumbras* (and, one might add, with *Eglamour*) are rather tenuous, and further caution is imposed by the defective nature of the Auchinleck MS.,[2] since this could originally have contained some others of the romances that seem to have left their mark on *Sir Thopas*. The theory remains an interesting one, even if it cannot be of much practical help to the present discussion. It may be added, incidentally, that Chaucer's use of such a 'fourteenth-century prototype' of C would be still easier to understand if, as seems likely, it had contained a smaller number of devotional pieces than the present collection, and had grouped its romances more tightly together; it would then have been still more obviously a collection of such works than its surviving descendant.

The Language of MS. Lambeth

The spellings of L indicate a type of ME. quite distinct from that of the archetype. Furthermore, its treatment of the more unexpected rhymes in that text is much less conservative than that of C, and suggests an antecedent manuscript history that was both more confused and more wide-ranging. At the following points the spelling of words in rhyme-position conflicts with the sound demanded by the rhyme:

1. WS. *ǽ* is represented by *a* in L 785, L 975, and L 1469.
2. 'Saxon' *ǽde* is written *eid* in L 849, *ayde* in L 1009 and L 1381.
3. POE. **gung* gives *yo(u)nge* everywhere.
4. OE. *y* is rendered as *i* or *y* much more frequently than the rhymes would allow.

[1] *Sir Thopas* has not been precisely dated, although J. M. Manly has suggested that it was composed in or shortly after 1383 (*E & S* xiii (1928), 73); see below, pp. 66 f.
[2] The sequence of numbers assigned to individual articles implies that certain of these have been lost: see A. J. Bliss, 'Notes on the Auchinleck MS.', *Speculum*, xxvi (1951), 652 ff. In its complete form it might have contained a text of *Sir Perceval* (see *Arthurian Literature in the Middle Ages*, ed. R. S. Loomis, Oxford, 1959, p. 480, n. 3), which seems to have provided both Chestre and Chaucer with material: see p. 35 above for Chestre's possible borrowings from it.

5. OE. *ā* gives *o* in L 64, L 1157, L 1160, and L 2051. In *strange* L 1427: *wrange*: *longe*: *fange* it is not clear whether the vowels are long or short.

6. POE. *ĕ*+*ld* gives *old* at all points.

7. POE. *ĕ*+*ll*+*i, j* is written *ell* in L 1322 and L 1921.

8. At L 1140 f. *fayne* and *slayne* are substituted for the *fawe* and *slawe* demanded by rhyme.

To these we may add the following distinctive features that are not (or not certainly) attested in rhyme:

9. OE. *a* before nasal consonants is normally written *a* although *o* is found in *gon, begon* and *con*.

10. OE. *e* is raised to *i* before *nd* in *hynde* L 1317 and between *f* and *l* in *fylle* L 1413.

11. OE. *i* is often represented by *e* in open syllables.[1]

12. OE. *u* in open syllable rhymes on *o* in *j-nome* L 1113: *some*: *come*: *grome*.[2]

13. Final *ng* has unvoiced to *nk* in *thinke* L 2088.

14. Final *nd* has simplified to *n* in *wyne* L 212, *lyne* L 1065, and *rowne* L 1597; note also the inverted spellings *bounde* L 476 and *bownde* L 894 and L 1200.

15. The group *ngþ* has given *nth* in *strenthe* L 175, L 1306, *lenthe* L 753, *leynthe* L 913, and L 1305.

16. The 3 sg. pr. ends in -is in *ridis* L 315 and *rydis* L 426, and *ledys* L 1467 (: *wedis*).

17. A present participle in -*ande* is *prickande* L 794.

18. The usual preterite forms of the auxiliary verb *ginnan* are *can(ne)* and *con(ne)*.

The above features reflect the confused textual history of L;[3] the general impression received is that the text is more Northern in character than either C or LD, but the absence of any secure examples of the retention of OE. *ā* prevents any more decisive interpretation.[4]

[1] This feature is prominent in the *Paston Letters*: see Luick § 394 and N. Davis, *The Language of the Pastons*, 1954, pp. 122, 126 and n. 14.

[2] In C the fourth rhyme-word is OE. *guma*.

[3] See p. 13, n. 1, above.

[4] It is noteworthy that the Ashmole text of LD also contains very few traces of this feature, in spite of some strikingly Northern forms within the line.

IV. THE STORY OF THE FAIR UNKNOWN
IN MEDIEVAL LITERATURE

Since limitations of space make it impossible to provide either detailed synopses of other versions of the story, or any full discussion of the points at which they radically diverge from each other, I have contented myself with giving, first, summary accounts of the eight principal cognates of LD, second, a brief discussion of the most important of the episodes of the story in the light of the evidence provided by these cognates, and, finally, the points at which Chestre's version appears significantly different from any other.

(a) *Li Biaus Descouneus* (BD) of Renaut de Beaujeu stands in its first half very close to LD. It lacks an introductory account of the hero's *enfances*, but summary details of his upbringing are given after the defeat of the enchanters. As in LD, he sets out from Arthur's court near the beginning of the romance, and there then follow, without a break, encounters with Blioblieris, the guardian of a ford (Wyllyam Selebraunche LD); the two giants; the three avengers; the huntsman knight, Orguillous de la Lande (Otes de Lyle LD); Giflet li fius Do, the knight who lays claim to the hawk (Gyffroun le Flowdous LD); Malgiers, the defender of the Île d'Or (Maugys LD); the seductive Pucele as Blances Mains (la Dame d'Amore LD); the steward Lanpart; the enchanters, Mabon and Evrain, and the transformed queen, Blonde Esmeree. All this, however, occupies little more than half of the total length of the romance, and after the preparations for the hero's marriage with the queen have been described, the action takes a turn that is quite without parallel in LD. Guinglain suddenly becomes filled with remorse at having deserted the lady of the Île d'Or, and on the advice of his squire Robert he returns to her land. When he meets her she is still very angry with him for having left her so abruptly, but once she has obtained her revenge by humiliating him with magical illusions she relents and becomes his mistress. All goes well until Arthur proclaims a tournament in order to lure Guinglain back to his queen; the enchantress warns him that he will never return if he leaves her now, but his desire to go is so strong that she is powerless to keep him.

At the tournament he wins great honour and subsequently marries Blonde Esmeree. The romance ends inconclusively, since Renaut leaves open the possibility of a third visit to the lady of the Île d'Or; if the poet can gain the favour of his own lady, he will once again unite Guinglain with his true love.

(b) Claude Platin's *Giglan*, a late and composite prose romance, fuses the story as told by Renaut with the quite distinct tale of Geoffroy de Maience that is found in the Provençal romance of *Jaufré*. Apart from a much reworked account of Gawain's rape of a maiden in a forest,[1] early in the romance, almost all the Fair Unknown material is very close to the form it had assumed in BD. What deviations exist are either straightforward pieces of elaboration—as in the much fuller accounts which the defeated knights give Arthur of the hero's prowess—or cross-references or linking passages made necessary by the double action of the romance; Platin, for example, exalts Giglan above Geoffroy by making him quite free from any trace of the uxorious indolence to which the latter is subject.

(c) The *Wigalois* (W) of Wirnt von Gravenberc also tells of the desertion of a beloved lady, but the incident there forms part of the adventures of Gawain which serve as a prologue to the career of Wigalois, his son. Gawain's liaison (which takes the form of a perfectly respectable marriage) is broken off by his desire to revisit his companions of the Round Table, and when he attempts to make his way back to his wife, his efforts are in vain. Twenty years later, his son sets out in search of him, is drawn to Arthur's court by news of a tournament, and is trained as a knight by Gawain himself (who knows nothing of their relationship). The maiden and dwarf then appear as in LD and BD, and the episodes that follow the hero's departure from court at first agree fairly closely with those of the English and French romances: Wigalois fights successively with a host accustomed to do battle with all comers, with two giants, a huntsman, and the villain of the combat for the bird; later in the romance he jousts with the steward of the oppressed lady, and—after a great deal of interpolated material—with Roaz, the enchanter. As in BD, however, this is not the end of the story; the hero's success is crowned by the arrival of Gawain

---

[1] Mentioned in LD 7-9 and alluded to in W 1511-16.

and three other knights of the Round Table, but just as the feasting is coming to an end a messenger arrives demanding vengeance for his lord and lady who have been murdered by Lion von Namur. Namur is besieged and conquered, and on his way home from there Wigalois learns that his mother has died of grief at her double loss of husband and son. He stays briefly with Arthur at Nantes, then returns with his wife (Larie, the princess rescued from the enchanter) to his own land.

W is undeniably a most important text, but its presentation of the traditional material is often very garbled indeed. Some parts of it have been greatly inflated (the episode of the prize of beauty now takes close on a thousand lines), while at other points individual motifs have been rearranged in completely new patterns. Most interesting of all in this respect is the treatment of material taken from the story of the transformed queen, since (1) Larie, the princess who corresponds most closely to the queen of Synadoun in other respects, retains her human shape and is in no immediate danger from the enchanter; (2) the transformation into animal shape and the tortures suffered at the hands of the enchanters have been transferred to Larie's father, the dead king who divides his time between enduring the purgatorial flames of Korntin and assuming the form of a guiding animal; (3) the serpentine form of the queen in LD is embodied in Pfetan, the dragon with which Wigalois fights shortly after his royal guide has left him. The meeting with this dragon occurs in the middle of the hero's journey to the enchanter's castle from Roimunt, the refuge of Larie and her mother, and forms part of what must be the most remarkable passage of amplification in the whole of the romance, since it tells how the hero is confronted, in turn, with a phantom tournament, Pfetan, the wild woman Ruel, the dwarf Karrioz, a perilous belt of black mist and a dangerous bridge, and the centaur-like Marrien. Some of the detail here can be related to episodes in BD or LD, but the total effect of these scenes is quite unlike anything to be found in the French and English romances, or—for that matter—in the first half of W itself.[1]

---

[1] See R. Bethge, *Wirnt von Gravenberg*, Berlin, 1881, p. 62, and F. Saran, 'Ueber Wirnt von Grafenberg und den Wigalois', (see Bibliography, p. 70), *passim.*

(*d*) *Le Chevalier du Papegau*, a prose romance of the fifteenth century, is closely related to W in its account of what follows the joust with the steward. After being guided by the trans-formed king, the hero meets with the ghostly tournament, the dragon, the wild woman, and the perilous bridge, although nothing is said about the dwarf, the black mist, or Marrien, and the whole treatment is very much terser than in W.[1] In the earlier parts of the romance the differences between W and *Papegau* far outweigh the similarities, and each romance has preserved some traditional material not to be found in the other: the encounters with the giants and the huntsman are found only in W; the hero's involvement with an enchantress, only in *Papegau*. These facts make it plain that the prose romance cannot derive directly from W; the elements which the two texts have in common must go back to a lost version, in which the story of the Fair Unknown had already been much modified.[2]

The most striking innovation is that the hero of the prose romance is no longer an unknown quantity but Arthur himself, recently crowned and eager to undertake the first adventure to present itself at his court. A natural corollary of this change is the absence of any version[3] of the conception and upbringing of the Fair Unknown, although some details belonging to such an account have found their way into the self-contained story of the dwarf with a giant son that is told near the end of the romance.[4] Also of interest is the fact that the hero no longer marries the lady rescued from the enchanter (contrast W); here as in BD it is the enchantress who seems to be the true heroine of the story. It was on her behalf that Arthur had set out from Camelot in the first place—the queen's messenger does not appear until after his triumphal entry into the Amoureuse Cité (Île d'Or BD)—and he returns to her briefly on his way back to the court. The competition of beauty has become the second of the adventures met with after setting out, and here, as in W,

---

[1] In the introduction to his edition of this text (Halle, 1896), Heucken-kamp points out that the author is increasingly prone to abridge his story as he gets nearer to the chief adventure (p. liii).

[2] For the relationship of the two texts, see Heuckenkamp, op. cit., pp. xxix–liv and Saran, op. cit., pp. 335–420.

[3] See p. 49, n. 2.

[4] See the note to L 13–24 in the Commentary.

the prize is no hawk but a parrot. This bird now completely
dominates its dwarf guardian and has, indeed, taken over two
of his most characteristic attributes—skill in music, and
a fondness for giving advice or information to the hero.[1]

(e) *Carduino*, the Italian representative of the story, offers
the smallest range of incident,[2] since the hero meets with only
three adventures before reaching the enchanted city: a brief
stay with an enchantress, a combat with an aggressive knight,
and another with two giants. The first of these corresponds to
the *second* visit to the Île d'Or in BD in that the lady plays
magical tricks on the knight; the third stands very close to
versions of the same scene in LD, BD, and W. As in W, the
hero has to fight with only one enchanter in the chief adventure,
but in this his opponent makes two quite separate attacks upon
him.[3] After the defeat of the enchanter not only the oppressed
lady but all the other inhabitants of the city are restored to
human shape from the animal forms they had been forced to
assume. The most significant peculiarities, however, occur in
the opening and closing sections of the poem, since the parts
played by both Gawain and the mother of the hero are very
different from what they are in LD, BD, and W. Gawain is no
longer the father of the Fair Unknown but one of the knights
responsible for that father's death, while the mother tells
Carduino of this murder and hints that he may one day avenge
it. And indeed the knight killed in the second of the episodes
following the departure from court proves to be one of the
murderers (and brother to Gawain). This lucky encounter
satisfies Carduino's desire for vengeance, and he at length
pardons the other knights who had been involved in the crime.

(f) *Erec et Enide* (E) and *Gereint vab Erbin* (G) resemble
Papegau in that they lack any account of the hero's *enfances*.[4]
The majority of the incidents proper to the story are preserved,

[1] No dwarf accompanies the female messenger from the Amoureuse
Cité, but the guardian of the parrot appears sufficiently early in the romance
for the latter to serve as Arthur's guide, philosopher, and friend for virtually
the whole of it.

[2] Only 856 lines have been preserved (eight stanzas describing the early
part of the scene at court are missing).

[3] See pp. 56 f.

[4] They also, with W, lack any clear mention of the motif of the Waste
City.

but are organized in a very unconventional way; the most
obvious innovation is that the hero (here an established knight
of the Round Table) is not drawn from Arthur's court by
messengers requesting help for an oppressed mistress, but goes
in pursuit of an aggressive knight met with casually in the course
of a scene of hunting. This knight subsequently proves to be
associated with a contest of beauty of which the prize is a hawk,
and in defeating him, Erec at once avenges the insult that he
had earlier done to Guenievre, and gains Enide as wife for himself. But he has not been married long before seriously harming
his fame by his uxorious indolence, and to restore his damaged
reputation he sets out in search of adventures, accompanied
only by his wife. At the end of four such adventures he meets, by
chance, with Arthur and his court in a forest (a hunt is once again
in progress) and is healed of his wounds. In spite of the en-
treaties of the king and all his knights, he then sets out once
more, and in the sequel fights with two giants, accepts the
rather dangerous hospitality of Evrain (Lambard LD) and, as
final proof of his rehabilitation, undertakes the dangerous
adventure of the Joie de la Cort, in which he fights with
Mabonagrain (Maugys/Maboun LD).

   The reworking here has been even more thorough-going than
in the source of the material common to W and *Papegau*.
As in these texts, material that in LD and BD is concentrated
in a single scene has occasionally been spread over a number of
episodes;[1] at other points, however, characters and actions that
were originally quite distinct have been combined. The most
striking example of such fusion is Enide herself, since she has
taken over the functions of no less than four characters who are
kept quite separate in BD (three of whom are also distinct in
LD): the lady whose beauty is championed (Margerie BD),[2]
the seductress (la Dame d'Amore LD), the hero's guide (Elene
LD), and his wife (the Queen of Synadoun LD). It could be
argued that the amalgamation of roles has in this case produced
a character who is more complex and interesting than any of

---

[1] The treatment of the forest encounter with a dwarf huntsman is particularly significant: see *Romania*, lxxxvii (1966), 33–58.
[2] In W and *Papegau* this character is also kept distinct from the female
messenger (contrast LD where Elene assumes both roles).

her counterparts in BD, but the example of Mabonagrain—the other important figure of mixed provenance in E—shows how easy it is for complexity to topple over into flat inconsistency under these circumstances.[1] Nor are the contradictions confined to Mabonagrain alone; the whole of the episode in which he figures abounds in them and is further weakened by the absence of some of the most evocative features of the cognate fight with the enchanters, as presented by LD and BD.

(g) Malory's *Tale of Gareth* has a more synthetic look about it than any of the other cognates,[2] but something must be said about its climactic scenes, since these have points in common with both the Île d'Or and Synadoun. They begin with Gareth's defeat of the Red Knight of the Red Laundes, who has long menaced Lyonesse, the heroine of the romance, and who—in accordance with a promise made to his (unnamed) mistress—has been accustomed to hang all the opponents defeated by him.[3] What follows this victory is as unexpected as it is unconvincing. Lyonesse suddenly refuses to grant the hero her love until a year has passed, but yet, once he has obediently taken himself away, persuades her brother Gryngamour to kidnap Gareth's dwarf servant, so that she may learn something concerning his identity. She and her sister Lyonet—who had guided Gareth to the adventure in the first place—then leave their own Castell Perelous for their brother's dwelling, the Ile of Avylyon. Gareth, in hot pursuit of the abductor of his dwarf, soon arrives there himself and sees his lady once more, but because of the change of location imagines her to be someone else, and falls desperately in love with her. Before long, however, he learns the truth of the matter and, after vowing perpetual love to each other, he and Lyonesse arrange that she is to come to his bed that night. As on a subsequent occasion, however, their union is frustrated by the sudden appearance of a knight with a battle-axe—a phenomenon engineered by the

---

[1] See Gaston Paris in *Romania*, xx (1891), 152-5.

[2] R. S. Loomis has characterized it as 'a pastiche' (*PMLA* xlviii (1933), 1023); R. H. Wilson as 'a conflation of end-products' (*PMLA* lviii (1943), 21).

[3] Compare the decapitation practised by Malgiers (BD), Mabonagrain (E), and Gyffroun (LD: see the note to L 750-3).

magically gifted Lyonet, who disapproves of her sister's *over-hasty* behaviour,[1] and the two are not finally united until after Gareth has greatly distinguished himself at a tournament held, with Arthur's approval, at the Castell Perelous, as a means reuniting Gareth and his family.

In this curious jumble the point of some traditional motifs has been seriously blunted. Unlike his counterparts in LD and BD, Gareth never really deserts his lady as a result of his infatuation with an enchantress, but by failing to recognize Lyonesse in the lady of the Ile of Avylyon he certainly imagines himself to be on the point of doing so. Lyonesse, for her part, has no need whatsoever to proclaim a tournament in order to lure an erring fiancé back to her side (as Blonde Esmeree does in BD), since Gareth is with her when she decides to hold one, but it is still represented as a means of reuniting everyone of importance at her castle. In these cases the primitive motifs have survived long after the circumstances which made them plausible have been superseded by others; elsewhere in *Gareth* we find that variant versions of a single motif have been implausibly combined. Thus the early pages of the story imply both of Philipot's types of the *enfances* of the Fair Unknown;[2] Gareth is at first presented as an overgrown youth whose mind is chiefly set on obtaining full board at Arthur's court,[3] but is later said to have been equipped from the outset with everything proper to be a knight. The apparently ignoble streak in his nature provokes the bitter hostility of Lyonet, his guide, and this is kept up by her for much longer than in any other cognate, giving a certain degree of relief to the otherwise tedious succession of combats that follow the departure from court. But neither in this section nor in the group of adventures that follow the tournament at the Castell Perelous do we find anything remotely like the encounters with the giants, the huntsman, the

---

[1] In this she reflects the scruples of the enchantress of BD (2449–58).

[2] He characterizes the upbringing of Lybeaus and Carduino, which is in ignorance of the world of chivalry, as *les enfances humaines*, that of Descouneus and Wigalois, who are carefully trained as knights, as *les enfances féeriques* (*Romania*, xxvi (1897), 297–300).

[3] Here held at Kynke Kenadonne, which must be a corruption of an earlier *Cenadon (Synadoun LD); see R. S. Loomis, *Arthurian Tradition and Chrétien de Troyes*, p. 116, n. 49.

suspect host or the transformed lady, that are so important in
LD and BD; the joust for the hawk, if preserved at all, survives
only as the merest aside in the description of the rules governing
the tournament.[1]

These romances by no means exhaust the number of the
cognates of LD—at more remote levels the stories of Degarre,
Perceval, and Lancelot could also be regarded as such—but
between them they provide almost all the material necessary
to the understanding of the ME. romance. It is highly unlikely
that Chestre can have been personally acquainted with any of
them but E and BD, and the first of these is so very individual
in its statement of the common themes that it could not possibly
have furnished him with the main lines of his story. BD is much
more likely to have provided these, but even so will not account
for all the traditional motifs to be found in LD.[2] The classic
solution of the difficulty, of course, would be to derive all such
motifs—both here and in the other cognates—from a single lost
archetype, but it is one that comes to seem increasingly
inadequate with familiarity with the network of parallels that
unites the individual romances. In the last resort we can hardly
avoid the conclusion that many of these parallels must result
from 'secondary' borrowings made between variant versions
of the story of Lybeaus—a conclusion that seems particularly
apt as far as LD is concerned, since Chestre has elsewhere
shown himself capable of using related stories in conjunction
to produce a new synthesis of his own.[3] Altogether then, without quite reverting to Kaluza's view of the supreme importance
of BD to Chestre,[4] we can at least accept as possible the theory
that he had been acquainted with some text of Renaut's poem

[1] It is stated that if the victor should be a married man he is to receive
'a coronall of golde . . . and a whyght jarfawcon' in place of the hand of
Lyonesse (*Works*, i. 341).

[2] Some important objections to BD as Chestre's source were put forward
by both Schofield (*Studies on the Libeaus Desconus*, pp. 59 ff.) and Philipot
(*Romania*, xxv (1896), 269 f.).

[3] In *Sir Launfal*, where joint use is made of the stories of Launfal and of
Graelent: see A. J. Bliss, *Sir Launfal*, pp. 24 ff., and *MÆ* xxxi (1962), 75 ff.
and xxxv (1966), 122 ff.

[4] See p. cxxxxi of his edition.

(not necessarily the one that has survived in MS. Chantilly 472) as well as with other related material. This last may have included *Erec*, but the evidence of parallels is here slender, and usually suggests a more remote connexion than that of direct borrowing from E into LD.[1] But however tenuous the direct relation of the two texts may be, Chrétien's romance is of the greatest importance to any attempt at reconstructing the probable form in which Chestre was acquainted with the crucial episodes of the romance: the Île d'Or, Synadoun, the prize of beauty, and the relationship between Lybeaus and his female guide.

1. The importance of the Île d'Or episode lies in its power to raise doubts about whether the Queen of Synadoun was meant as the true heroine of the romance, and in its relevance to our ideas about the length and organization of the primitive story as a whole. As we have seen, BD offers a mass of material which is absent from LD and which, at first sight, seems less likely to be 'authentic' than the product of Renaut's fondness for duplicating some parts of his source-material;[2] by this view, the blunt version of the affair with the enchantress that is given in LD 1399–1458 would be more authentic than Renaut's treatment of it in two instalments. But some support, at least, for the version of BD is provided by *Papegau*, in which Arthur pays a second visit to the Amoureuse Cité after he has defeated the enchanter, but still refrains from any permanent union with the lady. In themselves, these two versions of the double visit to the enchantress are too diverse either to establish its authenticity, or to throw much light on its original shape and content, but we come a little closer to achieving these aims if we consider the liaison with the seductress in conjunction with the theme of a tournament, commonplace in itself, but made significant within the context of *Lybeaus* by the frequency with which it is associated with the Île d'Or material.[3] In BD and *Gareth* the two episodes are explicitly related in that the tournament is

---

[1] See, however, *Romania* lxxxvii (1966), 46–48.

[2] See Schofield, op. cit., p. 110 and D. D. R. Owen in *Romania*, lxxx (1959), 478, n. 3.

[3] Like some other relatively sophisticated features, it is absent from both *Carduino* and LD.

proclaimed with the deliberate intention of luring the hero
back to his companions of the Round Table (as well as, in BD,
to his wife-to-be). In other cognates no such clear link is provided, but the two scenes remain juxtaposed. In E the tournament of Tenebroc immediately precedes Erec's lapse into
indolence; in W the hero hears news of such a tournament
immediately after he has left his mother's country (which was,
to Gawain, a land of uxorious bliss)[1] for the world of chivalry;
in *Papegau* two tournaments are mentioned at roughly the
same point in the story: the first is proclaimed by the enchantress herself, just before she finally grants her love to
Arthur, and is a means of demonstrating her absolute power
over him; the second, by the mysterious Duchess of Estrales,[2]
immediately after Arthur has left the enchantress to go to the
help of the oppressed queen.

Taken together, this evidence suggests that in an earlier form
of the story a tournament had—as in BD—played an essential
part in resolving the tangled love-life of the hero. A moment's
thought, however, will make it plain that if this episode is
accepted as a genuine complement to the affair at the Île d'Or,
it could hardly have been used to drag Lybeaus away from an
initial stay with the enchantress, since this would have preceded
the rescue of the oppressed queen (to effect which he had left
Arthur's court in the first place), and he could therefore be
brought to his senses—as in LD, BD, and *Papegau*[3]—by
a simple reminder from his companion that he was neglecting
his principal mission. In other words, the tournament could
only have been truly functional within the frame of the original
narrative if the chief adventure had already been successfully
terminated—a state of affairs reasonably close to that offered

---

[1] The *Erec*-motif also survives in W 1167–70, which tell of Gawain's
failure to take part in jousts (here because of his grief at losing contact with
his wife).

[2] For Estregales? Blonde Esmeree is said to be Queen of Gales in BD
3385 f., 5056, and 5215.

[3] There has been considerable confusion in this last, since Arthur sets
out from Camelot to rescue the enchantress and not to go to the aid of the
disinherited lady, but since the emissary of the latter obtains the king's
promise of support before he and the first lady have become lovers, she is
still able to reproach him with negligence of his duty after the manner of
her counterparts in BD and LD.

by BD. A further implication of the same argument is that
a second visit to the Île d'Or would hardly have been possible
if the lady had been as unsympathetically presented as she is
in LD[1] and *Carduino*. Of these, the Italian poem gives much
the more explicit account of the way in which she exercises her
magical powers: the hero has no sooner crossed the threshold
of her room than he imagines that he is hanging suspended over
a torrent.[2] In BD this illusion and a later fantasy that the hall
roof is crushing him likewise follow an attempt to reach the
lady's bed, but there are important differences in the way in
which the common material is presented in the two romances.
In *Carduino* the lady had actually called out to the hero to come
to her (although it must be added that she had earlier warned
him to do the exact opposite of her commands), is purely
malicious in her trickery, and is never again seen by him; in
BD, on the other hand, where the material is spread over two
visits to the Île d'Or,[3] she never directly invites him to enter
her room, and has some excuse for humiliating him as she
does. It may seem paradoxical to insist that BD could here
represent the original presentation of events more exactly than
Carduino, when the latter is in some respects so very much less
rationalized and more primitive—the absence of any previous
lover to correspond to Malgiers in BD, the motiveless malignity
of the lady and her lack of concern with orthodox morality
certainly belong to a less sophisticated mode of story-telling
than that of Renaut[4]—but this interpretation seems both possible in general terms, and probable in the light of the special
texture of *Carduino*. Possible, because the most primitive form
that a romance episode could assume within a given narrative
structure is not necessarily identical with that which it could
assume under any imaginable circumstances; probable, because
far from presenting us with something like the embryo from
which more complex versions have developed, *Carduino* here

---

[1] See the note to 1434.   [2] *Carduino*, ii, sts. 8–20.
[3] On his first visit, for example, he dreams that he holds her all night in
his arms (BD 2464–71); this may correspond to the statement in *Carduino*
ii. 14, that before she goes to her own room it seems to the hero that she
has been with him for a thousand years.
[4] Whose favourable characterization of her could have been prompted
by a desire to flatter his own mistress: see BD 4828 ff.

as elsewhere offers a primitive complex of incident in a condensed and rather confused way. It is, for example, odd that the hostess should behave in a way that makes the frustration of her desires almost inevitable, and still odder that a brief moment of time should seem like an infinitely longer period to her victim.[1]

The distinction between a motif in its most primitive form imaginable, and that which is most primitive within a given story-context, is one that must also be made when we turn to the account which these romances give of the relation of the enchantress to her previous lover. In general it may be said that whereas LD, BD, and *Papegau* present this in a way calculated to favour the lady, E (in the Mabonagrain episode) and *Gareth* do not. In BD a number of inconsistencies arise from the fact that the human qualities of the Pucele are stressed at the expense of her magical powers; although she has established the seven years' defence of a causeway as a proof of knightly excellence and sure guide to a good husband, Malgiers (who is measuring up to the test very well in his way) is represented as completely undesirable (BD 2035 ff.). Again, although the lady is skilled in all forms of magic (BD 1931–6) she appears to have no alternative but death to marrying her suitor if he should complete the period of probation (BD 2029–31). LD and *Papegau* avoid these difficulties by making the aggressor consistently monstrous[2] and by keeping back all mention of the lady's magical powers until after he has been defeated, but *Gareth* and E resolve the problem in a different way, since in both of these the mistress of the aggressive knight never has any intimate connexion with the hero who defeats him, and so is able to adopt some of the less flattering of the variant features available within the complex character-type that she represents. In *Gareth* she uses the Red Knight of the Red Laundes as a means of avenging the death of her brothers (i. 324 f.); in *Erec* she jealously keeps Mabonagrain from all contact with the outside world by compelling him to stay in the enchanted garden until he is defeated by one of the questing knights

---

[1] In most popular tales in which a mortal has a supernatural mistress it is more usual for a very long period of time to seem short than the other way about; see, for example, *Guingamor*, 533–40 (*Romania* viii (1879), 57 f.).

[2] L 1305–16; *Papegau*, pp. 14–18.

(E 5998–6067). This latter development means that Mabon-agrain now figures as a prisoner and not—like Mabon in BD and LD—as an enchanter who keeps others prisoner, and since in Brythonic legend Mabon had endured a cruel captivity,[1] the shift has the effect of making Mabonagrain revert to type in one important respect. We are therefore confronted with the paradox that E—which is fundamentally the most re-worked and 'advanced' of all the romances of *Lybeaus*—has chosen variant forms of certain important characters and motifs that are more 'primitive' than those which correspond to them in LD and BD, and which could hardly have coexisted with other aspects of the story in its earliest developed form.

2. In the episode at the enchanted city which culminates in the rescue of the Queen of Synadoun (the second 'heroine' of the story), LD and BD diverge less seriously than in their accounts of events at the Île d'Or. It is true that Chestre seems occasionally to have left out material contained in BD, but this impression can be misleading, since he has a habit of presenting traditional motifs in so laconic a form that their true significance is obscured.[2] In any case we are more often conscious of the different arrangement of such motifs than of their complete omission, and on occasion Chestre's patterns can look more 'traditional' than those of Renaut. This is above all true of his description of the phenomena which precede the entry of Maboun and Yrayn into the enchanted hall (LD 1801–18), since these (the sudden darkness, slamming of doors and windows, shower of stones, and earthquake) form themselves into a sequence that corresponds very closely to one found in other adventures at an enchanted castle in Arthurian romance, most notably to Bohort's visit to the Grail Castle that is described in the *Vulgate Lancelot* (v. 298 f.). This pattern is not reproduced in any other version of the story of *Lybeaus*; BD, which preserves many of the individual motifs, has distributed them very differently. For example, the phenomena are set in motion in the *Lancelot* by Bohort's act of sitting on the Perilous Bed[3] and in LD by the act of sitting at the raised table in the

---

[1] See W. J. Gruffydd, *Rhiannon*, pp. 91–94.   [2] See below, pp. 63 f.

[3] Mabonagrain appears as soon as Erec has sat down on the lady's bed (E 5844–50); no earthquake or thunder underlines the significance of the

hall, and in both they are followed by the sudden appearance of the hero's opponent(s). In BD, Descouneus actually goes to sleep on such a table (BD 3254), but only after he has fought with and defeated both Evrain and Mabon (BD 2926–3070), and endured a commotion and shower of missiles very like that in LD (BD 3074–89).[1]

But if we accept the episode in the *Vulgate Lancelot* as a valid pointer to the original shape of events in this case, we must also recognize the fact that it supports Renaut's version of the fighting with the enchanters against that offered by LD. For in making his hero fight first with Evrain and then—after the retreat of the latter into an inner room—with the more powerful Mabon, Renaut stands much closer to Bohort's fight against an opponent who makes two appearances that are separated by a brief (recuperative) spell in an inner chamber, than does Chestre, with his account of the simultaneous entry of Maboun and Yrayn and their habit of fighting jointly against Lybeaus for part of the time.[2] But even though Chestre seems less authentic in this respect, he still communicates the relative unimportance of Yrayn by devoting over twice as much space to his description of the fighting with Maboun as to that with his brother, and the climax of the scene is provided by five consecutive stanzas in which Yrayn plays no active part at all (LD 1903–62). What follows the death of Maboun is both confused in itself and inadequate as a resolution of the main adventure in the story. Lybeaus rushes back to the already seriously wounded Yrayn with the intention of killing him, but finds that he has vanished and fears that he will still be capable of harming him (LD 1972–83). The transformed queen attempts to set his mind at rest by twice remarking that *both* enchanters have been killed (LD 2020–2 and 2064–7), but her statements are too terse to carry much conviction, and the first of them does

---

action here, but at the same point in G, Gereint's occupying of an empty chair is at once followed by a 'great commotion' (*Mab.*, p. 272; WB., col. 449).

[1] It should also perhaps be noted that in the *Lancelot*, Bohort makes a second trial of the Perilous Bed after he has defeated his opponent, and becomes the target of a hail of arrows.

[2] The *Lancelot*-pattern is also reflected in *Carduino*, ii, sts. 56–58, where a single enchanter makes two distinct attacks on the hero.

not prevent Lybeaus from subsequently fearing that Yrayn had only been wounded (LD 2041–3 and 2054). In spite of Chestre's habitual carelessness over points of detail it seems less likely that this confusion originated in LD than that we find here, in aggravated form, an uncertainty about the fate of the second enchanter that was of very long standing in the story of Lybeaus. The starting-point of the confusion may well have been the fact that an early version of the story had told of two encounters with the same enchanter (compare *Carduino*),[1] who ran away from the hero at the end of the first, and was killed by him at the end of the second; in other words, that there existed a tradition of two combats but only one death. When Evrain came to take over the first of these, he took to flight in the approved fashion and was simply never heard of again;[2] Chestre, as we have seen, attempted in a random sort of way to set the reader's mind at rest, but the traditions had to be preserved even when they were unsatisfactory, and he refrained from writing in a passage that would have given greater weight to the assertions of the queen.[3]

Nothing has yet been said about this queen, although—since it was for her sake that Lybeaus set out at the beginning of the romance—she ought theoretically to be of considerable interest and importance. But in fact she is quite the least memorable part of the episode in which she figures; in those cognates in which her characterization has been unaffected by that of her rival of the Île d'Or, she is credited with all the qualities of mind and body obligatory in a romance heroine, but remains an essentially passive figure, who belongs to Lybeaus by right of conquest and has little complexity of any kind, either within the frame of a single version of the story or within the larger context of the romances as a whole. But when we turn to the third of the ladies championed by Lybeaus—the contender for the prize of beauty—we once again find great diversity of treatment, together with the complicating factor of

[1] See Schofield, op. cit., p. 127.
[2] See the note to 1963–74.
[3] Later redactors were less inhibited, since both the Percy text and those of Ashmole and Naples give graphic descriptions of the killing of Yrayn. See the Appendix, Sections (c) and (g), and *MÆ* xxxii (1963), 17.

occasional overlapping with the fourth 'heroine'—the guide
who leads the hero to Synadoun.

3. In BD, W, and *Papegau* there is no overt mention of any
liaison between Lybeaus and the lady he champions in this
scene, nor does she remain in his company after the fighting is
over, but even these texts preserve hints of a tradition in which
the two were more closely related. For one thing, both W and
Papegau make the prize of beauty remain with the hero and his
companion instead of being taken away by the lady to whom it
belongs; in the second the parrot is in any case Arthur's by
right (p. 11), while the same bird is angrily returned to Wigalois
by Elamie after he has refused to accompany her to her own
land (she tells him to give it, with his other winnings, to his
vriundin—Nereja, the guide to the enchanter (W 3247)). Even
in BD, where the atmosphere at parting is quite unstrained and
Margerie takes the prize with her, there is a hint of the turn of
events described in W, since all that Descouneus has won in
the course of the last two episodes is bestowed upon Margerie
by Helie, the guide.[1] These stray hints of a closer connexion
between Lybeaus and the lady he champions are decisively
realized in LD and E, since in both of these texts the latter is
identified with the guide (Elene LD, Enide E).[2] It is also
significant that in both of them a love-affair develops between hero and guide; in E the fact that Erec marries Enide
after winning the hawk for her leads to everything that follows;
in LD the relationship is of no importance in the sequel, but
its existence is put beyond doubt by two interesting passages.
In the later of these (which occurs within the episode of the
falcon), Lybeaus refers to Elene as his *lemman* (LD 805); in
the earlier, the reconciliation of the two after Elene's earlier
hostility is followed by what can hardly be anything other than
a night of love-making:

> He and þat mayde bryȝt
> To-gydere made all nyȝt
> Game and greet solas.
>   (LD 445–7)[3]

---

[1] In other words, Renaut may have stood the situation of W on its head.
[2] For Enide's function as a guide, see below, p. 60.
[3] See also the note to these lines in the Commentary.

These variants cannot all derive from a single pattern of relationships between Lybeaus and the lady; they rather suggest two such patterns, in one of which the lady's love was accepted, and in the other rejected, by the hero, and it may be that something of both has survived into LD, since the immediately preceding scene with the giants concludes with the rejection of his host's offer of his daughter, Vyolette, as wife (LD 688–99).[1] Altogether, the lady has more in common with the Dame d'Amore than at first appears, and it is not surprising that Chestre should have brought the episodes in which they appear still closer together by adopting motifs proper to each one of them into the other. The Dame d'Amore has the same kind of power over the hero's eyes as the lady of the hawk had possessed in BD,[2] while Gyffroun has taken over the motif of decapitating all defeated opponents, which properly belongs to Malgiers at the Îlle d'Or[3].

4. Finally we must say something about the hero's relations with his guide. The essence of these is a hostility that arises from the lady's doubts about his ability to cope with the perilous adventure that awaits him, and is only dispelled by practical demonstrations of his valour on the journey. The cognates differ considerably in fixing the point at which this hostility evaporates. In LD this happens after the fight with Selebraunche (LD 448–50), in BD after the battle with the giants (BD 841–52), but in W Nereja is not completely won over until after the defeat of Schaffilun in the fifth of the combats which follow the departure from court (W 3612–9), while Gareth has to emerge victorious from seven combats before Lyonet changes her attitude towards him (i. 312 f.).[4] Most interesting of all are G and E, which offer a version in which the friction between the pair dominates almost the whole of their journeyings together, although here, as we might

[1] Since this host corresponds to the *vavasor* of E a further link is established between Vyolette and the lady in the episode of the hawk.

[2] See the note 1426–34. The lady championed by the aggressive knight is very ugly in both BD (1727) and *Papegau* (p. 7).

[3] See also the note to L 750–3; the same knight is also very unsympathetically presented in *Papegau* (p. 9).

[4] In *Carduino* it is the dwarf who is most opposed to Arthur's choice of knight for the adventure (ii. 7).

expect, the basic material has been so thoroughly reworked that it is no longer easy to recognize. Philipot defined the change by saying that the guide's doubts about the powers of her champion have been metamorphosed into the anxiety of a young wife who believes that her husband's prowess and reputation are in decline,[1] but this is hardly the whole story: we must also note that Enide still preserves one or two traces of her primitive role as the *demoisele mesdisante* that Helie and Lyonet represent so vigorously: the actual words in which she expresses sorrow for her previous unguarded speech (E 3110–12) are quite in keeping with those uttered by Helie for a similar purpose (BD 841–52),[2] while in the more forthright version of G she not only continues to repeat these slanders after she and her husband have begun their journey,[3] but reacts to his first victory over a group of marauding knights in a manner worthy of Lyonet: 'sad and sorrowful was the maiden to see that'.[4] But for the greater part of their journey together the unhappy relationship between husband and wife is represented as the result of short temper on the part of the husband rather than of any bad manners in his companion, although Enide still keeps up her traditional function of pointing out sources of danger to the hero.[5] And as soon as Erec and Enide are reconciled they once more achieve complete happiness in their love (E 4879 ff., and 5199 ff.).[6]

Chestre's Version of the Story

Since it is not possible to construct a single watertight source for LD,[7] we are never able to say with absolute certainty that any given feature of the romance is the work of Chestre and of no one else; all the same, certain tendencies in his version are so persistent—and usually so distinct from anything to be

---

[1] *Romania*, xxv (1896), 265.

[2] In the new context of E the reproach refers to the fact that she had, at her husband's insistence, repeated the slanders of others to him.

[3] *Mab.*, p. 254; WB., col. 422.

[4] *trist ac aflawen oed y uorwyn yn ydrych ar hynny* (*Mab.*, p. 253; WB. col. 420).

[5] Compare LD 259–70, 719–38, 1238–54, and 1480–1506.

[6] These passages have something in common with LD 445–7, noted on p. 58, above.

[7] See pp. 50 f. above.

observed in the cognates[1]—as to seem worth mentioning. One fundamental habit is that of reshuffling motifs in a way that serves to link them with material with which they had not previously been associated; a practice which suggests that parts, at least, of LD were composed from memories of its source-material. On a small scale this seems to lie behind Selebraunche's protest about the iniquity of attacking an unarmed man;[2] on a larger one, in the ascription to Gyffroun instead of Maugys of the habit of beheading defeated knights.[3] It is also just possible that the arrangement of the first five episodes which follow the hero's departure from court may have been determined by lapses of memory, since the sequence (1) Selebraunche, (2) his avengers, (3) the giants, (4) the prize of beauty, and (5) the huntsman knight, of LD becomes (1), (3), (2), (5), (4) in BD. But as far as the first three adventures are concerned there is no external evidence that obliges us to rate Chestre's sequence as less authentic than that of Renaut; and although the latter's placing of the fight with the avengers after that with the giants achieves a certain degree of suspense that is lacking in the ME. account,[4] this could easily have originated in BD itself. More support can be found for the OF. arrangement of the fourth and fifth episodes, since both W and E offer parallels to the appearance of the prize of beauty *after* the meeting with the huntsman knight; but even here the issue is not quite clear, since the link which LD provides between (3) and (4)—a grateful host's offer of horse, arms, and daughter to the hero—which is quite absent from BD and W, is of very great importance in E.[5] Possibly there had existed two traditional groupings of the relevant scenes; one in which the forest meeting had preceded the competition of beauty, and another in which that competition was prefaced by the meeting with a grateful host. The source of BD and W would have known only

---

[1] Although *Carduino* to some degree parallels the mixture of terseness and 'primitivism' that is so typical of LD.

[2] See the note to 361–6.

[3] See the note to L 750–3.

[4] In that even if Descouneus defeats the giants he will still not be out of immediate danger.

[5] For a discussion of the incident, see R. S. Loomis, *Arthurian Tradition and Chrétien de Troyes*, pp. 81–84.

the first of these, that of LD only the second, but both would
have been fused in an antecedent form of E.

At other points in his romance, however, Chestre seems to
have modified the traditional material in a less accidental way.
He shares with other ME. redactors a fondness for sharpening
the moral focus of his narrative where this was traditionally
ambiguous, notably in respect of the uncertainty about the
relationship of the enchantress to the knight who barred the
approach to her (was it that of helpless victim and cruel suitor,
or of sovereign lady and besotted lover?), and the doubt about
which of the hero's women was his real love.[1] In LD both
Maugys and the Dame d'Amore are presented very much in
terms of black and white; the first becomes an aggressor of the
most repulsive kind; the second, a heartless seductress for
whom Lybeaus does not spare a thought once he is out of her
clutches, but in neither case is the reworking so thorough as to
leave no rough edges for later *disours* to smooth away.[2] Like
a number of other writers of the time, Chestre was always
liable to introduce fresh logical difficulties in the act of attempting to remove existing ones, and never more so than when—
as in his treatment of Maugys—he amplified the basic facts
with material taken over from the 'heroic' romances.[3] His
familiarity with these works has made of the guardian of the
Île d'Or an uncomfortable amalgam of knight and giant,[4] just
as it had made the forest battle between Otes and Lybeaus
bloodthirsty to a degree that makes their final friendship very
difficult to accept.[5] On the other hand this heroic streak is
perfectly consistent with the constant emphasis that is placed
upon the feudal bond that unites Lybeaus and Arthur, which
goes beyond anything comparable in the other romances.
Lybeaus, for example, entreats the king's blessing (243–6), con-
siders that he is bound to uphold the reputation of the Round

[1] These features lack clear definition within some single versions of the
story; they would have appeared still more ambiguous to Chestre if he had
been acquainted with more than one form of the episodes in which they
appear.

[2] For the work of such *disours*, see *MÆ* xxxii (1963), 11–23.

[3] Works such as *Arthour and Merlin*, which contain descriptions of
fighting between Christian heroes and pagan hordes.

[4] See the note to 1291–3.

[5] See Schofield, op. cit., pp. 162 f.

Table (190–2, 1286–8, 1526–30, 1651–3), and that any failure on his part is likely to reflect back on Arthur (1439–40, 1504–6, 1919–20). Not only does he order all the knights he has defeated to surrender themselves to Arthur (as in other cognates), but he sends back to the king any other prizes he has won in battle (682–4, 793–5, 973–5). Arthur, for his part, delights in his knight's prowess and dispenses treasure to him as the reward of a loyal vassal (979–90, L 1263–8).

The negative side of this 'heroic' approach is an almost total lack of interest in the more sentimental aspects of the story. The brusque account of the affair with the Dame d'Amore[1] offers nothing to correspond with the mental gymnastics of Renaut's hero at the same points in BD,[2] or with Arthur's complex relationship with the lady of the Amoureuse Cité in *Papegau*.[3] This lack of interest in the psychology of love has, of course, always been regarded as typical of ME. romances in general,[4] but in Chestre's case it forms part of a more widely diffused tendency to present important material in very laconic terms, and a failure to establish an overt connexion between individual parts of the stanza (most often, between the three-line units of which it is composed). The second of these characteristics is the one more apparent to the casual reader, since it from time to time prevents him from obtaining a clear notion of the exact chronology or geography of events, or of the motivation of the characters.[5] Chestre's terseness, on the other hand, is of great concern to the student of the story of Lybeaus as a whole, since some lines which appear from their imprecision to be no more than stanza-fillers, prove on closer examination to present material that was traditionally associated with the Fair Unknown. Thus L 1478 *She dyde hym traye and tene* is really a glancing allusion to the magical tricks of the

---

[1] See especially LD 1411–34.

[2] In particular, BD 2459–71, 4512–42, and 4600–30.

[3] At one point he rebels violently against the indignities she has made him suffer (p. 35).

[4] See, for example, W. P. Ker, *Medieval English Literature*, pp. 80 f., and J. E. Wells, *A Manual of the Writings in Middle English*, p. 2.

[5] Renaut is normally much more careful about such matters: compare LD 253–64 with BD 321–3 and LD 1081–1104 with BD 1370–1401 (for the movements of characters), and LD, 601–3 and 616–18 with BD 754–7 and 775–9 (for their motivation).

enchantress that are described at such length in BD 2385 ff. and 4487 ff., and *Carduino*, ii. 14–17, while LD 1774 f.

> Of mayne mor ne lasse
> Ne sawe he body ne face

stands as a highly condensed description of the Cité Gaste that is more fully presented in BD 2801–8 and 2871–9. Examples such as these, which can be glossed by making reference to less cryptic versions of the events which they describe, must make us cautious about dismissing as mere tags some other lines to which the cognates offer no obvious parallels.[1]

Such considerations increase the literary–historical interest of LD but hardly do anything to increase our respect for Chestre's craftsmanship, especially when we remember that what can be called his 'laconic' approach coexists with an antithetical weakness for loose and flabby writing. Of this the final cause seems to have been a determination to secure a proper quota of rhymes at whatever cost to the sense.[2] This is most clearly shown in Chestre's fondness for words and phrases of a highly conventional kind; it can also be seen in the extension of the meaning of certain words beyond what appears to have been their current semantic limits: good examples are afforded by *roun* and *skyll*.[3] In reality these apparently contradictory impulses are only different aspects of a single approach to composition, since Chestre's use of some favourite words is itself so various (that is, his obsession with rhyme has forced them into such a variety of contexts) as to deprive them of any precise meaning; from one point of view they have become as much tags as any of the stock-in-trade of phrases available to all writers of tail-line romance.

A Note on Thomas Chestre

It has at all points been assumed that LD, like the so-called 'Southern' *Octavian*, was the work of the Thomas Chestre who

---

[1] Even the least authentic-looking part of the romance—the fight against superior numbers in a forest, to which the 'heroic' romances contributed so markedly—is not without some traditional authority, in view of the parallels with E: see p. 47, n. 1.

[2] See p. 36.

[3] See the notes to 972 and 1844.

names himself at the end of *Sir Launfal*, and although there is not space here for a full vindication of this theory,[1] enough depends upon it to make it desirable to outline the kind of evidence by which it is supported. The most tangible part of this evidence—the part, indeed, upon which nineteenth-century scholars largely concentrated their attention—consists of parallels of wording, pattern, and theme that are offered by two or more of these romances.[2] Of these, the verbal and phrasal correspondences have the advantage of being easily and quickly assembled, but in most cases their value as evidence is greatly diminished by their highly conventional nature. However, even here we find a small number of examples of a kind more likely to occur in two works by a single author than in two by different hands—notably those in which words and phrases, commonplace in themselves, are yet conjoined in a sufficiently distinctive way.[3] To these we may add certain phrasal patterns[4] and narrative devices.[5] It is noteworthy that all of these may be used with a singular disregard for their aptness to context; indeed, their significance to the problem of authorship lies not only in the fondness for certain words, phrases, or formulae, to which they bear witness, but in the fact that this common material is used in a manner that betrays a consistent desire to meet the needs of rhyme, at whatever cost to stylishness and sense.[6] And if *Octavian*, *Launfal*, and *Lybeaus* resemble each other in the extent to which their total effect is weakened by this rather unscrupulous approach to language, they are no less akin in the way in which they present (or distort) specific points in their sources. All three are capable of communicating these in a style that is both terse in its statements and disjointed in its continuity,[7] and may also reshuffle authentic motifs to produce new and sometimes unsatisfactory sequences of incident.[8] Most curious of all, some of this half-remembered material is

---

[1] I have discussed the matter at some length in *MÆ* xxxi (1962), 88–109.

[2] See Kaluza's study of the problem in *ES* xviii (1893), 165–90.

[3] See the note to L 1629–36.

[4] One such is mentioned in the note to 284.

[5] See the note to 1219–21.

[6] Particularly illuminating is the use which Chestre makes of *roun* and *skyll*—two favourite words. See the notes to 972 and 1844 and, for a fuller discussion, *MÆ* xxxi (1962), 99–101.

[7] Ibid. 95–97.

[8] Ibid. 90–92.

F

allowed to persist into quite alien contexts without any serious attempt being made to tone down the discrepancies of mood and statement that result.[1] For once, the original redactor of a ME. romance would seem in his own way to have been almost as careless as any of the scribes who later handled his work.

The period during which this curious work was composed has been variously given as 1325–50 (Kaluza)[2] and 1350–1400 (Fischer).[3] The second of these seems much the more likely. Kaluza appears to have favoured the relatively early period in order to bring LD as close as possible in time to the Auchinleck MS. which he considered Chestre to have plundered so extensively;[4] in fact, however, not all of the parallels which exist between LD and such works as *Guy* and *Bevis* are to be accounted for by the texts preserved in Auchinleck,[5] and whether we interpret this as a sign that Chestre had supplemented these texts by other and later versions, or that he had made use of a quite distinct manuscript collection in the first place, the effect must be to weaken the claims of 1327–40— the date of Auchinleck—to provide a *terminus a quo* for LD. Kaluza's rejection of the date of *Sir Thopas* as a *terminus ad quem* is almost equally open to criticism. He argues[6] that Chaucer's mention of *sir Lybeux* (*Canterbury Tales*, vii. 900) was prompted by allusions to the hero in *The Squyr of Lowe Degre* (C 78 and 614), and that since the text of LD known to the author of the *Squyr* was already very corrupt,[7] a reasonable period of time must separate Chestre's original from *Sir Thopas*. But against this it must be urged that (1) the relevant passages in the *Squyr* may well be late interpolations;[8] (2) there is in any case no very cogent evidence that Chaucer had ever known this text in any form,[9] and (3) Chaucer's knowledge of LD almost certainly went beyond the limits of what he could have obtained

---

[1] Ibid. 97–99.   [2] *Libeaus*, p. clxvi.   [3] *Lautbestand*, pp. 197–9.

[4] He also claimed that the second quarter of the century would agree with the linguistic evidence, but this seems an attempt to rationalize a rather illogical conclusion.

[5] See especially the notes to 454–65, 1123–8, 1153–8, and 1333–62.

[6] Op. cit., pp. clxv f.

[7] Both of the '*Lybeaus*-passages' in Copland's text of the *Squyr* are given in the note to L 192.

[8] Thus Weyrauch, *ES* xxxi (1902), 182.

[9] See the Introduction to W. E. Mead's edition of this text, pp. lii–lxvi.

from the *Squyr*.[1] In other words, *Sir Thopas* may be reinstated
as the *terminus ad quem* for LD, and its own dating thus becomes
a matter of some importance. J. M. Manly, after taking note
of the number of points at which Chaucer satirizes the bourgeois
instincts of the Flemish knights, suggests that the parody
would have had most point if composed shortly after 1383—
the date of the Flemish embassy to London. If his reasoning is
correct, then LD could hardly have been written much later
than 1380; if not, then the latest possible date would be 1400,
the year of Chaucer's death.

Other features of LD that could be relevant to its date of
composition suggest the second half or more precisely the last
quarter of the fourteenth century. The armour described in
the romance is quite clearly 'mixed' (*mayl and plate* 1176), and
although most of the individual pieces that are mentioned
(*auentayle, barbe[l], gorgere,* and *pysane*) are already to be found
in texts contained in MS. Auchinleck, *krest* (352) in the sense
of an ornament or device on top of a helmet seems first to occur
in texts of the second half of the fourteenth century. This period
is also suggested by the treatment of final *-e*,[2] which may be
either sounded or suppressed, even though the 'mixed' prosody
of LD[3] makes it virtually impossible to produce exact statistics
on this point. Finally, a time of origin nearer the end than the
beginning of this half-century is implied by two important
linguistic developments that are attested in rhyme: the shift of
$[ou\chi t] > [au\chi t]$, and the lowering of $\bar{\rlap{e}}{}> \bar{e}$ before *r*.[4] Both of
these have been characterized as typical of the (early) fifteenth
century,[5] and even if we cannot accept this quite literally—
since other evidence makes it impossible to push the date
of LD beyond 1400[6]—they must make any time earlier than
the last quarter of the century seem most unlikely. We may
therefore place LD somewhere within 1375–1400, with

[1] See F. P. Magoun's article in *PMLA* xlii (1927), 833–44, and L. H.
Loomis in *Sources and Analogues*, p. 487 and n. 4.

[2] Jordan §§ 141, 290; Fischer, op. cit., p. 198.

[3] See above, pp. 20–22.   [4] See Section III, §§ 8 and 13.

[5] Jordan § 287; Dobson § 126.

[6] Even if we were to ignore the connexion with *Sir Thopas*, it would be
hard to accept that LD had been written later than 1400, since Chestre's
original would then have been virtually contemporary with MS. H—which
already has an elaborate history of textual corruption behind it.

Manly's dating of *Sir Thopas* suggesting the earlier, and the linguistic evidence the later part of this period.

V. SELECT BIBLIOGRAPHY

I. LIST OF ABBREVIATED TITLES

Manuscripts containing Lybeaus Desconus (LD)

C	British Museum, MS. Cotton Caligula A. ii.
L	Lambeth Palace, MS. 306.
H	Lincoln's Inn, MS. Hale 150.
A	Bodleian, MS. Ashmole 61.
N	Biblioteca Nazionale, Naples, MS. xiii, B. 29.
P	British Museum, MS. Additional 27879 (MS. Percy).

Printed texts

Amis   *Amis und Amiloun*, ed. E. Kölbing (*Altenglische Bibliothek*, ii), Heilbronn, 1884.

AM   *Arthour and Merlin*, ed. E. Kölbing (*Altenglische Bibliothek*, iv), Leipzig, 1890.

BD   Renaut de Beaujeu, *Li Biaus Descouneüs* (*Le Bel Inconnu*), ed. G. P. Williams (C.F.M.A. 38), Paris, 1929.

Bevis   *Sir Beves of Hamtoun*, ed. E. Kölbing (E.E.T.S., e.s. 46, 48, 65), London, 1885–94.

E   Chrétien de Troyes, *Erec et Enide*, ed. M. Roques (C.F.M.A. 80), Paris, 1955.

Giglan   [Claude Platin], *L'Hystoire de Giglan* (British Museum C. 47. f. 5), Lyon, no date. (Not paginated; all references are to the signatures.)

Guy   *Guy of Warwick*, ed. J. Zupitza (E.E.T.S., e.s. 42, 49, 59), London, 1883–91.

Kaluza   *Libeaus Desconus*, ed. M. Kaluza (*Altenglische Bibliothek*, v), Leipzig, 1890.

Mab.   *The Mabinogion*, trans. G. Jones and T. Jones, London, 1950.

Papegau   *Le Chevalier du Papegau*, ed. F. Heuckenkamp, Halle, 1896.

RCL   *Richard Cœur de Lion*, ed. K. Brunner (*Wiener Beiträge zur englischen Philologie*, xlii), Vienna, 1913.

SD   *Sir Degarre*, ed. G. Schleich (*Englische Textbibliothek*, 19), Heidelberg, 1929, and W. H. French and C. B. Hale in *Middle English Metrical Romances*, New York, 1930.

SL   Thomas Chestre, *Sir Launfal*, ed. A. J. Bliss, London, 1960.

SO   The 'Southern' *Octavian*, ed. G. Sarrazin (*Altenglische Bibliothek*, iii), Heilbronn, 1885.

SP   *Sir Perceval of Gales*, ed. J. Campion and F. Holthausen (*Alt- und mittelenglische Texte*, 5), Heidelberg, 1913.

W   Wirnt von Gravenberc, *Wigalois*, ed. J. M. N. Kapteyn
         (*Rheinische Beiträge und Hülfsbücher zur germanischen
         Philologie und Volkskunde*, 9), Bonn, 1926.
WB   *The White Book Mabinogion*, ed. J. G. Evans, Pwllheli, 1907.

Periodicals

ES   *Englische Studien*
E & S   *Essays and Studies*
MÆ   *Medium Ævum*
MLN   *Modern Language Notes*
MLR   *Modern Language Review*
PMLA   *Publications of the Modern Language Association of America*
RES   *Review of English Studies*

2. OTHER WORKS

ME. texts

Le Bone Florence of Rome, ed. W. Viëtor and A. Knobbe, Marburg,
   1893–9.
Sir Eglamour, ed. G. Schleich (*Palaestra*, 53), Berlin, 1906, and F. E.
   Richardson (E.E.T.S. 256), London, 1965.
The Erl of Tolous, ed. G. Lüdtke, Berlin, 1881.
Sir Gowther, ed. K. Breul, Oppeln, 1886.
Sir Ysumbras, ed. J. Zupitza and G. Schleich (*Palaestra*, 15), Berlin,
   1901.
Kyng Alisaunder, ed. G. V. Smithers (E.E.T.S. 227, 237), London,
   1952–7.
The King of Tars, ed. F. Krause in *ES* xi (1888), 33 ff.
The Works of Sir Thomas Malory, ed. E. Vinaver, Oxford, 1947.
Sir Orfeo, ed. A. J. Bliss, 2nd edn., Oxford, 1966.
The Squyr of Lowe Degre, ed. W. E. Mead, Boston, 1904.
Sir Tristrem, ed. E. Kölbing (*Die nordische und die englische Version der
   Tristan Saga*, ii), Heilbronn, 1878–82.

Other texts

Der Anglonormannische Boeve de Haumtone, ed. A. Stimming (*Biblio-
   teca Normannica*, vii), Halle, 1899.
Carduino in *Poemetti Cavallereschi*, ed. P. Rajna, Bologna, 1873.
The Didot Perceval, ed. W. Roach, Philadelphia, 1941.
Durmart le Galois, ed. E. Stengel (*Bibl. litt. Ver. in Stuttgart*, cxvi),
   Tübingen, 1873.
Octavian, ed. K. Vollmöller (*Altfranzösische Bibliothek*, iii), Heilbronn,
   1883.
Le Roman de Brut de Wace, ed. I. Arnold (S.A.T.F.), Paris, 1938–40.
The Sources and Analogues of Chaucer's Canterbury Tales, ed. W. F.
   Bryan and C Dempster, London, 1958.

La Vengeance Raguidel in Raoul de Houdenc, *Sämtliche Werke*, ed. M. Friedwagner, Halle, 1897–1909.
The Vulgate Version of the Arthurian Romances, ed. H. O. Sommer, Washington, 1909–13.

Literary studies and articles

R. Bethge, *Wirnt von Gravenberg*, Berlin, 1881.
W. J. Gruffydd, *Rhiannon*, Cardiff, 1953.
M. Kaluza, 'Thomas Chestre, *Verfasser* des *Launfal, Libeaus Desconus* und *Octovian*', *ES* xviii (1893), 165–90.
R. S. Loomis, 'The Visit to the Perilous Castle: A Study of the Arthurian Modifications of an Irish Theme', *PMLA* xlviii (1933), 1000–35.
—— *Arthurian Tradition and Chrétien de Troyes*, New York, 1949.
H. Newstead, *Bran the Blessed in Arthurian Romance*, New York, 1939.
H. R. Patch, *The Other World According to Descriptions in Medieval Literature*, Cambridge (Mass.), 1950.
E. Philipot, 'Un Épisode d'*Érec et Énide: La Joie de la cour*—Mabon l'enchanteur', *Romania*, xxv (1896), 258–94.
—— Review of Schofield's *Studies on the Libeaus Desconus*, *Romania*, xxvi (1897), 290–305.
F. Saran, 'Ueber Wirnt von Grafenberg und den Wigalois', *Beiträge zur Geschichte der deutschen Sprache und Literatur*, xxi (1896), 253–420.
W. Schofield, *Studies on the Libeaus Desconus* (*Harvard Studies in Philology and Literature*, iv), Boston, 1895.
A. McI. Trounce, 'The English Tail-Rhyme Romances', *MÆ* i (1932), 87–108, 168–82; ii (1933), 34–57, 189–98; iii (1934), 30–50.

Linguistic studies and works of reference

A. J. Bliss, 'The Spelling of *Sir Launfal*', *Anglia*, lxxv (1957), 275–89.
K. Brunner, *Die englische Sprache*, Halle, 1950–1.
E. J. Dobson, *English Pronunciation 1500–1700*, Oxford, 1957.
E. Fischer, *Der Lautbestand des südmittelenglischen Octavian* (*Anglistische Forschungen*, 63), Heidelberg, 1927.
R. Jordan, *Handbuch der mittelenglischen Grammatik* (bearb. H. C. Matthes), Heidelberg, 1934.
R. Kaiser, *Zur Geographie des mittelenglischen Wortschatzes* (*Palaestra*, 205), Leipzig, 1937.
A. Liedholm, *A Phonological Study of the Middle English Romance 'Arthour and Merlin'*, Uppsala, 1941.
K. Luick, *Historische Grammatik der englischen Sprache*, Stuttgart, 1964.
M. K. Pope, *From Latin to Modern French*, Manchester, 1952.

THE PRESENTATION OF THE TEXT

Emendation

BOTH C and L contain a large number of corrections to the text, but whereas almost all those of C involve deletion or expuncting within the line, and so must be the work of the original scribe, those of L were almost certainly made by a later corrector (in spite of a similarity of hand). Wherever a correction is of the first type, it has been incorporated into the body of the text; where of the second, it has usually been rejected in favour of the original reading, when this is recoverable. Very little is lost by relegating the work of the corrector of L to footnotes, since in spite of occasional sensible emendations (as at L 206), he obviously worked without the support of any better text of *Lybeaus*. I have, however, given in square brackets within the line any words that he has supplied that were necessary to the sense but omitted by the original scribe. Otherwise, I have only inserted such missing words where they are not present in the alternative text.

Expansion

As so often happens with manuscript copies of popular texts, it has proved impossible to be perfectly consistent in the treatment of the scribe's signs of contraction (or flourishes). Particular difficulties are presented by final -*o(u)n* in both C and L. In C, apart from the (very rare) -*on*, and -*oun*, we find the same forms with a horizontal flourish over the last two minims[1] (these more elaborate variants do not appear in the early pages of the text, but they become increasingly common in the last two-thirds); my practice has been to ignore the flourish over -*oun*, but to take it literally when it occurs over -*on*, by interpreting the second letter as *u*, and expanding to -*oun*. In L, final -*on* carries a flourish over the second letter in almost all cases, including a handful where it could only be expanded to -*onn* (L 1497 *vpon*); I have ignored it at all points.

[1] See the Frontispiece (as also for L 206).

Signs of contraction that are obviously meaningful have been silently expanded. The abbreviation for *-is* (in Latin) has been rendered as *-is* in L, but as *-es* in C, in accordance with the spelling of this syllable when it is written in full. In L this sign of contraction has sometimes been confused with the meaningless final flourish, and an otiose final *-is* produced as a result: *haukis* L 943, where the context requires *hauk*. I have emended in such cases. The abbreviation for *-us* (in Latin) has been taken literally, and the *j*-like capital *I* has been represented by *Ȝ* or *j*. Words in which the prefix is obviously separated from the rest are normally hyphenated, but I have used my discretion in presenting words with initial *a-*, since this tends to be written separately whether it is a true prefix or not (in *a none*, for example). Punctuation and capitals have been normalized in accordance with modern usage.

Kaluza's Edition

The line-numbering of this edition (which has been cited in all previous writing on LD) is given in the left-hand margin of the Lambeth text below.

LYBEAUS DESCONUS

f. 42vb

Jhesu Cryst our Sauyour
And hys modyr, þat swete flowr,
Helpe hem at her nede
þat harkeneþ of a conquerour,
Wys of wytte and why3t werrour   5
And dou3ty man yn dede.
Hys name was called Geynleyn,
Be-yete he was of Syr Gaweyn,
Be a forest syde;
Of stouter kny3t and profytable   10
Wyth Artour of þe Rounde Table,
Ne herde ye neuer rede.

þys Gynleyn was fayr of sy3t,
Gentyll of body, of face bry3t,
All bastard 3ef he were.   15

Hys modyr kepte hym yn clos
For douute of wykkede loos,
As dou3ty chyld and dere.

And for loue of hys fayr vyys,
Hys modyr clepede hym Bewfys,   20
And non oþyr name,

Above the first line: Incipit Lybeaus Disconus
4 harkeneþ: *loop (of* k?) *above* r   5 Wys: *loop (of* h?) *above* w   15 he
above line; caret after 3ef   21 non oþyr: *MS.* no noþyr

LAMBETH PALACE 306

Jhesu Criste ou[r]e Savyour
And his moder, þat swete ffloure,
Spede hem at her nede
That lysteneth of a conquerour,
Wise of witt and a wight wereour   5
A[nd] doughty man of dede.
His name was Sir Gyngelayne,
Gotten he was of Sir Gaweyne,
Vnder a forest syde;

K 10   A better knyght was neuer prophitable   10
With Arthur at the Roun Table:
Herde J neuer of redde.

Gyngelayne was fayre of sight,
Gentyll of body and of face bryght,
Bastard though that he were;   15
His moder hym kept[e] with hir myght
That he shulde se no knyght
J-armed in no maner,
For he was full [savage]

K 20   And gladly wold [do] oute-rage   20
To his ffellaves in fere;
And all for dred of wycke loose
His moder alwey kept[e] him close
As dughty childe and dere.

And for he was so fayre of ffyce,   25
His moder clept[e] him Bewfi3,
And none oþer name,

Above the first line: A tretys of one Gyngelayne othir wyse Namyd by Kyng
Arthure lybeus dysconeus that was Bastard son to sir Gaweyne. *Dot or*
oblique stroke inserted in the middle of lines 1–23   1 *Capital* J
in red, seven lines deep   oure: *superscript* r *added later*   6 And: nd *erased*
11 Arthur: *first* r *over erasure*   12 of *followed by superscript* nor
16 kepte: *final* e *erased here and in line 23*   19 savage *deleted and*
followed by sawge   20 do *deleted and* not *added above line*   26 clepte:
final e *erased*

And hym-self was full nys:
He ne axede naȝt, y-wys,
What he hyȝt, at hys dame.
As hyt be-felle vp-on a day,   25
To wode he wente on hys play,
Of dere to haue hys game;
He fond a knyȝt whar he lay,
Jn armes þat wer stout and gay,
J-sclayne and made full tame.   30

þat chyld dede of þe knyȝtes wede
And anon he gan hym schrede
Jn þat ryche armur.
Whan he hadde do þat dede,
To Glastyngbery he ȝede,   35
þer ley þe Kyng Artour.

f. 43ʳᵃ   He knelede yn þe halle,
Be-fore þe knyȝtes alle,
And grette hem wyth honour,
And seyde, 'Kyng Artour, my lord,   40
Graunte me to speke a word,
J pray þe par amour.'

þan seyde Artour þe kyng,
Anoon wyth-oute any dwellyng,
'Tell me þyn name aplyȝt: 45
For seþen Y was y-bore,
Ne fond Y me be-fore
Non so fayr of syȝt.'

31 þe: *superscript* e *to replace one blotted and expuncted after* þ   37 knelede:
i *expuncted before* l

And this childe was so nyse
He asked neuer, j-wysse,
f. 73ᵛ   K 30   Whate hight [off] his dame.   30
Tyll hit be-fell vppon a day,
The childe wente him forthe to playe,
Off dere to haue som game;
He fond a knyght þere he lay,
Jn armes stoutc and gayc,   35
Slayne and made ful tame.

He toke of that knyghtis wede;
Hym-sylffe þerin well fayre [c]an shrede,
All in that bryght armour.
K 40   Whan he had do that in dede,   40
To Glastynbury þe childe him yede,
Ther lay Kyng Arthure.
And whan he came to Arthurs hall
He fond him there and his lordis all;
This childe knelyd downe on his kne: 45
'Kyng Arthure, Criste þe saue and see!
J am come oute of fer contre
My mone to make to the.

J am a childe vnkowthe
K 50   And come out of the southe   50
And wolde be made a knyght;
Lorde, J pray the nowthe,
With thi mery mouthe,
To graunte me anone right.'
Than saide Arthure the kynge,   55
'To me childe, with-out dwellinge:
Whate is thi name aplight?
For neuer sethe J was born,
Sawe J neuer me be-forne
K 60   So semely to my sight.'   60

30 off *deleted and* onys *added above line*   38 can: g *over* c   49 vnkowthc:
e *over erasure*   50 come: e *over erasure*   56 To: o *altered from* e
59 me: e *over erasure*

þat chylde seyde, 'Be Seynt Jame!
J not what ys my name:　　　　　　　　50
J am þe more nys;
But whyle Y was at hame,
My modyr, yn her game,
Clepede me Beau-fyȝ.'
þanne seyde Artour þe kyng,　　　　　　55
'þys ys a wonder þyng,
Be God and Seynt Denys,
Whanne he þat wolde be a knyȝt
Ne wat noȝt what he hyȝt
And ys so fayr of vys.　　　　　　　　60

Now wyll Y ȝeue hym a name,
Be-fore yow alle yn same,
For he ys so fayr and fre;
Be God and be Seynt Jame,
So clepede hym neuer hys dame,　　　　65
What woman þat so hyt be.
Now clepeþ hym alle yn vs,
Lybeau Desconus,
For þe loue of me;
þan may ye wete a-rowe,　　　　　　　70
þe Fayre Vn-knowe,
Sertes so hatte he.'

f. 43rb　　　　Kyng Artour anon ryȝt
Made hym þo a knyȝt,
Jn þat selue day.　　　　　　　　　　75
And yaf hym armes bryȝt,
Hym gertte wyth swerde of myȝt:
For-soþe as Y yow say,
And henge on hym a scheld,
Ryche and ouer-geld,　　　　　　　　80
Wyth a gryffoun of say,

---

50 what: h _over_ a　　　　68 Lybeau _preceded by expuncted and deleted_ lyba
72 Sertes _followed by expuncted and deleted_ sert　　　　80 and _followed by_
expuncted and deleted e

Sayde Gyngelayn, 'Be Seint Jame!
f. 74ʳ J ne wote whate is my name:
J am the more nyse;
But while J was at home,
My moder, on hir game,   65
Clepped me Bewfice.'
Than sayde Arthur the kyng,
'This is a wonder thinge,
Be God and Seint Denyce,
K 70 [Whan] þat [he] wold be made a knyght   70
And wote not whate his name h[e]ght
And hathe so fayre a vice.

J shall if hym a name,
Amonge you all in [s]ame,
For he is fayre and fre;   75
Be God and be Seint Jame,
So clepped him neuer his dame,
Whate woman so she be.
Clepeth him in your vse,
K 80 Lybeus Disconeus,   80
For the loue of me;
Than mowe ye wit, on a rowe,
That the better ye mowe knowe
Certis so hight hee.'

Kynge Arthur anone right   85
[C]on make him a knyght,
Jn that sylffe daye.
'Now Kyng Arthur haþe made me knyght,
J thanke him with all my myght;
K 90 Bothe by day and nyght   90
With my fomen J will fight
Them to say with strok[e] of myght
And to juste in feer.'

67 Arthur: *a final* e *added*   70 Whan *erased and* Wo *one written over*
it   he *erased*   71 heght: y *over* e   73 if: *initial* g *added later*
74 samc: *cross-stroke drawn through* s   85 Arthur: *as in lines* 88, 95 *and*
100 *a final* e *added subsequently*   86 Con: G *over* C   92 stroke: *con-*
traction for is *over* e   93 feer: *perhaps* feere

And hym be-tok hys fadyr Gaweyn
For-to teche hym on þe playn
Of ech kny3tes play.

Whan he was kny3t j-made,   85
Anon a bone þer he bad
And seyde, 'My lord so fre:
Jn herte Y were ry3t glad
þat ferste fy3te yf Y had
þat ony man askeþ þe.'   90
þanne seyde Artour þe kyng,
'J grante þe þyn askyng,
What batayle þat so hyt be;
But me þyngeþ þou art to 3yng
For-to done a good fy3tynge,   95
Be aw3t þat Y can se.'

Wyth-oute more resoun,
Duk, erl and baroun
Whesch and yede to mete.
Of all manere fusoun,   100
As lordes of renoun,
Y-now3 þey hadde ete.
Ne hadde Artour sete bote a whyle,
þe mountance of a myle,
At hys table y-sete,   105
þer com a mayde ryde
And a dwerk be here syde,
All be-swette for hete.

f. 43ᵛᵃ   þat mayde was clepede Elene,
Gentyll, bry3t and schene: 110
A lady messenger.
þer nas contesse ne quene
So semelych on to sene
þat my3te be her pere.

---

95 a *followed by expuncted and deleted* d   98 erl: (*loop of another* l?) *above* r
103 *caret after* Artour; sete *in right-hand margin*

f. 74ᵛ   Whan he was a knyght made,
                      Off Arthur a bone he bade   95
                      And sayde, 'My lorde fre:
K 100   Jn hert J were full glad
                      The first fyghtinge þat ye hadde
                      That men will aske of the.'
                      Than saide Arthur þe kynge,   100
                      'J graunte the thine askynge,
                      Whate batayll so it bee;
                      But me thinkeþ þu arte to yonge
                      To do a gode ffyghtynge,
                      Be ought that J can see.'   105

                      With-outen eny more reyson,
K 110   Duke, erle and baron
                      Wesshed and went to mete.
                      Volatyle and venyson,
                      As lordis of grete renon,   110
                      J-now they had to ete.
                      Nade Arthure syt but a while,
                      The mountence of a myle,
                      Att his tabyll [sett],
                      The[r] con a mayde in ryde   115
                      And a dwerffe by hir syde,
K 120   All be-swett for hete.

                      The may hight Ell[y]ne,
                      Gentyll, bryght and shene:
                      A lovely messengere.   120
                      Ther nas countes nor quene
                      So semely on to sene
                      That myght be hir pere.

114 sett: *deleted and partially erased, followed by* sete   115 Ther: *MS.*
The   118 Ellyne: e *over erased* y   122 on: *a final* e *added; oblique
stroke between this and next word*

Sche was clodeþ in tars,   115
Rowme and nodyng skars,
Pelured wyth blaunner;
Her sadell and her brydell yn fere
Full of dyamandys were:
Melk was her destrere.   120

þe dwerke was clodeþ yn ynde,
Be-fore and ek be-hynde:
Stout he was and pert.
Among alle Crystene kende
Swych on ne schold no man fynde;   125
Hys surcote was ouert.
Hys berd was yelow as ony wax,
To hys gerdell henge þe plex:
J dar well say yn certe.
Hys schon wer wyth gold y-dyȝt   130
And kopeþ as a knyȝt,
þat semede no pouert.

Teandelayn was hys name:
Well swyde sprong hys name,
Be norþ and be souþe;   135
Myche he couþe of game
Wyth sytole, sautrye yn same,
Harpe, fydele and crouþe.
He was a noble dysour
Wyth ladyes of valour: 140
A mery man of mouþe.
He spak to þat mayde hende,
'To telle þyn erynde,
Tyme hyt were nouþe.'

f. 43ᵛᵇ   þat mayde knelede yn halle   145
Be-fore þe knyȝte alle
And greette hem wyth honour

---

119 were: *loop (of* h?) *over first* e   144 nouþe: *deleted descender to second minim of* u

She was clothed in tarse,

Rownd and nothinge scarse, 125
J-pured with blawndenere;

Hir sadill was ovir-gilt
And with diamondis ffyltt:
Milke white was hir destere.

The dwerff was cloþed in ynde, 130
By-fore and eke be-hinde:
Stoute he was and pertte.
Amongis all Cristyn kyng
Suche sholde no man fynde;
Hi[s] surcote was so ryche bete. 135
His berde was yelewe as wax,

To his girdyll hange his fax:
The sothe to say in sertente.
Off gold his shone were dight
And coped as a knyght: 140
That signyfied no povert.

Theodeley was his name:
Wyde [wher] spronge his fame,
By northe and eke by southe;
Mekyll he couthe of game, 145
Sotill, sawtrye in same,

Harpe, fethill and crowthe.
He was a gentill boourdour
Amonge ladyes in boure:
A mery man of mouthe. 150
He spake to the mayde hende,
'For-to tell thine erende,
Tyme hit were nouthe.'

The mayde knelyd in hall
Be-for the knyghtis all
And sayde, 'My lorde Arthur, 155

130 dwerff: *preceded by expuncted and deleted* dew   131 fore: *above line*
before deleted and partially erased fore   135 His: *MS.* Hir   surcote:
e *over erasure*   143 were *over erased* wher   152 erende: *second* e
over erasure   156 Arthur: *a final* e *added subsequently*

And seyde, 'A cas þer ys y-falle,
Worse wyth-yn walle
Was neuer non of dolour: 150
My lady of Synadowne
Js broȝt yn strong pryson,
þat ys greet of valour;
Sche prayd þe sende her a knyȝt,
Wyth herte good and lyȝt,   155
To wynne her wyth honour.'

Vp start þe yonge knyȝt,
Hys herte was good and lyȝt,
And seyde, 'Artour my lord,
J schall þo þat fyȝt   160
And wynne þat lady bryȝt,
ȝef þou art trewe of word.'
þan seyde Artour, 'þat ys soþ,
Certayn wyth-outen oþ,
þer-to Y bere record.   165
God grante þe grace and myȝt
To holde vp þat lady ryȝte
Wyth dente of þy sword.'

þann gan Elene to chyde
And seyde, 'Alas þat tyde   170
þat J was hyder y-sent!
þys word schall sp[r]yng wyde:
Lord kyng, now ys þy prede
And þy manhod y-schent,
Whan þou schalt sende a chyld   175
þat ys wytles and wylde
To dele þoȝty dent,
And haste knyȝtes of mayn:
Launcelet, Perceual and Gaweyn,
Prys yn ech turnement.'   180

164 wyth-outen oþ: *MS.* wᵗ oute noþ   172 spryng: *MS.* spyng

f. 75ᵛ K 160   A casse is nowe beffall,
                A worsse with-in wall
                Was neuer yitt of doloure:
                Mi lady of Synadowne   160
                Js brought in stronge prison,
                That was of grete valure,
                And pray you sond hir a knyght
                That is of wer wyse and wight,
                To wynne hir with honoure.'   165

                Vppe startte that yonge knyght,
K 170   With her[t] mery and light,
                And sayde, 'Arthur my lorde,
                J shall do that fight
                And wyn that lady with myght,   170
                Jf ye be trewe of worde.'
                Than sayde Arthoure, 'þat is sothe,
                Certeyn with-outen othe,
                Therto J ber recorde.
                God yf the strenthe and myght   175
                To holde that ladyes right
K 180   With dynte of sper and swerde.'

                The mayde be-gan to chide
                And sayde, 'Alas that tyde
                That J was heder j-sentt!   180
                Thy worde shall sprynge wide:
                For-lorne is thy pryde
                And thi lose shentt,
                When thou wilt send a childe
                That is witles and wylde   185
                To dele eny doughty dent,
K 190   And haste knyghtis of renon:
                Syr Persyfale and Syr Gawyn,
                That ben abled in turment.'

166 Vppe: *capital* V *in red, two lines deep*   167 hert: *MS.* her
174 ber: *a final* e *added subsequently; oblique stroke between this and word
following, as with* 177 sper   189 ben: *a final* e *added subsequently; oblique
stroke between this word and next*

f. 44ra

Lybeaus Desconus answerede,
'ȝet was Y neuer aferde
For doute of mannys awe.
To fyȝte wyth spere or swerd
Somdell Y haue y-lerde,   185
þer many men were y-slawe.
He þat fleþ for drede,
J wolde be way or strete

Hys body wer to-drawe.

J wyll þat batayle take   190
And neuer on for-sake,
As hyt ys Artours lawe.'

þan seyde Artour anon ryȝt,
'þou getest non oþer knyȝt,
Be God þat boȝte me dere!   195
ȝef he þyngyþ þe not wyȝt,
Go gete þe on wher þou myȝt,
þat be of more powere.'

f. 76ʳ   The dwerffe with grete erroure   190
                          Went to Kynge Arthowre
                          And saide, 'Kynde kynge:
                          This childe to be weroure
                          And to do suche labour
                          Js not worthe a fferthinge!   195
                          Or that he that lady see,
K 200   He shall do bataylles thre,
                          Wyth-oute eny lesynge;
                          At Poynte Perilowse,
                          Be-syde the Chapell of Awntrous,   200
                          Shall be his begynynge.'

                          Syr Lybeus than answerde,
                          'Yett was J neuer a-ferde
                          For dred of wordys awe.
                          To fyght with spere and swerde   205
                          Somdell haue J [lerned],
K 210   Ther many man hathe be slawe.
                          That man that fleyth by wey or strete,
                          J wolde the devyll had broke his nek,
                          Wher-euer he hym take;   210
                          Also J wolde he were to-drawe
                          And with the wyne to-wawe,
                          Till the devill him take.
                          The batayll J vndir-take
                          And neuer none for-sake,   215
                          As hit is londis lawe.'

                          The kynge said anone right,
                          'Thou ge[t]tist here none oþer knyght,
                          By Him that bought me dere!
K 220   Jff ye thinke the childe not wyght,   220
                          Get the anoþer wher thou myght,
                          That is of more power.'

196 lady: *preceded by deleted* lay see   206 lerned: (d)ed *erased and*
de *substituted, the whole word then deleted and followed by* leerde   207
Ther: *a final* e *added subsequently*   many: *preceded by expuncted and deleted*
may   215 for: *followed by deleted* sar   218 gettist: *first* t *altered from* s

þat mayde for wreþþe and hete
Nolde neydyr drynke ne ete,   200
For alle þo þat þer were,
But satte down all þysmayd
Tyll þe table was y-layd,
Sche and þe dwerke yn fere.

Kyng Artour, yn þat stounde,   205
Hette of þe Table Rounde
Four þe beste knyȝtes,
Jn armes hole and sounde,
þe beste þat myȝte be founde,
Arme Lybeaus anoon ryȝtes;   210
And seyde, 'þorȝ helpe of Cryst,
þat yn þe flome tok baptyste,
He schall holde all hys hestes,
And be good champyoun
To þe lady of Synadoun   215
And holde vp alle her ryȝtes.'

f. 44rb   To army þer knyȝtes wer fayn:
þe ferste was Syr Gaweyn,
þat oþer, Syr Perceuale,
þe þyrþe, Syr Eweyn,   220
þe ferþde was Syr Agrafrayn:
So seyþ þe Frenȝsch tale.
þey caste on hym a scherte of selk,
A gypell as whyte as melk,
Jn þat semely sale,   225
And syȝt an hawberk bryȝt
þat rychely was a-dyȝt
Wyth mayles þykke and smale.

Gaweyn, hys owene syre,
Heng abowte hys swyre   230
A scheld wyth a gryffoun;

212 flome: f *over loop* (*of initial* l?)

f. 76ᵛ   The mayden for jre and hete
           Wolde neyþer drynke ne ete,
           For none that there were;   225
           She sate downe dismay[de]
           Tyll the table was raysed,
           She and the dwerffe in fere.

           Kyng Arthour, in that stounde,
K 230   Comaunded of the Tabill Rownde   230
           Foure of the best knyghtis,
           Jn armys hole and sownde,

           To arme him anone rightis;
           And sayde, 'Throwe þe helpe of Criste,
           That in the fflome was baptiste,   235
           He shall holde vppe all his hight[is],
           And be gode champyon
           To the lady of Synadon
K 240   And fellen hir foon in fyght[is].'

           To armen him þe knyghtis were fayne: 240
           The fyrst was Syr Gawayne,
           That oþere, Syr Persyuale,
           The third was Syr Jwayne,
           The fourthe highte Agfayne:
           Thus telleth the Frensshe tale.   245
           They kestyn on him of sylke
           A sorkett white as mylke,
           That semely was in sale;
K 250   Ther-on an haubryk bryght
           That richely was dyght   250
           With mayles thik and smale.

           Syr Gawyn, his owe syre,
           Henge abo[u]te his swyre
           A shelde with one chefferon;

---

225 were: *final* e *over another letter*   226 dismayde: sed *over erased* de
229 Arthour *and* 249 Ther: *a final* e *added subsequently*   236 hightis *and*
239 fyghtis: *MS.* hight *and* fyght   253 aboute: w *over* u

And Launcelet hym broȝt a sper,
Jn werre wyth hym well to were,
And also a fell fachoun;
And Syr Oweyn hym broȝt a stede   235
þat was good at euerych nede
And egre as lyoun;
And an helm of ryche atyre
þat was stele and noon yre
Perceuale sette on hys croun.   240

þe knyȝt to hors gan spryng
And rod to Artour þe kyng
And seyde, 'My lord hende:
ȝef me þy blessynge,
Anoon wyth-oute dwellynge: 245
My wyll ys for-to wende.'
Artour hys hond vp-haf
And hys blessynge he hym yaf,
As korteys kyng and hende,
And seyde, 'God graunte þe grace   250
And of spede space,
To brynge þe lady out of bende.'

f. 44ᵛᵃ   þe mayde stout and gay
Lep on her palfray;
þe dwerk rod hyr be-syde.   255
And tyll þe þyrde day,
Vp-on þe knyȝt alwey
Euer sche be-gan chyde;
And seyde, 'Lorell and kaytyf,
þey þou wher worþ swy[ch] fyfe,   260
Y-tynt now ys þy pryde!
þys pase be-fore kepeþ a knyȝt
þat wyth ech man wyll fyȝt:
Hys name ys spronge wyde.

237 egre: *preceded by deleted* er   260 swych: *MS.* swyw

And an helme of riche atyre   255
That was stele and none jre

Sir Percyvale sett on his crowne;
Lawncelett brought him a spere,

K 260   Jn armes him with to were,
And a fell fa[u]chone;   260
Jwayne brought him a stede
That was gode at nede
And egir as eny lyon.

The knyght to hors gan sprynge
And rode to Arthure the kynge   265
And sayde, 'My lorde hende:
Yeff me thy blessynge,
With-oute eny dwellynge:

K 270   My will is nowe to wende.'
Arthur his honde vp-haffe   270
And his blessyng him yaffe,
As curteys kynge and kynde,
And sayde, 'God yf the grace,
Off spede and eke of space,
To brynge that byrde oute of bonde.'   275

The messanger was sto[u]te and gaye
And leppt[e] on her palfraye;
The dwerffe rode by hir syde.

K 280   Tyll on the thirde day,
On that knyght alwaye   280
Faste he gan to chide;
And saide, 'Lorell, cayty[ff]e,
Though þu were worþe suche fyve,
Lorne is thy pryde!
This place be-forne kepith a knyght   285
That wit[he ee]che man will fight:
His wordis spryngen full wyde.

260 fauchone: v *over* u   270 haffe: *later cross-stroke through* a *as in* 271
yaffe; ff *over erasure in* 271   276 messanger: *a final* e *added subsequently*
stoute: v *over* u   277 leppte: *final* e *erased*   281 he: *a* t *erased before* h
282 Lorell: o *over another letter*   caytyffe: v *over erased* ff   285 place:
la *over erasure*   286 withe eeche: h e *over erased* he ee; *erased* The which
in left-hand margin.

Wylleam Celebronche: 265
Hys fyȝt may no man staunch,
He ys werrour so wyth;
þoruȝ herte oþer þoruȝ honche,
Wyth hys sper he wyll launche
All þat aȝens hym ryȝtte.'   270
þan seyd Lybeaus Desconus,
'Js hys feȝtynge swych v[u]s,
Was he neuer y-hytte?
What-so-euer me be-tyde,
To hym Y wyll ryde   275
And loke how he sytte!'

Forþ þey ryden all þre,
Wyth merþe and greet solempnyte,
Be a castell aunterous,
And þe knyȝt þey gon y-se,   280
J-armeþ bryȝt of ble,
Vp-on þe Vale Perylous.
He bare a scheld of grene
Wyth þre lyouns of gold schene:
Well prowdc and precyous;   285
Of [s]wych lengell and trappes:
To dele ech man rappes
Euer he was fous.

f. 44ᵛᵇ   And whan he hadde of hem syȝt
To hem he rod full ryȝt   290
And seyde, 'Welcome, beau frer!
Ho þat rydyȝt her day oþer nyȝt
Wyth me he mot take fyȝt
Oþer leue hys armes here.'
'Well,' seyde Lybeaus Desconus,   295
'For loue of swete Jhesus,
Now let vs passe skere:
We haueþ for-to wende
And beþ fer from our frende,
J and þys meyde yn fere.'   300

272 vus: y _over_ u   286 swych: _MS._ wych

He hat Syr William Delara[u]nche:
K 290   His ffyght may no man staunche,
f. 77ᵛ   He is a werreour oute of wytt;   290
Throwe herte oþer throwe haunche,
His spere he will throwe launche
Whoso agayne hym sytt.'
Quod Lybeous Disconeous,
'Js his fyght of suche vse,   295
Was he neuer j-hitt?
For ought that may betyde,
Ayenes him will J ride
K 300   To se how he will sytte!'

They redyn forthe all thre   300
Vpon that fayre cause
Ryght to Chapell Auntours;
The knyght they con see,
Jn armys bryght of blee,
Vppon the Poynte Perylous.   305
He bare a shelde of grene
With iij lyons of gold shene:
Well proude and precious;
K 310   Off sute lynnell and trappes:
To dele strokys and rappes   310
That knyght was evyr vyous.

Whan he sawe Lybeous with syght
Agayne him he rode right
And sayde, 'Well-come bewfere!
Whoso ridi[s] here day or nyght   315
He most nedys with me fight
Or leven his armes here.'
Quod Lybeous Disconeus,
K 320   'For the loue of Jhesus,
Lett vs nowe passe here: 320
We be fer from any frende
And have wylde wey to wende,
f. 78ʳ   J and this mayden in fere.'

288 Delaraunche: v *over* u   299 sytte: *later cross-stroke through* s
315 ridis: th *over erased* s

Wylleam answerede þo,
'þou myȝt not skapy so,
So God ȝef me good reste!
We wylleþ, er þou go,
Fyȝte boþe two,   305
A forlan[g] her be weste.'
þan seyde Lybeaus, 'Now Y se
þat hyt nell non oþer be:
Jn haste þo dy beste.
þou take þy cours wyth schafte,   310
Ȝef þou art knyȝt of crafte,
For her ys myn all preste.'

No lengere þey nolde abyde;
To-gedere þey gonne ryde
Wyth well greet raundoun.   315
Lybeaus Desconus þat tyde
Smot Wylleam yn þe syde
Wyth a sper feloun;
And Wylleam sat so faste
þat hys styropes to-braste   320
And hys hynder arsoun.
Wylleam gan to stoupe
Mydde hys horses kroupe
þat he fell adoun.

f. 45ra   Hys stede ran away;   325
Wylleam ne naȝt longe lay
But start vp anoon ryȝt
And seyde, 'Be my lay!
Be-fore þys ylke day
Ne fond Y non so wyȝt.   330
Now my ste[de] ys a-go,
Fyȝte we a-fote also,
As þou art hendy knyȝt.'

306 forlang: *followed by contraction for* -is   311 crafte: *loop (of another*
f?) *above* r   331 stede: *MS.* ste

William answerd thoo,
'Thowe shalt not scape soo,   325
So God yf me rest!
We shall bothe twoo
Fyght or than we goo,
K 330   A forlonge here be weste.'
Quod Lybeus, 'Nowe Y see   330
Hit will no[n] oþer bee:
J[n] haste do thi best.
Take thi course with thi shafte,
Jff þu conne thy crafte,
For here is myne all prest.'   335

They wolde no lenger abyde,
But to-geder con þey ryde
With well grete raundon.
K 340   Lybeus Disconeus that tide
Smote William vnder the syde   340
With a sper ffelloune;
But Will[iam] sate so faste
That bothe his styropis to-brast
And his hynder arsoune,
That he be-gann to stoupe   345
Ouer his hors crowpe,
And in the felde fell downe.

His stede ranne away,
K 350   But William nought longe laye
But stertt vp anone ryght   350
And sayde, 'Be my faye!
Nevyr a-for this daye
Ne fonde J none so wyght.
My stede is nowe a-goo:
f. 78ᵛ   Sir, ffyght on fote also,   355
Yff thou be a gentyll knyght.'

---

331 non oþer: *MS.* no noþer   332 Jn: *MS.* J   341 ffelloune
and 344 arsoune: *perhaps* fellonne, arsonne   342 William: *MS.* Will
352 a-for: *a final* e *added subsequently*

þo seyde Lybeau Desconus,
'Be þe loue of Jhesus,   335
þer-to Y am full ly3t.'

To-gedere þey gonne spryng;
Fauchouns hy gonn out-flyng
And fo3te fell and faste.
So harde þey gonne drynge   340
þat feer, wyth-oute lesynge,
Out of har helmes braste;
But Wylleam Selebraunche
Lybeau Desconus gan lonche
þor3-out þat scheld yn haste;   345
A kantell fell to grounde:
Lybeau, þat ylke stounde,
Jn hys herte hyt kaste.

þanne Lybeaus, wys and why3t,
Be-fore hym as a noble kny3t,   350
As werrour queynte and scle3,
Hawberk and krest yn sy3t
He made fle doun ry3t
Of Wylleames helm an he3;
And wyth þe poynt of hys swerd   355
He schauede Wylleamys berd
And com hy[s] flessch ry3t ney3.
Wylleam smot to hym þo
þat hys sword brast a-two,
þat many man hyt sey3.   360

f. 45ʳᵇ   þo gan Wylleam to crye,
'For loue of Seynt Marye,
Alyue let me passe!
Hyt wer greet vylanye
To þo a kny3t to deye,   365
Wepene-les yn place.'

341 wyth-oute: *preceded by deleted* out   357 hys: *MS.* hy

Sayde Libeus Disconeus,
'By the leue of Jhesus,
K 360   Ther-to J am full lyght.'

To-geder con they dynge   360
And ffauchones oute to flynge
And faughten ffrely faste.
Dyntis con they dynge
That fyre, with-oute lesynge,
From helme and basnett oute-braste;   365
But Wylliam Sellabraunche
To Lybeus con launche
Through his shelde on highe.

K 370

Lybeus anone ryght
Deffended him with myght,   370
As werreor queynte and slygh;
Barbe and crest in syght
He made to fle downe ryght
Off Williams helme on highe;
And with the poynte of the swerde   375
K 380   He shove Williams berde
And came the fflesshe not nyghe.
William smote to Lybeus soo
That his swerd barst a-two,
That many a man hit sy3e.   380

Tho can William to crye,
'For the loue of Mary,
On lyve now lett me passe!
Hit were a grete vylonye
To do a knyght to dye,   385
K 390   Wepenles in a pla[s]se.'

386 plasse: *first* s *erased*
C 4342   H

þan seyde Lybeaus Desconus,
'For loue of swete Jhesus,
Of lyue hast þou no grace
But ȝef þou swere an oþ   370
Er þan we two goþ,
Ryȝt her be-fore my face.

Jn haste knele adoun
And swer an my fachoun
þou schalt to Artour wende   375
And sey, "Lord of renoun,
As ouer-come and prysoun,
A knyȝt me hyder gan sende,
þat ys y-clepede yn vs
Lybeaus Desconus,   380
Vn-knowe of keþ and kende." '
Wylleam on knees doun sat
And swor, as he hym hat,
Her farward word and ende.

þus departede þey alle: 385
Wyllyam to Artours halle
Tok þe ryȝte way.
As kas hyt be-gan falle,
Knyȝtes proud yn palle
He mette þat selue day.   390
Hys susteres sones þre
Wher þe knyȝtes fre
þat weren so stout and gay.
Whann þey sawe Wyllyam blede,
As men þat wold awyede   395
þey made greet de-ray.

f. 45ᵛᵃ   And seyde, 'Eem Wylleam,
Ho haþ don þe þys scham
þat þou bledest so ȝerne?'

383 as: *preceded by beginning of another letter* (h?)   398 don: *perhaps* donn

f. 79^r Quod Lybeus Disconeus,
'By the l[ou]e of Jhesus,
Off lyfe gettest þu no grace
But þu swere me an othe   390
Or than ye hense gothe,
Right be-for my face.

Jn haste knele downe
And swere on my ffauchon
Thou shalt to Artor wende   395
K 400   And say, "Lord of renon,
As ouer-come person,
A knyght me heder ganne sende,
That ye cleppen in your vse
Lybeus Disconeus,   400
Vnkothe of right and k[y]nde." '
William on kneis him sett
And swore, as he hym hett,
Her fo[r]ward worde and ende.

Thus they departed all: 405
K 410   William to Arthours hall
Toke the right waye.
A case ther can be-fall:
Thre prynces proude in palle
He met that ylke daye.   410
The knyghtis all thre
Weren his syster sonnes free,
That weren so stoute and gaye.
Whan they sawe William blede,
As men that wolden wede   415
K 420   They maden grete deraye.

f. 79^v And seyde, 'Eme William,
Who hathe wrought the this shame?
Why bledest thou so yeren?'

388 loue: ev *over* ou   392 be-for: *a final* e *added subsequently*
393 *caret after* knele; þu *added above line*   394 ffauchon: *an* e *added*
subsequently   401 kynde: y *partially erased,* e *over it, followed by caret*
and second e *above line*   404 forward: r *added above line*

He seyde, 'Be Seynt Jame,   400
On þat [nys] naȝt to blame:
A knyȝt stout and sterne.

A dwerk ryȝt her be-fore,
Hys squyer as he wore,
And ek a well fayr wyȝt.   405

But o þyng greuyþ me sore:
þat he haþ do me swore
Vp-on hys fawchoun bryȝt
þat Y ne schall neuer-more,
Tyll Y come Artour be-fore,   410
Soiourne day ne nyȝt.
For prysoner Y mot me yeld
As ouer-come yn feld
Of hys owene knyȝt,
And neuer aȝens hym bere   415
Noþer scheld ne spere:
All þus Y haue hym hyȝt.'

þanne seyde þe knyȝtes þre,
'þou schalt full well a-wreke be:
For-soþe wyth-out fayle!   420
He alone aȝens vs þre
Nys naȝt worþ a stre
For-to holde batayle.
Wend forþ eem and do þyn oþe,
And þe traytour, be þe roþe,   425
We schull hym asayle,
Ryȝt be Godes grace
Yer he þys forest passe,
þauȝ he be dykke of mayle!'

---

401 nys: *MS. deleted* nyȝt *or* nyȝs   405 fayr: y *written over* þ
427 grace: *followed by expuncted and deleted* he

'By God and be Seint Jame,   420
Of that he is nought to blame,
A knyght wel stoute and sterne.
Lybeus Disconeus he highte:
To fell his fone in fyght
He nys noþinge to leren.   425
K 430 A dwerffe ryd[is] him by-fore,
His squyer als he were,
And eke a well fayre berne.

But o thinge grevis me sore:
That he hathe made me swere   430
By his ffauchone bryght
That J shall neuer-more,
Till J be Artour be-fore,
Stynte day nor nyght.
To hym J mot me yelde   435
K 440 As ouercomen in felde
Of his owne knyght;
J shall neuer ayenes him bere
Noþer sheld noþer spere:
Thus haue Y him hight.'   440

Than said the knyghtis free,
'Thou shalt a-wroken bee:
Sertys with-oute fayle!
Hym agayne vs thre
Ys not worthe a stree   445
K 450 For-to holde batayle.
f. 80r   Wende thedyr and do thine othe,
And though the traytour be wrothe
We shall him assayll;
Or he this forest passe   450
His hambrek we will to-rasshe,
Though hit be thike of mayle!'

426 rydis: eth over erased is

Now lete we Wylyam be,   430
þat wente yn hys jorne
Toward Artour þe kyng.
Of þese kny3tes þre,
Harkeneþ, lordynges fre,
A ferly fayr fy3tynge!   435

f. 45vb   þey armede hem full well
Yn yren and yn stel,
Wyth-out ony dwellyng,
And leptede on stedes sterne
And after gon y-erne   440
To sle þat kny3t so yenge.

Her-of wyste no wy3t
Lybeaus þe yonge kny3t,
But rod forþ pas be pas.
He and þat mayde bry3t   445
To-gydere made all ny3t
Game and greet solas.
Mercy hy gan hym crye
þat hy spak vylanye:
He for-3af here þat trespas.   450
De dwerke was her squyer
And seruede her, fer and ner,
Of all þat nede was.

A-morn, whan þat hyt was day,
þey wente yn har jornay   455
To-ward Synadowne.
þanne saw þey kny3tes þre,
Jn armes bry3t of ble,
Ryde out of Karlowne:
All y-armed yn-to þe teþ,   460
Euerych swor hys deþ,
An stedes baye browne,
And cryde to hym full ry3t:
'þef, turne agayn and fy3t,
Wyth þe we denkeþ roune!'   465

436 hem: *followed by expuncted and deleted* yn

K 460

Her-of wyst no wyght
K 470   Syr Lybeus that yonge knyght,
But rode forthe pase by pase.   455
He and that mayden bright
Made to-geder that nyght
Gamen and grete solas.
Mercy she con hym crye
For she had spoken hym vylonye: 460
He for-yaue hir that trespas.
The dwerff was hir squyer
And serued hem bothe in fere
K 480   Off alle that worthi was.

On morowe, whan it was daye,   465
They redyn on her jornaye
Taward Synadon.
Then met they in the way
Thre knyghtis stoute and gaye,
Rydynge from Carboun.   470

K 490   To hym they cryed aright:
'Traytor, torne agayne and fight,
Or leve here thi rennoun!

453 Her-of: e *added after* r, *followed by oblique stroke*   467 Synadon:
final ne *added subsequently*   470 Carboun *and* 473 rennoun: *perhaps*
Carbonn, rennonn

Lybeaus Desconus þo kryde,
'J am redy to ryde
Aȝens yow alle y-same!'
He prykede, as pryns yn pryde,
Hys stede yn boþe syde,   470

Jn ernest and yn game.
þe eldest broþer gan bere
To Syr Lybeaus a spere:
Syr Gower was hys name,
But Lybeaus hym so nyȝ   475
þat he brak hys þeȝ,
And euer efte he was lame.

þe knyȝt gronede for payne;
Lybeaus, wyth myȝt and mayne,
Felde hym flat adowun.   480
þe dwerk Teondeleyn
Tok þe stede be þe rayne
And lep yn-to þe arsoun,
And rod hym, also sket,
þer þat þe mayde set   485
þat was fayr of fasoun;
þo louȝ þat mayde bryȝt
And seyde, 'þys yonge knyȝt
Ys chose for champyon!'

f. 46ᵗᵃ

480 adowun: *perhaps* adownn

For here we westward wende
Thyne haubrek we shall rende: 475
Ther-to we bethe ffull bounde.'

Syr Lybeus to hem cryed,
'J am redy to ride
Ayenes you all in same!'
As prince prouude in pride,   480
He prekyd his stede on eche syde
And to them stoutly con r[e]de
On ernest and nought in game.
The eldest broþer can bere
To Sir Lybeus a spere: 485
Gower was his name;
Lybeus rode Gower so n[e]gh[e]
That he to-brake Gowers thiegh,
And evyr after was lame.

The knyght gronyd for payne;   490
Lybeous, with myght and mayne,
Held hym fast adowne.
The dwerffe of Theodoleyn
Toke the stede by the rayne
And lepte vp in the arson,   495
And rode forthe, also skette,
Ther the mayde Elyne sette
That faire was of ffassyon;
Than loughe this mayden bright
And seide that this yonge knyght   500
Js chose for champyon.

The medyllest broþere be-helde
How his brother in the felde
Had lorne bothe mayne and myght;
He smote, as it is tolde,   505
Syr Lybeous in the shelde
With his spere full right.

f. 80ᵛ

K 500

K 510

K 520

482 rede: y *over first* e   487 neghe: y *over first* e *and final* e *erased*
497 sette: ette *over erasure*

þe myddell broþer com ȝerne   490
Vp-on a stede sterne,
Egre as lyoun:
Hym þoȝte hys body wold berne
But he myȝt, also ȝerne,
Fell Lybeaus adoun.   495
As werrour out of wytte
Lybeaus on helm he smyt
Wyth a fell fachoun;
Hys strok so harde he set,
þorȝ helm and basnet,   500
þat sword tochede hys croun.

þo was Lybeaus agreued
Whan he feld on hedde
þat sword wyth egre mode;
Hys brond abowte he weuede: 505
All þat he hyt he cleuede,
As werrour wyld and wode.
f. 46ʳᵇ   'Allas,' he seyde þo,
'Oon aȝens two,
To fyȝte, þat ys good!'   510
Wel faste þey smyte to hym,
And he, wyth strokes grym,
Well harde aȝens hem stode.

The shafte a-two did brest,
The hede steked faste
Jn place ther hit was pight;   510
Lybeous than can ber
With the poynte of his spere
The helme awey of the knyght.

f. 81ʳ   The yongest broþer ffull yerne
K 530   Vpon a stede full sterne   515
             As egir as eny lyon,
             Hym thought his body can bren
             But he myght, also yern[e],
             Ber Lybeous downe.
             As werour oute of witt   520
             Lybeous on the helme he hit
             With a ffell fauchon;
             So styffe a stroke he set[t],
             Throwe helme and basnet[t],
K 540   Hit clave in Lybeous crowne.   525

             Tho wax Lybeous agreved
             When he felte on his hed[e]
             The swerde with egir mode;
             His bronde aboute he wende:
             All that he hit he shende,   530
             Als[e] werreour wilde and wode.
             Full fast men saide tho[o],
             'A man agaynes two,
             To fyght is nothinge gode!'
K 550   Harde he hewe on him,   535
             And he, with strokys grym[e],
             Styfly ayenes him stode.

513 *followed by catchword*: the yongest broþer   518 yerne: *final* e *erased,*
flourish added to n   519 Ber: *a final* e *added subsequently*   523 styffe:
fe *over erasure*   sett: *second* t *erased, as in* 524 basnett   527 hede: *final* e
erased   530 hit *followed by oblique stroke*   531 Alse: *final* e *erased*
532 thoo: *second* o *erased*   536 gryme: *final* e *erased*

þo sawe þese knyȝtes
þey ne hadde no myȝtes   515
To feȝte aȝens her fo;
To Syr Lybeaus þey gon vp-ȝelde
Boþe har sperys and har schelde
And mercy cryde hym þo.

Lybeaus answerede, 'Nay,   520
Ye ne askapeþ so away,
Be God þat schop mankende!
þou and þy brederen twayne
Schull plyȝt her your fay
To Kyng Artour to wende,   525
And sey, "Lord of renounnes,
As ouer-come and prysouns,
A knyȝt vs hyder gan sende:
To dwelle yn your bandwon
And ȝelde you tour and toun,   530
Ay wyth-outen ende."

And but ye wyllen þo so,
Sertes, Y schall you slo,
Er þan hyt be nyȝt.'
þe knyȝtes sweren þo   535
þey wolde to Artour go,
And trewes þer þey plyȝt.
þus departede day,
Lybeaus and þat may,
As þey hadden tyȝt.   540

But throwe Godis grace,
That oþer brother he canne brace
Vnder his right arme tho[o];   540
He threwe him in that place
And in that selfe space
His lyfte arme brast atwo[o].
The yongest say with sight
K 560   That he ne had mayne n[o] myght   545
To fyght agaynes his foo;
f. 81ᵛ   To Lybeous vp he helde
His spere and eke his shelde
And mercy cryed hym thoo.

Lybeous answerd, 'Naye,   550
Thou ascapest not so away,
By Hym that holpe mankynde!
Thou and thi breþeren tweyne
Shull plight me your fayne
K 570   Ye shullen to Artor wende;   555
And sey, "Lord of renon,
As ouer-come [of] persoune,
A knyght me hedyr can sende:
To yelde you toure and towne
And dwell in your bawndon,   560
Ever with-oute ende."

And but ye will so doo,
Certis, J will you sloo,
Longe or hit be nyght.'
K 580   The knyghtis sworne two   565
They shulde to Arthur goo,
Her trowythe ther they plight.
Lybeus and that may
Rydden in her jornaye
Ther they haden tight.   570

---

540 thoo: *second o erased, as in* 543 atwoo   545 no: o *altered to* e,
followed by oblique stroke   557 of: *erased*   562 And: *capital* A *in*
red, two lines deep

Tyll þe þyrde day
þey ryde yn game and play,
He and þat mayde bryȝt.

f. 46ᵛᵃ   And euer þey ryden west
Jn þat wylde forest
To-ward Synadowne;   545
þey nyste what ham was best:
Taken þey wolde reste
And myȝt not come to toun.
A logge þey dyȝte of leues   550
Jn þe grene greues,
Wyth swordes bryȝt and broune;
þer-jnne þey dwellede all nyȝt,
He and þat mayde bryȝt,
þat was so fayr of fasoun.   555

And þe dwerk gan wake
For noo þef ne schuld take
Har hors away wyth gyle.
For drede he gan to quake,
For gret fer he sawe make,   560
þannes half a myle.
'Arys,' he seyde, 'yong knyȝt!
To horse þat þou wer y-dyȝt,
For dowte of peryle;
For J here greet bost   565
And fer smelle rost,
Be God and Seynt Gyle!'

Lybeaus was stout and fer
And lepte on hys destrer,
Hente scheld and spere   570
And rod toward þe fyer,
And whanne he nyȝede ner,
Two geauntes he saw þer.

560 gret: r *over* e

Tyll that the ther[d] day
They reden in game and playe,
He and that mayden bryght.

        They reden even weste
K 590   Jn-to the wilde forest   575
        Taward Synadoun;
        They nuste whate hem was best:
        Taken they wolde fayne reste
        And myght not come to tow[n]e.
f. 82ʳ   Jn the grene greves   580
        Thei dight a loge of leves,
        With swerdys bryght and brow[n]e;
        There-in they dwelled al nyght,
        He and that mayden bright,
K 600   That was of fayre fassyon.   585

        And evyr the dwerff cann wake
        That nothinge shulde be-take
        Her[e] hors aweye with gyle.
        For dred he ganne quake:
        Grete ffyre he sawe make,   590
        Thensse halfe a myle.
        'Aryse, sir,' he sayde, 'knyght!
        To hors that ye were dight,
        For dred of more perile;
K 610   Certis, J h[i]re boste   595
        And fele grete smylle of roste,
        Be God and be Seint Gyle!'

        Lybeous was stoute and fayre
        And lepte vpon his desteyre
        And hent shelde and spere,   600
        And whan that he nyȝhed nere,
        As he rode tawarde the f[y]re,
        Two gyauntes he sawe there.

571 therd day: *MS.* therday   579 towne: *MS.* towe   582 browne:
MS. browe   588 Here: *final* e *erased*   590 sawe: s *over* c   595 hire:
e *over* i   599 desteyre: eyre *over erasure*   602 fyre: e *over erased* y

þat on was red and loþlych
And þat oþer swart as pych: 575
Grysly boþe of chere!
þat oon held yn hys barme
A mayde y-clepte yn hys arme:
As bryȝt as blos[m]e on brere.

f. 46ᵛᵇ   þe rede geaunt sterne   580
A wylde boor gan terne
Abowte vp-on a spyte.
þat fyer bryȝt gan berne,
þe mayde cryde yerne
þat som man schuld her þer wete,   585
And seyde, 'Wellaway!
þat euer J bode þys day
Wyth two fendes to sette!
Now help, Marie mylde,
For loue of þy chylde,   590
þat Y be naȝt for-ȝette!'

þan seyde Lybeaus, 'Be Seynt Jame!
To saue þys mayde fro schame,
Hyt wer a fayr apryse;
To fyȝte wyth boþe yn same,   595
Hyt wer no chyldes game,
þat beþ so grymme and gryse!'
He tok hys cours wyth schafte,
As knyȝt of kende crafte,
And rod be ryȝt asyse.   600
þe blake geaunt he smot smert
þorȝ þe lyuere, longe and herte,
þat neuer he myȝte aryse.

þo flawe þat mayde schene
And þankede Heuene Quene   605
þat swych socour her sente;

179 blosme: *MS.* blosle   605 þankede: k *over* g

That one was rede and lothelych,
K 620   That oþer black as eny pyche: 605
Gressly bothe of chere!
The black helde in his arme
A mayde j-clypped in his barme:
So bryght as blossom on brere.

The rede giaunte full yerne   610
A wylde bore canne torne
Aboute apon a spytt.
The fyre bright can bren,
f. 82ᵛ   The mayde cryed yerne
K 630   For some man shuld it wit,   615
And sayde euer, 'Wayle-a-waye!
That euer J shulde bide this daye
With two devylles to sitt!
Helppe me, Mary mylde,
For love of thine childe,   620
That J be nought for-yett!'

Than Lybeous: 'Be Seint Jame!
To saue this maiden from shame,
Hit were enpure enpri[c]e;
K 640   But for-to fight with bothe in same,   625
Hit is no childes game:
They be so grym and gryse!'
He toke his course with a shafte,
As knyght of kynde crafte,
And rode be right assyse.   630
The blacke giaunte can to smertt
Thorugh lounge and hert,
That neuer after cann rysse.

Tho flye the mayden shene
K 650   And thanked tho heven quene   635
That suche socoure hir sentt;

605 pyche: *caret between* y *and* c; t *added above line*   624 enprice: s *over*
erased c   629 a *inserted subsequently between* As *and* knyght   632 *caret*
after and; eke thorught *added above line*   633 rysse: ss *over* d

C 4342   I

Þo com þat mayde Elene,
Sche and her dwerk y-mene,
And be þe hond her hente,
And ladde her yn-to þe greues,   610
Jn-to þat logge of leues,
Wyth well good talent,
And prayde swete Jhesus
Helpe Lybeaus Desconus
þat he wer naȝt y-schent.   615

f. 47ra   Þe rede geaunt þore
Smot to Lybeaus wyth þe bore
As man þat wold awede.
Þe strokes he sette so sore
þat hys cursere þer-fore   620
Deed to grounde ȝede.
Lybeaus was redy boun
And lepte out of þe arsoun
As sperk þoȝ out of glede
And, egre as a lyoun,   625
He fauȝt wyth hys fachoun
To quite þe geauntes mede.

Þe geaunt euer fauȝt,
And at the seconde drauȝt
Hys spyte brak a-two;   630
A tre yn honde he kauȝt
As a man þat wer vp-sawȝt
To fyȝte aȝens hys fo,
And wyth þe ende of þe tre
He smot Lybeaus scheld a-þre,   635
And þo was Lybeaus well wo;
And er he eft þe tre vp-haf,
A strok Lybeaus hym yaf:
Hys ryȝt arm fell hym fro.

639 ryȝt: *followed by deleted beginning* (*of* h?)

Tho came the mayde Ele[yn],
She and the dwarffe by-dene,
And by the hande hir hentte,
And lad hir in-to the greves,   640
Jn-to the loge of levys,
With well gode entent,
And be-sought swete Jhesus
Helpe Lybeus Disconeus
K 660   That he ne[r] nought shent.   645

The rede gyaunte smote thore
To Sir Lybeous withe the bore
f. 83ʳ   As wolfe oute off wede.
His dynnte he smote so sore
That Lybeous stede th[o]re-for   650
Downe to grownde yede.
Lybeous was redy bounde
And lepte on his arson
As sparkyll dothe on glede;
K 670   With hartt egyr as a lyon,   655
He faught with his fauchon
To quyte the gyaunte his mede.

Euer the gyaunte ffaught[e],
But at the secunde draught
His spere barst evyn a-twoo;   660
As man that was vnsawght
A tronchon oute he laught[e]
To fyght agaynes his foo,
And with the hede of the tre
K 680   He smote Lybeous shelde in thre: 665
Than was Lybeous woo.
As he his tronchon vp-haffe,
Syr Lybeous a stroke him gaffe:
His right arme fell hym froo.

637 Eleyn: ne *over erased* yn   645 ner: *MS.* ne   650 thore-for: *first*
o *altered to* e; *a final* e *added*   658 ffaughte: *final* e
erased as in 662 laughte

þe geaunt fell to grounde: 640
Lybeaus, þat ylke stounde,
Smot of hys hedde ryȝt.
Hym þat he yaf er wounde,
Jn þat ylke stounde,
He seruede so aplyȝt.   645
He tok þe heddes two
And yaf hem þe mayden þo,
þat he hadde fore þat fyȝt;
þe mayde was glad and blyþe
And þonkede God fele syde   650
þat euer was he made knyȝt.

f. 47ʳᵇ   þan seyde Lybeaus, 'Gentyl dame,
Tell me what ys þy name
And wher þou wer y-bore.'
Sche seyde, 'Be Seynt Jame,   655
My fader ys of ryche name,
Woneþ her be-fore:
An erl, an hold hore knyȝt,
þat haþ be a man of myȝt:
Hys name ys Syr Antore.   660
Men clepeþ me Vyolette:
For me þese geauntes be-sette
Our castell full ȝore.

ȝesterday yn þe mornynge,
Y wente on my playnge   665
And noon euell ne þouȝte.
þe geauntes, wyth-out lesynge,
Out of a kaue gonne sprynge
And to þys fyer me brouȝt;
Of hem Y hedde ben y-schent   670
Ne God me socour hadde y-sent,
þat all þys world wrouȝt.
He ȝelde de þys good dede,
þat for vs gan blede
And wyth hys blod vs bouȝt.'   675

642 Smot: *followed by deleted beginning* (*of* h?)   661 Men: *letter erased*
after n

The gyaunte fell to grownde: 670
Syr Lybeous, in that stownde,
Smote of his hede full right.
Jn Frensshe as it is j-ffounde,
He that he gave the fyrste wounde,
K 690   He servyd hym so aplyght.   675
And then toke the hedis two
And bare the mayden thoo,
For whom he made that ffyght;
The mayde was glade and blythe
And thanked God ffele sythe   680
f. 83ᵛ   That euer he was made knyght.

Quod Lybeous, 'Gentil dame,
Tell me whate is thi name
And where ye were y-bore.'
K 700   'Syr,' she sayde, 'be Seynt John,   685
My ffader is of riche fame
And wonnes yonder be-forne:
An erle, an olde hore knyght,
That hathe ben man of myght:
His name is Syr Anctour.   690
They clepen me Violet:
The gyauntes had me be-sett
Aboute our castell yore.

Yesterday in the evenynge,
K 710   J went on my playenge: 695
None harme Y ne thoughte.
The gyaunte, with-oute lesynge,
Oute of the busshes con sprynge
And to this fyre me brought;
Off hem J had be shent   700
Nad God me socoure sent,
That all the worlde wrought.
He quyte the thy mede,
That for vs canne blede
K 720   And with his body vs bought.'   705

Wyth-out ony more talkynge,
To horse þey gon sprynge
And ryde forþ all yn same.
He tolde þe erl tydynge
How he wan yn fyȝtynge　　　　　　　　680
Hys chyld fram wo and schame.
þe two heddes wer y-sent
Artour þe kyng to present,
Wyth mochell gle and game;
þanne ferst yn court aros　　　　　　　　685
Lybeaus Desconus los
And hys gentyll fame.

f. 47va　　　þe Erl Antore also blyue
Profrede hys doftyr hym to wyue,
Vyolette þat may;　　　　　　　　690
And kasteles ten and fyue
And all after hys lyue
Hys lond to haue for ay.
þan seyde Lybeaus Descono[u]s,
'Be þe loue of swete Jhesus!　　　　　　　　695
Nauȝt wyue yet Y ne may:
J haue for-to wende
Wyth þys mayde so hende,
And þer-fore haue good day!'

þe Erl, for hys good dede,　　　　　　　　700
Yaf hym ryche wede:
Scheld and armes bryȝt,
And also a noble stede
þat douȝty was of dede
Jn batayle and yn fyȝt.　　　　　　　　705
þey ryde forþ all þre
Toward þe fayre cyte:
Kardeuyle for-soþ hyt hyȝt.
þanne sawe þey yn a park
A castell stout and stark　　　　　　　　710
þat ryally was a-dyȝt.

694 Desconous: *MS.* Desconois　　　　708 hyt: t *over* ȝ

With-oute more talkynge,
To hors con they sprynge
And reden forthe all in same,
And tolde the erle tydynge
Howe he wanne in fightynge   710
His doughter fro woo and shame.
Than were the hedis sent
To Kynge Arthour in present,
f. 84ʳ   With mekyll glee and game;
K 730   And tho in courte ffast roose   715
Syr Lybeous Dysconeus noble loose
And all his gentill fame.

K 740

The Erle, for his gode dede,
Yaue him full riche mede:
Shelde and armes bryght,   720
And also a noble stede
That was gode at nede
K 750   Jn turnament and in fyght.
Lybeus and that maye
Redyn in her jurnaye,   725
Ther they logen tyght;
Thanne sawe thei in a parke
A castell store and starke
That richely was y-dight.

718 The: *capital* T *in red, two lines deep*

Swych saw þey neuer non,
J-made of lyme and ston,
J-karneled all abowte.
'Oo!' seyde Lybeaus, 'Be Seynt Jon!   715
Her wer a wordly won
For man þat wer yn dowte.'
þo loȝ þat mayde bryȝt
And seyde, 'Hyt owyþ a knyȝt,
þe beste her abowte: 720
Ho þat wyll wyth hym fyȝt,
Be hyt be day oþer nyȝt,
He doþ hym lowe lowte.

f. 47vb

For loue of hys lemman,
þat ys so fayr a woman,   725
He haþ do crye and grede
Ho þat bryngeþ a fayryr oon,
A jerfaukon, whyt as swan,
He schall haue to mede.
Ȝef sche ys naȝt so bryȝt,   730
Wyth Gyfroun he mot fyȝt
And ye may not spede,
Hys hed schall of be raft
And sette vp-on a sper schaft
To se yn lengþe and brede.   735

And þat þou mayst se full well:
þer stant yn ech a karnell
An hed oþer two vp-ryȝt.'
þan seyde Lybeaus also snell,
'Be God and Seynt Mychell!   740
Wyth Gyffroun Y schall fyȝt
And chalaunge þe jerfawucon
And sey þat Y haue yn þ[y]s toun
A lemman to so bryȝt;
And ȝef he her wyll se,   745
Y wyll hym schewy þe,
Be day oþer be nyȝt!'

740 Mychell: *preceded by deleted* p   743 þys: *MS.* þ^o

Fayre walled hit was with stone: 730
Suche sawe he neuer none,
With cornyllus styff and stoute.
K 760   Sayd Lybeous, 'Be Seynt John!
This were a worthy wone,
Who had hit wonne with dyntt.'   735
Than lough that byrd bryght
And sayde, 'Alwey a knyght,
The best here all aboute,
Whoso will with h[i]m fyght,
By day or by nyght,   740
Lowe he maketh him loute.

For love of his leman,
K 770   That is so fayre a woman,
He hathe done crye and grede
Whoso bryngeth a fayrer on,   745
A gerfawkon, white as swanne,
f. 84ᵛ   He shall haue to his mede.
And yf she is not so bright,
With Jeffron he most fight
And yf he may not spede,   750
His hede shall him be rafte
And sett vpon a shafte
K 780   To seen in lenthe and brede.

The sothe to se wele

An hede or two vp-ryght.'   755
Saide Lybeous als snelle,
'By God and Saint Michelle!
With Jeffran Y will ffyght
And chalaunge that faukon
And sey J haue in towne   760
A lemman two so bright;
K 790   And when he will hir a-see,
J shalle shewe him thee,
By day other by nyghte!'

739 him: *MS.* hō   745 fayrer: *beginning of* e *before first* r

þe dwerk seyde, 'Be Jhesus!
Gentyll Lybeaus Desconus:
þat wer a greet peryle.   750
Syr Gyffroun le Flowdous
Jn fyȝtyng he haþ an vs
Knyȝtes to be-gyle.'
Lybeaus answerede þar,
'þer-of haue þou no kar,   755
Be God and be Seynt Gyle!
J woll y-se hys face,
Er Y westward pace
From þys cyte a myle.'

f. 48ra   Wyth-oute a more resounne   760
þey tok har yn in þe toune
And dwellede stylle yn pese.
A-morn Lybeaus was boun
For-to wynne renoun
And ros, wyth-oute les;   765
And armede hym full sure
Jn þat selue armure
þat Erl Antores was.
Hys stede he be-gan stryde,
þe dwerk rod hym be-syde   770
Toward þat prowde palys.

Syr Gyffroun le Fludous
Aros, as was hys vus,
Jn þe morn tyde;
And whan he com out of hys hous   775
He saw Lybeaus Desconus
Com pryky[n]de as pryns yn pryde,
Wyth-out a more abood;
And aȝens hym he rod
And þus to hym he cryde   780
Wyth voys þat was schylle:
'Comyst þou for good oþer for ylle?
Tell me and naȝt ne hyde!'

777 prykynde: *MS.* prykyde

The dwerffe said, 'By Jhesus!   765
Gentill Lybeous Disconyous,
Thou puttist þe in grete perille.
Jeffron le Freudous
Jn syght hathe a queynte vse
Knyghtis to be-gylle.'   770
Lybeous answerd ther,
K 800   'Ther-of haue J no care,
Be God and be Seint Gile!
J shall see his face,
Or Y esteward passe   775
From this cite a myle.'

f. 85ʳ   Wyth-oute more renowe[n]
They dwellyd still in towne
All that nyght in pease.
On morowe Lybeous was bowne   780
To wyne him renon
K 810   And rose, with-oute leese;
And armed him right sever
Jn that noble armwre
That er Aunctours was.   785
His stede ganne to stride,
The dwarffe rode him be-side
Taward the proude palleys.

Jeffrond le Freudys,
He rose and was with vs,   790
Jn that morowe tide
K 820   To honour swete Jhesus
And ses Lybeus Disconyous
Come prickande with pryde.
With-oute any abode,   795
Agayne Libeous he rode
And lowde to hym can crye
With vaise sharpe and shille:
'Comest þu for gode or jlle?
Tell me anone in hiȝe!'   800

777 renowen: *final* n *in lighter ink*   789 Freudys: *perhaps* Frendys

þan seyde Lybeaus also tyte,
'For Y haue greet delyte   785
Wyth þe for-to fyȝt.
For þou seyst greet despyte,
þat woman half so whyt
As þy lemman be ne myȝt,
And Y haue on yn toune   790
Fayryr of fassyoune,
Jn cloþes whan sche ys dyȝt.
þer-fore þy gerfawcoun
To Artour þe kyng wyth kroun
Bryng Y schall wyth ryȝt.'   795

f. 48ʳᵇ   þan seyde Gyfroun, 'Gentyll knyȝt,
How scholl we preue þys syȝt
Whych of hem fayrer be?'
Lybeaus answerede aplyȝt,
'Jn Cardeuyle cyte ryȝt,   800
þer ech man may hem se,
And boþe þey schull be sette
Amyddes þe market,
To loke on boþe bond and fre.
Yf my lemman ys broun,   805
To wynne þe gerfawcoun
Fyȝte Y wyll wyth þe.'

þann seyde Gyfroun also snell,
'To all þys Y graunte well;
þys day at vnderne tyde,   810
Be God and be Seynt Mychell!
Out of þys castell
To Karlof J schall ryde!'
Har gloues vp þey held
Jn forward as Y teld,   815
As prynces prowde yn pryde.
Syr Lybeaus also snell
Rod hom to hys castell:
No leng he nolde abyde.

785 delyte: d *over loop of* l   788 half: *preceded by expuncted and deleted*
alf

Quod Lybeous also tite,
K 830   'J haue grete delyte
With the for-to fighte.
Thou seyste a foule dispite,
Ther is no woman so white   805
As thy leman be lighte,
And J haue one in towne
Well fayre of ffassyon,
Jn clothis when she is dight.
f. 85ᵛ   Therfor the gerfaukon   810
To Arthur kynge with crowne
K 840   Bringe J shall with right.'

Qu[o]d Jeffrey, 'Gentyll knyght,
We shull prouen aright
Whether the fayrer bee.'   815
Quod Lybeous anone right,
'Jn Cordile cite with sight,
That eche man may hir see,
And amyddis the market
Bothe thei shull be sette,   820
To loke on bonde and free.
K 850   Yff my leman is browne,
To wyn the jerfaukon
Juste Y will with the.'

Quod Jeffrounse also snell,   825
'For-sothe J graunte it wele;
This daye at vndertide,
By God and by Seint Michell!
Oute atte this castell
To Cardyle we shull ride!'   830
Her glovis vp they helde
K 860   Ther right in the felde,
As prynce proude in pryde.
Lybeus also snelle
Rode home to his ostell: 835
He nolde no lenger abide.

813 Quod: *MS.* Qud   819 And: *capital* A *in red, two lines deep, guide letter to*
right   825 Jeffrounse: *perhaps* Jeffronnse (*as in other forms of this name in* L)

And commande mayde Elene,   820
As semelekest on to sene,
Buske her and make her boun.
'J say, be Heuene Quene,
Gyffrouns lemman schene
þys day schall come to toun;   825
And boþe men you schull y-se
Amydward þe cyte,
Boþ body and fasoun;
ȝef þou be naȝt so bryȝt,
Wyth Gyffroun J mot fyȝt   830
To wynne þe gerfaucoun.'

f. 48ᵛᵃ   Mayde Elene, also tyte,
              Jn a robe of samyte
              Anoon sche gan her tyre
              To þo Lybeaus profyte,   835
              Jn keue[r]chers whyt
              Arayde wyth gold wyre.
              A veluwet mantyll gay
              Pelured wyth grys and gray
              Sche caste abowte her swyre;   840
              A sercle vp-on her molde
              Of stones and of golde:
              þe best yn þat enpyre.

831 gerfaucoun: *loop (of* k?) *above* o   836 keuerchers: *MS.* keuechers

                    And hit the mayde Elyne,
                    That semely was to sene,
                    To buske and make hir bownde;
                    And seyde, 'By Heuen Quene,   840
                    Geffrouns lemman the shene
f. 86ʳ   K 870 Today shall come to towne;
                    Amydward the cite
                    That all men shall you see,
                    Off wede and fassyon;   845
                    Yff þu arte not so bryght,
                    With Jeffroun J mot fight
                    To wynne the jerffaukon.'

                    The dwerff answerd and seid,
                    'Thow doste a savage dede,   850
                    For any man j-borne!
K 880   T[h]ow wilt not do be rede
                    But faryst with thi madd-hede
                    As lorde that will be lorne.
                    For his loue forthe we wende   855
                    That died for all mankynde
                    And in Bedlem was borne!'
                    Lybeous said, 'That were shame:
                    J hadde levyr, be Seint Jeme,
                    With wilde hors to be torne!'   860

                    The mayde Ellyne, also tiȝth,
K 890   Jn a robe of sa[m]yte
                    Gaylie ganne hir atyre
                    To do Lybeous prophite,
                    Jn kerchevys fayre and white   865
                    Aryved with gold wyre.
                    A velvet mantill gaye
                    Purfild with gryce and graye
                    She did aboute hir swyre;
                    The serkell vpon hir moolde   870
                    Off precious stones and goolde:
K 900   The best of that empire.

852 Thow: *MS.* Tow   862 samyte: *MS.* sanyte   863 atyre: raye
expuncted and deleted after a

Vp-on a pomely palfray
Lybeaus sette þat may,   845
And ryden forþ all þre.
þanne ech man gan to say,
'Her comeþ a lady gay
And semelych on to se!'
Jnto þe market sche rode   850
And houede and abode,
Amydward þe cyte;
þan syȝ þey Gyffroun come ryde
And two squyeres be hys syde,
Wyth-out a more mayne.   855

He bar þe scheld of goules,
Of syluer þre whyte oules,
Of gold was þe bordure.
Of þe selue colours
And of non oþer flowres   860
Was lyngell and trappure.
Hys squyer gan lede
Be-fore hym vp-on a stede
þre schaftes good and sure;
þat oþer bar redy boun   865
þe whyte gerfawcoun
þat leyd was to wajour.

f. 48vb   After hym com ryde
A lady proud yn pryde,
Was clodeþ yn purpel pall.   870
þat folk com fer and wyde
To se her bak and syde:
How gentyll sche was and small.
Her mantyll was rosyne,
Pelured wyth ermyne,   875
Well ryche and reall.
A sercle vp-on her molde
Of stones and of golde,
Wyth many amall.

855 more: *preceded by expuncted and deleted* r   865 redy: *loop (of* b?)
above r

Lebeous sate that daye
f. 86ᵛ   Vpon a gode palfraye,
And reden forthe all three.   875
Eche man to other ganne saye,
'Here cometh a lady gaye:
Js semely vn-to see!'
Jn-to the marke[t]e þei rode
And boldly ther abode,   880
Amydward the citee;
K 910   Then sawe thei Jeffron com ryde
And two squyers by his syde
And no more mayne.

He bare the shelde of gowlys,   885
Off syluer thre white owlys,
And of gold the bordure;
And of that same colours
And of that other floures
Was fyne golde and trappure.   890
The squiers that by him rode
K 920   That one bare shaftis gode,
Thre shaftis gode and sewre;
That other lade redy bownde
The joly gentill jerfaukowne: 895
The two ladyes were there.

And aftir hym come ryde
A lady proude in pryde,
J-clothed in purpyll palle.
The folke came fer and wide   900
To se them bac[k] and syde:
K 930   Howe gent she was and smalle.
f. 87ʳ   Hir mantill was ryght ffyne,
J-powderd with ermyne,
Well riche and ryalle.   905
The sercle on hir molde
Of stones and of goolde
And many a ryche amayle.

879 markete: *MS.* markeke   901 back: *MS.* backis

As þe rose her rode was red;   880
þe her schon on hyr heed
As gold wyre schyneþ bryȝt.
Ayder browe as selken þrede
Abowte yn lengþe and yn brede;
Hyr nose was strath and ryȝt.   885
Her eyen gray as glas,
Melk whyt was he[r] face:
So seyde þat her sygh wyth syȝt.
Her swere long and small;
Her beawte telle all   890
No man wyth mouþe ne myȝt.

To-gedere men gon hem bryng
Amydward þe chepyng,
Har beawte to dyscryue.
þey seyde, olde and yenge,   895
For-soþ wyth-oute lesyng,
Be-twene hem was partye:
'Gyffrouns lemman ys clere
As ys þe rose yn erbere,
For-soþ and naȝt to lye!   900
And Elene þe messengere
Semeþ but a lauendere
Of her norserye.'

f. 49ra   þan seyde Gyffroun [l]e Fludous,
'Syr Lybeaus Desconus,   905
þys hauk þou hast for-lore!'
þan seyde Lybea[u]s Desconus,
'Nay, swhych nas neuer myn vus:
Justy Y well þer-fore.
And yef þou berest me doun,   910
Tak my heed þe fawkoun,
As forward was be-fore;
And yf Y bere doun þe,
þe hauk schall wende wyth me,
Maugre þyn heed hore.'   915

887 her: MS. he   890 beawte: preceded by deleted ba   904 le: MS.
be   907 Lybeaus: three minims after a

As rose hir rudde was rede;
The here shone on hir hede   910
As gold wyre shynynge bryght.
K 940   Hir browes also blacke as sylke threde
J-bent in leynthe and brede;
Hir nose was streght and right.
Hir eyen gray as glasse,   915
Milke white was hir face:
So seid they þat sawee þat syght.
Hir swyre longe and smale;
Hir bewte to tellen alle
No man with mowthe myght.   920

But tho men did hem brynge
K 950   Two cheyers in-to the chepyng,
Her bewtees to discryve.
Then seid bothe olde and yonge,
Forthe-withe with-oute lesynge,   925
Be-twene hem was partye:
'Geffroune leman is clere
As rose on rise or in erbere,
For-sothe and nought to lye!
Ellyne the messangere   930
Ne were but a lawnder:
K 960   Off hir no loose make J!'

f. 87ᵛ   Quod Geffrounde ly Froundes,
'Sir knyght, by swete Jhesus,
This hau[k] thou haste lore!'   935
Qu[o]d Lybeous Disconeous,
'Suche was neuer myne vse;
Juste J will ther-fore.
Yf thowe berest me downe,
Take my hede and the faukon,   940
As forwarde was thore;
K 970   And yf J ber downe the,
The hau[k] shall wend with me,
Magre thyne hede hore.'

935 hauk: *MS.* haukys   936 Quod: *MS.* Qud   943 hauk: *MS.*
haukis

What help mo tales telld?
þey ryden yn-to þe feld
And wyth ham greet partye;
Wyth coronals stef and stelde
Eyþer smyt oþer in þe scheld   920
Wyth greet enuye.
Har saftes breke asonder,
Har dentes ferþe as þonder
þat comeþ out of þe skye;
Taborus and trompours,   925
Herawdes, goode descouerou[r]s,
Har strokes gon descrye.

Syr Gyffroun gan to speke:
'Breng a schaft þat nell naȝt breke,
A schaft wyth a cornall!   930
þys yonge ferly frek
Ys yn hys sadell steke
As stone yn castell wall;
þauȝ he wer whyȝt werrour
As Alysander oþer Artour,   935
Launcelet oþer Perceuale,
J wyll do hym stoupe
Ouer hys horses croupe
And yeue hym euele fall!'

f. 49rb   þe knyȝtes boþe two   940
               To-gydere þey ryden þo,
               Wyth well greet raundoun;
               Lybeaus smot Gyffroun so
               þat hys scheld fell hym fro
               Jn þat feld adoun.   945
               þo louȝ all þat þer wes
               And seyde, wyth-oute les,
               Duke, erl and baroun,

---

916 help: *preceded by deleted* hepl   telld: d *over* e   924 skye: *preceded
by deleted and expuncted* k   925 trompours: s *added by scribe*
938 horses: ses *added over original final* s   946 louȝ: *preceded by two
deleted letters (the first,* l)

With-oute more tale to telle,   945
They redyn downe in þe felde
And with hem grete partye;
With cornellus styff and shelde
Eythir agayne othir in the felde
With well grete envye.   950
Her shaftis brosten asondre,
K 980   Her dyntis ferden as thonder
That cometh oute of the skey;
Tabowres and trompours,
Heroudes and dissoures,   955
Her strokys con discrye.

Tho can Geffroune to lepe
And said, 'Gyve me that will not breke:
A shaffte with-oute cornall!
This yonge frely freke   960
Sytteth in his sadyll sete
K 990   As stone in castell wall;
J shall do him stoupe
Ovyr his hors crowpe
f. 88ʳ   And gyve hym an evill falle: 965
Though he be as wise wereour
As Alysaunder or Kyng Arthur,
Lawncelot or Syr Percevalle.'

The knyghtis bothe twoo
Redyn to-geder thoo,   970
With well grete rawndon;
K 1000   Lybeos smote Jeffroun soo
That his shelde smote him froo
Jn-to the felde adowne.
Then lowe all that ther was   975
And sayde, with-oute lees,
Dukes, erle and baron,

þat ȝet neuer þey ne seyȝ
Man þat myȝte dreyȝ   950
To justy wyth Gyffroun.

Gyffroun hys hors out-ryt
And was wode out of wyt
For he myȝte naȝt spede.
He rod agayn as tyd   955
And Lybeaus so he smyt,
As man þat wold awede.
But Lybeaus sat so faste
þat Gyffroun doun he caste,
Boþe hym and hys stede: 960
Gyffrounys regge to-brak
þat men herde þe krak
Aboute yn lengþe and brede.

þo seyde alle þo þat þer were
þat Gyffroun hadde for-lore   965
þe whyte gerfawkoun;
To Lybeaus þay hym bore
And wente, lasse and more,
Wyth hym yn-to þe toune.
Syr Gyffroun vp-on hys scheld   970
Was y-bore hom fram þe feld
Wyth care and rufull roun;
þe gerfawkoun y-sent was
Be a knyȝt þat hyȝt Gludas
To Artour, kyng wyth kroun.   975

f. 49ᵛᵃ   And wryten all þe dede
Wyth hym he gan lede:
þe hauk how þat he wan;
þo Artour herde hyt rede,
To hys knyȝtes he sede,   980
'Lybeauus well werry kan!

---

956 he: *above line before expuncted and deleted* hym   966 gerfawkoun:
k *over* c

That neuer yette they seye
A man that myght durye
A cours of Syr Jeffroune.   980

K 1010
    Geffroun toke his cours oute-ryght
And was nyghe oute of his witte
For he myghte not spede,
And rode ayene als tighte
And Lebeous on the helme he hitte,   985
As wolfe that wolde at wede.
But Libeous sate so faste
That Jeffroune downe caste
Bothe hym and his stede:
Geffrounes backe to-brake   990
That men herd the crake
K 1020
Aboute in leynthe and brede.

Than sayde all that ther weren
That Jeffroun had j-lorne
The gentill jerfaukon;   995
To Lybeous they hym bare
f. 88ᵛ
And went, bothe lesse and more,
With hym in-to the towne.
Geffroun oute of the felde
Was borne home on his shelde   1000
With care and reuthefull row[n]e;
K 1030
The gerfaukon j-sent was
By a knyght that hight Cadas
To Arthur, kynge with crowne.

And wretyn alle the dede   1005
With him he can to lede
The hau[k] tho Lybeous wan;
Tho Arthure hard hit redde,
To his knyghtis he sayde,
'Lybeous well wer can!   1010

1001 rowne: *MS*. rowme   1007 hauk: *MS*. haukis

He haþ me sent þe valour
Of noble dedes four,
Seþe he ferst be-gan.
Now wyll Y sende hym tresour　　　　　　　985
To spendy wyth honour,
As falleþ for swych a man.'

A[n] hundred pound honest
Of floryns wyth þe best
He sente to Cardelof þan.　　　　　　　　990
þo Lybeauus held hys feste
þat fourty dayes leste,
Of lordes of renoun.
þan Lybeauus and þat may
Token hyr ryȝte way　　　　　　　　　　995
Toward Synadowne,
And fayre her leue token þay
To wende yn-to anoþer contray,
Of duk, erl and baroun.

As þey ryden an a lowc,　　　　　　　　1000
Hornes herde þey blowe,
þer-vnþer þe doune,
And houndes ronne greet and smale;
Hontes grette yn þe vale.
þe dwerke seyde, þat drowe,　　　　　　　1005
'For-to telle soþ my tale,
Fele yeres ferly fale,
þat horn well Y þede knowe:
Hym blowyþ Syr Otes de Lyle,
þat seruede my lady som-whyle　　　　　　1010
Jn her semyly sale.
Whanne he was take wyth gyle,
He flawe for greet peryle
West yn-to Wyrhale.'

988 An: *MS.* And　　　989 floryns: y *over* n　　　997 fayre: *preceded by*
expuncted and deleted fare　　her: r *added*　　　999 erl: *preceded by expuncted*
and deleted El　　1003 greet: r *over* e

He hathe sent me with honour
K 1040   Off foure fightis the floure,
Sethen he fyrst by-ganne.
J will him send tresoure
To spend with honour,   1015
As falleth for suche a man.'

An hondered pounde honeste
Off floreyns with the best
He sent to Kardill towne.
Ther Lybeous made a feste   1020
That [.xl.^{ti}] dayes it leste,
K 1050   As lord of grete renowne;
And at the vj. wokis ende
They toke her leve to wende:
Duke, erle and baroune.   1025
Syr Lybeous and that may
Tokyn her right waye
Tawarde Synadowne.

As they redyn by a lowe,
f. 89^r Hornes herd they blowe   1030

And huntynge grete of gile.

K 1060   The dwerf saide, in a thorowe,

'That horne wele J knowe,
For youre frely sale:
Hit blowis motis jolelye,   1035
That servid some-tyme my lady,
Semely in hir sale.
When she was takyn with gile,
He ffled for grete perile
West in-to Wyralle.'   1040

1021 .xl.^{ti}: *deleted within line; rewritten in left-hand margin*   1029 As:
capital A *in red; line followed by catchword* hornes herd

As þey ryde talkynge,   1015
A rach þer com flyngynge
Ouer-twert þe way.
þanne seyde old and ynge,
Fram her ferst gynnynge,
þey ne sawe hond neuer so gay: 1020
He was of all colours
þat man may se of flours
Be-twene Mydsomer and May.
þat mayde sayde, also snell,
'Ne sawe Y neuer no juell   1025
So lykynge to my pay.

God wold þat Y hym auȝte!'
Lybeauus anoon hym kaȝte
And yaf hym to mayde Elene.
þey ryden forþ all yn saȝt   1030
And tolde how knyȝtes faȝt
For ladyes bryȝt and schene.
Ne hadde þey ryde but a whyle,
þe mouuntance of a myle,
Jn þat forest grene,   1035
þey sawe an hynde com st[r]yke
And two grehoundes y-lyke,
Be þat rech þat Y er of mene.

þey houede vnþer a lynde
To se þe cours of þe hynde,   1040
Lybeaus and hys fere.
þanne seyȝ þey come [b]y-hynde
A knyȝt j-clodeþ y[n] ynde
Vp-on a bay destrere;
Hys bugle he gan to blowe   1045
For hys folk hyt schuld knowe
Jn what stede he wer.

1027 auȝte: *preceded by expuncted and deleted* hadde   1029 Elene:
loop above second e   *Between* 1035 *and* 1036 þey seyȝ an hounde come
stryke *deleted*   1036 stryke: *MS.* styke   1042 by-hynde: *MS.* ly
hynde   1043 yn: *MS.* y

As they redyn talkynge
K 1070　　They sawe a rache com renynge
Ouer-thwerte the waye.
Than said olde and yonge,
From her first begyn[y]nge,　　　　　1045
Thay sawe neuer none so gaye:
He was of all coloures
That man may se of ffloures
By-twene Mydsomer and Maye.
The mayde saide, alse snell,　　　　　1050
'Sawe J neuer no jowell
K 1080　　So lykinge to my paye:

So that J hit aught!'
Lybeous as tight it caught
And toke hit the mayden clene.　　　　1055
Thay ridden forthe all soffte
And tolde howe knyghtis faught
For birdes bryght and shene.
Ne had they redyn but a while,
The mountence of a myle,　　　　　1060
Jn that forest grene,
f. 89ᵛ K 109　　They sawe an hynde come strike
And two grewndis like
The racche that J of mene.

They hovyd vnder a lyne　　　　　1065
And sawe the course of the hynde,
Lybeous that was so fre.
Then sawe they come [b]e-hynde
A knyght j-clothed in jende
Vppon a baye destre;　　　　　1070
His bugill canne he to blowe
K 1100　　For houndis shulde him knowe
Jn whate stede that he were.

1045 begynynge: MS. begȳnge　　1068 be-hynde: MS. he hynde

He seyde to hem þat þrowe,
'Syr, þat rach was myn owe,
Y-gon for seuene yere.   1050

Frendes, leteþ hym go!'
Lybeauus answerede þo,
'þat schall neuer be-tyde:
For wyth myn handes two
J hym yaf þat mayde me fro   1055
þat houeþ me be-syde.'
þo seyde Ser Otes de Lyle,
'þan artow yn peryle,
Byker ȝef þou abyde.'
þo seyde Lybeauus, 'Be Seynt Gyle,   1060
J ne yeue naȝt of þy gyle,
Cherll, þouȝ þou chyde!'

þan seyde Syr Otes de Lyle,
'Syr, þyn wordes beþ fyle,
Cherll was neuer my name.   1065
My fader an erll was whyle,
þe countesse of Karlyle,
Certes, was my dame.
Wer ych y-armed now,
Redy as art þou,   1070
We wolde feyȝte yn same.
But þou þe rach me leue,
þou pleyyst, er hyt be eue,
A wonder wylde game!'

þo seyde Lybeauus, also prest,   1075
'þer-of þo þy best!
þys rach schall wyth me wende.'
þey tok har way ryȝt west
Jn þat wylde forest,
Ryȝt as þe dwerk hem kende.   1080

1049 owe: *preceded by expuncted and deleted* ow *and third (illegible) letter*
1067 countesse: t *over descender of another letter*

He seide to hem that throwe,
'That racche do J owee,   1075
A-gone is viij yere.

Frendis, lettes him goo!'
Lybeous answerd thoo,
'That shall neuer be-tide:
With myn hondis two   1080
J gave it the mayden me froo
K 1110   That hovith me by-syde.'
Quod Sir Otis de Lile,
'Thou puttist the in grete perile,
To bycker and thou abide.'   1085
Lybeous sayde, 'Be Seint Gile,
J ne gyff nought of thi gile,
Chorle, though thou chide!'

Qu[o]d Sir Otys de Lyle,
'Syr, thi wordis ar wile,   1090
Chorle was neuer my name.
K 1120   My ffader an erle was awhile,
And the countesse of Carlehille,
f. 90ʳ   For-sothe, was my dame.
Yff J were armed nowe,   1095
Redy as arte thowe,
We shulden ffight in same.
But yf thow the racche levyn,
Thowe pleyest, longe or evyn,
A wondyr wilde game!'   1100

Qu[o]d Lybeous, also prest,
K 1130   'Ther-of, sir, do thy beste:
The rache with me shall wende.'
Thay token her way evyn west
Jn-to that faire forest,   1105
As the [d]werff he[m] kende.

1077 lettes: l *over* t   1089 and 1101 Quod: *MS*. Qud   1106 dwerff:
MS. dewerff   hem: *MS*. hen

þe lord, wyth greet errour,
Rod hom to hys tour
And after hys frendes sende;
And tolde hem anon ryȝtes
þat on of Artourys knyȝtes   1085
Schamelych gan hym schende,

f. 50ʳᵇ
And hadde hys rach y-nome.
þanne seyde alle and some,
'þe traytour schall be take!
And neuer ayen hom come,   1090
þauȝ he wer þoȝtyer gome
þan Launcelet du Lake.'
þo dyȝte þey hem all to armes
Wyth swerdes and wyth gysarmes,
As werre schold awake.   1095
Knytes and squyeres
Lepte on her destrerys,
For har lordes sake.

Vp-on an hell well hyȝe
Lybeauus þer þey syȝe;   1100
He rod pas be pas.
To hym þey gon crye,
'Traytour, þou schalt dye
For þy wykkede trespas!'
Syr Lybeauus aȝen be-held   1105
How fulfelde was þe feld,
So greet peple þer was;
He seyde, 'Mayde Elene,
For our rach, Y wene,
Vs comeþ a karfull cas!   1110

J rede þat ye drawe
Jn-to þe wode schawe,
Your heddes for-to hyde;
For Y am swyde fawe,
þauȝ ych schulde be slawe,   1115
Bykere of hem Y woll abyde.'

1095 schold: l *over* d   1107 greet: r *over beginning of* e

Syr Otis, with grete errour,
Rode home to his toure
And after his frendis did send;
And tolde hem anone right[is]   1110
Howe one of Arthur is knyghtis
K 1140   So shamefully canne him shende;

And his racche was j-nome.
Than sware they, all and some,
That traytur shulde ben j-take   1115
And neuer ayene home come,
Though he were the grymmer grome
Than Launcelet de Lake.
They dighten hem to armes
With swerdys and giȝarnes,   1120
As werre that shulde awake.
K 1150   Knyghtis and squyers
Leppyn on her desters,
For her lordis sake.

Vpon an hill full hie   1125
Syr Lybeous ther he seye,
f. 90ᵛ   Rydinge forthe pase by pase.
To hym they con crye,
'Traytor, thou shalt die,
To-daye for thye trespace!'   1130
Lybeus ayene be-helde
K 1160   Howe full was the felde,
So mekyll folke that ther was;
He sayde, 'Mayde Ellyne,
For this racche, Y wene,   1135
Me cometh a carefull case.

J rede ye you with-drawe
To the wode shawe,
Youre hedis for-to hide;
For Y am frely fayne,   1140
Though Y shulde be slayne,
K 1170   Bekyr with hem to abyde.'

1110 rightis: *MS.* right

Jn-to þe wode þey rode
And Lybeauus þer-out aboþe
As aunterous knyȝt yn pryde.
Wyth bowe and wyth arblaste,   1120
To hym þey schote faste
And made hym woundes wyde.

f. 50va Lybeauus stede ran
And bar doun hors and man,
For noþyng nolde h[e] spare.   1125
þat peple seyde þan,
'þys ys fend Satan,
þat mankende wyll for-fare.'
For wham Lybeauus arafte,
After hys ferste drawȝte   1130
He slep for euer-mare;
But sone he was be-sette,
As þeer ys yn a nette,
Wyth grymly wondes sare.

Twelf knyȝtes, all prest,   1135
He saw come yn þe forest,
Jn armes cler and bryȝt.
Alday þey hadde y-rest
And þouȝ yn þat forest
To sle Lybeauus þe knyȝt.   1140
Of sute were all twelfe,
þat on was þe lord hym-self,
Jn ryme to rede aryȝt.
þey smyte to hym all at ones
And þoȝte to breke hys bones   1145
And felle hym doun yn fyȝt.

þo myȝte men her dynge
And swordes lowde rynge,
Amang hem all yn fere;
So harde þey gonne þrynge,   1150
þe sparkes gonne out-sprynge
Fram scheld and helmes clere.

1121 faste: *preceded by expuncted and deleted* fe   1125 he: *MS.* her
1137 armes: *beginning of loop above* a

Jn-to the fforest he rode
And ther he boldly abode.
As avauntors proude in pryde, 1145
With bowes and arblast,
They shotten to him faste
And made hym woundis wyde.

Syr Lybeous stede ranne
And bare downe hors and man, 1150
For nothinge wolde he spare.
K 1180 All men sayde than,
'This is the devyll Satan,
That mankynde will forfare.'
For whomso Lybeous araught 1155
At his fyrst drawght,
He slepte for euer-more;
But sone he was be-sette,
f. 91ʳ As dere is in the nette,
With grymly woundis sore. 1160

For xij knyghtis, all prest,
K 1190 He sawe come oute of the west,
Jn armys bryght and clere.
Alday thay haden y-rest
And thoughtyn in that fforest 1165
To slee Lybeous that knyght.
Off sewte they weren all twelue,
That one was the lorde him-selue,
Jn ryme to redyn a-right.
They smotyn to hym at onys 1170
And thoughten to breke his bonys
K 1200 And to fellyn hym in ffyght.

Tho myght men hire dynge
And rounde rappis rynge,
Amonges hem all in ffeere: 1175
The sparkylles conne to-sprynge,
Forthe withe-oute lesynge,
From sheld and helmes clere.

Lybeauus slouȝ of hem þre,
And þe four gonne to fle
And þorst naȝt nyȝhe hym nere.   1155
þe lord dwellede yn þat schour
And hys sones four,
To selle har lyues þere.

þer ronne þo rappes ryue:
He aȝens hem fyue   1160
Fauȝt as he were wod.
Neyȝ doun þey gonne hym dryue;
As water doþ of clyue,
Of hym ran þe blode.
As he was neyȝ y-spylt,   1165
Hys swerd brast yn þe hylt:
þo was he mad of mode.
þe lord a strok hym sette
þ[r]ouȝ helm and basnet,
þat yn þe scheld hyt stode.   1170

A-swogh he fell adoun
An hys hynder arsoun,
As man þat was mate.
Hys fomen wer well boun
To perce hys acketoun,   1175
Gypell, mayl and plate.
As he gan sore smerte,
Vp he pullede hys herte
And keuerede of hys state;
An ex he hente all boun   1180
At hys hynder arsoun:
All-mest hym þouȝte to late.

þan be-sterede he hym as a knyȝt:
þre stedes heeddes doun ryȝt
He smot at strokes þre.   1185

1162 *caret after* Neyȝ; doun *inserted above the line*   1163 doþ: *preceded by deleted* þoȝ   1164 hym: *preceded by expuncted* **and deleted** ham
1169 þrouȝ: *MS.* þouȝ

Lybeous slowe of hem three,
The fourthe be-gon to flee   1180
And durste nought neȝe him nere.
K 1210   The lorde lefte in the stoure
And his sonnes foure,
To syllen her lyves dere.

Tho runne rappes ryffe: 1185
He one agaynes fyve
Faughte as he were wode.
Nye downe they con hym dryve;
So watyr dothe of the skythe,
Off hym ranne the bloode.   1190
f. 91ᵛ   Whan Lybeous was ney spilte,
K 1220   His swerde barst in the hilte:
Than was he madde of mode.
The lord a stroke he sete
Throwe helme and basnett,   1195
That in the skolle hit stode.

Jn swounynge he fel downe
Vpon his ferther arsoune,
As man that was all mate.
His fone weren full bownde   1200
To persyne his aketowne,
K 1230   Bothe mayle and plate.
When he ganne sore to smerte,
He pulled vp his herte
And sterryd vp his state;   1205
An ax he hente him nyghe,
That henge by his thighe:
Almost him thought to late.

Tho he steryd him as a knyght:
Thre stedis adowne right   1210
He slowe at strokys three.

þe lord saw þat sy3t
And on hys courser ly3t
Awey he gan to fle.
Lybeauus no lenger abode
But aftyr hym he rode   1190
And vnþer a chesteyn tre
þer he hadde hym quelþe,
But þe lord hym yeld
At hys wylle to be,

f. 51ᵃ   And, be sertayne extente,   1195
               Tresour, lond and rente,
               Castell, halle and bour:
               Lybeauus þer-to consente,
               Jn fo[r]ward þat he wente
               To þe Kyng Artour.   1200
               'And seye, "Lord of renoun,
               As ouer-come and prysoun,
               Y am to þyne honour."'
               þe lord grauntede to hys wylle,
               Boþe lowþe and stylle,   1205
               And ledde hym to hys bour.

               Anoon þat mayde Elene
               Wyth gentyll-men fyftene
               Was fet to þat castell.
               Sche and þe dwerke by-dene   1210
               Tolde dedes kene
               Of Lybeauus how hyt fell:
               Swyche presentes four
               He hadde y-sent Kyng Artour,
               þat he wan fayr and well.   1215
               þe lord was glad and blyþe
               And þonkeþ fele syde
               God and Seynt Mychell.

1189 no: *preceded by* o *and first minim of* n   1190 aftyr: *loop* (*of* h?)
over t   1199 forward: *MS.* foward   1202 As: *followed by expuncted*
and deleted e   1217 þonkeþ: *preceded by expuncted and deleted* þonged[e]

K 1240 The lorde sawe that in sight
       And of his stede he alyght:
       Away he began to fflee.
       Lybeous no lenger abode   1215
       But aftyr hym he rode;
       Vnder a chesteyne tree
       Ther he hadde him qwelled,
       But that the lorde hym yelde
       At his will for-to bee,   1220

       And, by certeyne stente,
K 1250 Tresure, londe and rentte,
f. 92ʳ Castell, hall and boure:
       Lybeous therto assente,
       By forward so that he wente   1225
       Vnto Kynge Arthure
       And sayde, 'Lorde of renowne,
       As ouer-come and prisowne,
       J am to thine honowre.'
       The lorde graunted his wille,   1230
       Bothe lowde and stylle,
K 1260 And ladde him to his toure.

       Anone the mayden Ellyne
       With gentill-men fyftene
       Was j-fett to the castell.   1235
       She and the dwerffe bydene
       Tolden all the dedis kene
       Off Lybeous howe it be-fell:
       And whiche persones foure
       He sent to Kynge Arthure,   1240
       That he wanne fayre and wele.
K 1270 The lord was well blythe
       And thanked fele sythe
       God and Seint Michell

Now reste we her a whyle
Of Syr Otes de Lyle   1220
And telle we oþer tales:
Lybeauus rod many a myle
Among aventurus fyle
Jn Yrland and yn Wales.
Hyt be-fell yn þe monþ of June,   1225
Whan þe fenell hangeþ yn toun,
Grene yn semely sales;

1222 myle: y *over beginning of* e

That swyche a nobyll knyght   1245
Shulde with werre in fyght
Wynne his lady ffree.
To covere with mayne and myght,
Lybeous a fourtenyght
Ther with him canne lende.   1250
He did helen his wounde
K 1280   And made hym hole and sownde
By the fowrtenyght ende;
f. 92ᵛ   Than Lybeous and that maye
Toke her right waye   1255
To Synadon to wende.

The lorde, with-oute dwellynge,
Went to Arthur the kynge
And for presowne hym yelde,
And tolde him the begynnynge   1260
Howe suche a knyght in ffyghtyng
K 1290   Wan hym in the ffelde.
Kynge Arthur had gode game
And so had alle in same
That herde that tale y-tolde;   1265
And chosyn hym prophytable
Knyght of the Rounde Table,
To ffyght with spere and shelde.

Nowe rest we here a while
Of Sir Otys de Lyle   1270
And tell we forthe oure talis,
K 1300   Howe Lybeous rode many a myle
And sey awntours the while
And Jrlande and in Walys.
Hytt be-fell in June, Y wene,   1275
Whan ffenell hangeth al grene
Abowte in semely saale;

1267 Knyght: *preceded by deleted* ky   1269 Nowe: *capital* N *in red, two
lines deep*   1270 de: *preceded by blotted letter*   1275 Hytt: *capital* H
in red, two lines deep; wene: *loop (of* l?) *above* n

þys somerys day ys long,
Mery ys þe fowles song
A[nd] notes of þe nyȝtyngales.   1230

þat tyme Lybeauus com ryde
Be a ryuer syde
And saw a greet cyte
Wyth palys prowd yn pryde
And castelles heyȝ and wyde   1235
Wyth gates greet plente.
He axede what hyt hyȝt;
þe mayde seyde anon ryȝt,
'Syr, Y telle hyt þe:
Men clepeþ hyt Yle d'Or,   1240
Her haþ be fyȝtynge mor
þanne owher yn any countre.

For a lady of prys,
Wyth rode reed as rose on ryse,
þys countre ys yn dowte;   1245
A geaunt hatte Mauugys,
Nowher hys per þer nys,
Her haþ be-leyde abowte.
He ys blak as ony pych,
Nower þer ys non swych   1250
Of dede sterne and stoute;
Ho þat passeþ þe bregge
Hys armes he mot legge
And to þe geaunt alowte.'

The somerys day is longe,
Mery is the ffowlis songe
And notis of the nyghtyngale.   1280

That tyme Lybeous canne ryde
K 1310   Be a reueres syde
And sawe a fayre cite
With palys prowde in pryde
And castelles high and wyde   1285
And gates grete plente.
f. 93ʳ   He axed whate hit hight;
The mayden sayde anone right,
'Syr, J will telle the:
Men clepeth this Jl de Ore,   1290
Here be fightis more:
K 1320   Ther is werr in euery countre.

For a lady of price,
Roddy as rose on rice,
This contre is in dowte;   1295
A gyaunt that heght Maugys,
Nowhere his pere is,
Hir hathe be-sett aboute.
He is as blacke as pyche,
Nowher is none suche   1300
Off dedis sterne and stowte;
K 1330   Whate knyght so passyth the bryge
His armys he moste downe legge
And to the gyaunte alowte.

He is thirty fote on leynthe   1305
And myche more of strenthe
Than other knyghtis fyve;
Syr Lybeous, woll be-thynke the
That thou with him ne macched bee:
He is gryme to discryue.   1310

1282 reueres: *followed by dot*

þo seyde Lybeauus, 'Mayde hende,   1255
Schold Y wonde to wende
For hys dentys ylle?
Yf God me grace sende,
Er þys day come to ende
Wyth fyȝt Y schall hym spylle.   1260
J haue y-seyn grete okes
Falle for wyndes strokes;
þe smale han stonde stylle.
þey Y be ȝyng and lyte,
To hym ȝyt wyll Y smyte,   1265
Do God all hys wylle!'

f. 51ᵛᵃ   þey ryden forþ all þre
Toward þat fayre cyte,
Me clepeþ hyt Ylle d'Ore.
Mauugeys þey gonne y-se   1270
Vp-on þe bregge of tre,
Bold as wylde bore.
Hys scheld as blakke as pych,
Lyngell, armes, trappur was swych:
þre mammettes þer-ynne wore,   1275
Of gold gayly[c]h y-geld;
A schafte an honde he held
And oo scheld hym be-fore.

He cryde to hym yn despyte,
'Say, þou felaw yn whyt,   1280
Tell me what art þou!
Torne hom agayn all-so tyt,
For þy owene profyt,
Yef þow louede þy prow.'

1276 gaylych: *MS.* gaylyth

He berreth on euery browe
K 1340   As it were brystillus of a sowe;
His hede grete as an hyve,
His armys the lenthe of an elle,
His fystis arne full felle   1315
Dyntys with to dryve.'

Quod Lybeous, 'Mayden hynde,
f. 93ᵛ   My way nowe will Y wende
For alle his strokys ylle.
Jff God will me grace sende,   1320
Or this day come to ende
K 1350   With fight Y hoppe hym fell.
J haue sene grete okys
Fallyn with wyndes and strokys,
And the lytell stande full stille.   1325
Thoughe that Y be litell,
To hym will J smyte,
Let God do his wylle!'

They roden forthe all three
Tawarde that fayre cite   1330
That men calleth Jle Dolour.
K 1360   Maugys they con see
Vpon a bryge of tree,
Bolde as a wilde bore.
His shelde was blacke as pycche,   1335
And all his armour suche:
Thre mawmentis ther-in were,
Off gold gayly gilte;
A spere in honde he helde
And his childe him be-fore.   1340

He kryede to hym in spyte,
K 1370   'Sey, thou ffellave in white,
Tell me whate arte thowe!
Torne home ayene tite,
For thyne owne prophite,   1345
Yf thow lovyst thy prowe.'

Lybeauus seyde anoon ry3t,   1285
'Artour made me kny3t,
To hym J made avow
þat Y ne schulde neuer turne bak;
þer-fore, þou deuell yn blak,
Make þe redy now!'   1290

Syr Lybeauus and Maugys
On stedes prowde of prys
To-gedere ryde full ry3t.
Boþe lardes and ladyes
Leyn out yn pomet tours   1295
To se þat sely sy3t;
And prayde wyth good wyll,
Boþe lode and styll,
Helpe Lybeauus þe kny3t,
And þat fyle geaunt   1300
þat leuede yn Termagaunt,
þat day to deye yn fy3t.

f. 51ᵛᵇ   Har scheldes breeke asonder,
Har dentes ferd as donder:
þe peces gonne out-sprynge.   1305
Ech man hadde wonder
þat Lybeauus ne hadde y-be vnþer
At þe ferst gynnyng.
þanne drou3 dey swordes boþe
As men þat weren wroþe   1310
And gonne to-gedere dynge;
Lybeauus smot Mauugys so
þat hys scheld fell hym fro
And yn-to þe feld gan flynge.

Maugys was queynte and quede   1315
And smot of þe stedes heed
þat all fell out þe brayne;
þe stede fell doune deed,
Lybeauus noþyng ne sede
Bot start hym vp agayn.   1320

1303 breeke: *perhaps* brecke

Lybeous sayde anone right,
'Kynge Arthure made me knyght,
f. 94^r   To hym Y made avowe
That J shulde neuer turne my backe;   1350
Therfor, thow devyll black,
K 1380   Make the redy nowe!'

Syr Lybeus and Maugis
On stedis proude in prise
To-geder redyn full ryght.   1355
Bothe lordis and ladyes
Laynen in her toures
For-to se that syght;
And praied to God bothe lowde and stille,
Yff it were his swete wille,   1360
Save that Crysten knyght,
K 1390   And that ffyle gyawnte
That levyd on Turmagaunte,
This day to dye in fighte.

Her shaftes borsten on sonder,   1365
Her dyntis ferd as thonder:
The pecis canne of-sprynge.
Euche man had wonder
That Lybeous ne had gon vnder
At the fyrste begynnynge.   1370
They drewe swerdis bothe
K 1400   As men that were wrothe
And gonne to-gedir dynge;
Sir Lybeous smote Maugis soo
That his shelde fell him froo   1375
And in the [f]elde canne flynge.

Maugis was qweynt and qwede
And smote Lybeous stede on the hede
And dasshid oute the brayne;
The stede fell downe dede,   1380
Syr Lybeous nought sayde
f. 94^v K 1410   But stertt hym vp agayne;

1376 felde: *MS.* flelde

An ax he hente boun
þat heng at hys arsoun
And smot a strok of mayn
þoruȝ Maugys stedes swyre
And for-karf bon and lyre: 1325
þat heed fell yn þe playn.

A-fote þey gonne to fyȝte
As men þat wer of myȝte;
þe strokes be-twene hem two
Descryue no man ne myȝte,   1330
For þey wer vn-syȝt
And eyder oþres fo.
Fram þe our of pryme
Tyll hyt was euesong tyme,
To fyȝte þey wer well þro.   1335
Syr Lybeauus durstede sore
And seyde, 'Maugys, þyn ore!
To drynke lette me go.

f. 52ra

And Y schall graunte þe
What bone þou byddest me,   1340
Swych cas yef þat be-tyt.
Greet schame hyt wold be
For durste a knyȝt to sle,
And no mare profyt.'
Maugys grauntede hys wyll   1345
To drynke all hys fyll,
Wyth any despyte.
As Lybeauus ley on þe bank
And þoruȝ hes helm he drank,
Maugys a strok hym smyt   1350

þat yn þe ryuer he fell:
Hys armes ech a dell
Was weet and euell a-dyȝt;

1335 þro: *perhaps* þra   1353 euell: *preceded by expuncted and deleted* e[w]

And an ax hent y-bowne
That henge by his arsowne
And stroke to hym with mayne   1385
Through Maugis stede swyre:
He for-karve bone and lyre
That the hede fell in the playne.

On fote bothe they fyghte,
Discryven no man myght   1390
The strokys be-twis hem two;
K 1420   Bothe woundes they laughte,
For they were vnsaught
And eiþer other is foo.
From the oure of pryme   1395
Tyll hit were evensonge tyme,
To fyghtyn they were throo.
Sir Lybeous thrested soore
And sayde, 'Maugis, thine ore!
To drinke thou lett me goo.   1400

And Y shall graunte the
K 1430   Whate bone thowe aske of me,
Swiche case if the be-tide;
For grete shame hit wolde be
A knyght for thurste to slee,   1405
And no maner parfyte.'
Maugis graunted his will
To drynke all his fille,
With-oute more dispite.
As he lay on the banke   1410
And throw his helme dranke,
K 1440   Maugis smertly hym smytte

That in the reuer he fylle:
His armoure euery dele
f. 95ʳ   Was wette and evill y-dight;   1415

1413 fylle: *preceded by expuncted and deleted* ffiye

But vp he start snell
And seyde, 'Be Seynt Mychell,   1355
Now am Y two so ly3t!
What, wendest þou, fendes fere,
Vn-crystenede þat [Y] were
Tyll Y saw þe wyth sy3t?
J schall for þys baptyse   1360
Ry3t well quyte þy seruyse,
þoru3 grace of God almy3t!'

þanne newe fy3t þey be-gan:
Eyþer tyll oþer ran
And delede dentes strong;   1365
Many a gentylman
And ladyes whyt as swan
For Lybeauus handes wrong;
For Maugys yn þe feld
For-karf Lybeauus scheld   1370
Wyth dente of armes long.
þanne Lybeauus ran away
þer þat Maugys scheld lay
And vp he gan hyt fonge.

f. 52rb   And ran agayn to hym;   1375
Wyth strokes s[t]out and grym
To-gydere þey gonne asayle.
Be-syde þat ryuer brym
Tyll hyt derkede dym
Be-twene hem was batayle.   1380
Lybeauus was werrour wy3t
And smot a strok of my3t
þoru3 gypell, plate and mayll;
Forþ wyth þe scholder bon
Maugys arm fyll of anoon   1385
Jn-to þe feld, saun3 fayle.

1358 Y omitted in MS.   1376 stout: MS. strout   1377 asayle: first
a followed by expuncted and deleted sale

But vp he sterte as snelle
And seyd, 'Be Seint Michell,
Nowe am Y two so light!
Weneste thou, fendys fere,
Vncristened that Y were   1420
Tylle Y sawe the with sight?
K 1450   J shall for this baptyse
Quyte well thi service,
Thorough grace of God almyght!'

Then newe fyght by-ganne: 1425
Eyther to other ranne
And deltyn dyntes strange;
Well many a gentilman
And ladyes as white as swanne
For Lybeous her hondys wrange;   1430
For Maugis in the felde
K 1460   For-karffe Lybeous shelde
Thorough dynte of armes longe.
Than Lybeous ranne awaye
There Maugis shelde laye   1435
And vp he gan hit fange.

And ran agayne to hym;
With strokys sharpe and gryme
Eyther other ganne assayle.
Till the day was dymme   1440
Vpon the watir brym
K 1470   By-twene hem was bataylle.
Lybeous was werreour wight
And smote a stroke of myght
Thorowe jepowne, plate and mayle,   1445
Thorowe the shulderbone
That his right arme anone
f. 95ᵛ   Fell in the felde, saunce fayle.

þe geaunt þys gan se,
J-slawe þat he schulde be,
And flauȝ wyth myȝt and mayn.
Lybeauus after gan fle   1390
Wyth sterne strokes þre
And smot hys bak a-tweyn.
þe geaunt þer be-leueþ;
Lybeauus smot of hys heed
And of þe batayle was fayn.   1395
He wente yn-to þe toun;
Wyth fayr processioun
þat folk com hym agayn.

A lady whyt as flowr,
þat hyȝte la Dame d'Amore,   1400
Afeng hym fayr and well
And þankede hys honour
þat he was her socour
Aȝens þe geaunt so fell.
To chambre sche gan hym lede   1405
And dede of all hys wede
And clodede hym yn pell,
And proferede hym wyth word
For-to be her lord
Jn cyte and castell.   1410

f. 52ᵛᵃ   Lybeauus grauntede yn haste
And loue to her he caste,
For sche was bryȝt and schene.
Alas he ne hadde y-be chast!
For aftyr-ward at last   1415
Sche dede hym greet tene.
For twelf monþe and more
Lybeauus dwellede þore
And mayde Elene,
þat neuer he myȝte out-breke   1420
For-to help awreke
Of Synadowne þe quene.

1403 her: *followed by expuncted and deleted* co

The gyaunte this ganne see,
That he shulde slayne bee: 1450
He ffledde with myght and mayne.
K 1480   Syr Lybeous after ganne tee
With sterne strokys thre
He smote his backe on twayne.
The gyaunte ther belevyde;   1455
Syr Lybeous smote of his heved:
There-of he was fayne.
He bare the hede in-to the towne;
With a fayre processyoune
The folke come hym agayne.   1460

A lady bright as floure,
K 1490   That men calleth la Dame Amoure,
Resseyued him wele and fayre
And thanked hym with honour
That he was hir socoure   1465
Agayne that giaunte file.
To chambyr she him ledys
And did of all his wedis
And clothed hym in palle,
And profirde him with worde   1470
For-to be hir lorde
K 1500   Off cite and castell.

Lybeous graunted hir in haste
And loue to hir ganne caste,
For she was bright and shene.   1475
Alas she hadde be chaaste!
For euer at the laste
She dyde hym traye and tene.
For xij monthes and more
f. 96ʳ   As Lybeous dwelled thore   1480
He for-gate mayde Elyne,
K 1510   That neuer he myght oute-breke
For-to helpe to awreke
Off Synadowne the qwene.

For þys fayr lady
Kowþe moch of sorcery,
More þen oþer wycches fyfe;   1425
Sche made hym melodye
Of all manere menstracy
þat man myȝte descryue.
Whan he seyȝ her face
Hym þouȝ he was   1430
Jn paradys alyue;
Wyth fantasme and fayrye
þus sche blerede hys yȝe,
þat euell mot sche þryue.

Tyll hyt fell on a day   1435
He mette Elene þat may
Wyth-jnne þe castell tour;
To hym sche gan to say,
'Syr knyȝt, þou art fal[s] of fay
Ayens þe Kyng Artour!   1440
For loue of a woman
þat of sorcery kan
þou doost greet dyshonour:
þe lady of Synadowne
Longe lyȝt yn prysoun,   1445
And þat ys greet dolour!'

f. 52ᵛᵇ   Lybeauus herd her so speke;
Hym þouȝ hys hert wold breke
For sorow and for schame,
And at a posterne vn-steke   1450
Lybeauus gan out-breke
Fram þat gentyll dame,
And tok wyth hym hys stede,
Hys scheld and hys ryche wede,
And ryde forþ all y-same.   1455

1424 of *followed by deleted* s   1426 hym *followed by deleted* e
1432 fantasme: *preceded by deleted* fanst   1434 euell: *preceded by ex-*
puncted and deleted el   1439 fals: *MS.* falf   1443 greet: r *over* e
1447 speke: k *over* e

For the faire lady   1485
Cowthe more of sorcerye
Than other suche fyve;
She made hym suche melodye
Off all maner mynstralsye
That any man myght discryue.   1490
Whan he sawe hir face
K 1520   Hym thought that he was
Jn paradice on lyve;
With false lies and fayre
Th[u]s she blered his eye: 1495
Evill mote she thryue!

Till it be-fell vpon a daye
He mete Elyne that may
Be-side that castell toure;
To hym than ganne she saye,   1500
'Knyght, thou arte false in thi laye
K 1530   Ageynes Kynge Arthure!
For the love of o woman
That mekyll of sorcery canne
Thow doste the grete dissehonour: 1505
My lady of Synadowne
May longe lye in preson,
And that is grete doloure!'

Syr Lybeus herde hir speke;
Hym thought his hert gan breke   1510
For sorowe and for shame.
f. 96ᵛ K 1540   At a postren j-steke
There he ga[nn]e oute-breke
Fro that gentyll dame,
And toke with hym his stede,   1515
His shelde, his jren wede,
And reden forthe all in same.

1495 Thus: MS. This   1513 ganne: *three minims after* a

Her styward stout and sterne
He made hys squyere:
Gyfflet was hys name.

And ryde as faste as þey may
Forþ yn her jornay   1460
On stedes bay and browne.
Vp-on þe þyrdde þay
þey saw a cyte gay:
Me clepeþ hyt Synadowne;
Wyth castell hey3 and wyde   1465
And palys prowd yn pryde,
Werk of fayr fassoune;
But Lybeauus Desconus,
He hadde wonder of an vus
þat he saw do yn toune.   1470

For gore and fen and full wast
þat þer was out y-kast
To-gydere þey gaderede y-wys.
Lybeauus axede yn hast,
'Tell me, mayde chast,   1475
What amounteþ þys?
þey takeþ all þat hore
þat er was out y-bore:
Me þyngeþ þey don amys.'
þanne seyde mayde Elene,   1480
'Syr, wyth-outen wene,
J schall þe telle how yt ys.

f. 53ra   No kny3t, for nessche ne hard,
               þey he schold be for-fard,
               Ne geteþ her non ostell,   1485
               For loue of a styward:
               Men clepeþ hym Syr Lambard,
               Constable of þys castell.

1457 squyere: *preceded by deleted* sqy   1473 þey: *followed by deleted* d

Hir stywarde stoute and ffayre
He made his squyer:
Jurflete was his name.   1520

They rodyn ffaste as they maye
K 1550   Forthe on her jornaye
On stedis baye and browne;
Till on the third daye
They saue a cite gaye: 1525
Men clepen hit Synadowne;
With castelles high and wide
And palysed proude in pryde,
Worke of fayre ffacion;
But Lybeous Disconyous   1530
Had wonder of that vse
K 1560   That he saye men do in towne.

Cor and fenne full faste,
That men hade ere oute-caste,
They gadered ynne j-wysse.   1535
Syr Lybeous axid in haste,
'Tell me, mayden chaste,
Whate be-tokeneth this?
They taken in the goore
That ar was oute y-boore: 1540
Me thynketh they do amysse.'
K 1570   Than seyd mayde Ellyne,
'Syr knyght, with-oute wene,
J tell the whate hit is.

f. 97ʳ   No knyght, for nesshe ne harde,   1545
Though he shulde be for-ffarde,
Getteth here none ostell,
For doute of the stywarde
That hight Syr Lanwarde,
Constable of that castelle.   1550

1544 *followed by catchword* No knyght   1545 No *written over* Ar

Ryde to þat est gate
And axede þyn jn þer-ate,   1490
Boþe fayre and well;
And er he bete þy nede,
Justes he wyll þe bede,
By God and Seynt Mychell!

And yf he beryþ þe doun   1495
Hys trompys schull be boun
Har bemes for-to blowe,
And þoruȝ-out Synadowne
Boþe maydenes and garssoun
Fowyll fen schull on þe þrowe;   1500
And þanne to þy lyues ende,
Jn whett stede þat þow wende,
For coward werst þou knowe;
And þus may Kyng Artour
Lese hys honour   1505
þoruȝ þy dede slowe.'

þan seyde Lybeauus also tyt,
'þat wer a greet dyspyt
For any man alyue!
To þo Artour profyt   1510
And make þe lady quyt
To hym Y wyll dryue.
Syr Gyfflette make þe yare,
þyder we wyllyþ fare
Hastely and blyue.'   1515
þey ryde þe ryȝt gate
Euen to þe castell yate,
Wyth fayre schaftes fyfe.

f. 53rb   And at þe fayr castell
þey axede her ostell   1520
For aunterous knyȝtes;
þe porter fayre and well
Lette ham yn also snell
And axede anon ryȝtes,

1500 fen: *loop of* l *or* h *above* e   1507 seyde: d *written over* l

Go ryde in-to the castell gate
K 1580 And axe thine jnne ther-atte,
Bothe fayre and wele;
And ere he do thi nede,
Off justis he will the bede,   1555
Be God and be Seint Michell!

And yf he beryth the downe
His trumpetis shall be bowne
Her bemes high to blowe;
Then ouer all Synadowne   1560
Bothe mayde and garson
K 1590 This fen on the to thorowe.
To whiche lond that yowe wende,
Euer to youre lyves ende,
For kowarde thou worthe knowe;   1565
And thus may Kynge Arthure
Lesyn his honoure
For thyn dedis slowe.'

Quod Lybeous als tite,
'That were a foule disspyte   1570
For any knyght on lyue!
K 1600 To do Arthure prop[h]yte
And maketh that lady quyte
Thedyr will Y dryve.
Syr Gyrflete, make the yare,   1575
To juste with þe will not spare,
f. 97ᵛ   Hastely and blyue.'
They reden forthe at the gate
Right to the castell yate,
With faire shaftis fyve.   1580

And axed ther ostell
K 1610 At that fayre castell
For auntors knyghtis;
The porter faire and wele
Lete hym yn full snell   1585
And axed him anone rightis

1570 disspyte: p over t   1572 prophyte: MS. propfyte

'Ho ys yowre gouernowre?'   1525
þey seyde, 'Kyng Artour,
þat ys man most of myȝtes,
And welle of curtesye
And flowr of chyualrye
To felle hys fon yn fyȝtes.'   1530

þe porter profytable
To hys lord þe constable
þus hys tale tolde:
'And, wyth-oute fable,
Syr, of þe Rownde Table   1535
Beþ come knyȝtes bolde,
þat beþ armed sure
Jn rose reed armure
Wyth þre lyouns of gold.'
Lambard þer-of was fayn   1540
And swore oþ sertayn
Wyth hem juste he wolde.

And bad hem make yare
Jn-to þe feld to fare,
Wyth-oute þe castell gate.   1545
þe porter nold naȝt spare:
As grehond doþ þe hare
To ham he ran full wate
And seyde anon ryȝtes,
'Ye aunterous knyȝtes,   1550
For noþyng ye ne late:
Lokeþ your scheldes be strong,
Ȝour schaftes good and long,
Ȝour saket and faunnplate,

f. 53va   And rydeþ yn-to þe feld: 1555
My lord, wyth sper and scheld,
Comeþ wyth yow to play.'

Who was here gouernours;
And they seid, 'Kynge Arthure,
Man of moste myght[is];
Well of curtaysie   1590
And ffloure of chevalrye
K 1620   To ffellen his fone in fight[is].'

The porter prophitable
To his lorde the constable
Sone this tale tolde;   1595
And sayde, 'With-oute fable,
Syre, of the Rowne Table
Ar comen two knyghtis bolde;
That one is armyd full seuere
Jn roose rede armoure   1600
With thre lyons of goolde.'
K 1630   The lord was glad and blythe
And sayde, also swythe,
Justyn with hym he wolde.

And bade hem make hem yare   1605
Jn-to the felde to fare,
With-oute the castell gate.
f. 98ʳ   The porter wolde not spare:
As a g[r]eyhounde dothe to an hare
To hem ranne to the gate   1610
And sayde anone rightis,
K 1640   'Ye auntrous knyghtis,
For nothinge ye latte:
Looke your sheldis be stronge
And your shaftis longe,   1615
Soketys and vaumplate,

And rydeth in-to the felde:
My lord, with shafte and shelde,
Will with you playe.'

1589 myghtis *and* 1592 fightis: *MS.* myght, fight   1609 greyhounde:
MS. geyhounde

Lybeauus spak wordes bold:
'þat ys a tale y-told
Well lykynge vn-to my pay!'   1560
Jn-to þe feld þey ryde
And houede and abyde
As best broȝt to bay.
þe lord of-sente hys stede,
Hys scheld, hys ryche wede: 1565
Hys atyre was stout and gay.

Hys scheld was of gold fyn,
þre bores heddes þer-jnne
As blak as brond y-brent;
þe bordur of ermyne: 1570
Nas non so queynte of gyn
Fram Karlell yn-to Kent;
And of þe same paynture
Was lyngell and trappure,
J-wroȝt well fayre and gent.   1575
Hys schaft was strong wyth-all,
þer-on a stef coronall
To dely doȝty dent.

And whane þat stout styward,
þat hyȝte Syr Lambard,   1580
Was armede at all ryȝtes,
He rood to þe feld-ward,
Lyȝt as a lybard,
þer hym abyde þe knyȝtes.
He smote hys schaft yn grate: 1585
Almest hym þouȝ to late
Whanne he seyȝ hem wyth syȝte.
Lybeauus rood to hym þare
Wyth a schaft all square,
As man most of myȝte.   1590

f. 53vb   Eyþer smot oþer yn þe scheld:
                  þe peces fell yn-to þe feld
                  Of her schaftes schene;

1581 caret before all; at above line

Sir Lybeous spake wordis bolde: 1620
'That is a tale y-tolde
K 1650   Lykyng to my paye!'
Jn-to the felde they rode
And boldly ther abode
As bestis brought to baye.   1625
Lambard sent his stede,
His shelde, his jren wede:
His tire was stoute and gaye.

His shelde was asure fyne,
Thre beer hedis ther-jnne   1630
As blacke as bronde y-brent;
K 1660   The bordure of ermyne:
Was none so quaynte a gynne
Fro Carlile in-to Kentt;
And of that silfe peyntoure   1635
Was surcott and trappoure,
Jn worlde wher-so he went.
Thre squiers by hym ryde,
Thre shaftis thei bare him myde
To dele with doughty dynte.   1640

f. 98ᵛ   Tho that stoute stywarde,
K 1670   That hight Sir Lancharde,
Was armed to the ryghtis,
He rode to the ffelde-warde
As it were a lebarde,   1645
And ther abode thes knyghtis.
He sette his shelde in grate:
Almoste hym thought to late
When he hym seiȝe with sight[is].
Lybeous rode to hym thare   1650
With a shafte all square,
K 1680   As man of moste myght[is].

Ayther smote oþer in the shelde
That the peces flowen in the felde,
Sothe with-oute wene;   1655

1649 sightis *and* 1652 myghtis: *MS.* sight, myght

All þo þat hyt be-held,
Ech man to oþer teld,   1595
'þe yonge knyȝte ys kene!'
Lambard was aschamed sore,
So nas he neuer yn feld be-fore,
To wyte and naȝt to wene.
He cryde, 'Do come a stranger schaft;   1600
Ȝyf Artours knyȝt kan craft,
Now hyt schall be sene!'

þo he tok a schaft rounde
Wyth cornall scharp y-grounde
And ryde be ryȝt resoun.   1605
Ayder prouede yn þat stounde
To ȝeue oþer dedys wounde,
Wyth fell herte as lyoun.
Lambard smot Lybeauus so
þat hys scheld fell hym fro   1610
Jn-to þe feld adoun:
So harde he hym hytte
Vnneþe þat he myȝte sytte
Vp-ryȝt yn hys arsoun.

Hys schaft brak wyth greet power;   1615
Lybeauus hytte Lambard yn þe launcer
Of hys helm so bryȝt,
þat pysane, auentayle and gorgere
Fell yn-to þe feld fer,
And Syr Lambard vp-ryȝt   1620
Sat and rokkede yn hys sadell
As chyld doþ yn a kradell,
Wyth-oute mannys myȝt.
Ech man tok oþer be þe hod
And gonne for to herye good: 1625
Borgays, baroun and knyȝt.

1601 Artours: s _an afterthought_   1619 feld: _a second_ l _expuncted_
before d

Euche man to other tolde,
Bothe yonge and olde,
'This yonge knyght is kene!'
Lambarte his cours oute-right
As werour oute of wytte,   1660
For jre and herte tene,
K 1690   And sayde, 'Brynge me a shafte;
Yff this knyght con his crafte,
Right sone hit shall be sene!'

Tho toke the[y] shaftis rownde   1665
With cornelys sharpe y-grownde
And reden with grete raundon.
Eyther provyd that stownde
To gyve other dethes wounde,
With herte eger as a lyon.   1670
Lambarte smote Lybeous soo
K 1700   That his shylde fell him ffroo
f. 99ʳ   And in the ffelde fell adowne:
So harde he hym hitte
That vnnethis he myght sytte   1675
Vpryght in his arsoune.

His schafte brake with power;
Lybeous smote hym in the laynore
On his helme so bryght:
Pesawe, ventayle and gorger   1680
Fly forthe withe the helme so clere,
K 1710   And Sir Lambarde vp-right
Sate and rocked in his sadylle
As a childe in his cradill,
With-outen mayne and myght.   1685
Euery man toke othir by the lappe
And lowȝen and couthe her handis clappe:
Barowne, burgeys and knyght.

1665 they: MS. the

f. 54ra

Ayen to ryde Lambard þouȝt:
Anoþer helm hym was brouȝt
And a schaft vn-mete;
Whan þey to-gydere mette   1630
Ayder yn oþer scheld hytte
Strokes grymly greete.
Syr Lambardys schaft to-brast,
And Syr Lybeauus sat so faste,
Jn sadelys as þey setten,   1635
þat þe styward, Syr Lambard,
Fell of hys stede bakward:
So harde þey two metten.

Syr Lambard was aschamed sore;
þan seyde Lybeauus, 'Wyltow more?'   1640
And he answerede, 'Nay!
Neuer seþe Y was y-bore
Ne syȝ Y come her before
So redy a knyȝt to my pay.
A thoȝth Y haue myn herte wyth-jnne   1645
þat þou art com of Gawenys kynne,
þat ys so stout and gay.
Ȝef þou schalt for my lady fyȝt,
Well-come to me, syr þou knyȝt,
Jn loue and sykyr fay!'   1650

Lybeauus answerede, 'Sykyrly,
Feyȝte Y schall for a lady,
Be heste of Kyng Artour;
But Y not wherfore ne why,
Ne who her doþ swych vylany,   1655
Ne what ys her dolour;
A mayde þat ys her messengere
And a dwerke me brouȝt her,
Her to do socour.'
þe constable seyde, 'Well founde!   1660
Noble knyȝt of þe Table Rounde,
J-blessed be Seynt Sauour!'

1629 a: *added above line; caret after* And   1645 myn: y *over* a
1658 a: *preceded by deleted* aw

Syr Lambartt thought to juste bett:
Anoþer helme hym was y-fett   1690
And a shafte vn-mete,
K 1720   And wan they to-geder mette
Eythir to other his shelde sette
Strokys grysly and grete.
Syr Lambartis shafte to-braste,   1695
And Lybeous shoved soo faste,
Jn sadylles ther they sete,
That the constable, Sir Lambertt,
Felte ouer his hors backwarde,
With-oute more be-yete.   1700

Syr Lamberd was ashamed sore;
K 1730   Qu[o]d Sir Lybeous, 'Wilt thou more?'
And he answerd, 'Naye!
Sethe the tyme that Y was borne
Sawe J neuer me be-forne   1705
f. 99ᵛ   So rydynge to my paye.
Be my trouthe my herte is thine:
Thowe arte of Sir Gawynes kynne,
That is so stoute and gaye.
Yf thou shalt for my lady ffyght,   1710
Welcome to me this nyght
K 1740   Jn sekyr and trouthe in faye!'

Lybeous sayd, 'Sekerlye,
Fyght Y shall for thy ladye,
By heste of Kynge Arthure;   1715
But Y ne wote wherfor ne whye,
Ne who dothe hyr that tormentrye,
To brynge hir in dolour;
A mayde that was hir messanger
And a dwerff brought me here,   1720
Her to socoure.'
K 1750   Lambarde sayde at that stownde,
'Welcome, knyght of the Table Rownde,
Be God and Seint Saueour!'

1702 Quod: *MS.* Qud

f. 54rb

Anon þat mayde Elene
Was fette wyth kny3tes ten
Be-fore Syr Lambard.   1665
Sche and þe dwerk y-mene
Tolde seuen dedes kene
þat he dede dydyr-ward,
And how þat Syr Lybeauus
Fau3t wyth fele schrewys   1670
And for no deþ ne spared.
Lambard was glad and blyþe
And þonkede fele syde
God and Seynt Edward.

Anon wyth mylde chere   1675
þey sete to þe sopere
Wyth moch gle and game.
Lambard and Lybeauus yn fere
Of auenturus þat þer wer
Talkede boþe yn same.   1680
þan seyde Lybeauus, 'Syr constable,
Tell me, wyth-out fable,
What ys þe kny3tes name
þat halt so yn prysoune
þe lady of Synadowne,   1685
þat ys so gentyll a dame?'

'Nay syr, kny3t ys he non,
Be God and be Seynt Jon!
þat dorst away her lede:
Two clerkes beþ her fon,   1690
Well fals of flessch and bon,
þat haueþ y-do þys dede.
Hyt beþ men of maystrye,
Clerkes of nygremansye,
Hare artes for-to rede.   1695

1671 deþ: *preceded by deleted* d *and another letter*   1681 Syr: *followed*
by deleted s   1693 of: *followed by blotted and deleted* a   1694
nygremansye: *preceded by expuncted and deleted* nyge

And the mayden Elyne   1725
Was sen for with knyghtis kene
By-for Sir Lambarde.
She and the dwarffe by-dene
Tolde of the dedis kene
That he did thedirwarde,   1730
And how that Sir Lybeous
K 1760   Faught with fele shrewes
And hem nothinge spared.
Tho were they all blythe
And thanked God fele sythe,   1735
God and Seint Leonarde.

Anone with mylde chere
They sett hym to sopere
With mekell gle and game.
f. 100ʳ   Lybeous and Lambard y-ffere   1740
Off auentours that ther were
K 1770   Talkeden bothe in same.
Lybeous, with-oute ffable,
Seyd, 'Sir constable,
Whate is the knyghtis name   1745
That holdeth in prisoune
That lady of Synadon,
That is gentyll a dame.'

Quod Lambert, 'Be Seint John!
Knyght, sir, is ther none   1750
That durste hir away lede:
K 1780   Twoo clerkys ben hir foone,
Fekyll off bloode and bone,
That hauyth y-doo this dede.
They ar men of mynstrye,   1755
Clyrkys of nigermansye,
Here arte for-to rede.

Syr Maboun hatte þat oþer
And Syr Jrayn hys broþer,
For wham we beþ yn drede.

Þys Yrayn and Maboun
Haue j-made of our toun   1700
A palys queynte of gynne:
þer nys knyȝt ne baroun
Wyth herte harde as lyoun,
þat þorste come þer-jnne.
Hy[t] ys be nygremauncye   1705
Y-makeþ of fayrye,
No man may hyt wynne;
þer-jnne ys yn prysoun
þe lady of Synadowne,
Ys come of knyȝtes kynne.   1710

Ofte we hereþ her crye
But her to se wyth eye,
þer-to haue we no myȝte.
þey doþ her turmentrye
And all vylanye,   1715
Be dayes and be nyȝt.
Þys Maboun and Jrayn
Haueþ swor her deþ certayn,
To deþe þey wyll her dyȝte,
But sche graunte hem tylle   1720
To do Mabouunys wylle
And yeue hem all her ryȝt.

Of alle þys dukdom feyr
þat ylke lady ys eyr
And come of knyȝtes kenne.   1725
Sche ys meke and boneyre,
þer-fore we beþ in despeyre
þat sche be dyȝt to synne!'

our: *preceded by deleted* or   1705 Hyt: *MS*. Hys   1706 fayrye:
second y *over* e   1721 Mabouunys: *perhaps* Mabounnys

Jrayne ys that o brother
And Mabon is that other,
For whome we ar in dred.   1760

Jran and that Mabon
K 1790   Haue made in this towne
A paleys queynte of gynne:
Ther nys erle nor baroun
That bereth hert as a lyon,   1765
That durst come ther-in.
Hit is by nygrymauncye
J-wrought with ffayreye,
That wondir hit is to wynne;
Therin lyeth in presowne   1770
My lady of Synadon,
K 1800   That is of knyghtis kynne.

Oftyn we hire hir crye:
f. 100ᵛ   To sene hir withe none eye,
Ther-to haue we no myght.   1775
They do hir torment[ry]e
And all the velenye
And dreche hir day and nyght.
This Mabon and Yrayne
Haue sworne her othe certayne   1780
To dethe they will hir dight,
K 1810   But she graunte hem tyll
To do Mabones will
And yeven him hi[r] right.

Off all this kyngdome fayre   1785
Than is my lady ayre,
To wel[d]e all with wynne.
She is meke and bonoure,
Therfor we ar in spere
Luste they done hir synne.'   1790

1776 tormentrye: *MS.* tormentyre   1784 hir: s *over* r   1787 welde:
MS. wele

þan seyde Lybeauus Desconus,
'Be þe grace of Jhesus,   1730
þat lady Y schall wynne
Of Maboun and Yrayn;
Schame J schall, certayne,
Hem boþe wyth-out and wyth-jnne.'

f. 54vb

þo toke þey har reste   1735
Jn lykynge as hem leste
Jn þe castell þat ny3t.
A-morow Lybeauus hym þrest
Jn armes þat wer best
And fressch he was to fy3t.   1740
Lambard ladde hym forþ well whate
And bro3te hym at þe castell gate
And fond hyt open ry3t.
No ferþer ne dorste hym brynge,
For-soþ wyth-out lesynge,   1745
Erll, baroun ne kny3t.

But turnede hom agayn,
Saue Syr Gylet hys swayn
Wolde wyth hym ryde.
He swor hys oþ serteyn   1750
He wold se hare brayn
Yf þey hym wold abyde.

Quod Lybeous Disconyous,
K 1820   'By the love of Jhesus,
That lady shall Y wynne:
Bothe Mabon and Jrayne
J shall hewen in the playne   1795
The hedys by the chynne.'

Tho was no-more tale
J[n] the castell, grete and smale,
But [s]ouped and made hym blythe.
Baronys and burgeyses fale   1800
Comyn to that semely sale
K 1830   For-to listen and lithe
Howe Sir Lambert had wrought
And yf the knyght were oughte,
His crafte for-to kythe.   1805
They fownden hem sette in fere
And talkynge at her sopere
f. 101ʳ   Of knyghtis stoute and stythe.

Tho toke they ease and reste
And lykynges of the beste   1810
Jn the castell that nyght.
K 1840   On morowe was Lybeous prest
Off armes of the best:
Full ffresshe he was to fight.
Lambarde lad him that gate   1815
To the castell yate
And fonde it full vp-right.
Further durste hym none brynge,
Forsothe with-oute lesynge,
Barowne, burgeys ne knyght.   1820

But turned home agayne,
K 1850   Save Sir Jerflete his swayne
Wolde with hym ryde.
Lybeous swore, certayne,
That he wolde see his brayne   1825
Yf he wolde lenger abyde.

1798 Jn: *MS.* J   1799 souped: *MS.* stoupeh   1809 Tho: *followed*
by loop of h *or* k

To þe castell he rod
And houede and abod,
To Jhesu bad and tolde   1755
To sende hym tydynge glad
Of ham þat longe had
þat lady yn prysoun holde.

Syr Lybeauus, kny3t corteys,
Rod yn-to þe palys   1760
And at þe halle aly3te;
Trompes, schalmuses
He sey3 be-for þe hye3 deys
Stonde yn hys sy3te.
Amydde þe halle flore   1765
A fere stark and store
Was ly3t and brende bry3t.
Ner þe dore he 3ede
And ladde yn hys stede,
þat wont was helpe hym yn fy3t.   1770

f. 55ra   Lybeauus jnner gan pace
To se ech a place:
þe hales yn þe halle;
Of mayne mor ne lasse
Ne sawe he body ne face   1775
But menstrales y-clodeþ yn palle.
Wyth harpe, fydele and rote,
Orgenes and mery note,
Well mery þey maden alle;
Wyth sytole and sawtrye,   1780
So moche melodye
Was neuer wyth-jnne walle.

Be-fore ech menstrale stod
A torche fayr and good,
Brenny[n]ge fayre and bry3t.   1785
Jnner-more he 3ede
To wyte wyth egre mode
Ho scholde wyth hym fy3te.

1785 Brennynge: *MS.* Brennyge

To the castell he rode
And with Lambard abode,
To Jhesus than they cryed
He shulde hem send tidyngis glad   1830
Of hem that longe hadde
K 1860   Distroyed ther welthes wide.

Syr Lybeous, knyght curtays,
Rode in-to the paleys
And at the hall he alight;   1835
Trumpys, hornys, sarvysse,
Right by-for that highe deys,
He herde and saughe with sight,
And amydd the hall floore
A ffyre well starke and store   1840
f. 101ᵛ   That tente and brende bright.
K 1870   Ferther in he yede
And toke with hym his stede,
That halpe him in his ffyght.

Lybeous jnner ganne passe   1845
To be-holde that place:
The halys in the halle;
Off men more nor lasse
Ne sawe he body nor fface
Butt mynstralis cladde in palle.   1850
With harpe, lute and roote
K 1880   And orgone noyse of note,
Grete gle they maden all;
With sotill and sawtery,
Suche maner mynstralsye   1855
Was neuer with-in wall.

By-for euche mynstrale stode
A torche bothe fayre and gode,
J-tende and brente bright.
Sir Lybeous jnner yode   1860
To witten with egir mode
K 1890   Who shulde with hym fight.

He ȝede yn-to þe corneres
And lokede on þe pylers   1790
þat selcouþ wer of syȝte.
Of jasper and of fyn crystall,
Swych was pylers and wall:
No rychere be ne myȝte.

þe þores wer of bras,   1795
þe wyndowes wer of glas,
Florysseþ wyth jmagerye;
þe halle y-paynted was:
No rychere neuer þer nas
þat he hadde seye wyth eye.   1800
He sette hym an þat deys:
þe menstrales wer yn pes,
þat were so good and trye;
þe torches þat brende bryȝt
Quenchede anon ryȝt: 1805
þe menstrales wer aweye.

f. 55ʳᵇ   Dores and wyndowes alle
Beten yn þe halle
As hyt wer voys of þunder;
þe stones of þe walle   1810
Ouer hym gon falle:
þat þouȝt hym mych wonþer.
þat deys be-gan to schake,
þe erþe be-gan to quake;
As he satte hym vnder,   1815
þe rof aboue vn-lek
And þe fauusere ek,
As hyt wolde asonder.

As he sat þus dysmayde
And held hym-self be-trayde,   1820
Stedes herde he naye;

1804 torches: *preceded by expuncted and deleted* torke[s]

He yede in-to the corners
To be-holde the pilleres
That semely was of sight.   1865
Off jasper and of fyne cristale,
J-fflorysshed with amyall,
That was of moche myght.

The dores weren of brasse,
The wondowes all of glasse,   1870
Wrought with jmagerye;
K 1900   The halle y-peynted was:
Nowher none fayrer nas
That he hade seyne withe eye.
f. 102ʳ   He sett hym on the deys: 1875
The mynst[r]ales weryn in pees,
That were so tryste and trye;
The torchis that brent bright
They queynte anone right:
The mynstrellys weren awaye.   1880

The dorres and wyndowes all
K 1910   They betten in the hall
As hit were dynte of thonder;
The stones of the walle
On hym conne they falle,   1885
And ther-off had he wonder.
The deys be-gan to shake,
The erthe be-gan to quake;
As he sate ther-vnder,
The halle roofe vnlyke   1890
And the vasure eke,
K 1920   As it wolde all in sonder.

As he sate thus dismayed,
He holde hym-selfe dysseyved,
Sertis, herde he nyȝe;   1895

1876 mynstrales: *MS.* mynstales

þanne was he bette y-payd
And to hymself he sayd,
'ȝet Y hope to playe!'
He lokede yn-to a feld,   1825
þer he sawe, wyth sper and scheld,
Come ryde knytes tweye,
Of purpur jnde armure
Was lyngell and trappure,
Wyth gold garlaundys gay.   1830

þat on rod yn-to þe halle
And þer he gan to kalle,
'Syr knyȝt aunterous!
Swych cas þer ys be-falle,
þauȝ þou be proud yn palle   1835
Fyȝte þou most wyth vs!
Queynte þou art of gynne
Yf þou þat lady wynne
þat ys so precyous.'
þo seyd Lybeauus anon ryȝt,   1840
'All fressch J am to fyȝt,
þoruȝ help of swete Jhesus!'

f. 55ᵛᵃ   Lybeauus wyth good wyll
Jn-to hys sadell gan skyll
And a launce yn hond he hent;   1845
Quyk he rod hem tyll:
Jn feld hys fon to fell,
þer-to was hys talent.
To-gedere whan þey mette,
Vp-on har scheldes þey sette   1850
Strokes of þouȝty dent;
Mabouunys schaft to-brast,
þo was he sore agast
And held hym-self y-schent.

And wyth þat strok feloun   1855
Lybeauus bar hym adoun
Ouer hys horses tayle;

1829 trappure: *first* r *over* a   1852 Mabouunys: *perhaps* Mabounnys

Thoo he was better apayde
And to hym-selfe sayde,
'Yett Y hope to playe!'
He loked in-to the felde
And sawe, with spere and shelde,   1900
Men in armes twayne,
K 1930   Jn pured pure armoure
Was lyngell and trappure,
Wyth golde gaylye dight.

That one rode in-to the hall   1905
And by-ganne for-to call,
'Syr knyght auntours!
Suche case is nowe be-ffall,
f. 102ᵛ   They thou be knyght in palle
Fyght thou moste with vs!   1910
J holde the qwaynte of gynne
K 1940   And thou that lady wynne
That is so precious.'
Quod Lybeous anone ryght,
'Fresshe Y am to ffight,   1915
By the helpe of Jhesus!'

Syr Lybeous with gode will
And in-to his sadyll gan skylle,
A launce in honde he hente,
And titely rode hem tyll: 1920
His fomen for-to felle,
K 1950   Suche was his talent.
Whanne thaye to-geder smete,
Vpon her shelde hit sette,
With sperys doughtely of dynte;   1925
Mabounes launce to-braste,
Tho was he sore agaste
And helde hym shamely shent.

And with that stroke ffellowne
Syr Lybeous bare Maboune   1930
Ouere his hors tayle;

1911 the: *followed by deleted loop (of* k?) 1926 Mabounes: *perhaps*
Mabonnes (*as in other forms of this name in* L)

For hys hynder arsoun
To-brak and fyll adoun
Jn þat feld saunȝ fayle; 1860
And neyȝ he hadde hym sclayn:
Wyth þat come ryde Yrayn
Wyth helm, hauberke and mayle;
All fressch he was to fyȝt,
He þouȝt wyth mayn and myȝt 1865
Syr Lybeauus for-to asayle.

Lybeauus of hym was war
And sper to hym he bar
And lette hys broþer stylle;
Swych dent he smot dar 1870
þat hys hauberke to-tar,
And þat lykede Yrayn ylle.
Har launces þey brak a-two,
Swerdes þey þrouȝ out þo,
Wyth herte grym and grylle; 1875
And gonne for-to fyȝte,
Eyder preuede hys myȝt
Oþer for-to spylle.

f. 55ᵛᵇ As þey to-gedere hewe,
Maboun, þe mare schrewe, 1880
Jn feld vp aros;
He sawe and well knew
þat Yrayn smot dentys fewe:
þer-fore hym grym agros.
To Yrayn he ran ryȝt 1885
To helpe sle yn fyȝt
Lybeauus þat was of noble los;
But Lybeauus fauȝt wyth hem boþe,
þauȝ þey wer neuer so wroþe,
And kepte hym-self yn clos. 1890

Whan Yrayn saw Maboun
He smot a strok feloun
To Syr Lybeauus wyth yre;

K 1960 For his hynder arson
Brake and fell adawne
Jn-to the felde saunce fayle;
And neygh he had him slayne, 1935
But there come Sir Jrayne,
Jn helme, hawbrek of mayle;
So ffresshe he was to ffight,
He thought anone righte
Syr Lybeous to assaylle. 1940

Syr Lybeous was of hym ware,
f. 103ʳ K 1970 A spere to hym he bare
And lefte his brother stille;
Suche a dynte he yaue thare
That his haumbryk to-tare: 1945
That liked Jrayne ylle.
He[r] lawnses they borsten a-two,
Her swerdys they drewen thoo,
With hert grym and grylle;
They con to-geder fight, 1950
Eyther provid with right
K 1980 Other for-to spyll.

As they to-gedyr gan hewe,
Maboune, the more shrewe,
Jn ffelde vp aroos; 1955
He herde and well knewe
That Jrayne yaue dyntis fewe:
Ther-of hym sore agroos.
To hym he went full right
To helpe to fellen in fight 1960
Lybeous of noble loose;
K 1990 But Lybeous faught with bothe,
Though they weren wrothe,
And kepte hym-selffe close.

Tho Yran sawe Maboune 1965
He smote strokys fellon
To Sir Lybeous withe jre

1946 Jrayne: *preceded by deleted* vr   1947 Her: *MS.* He

Be-fore forþer arsoun
Als sket he karf adoun   1895
Of Lybeauus stedes swyre.
But Lybeauus was werrour sleȝ
And smot of hys þeyȝ,
Fell and bone and lyre;
þo halp hym naȝt hys armys,   1900
Hys chauntement ne hys charmys:
Adoun fell þat sory syre.

Lybeauus adoun lyȝt
A-fote for-to fyȝt:
Maboun and he yn fere.   1905
Swych strokes þey gon dyȝte
þat sparkes sprong out bryȝt
Fram scheld and helmes clere;
As þey to-gedere sette,
Har swerdes to-gedere mette: 1910
As ye may lyþe and lere.
Maboun, þat more schrewe,
To-karf þat sworde of Lybeawe
A-twynne quyt and skere.

f. 56ra   Lybeauus was sore aschamed   1915
And yn hys herte agramede,
For he hadde y-lore hys sworde,
And hys stede was lamed
And he schulde be defamed
To Artour kyng hys lord.   1920
To Yrayn þo he ran,
Hys sword he drouȝ out þan:
Was scharp of egge and ord.
To Maboun he ran ryȝt,
Well faste he gan to fyȝt: 1925
Of loue þer nas no word!

1897 was: w *over another letter* (*perhaps* s)   1913 Lybeawe: w *over* u
1916 y-lore: l *over* e   1920 kyng: *preceded by expuncted and deleted* kny

That evyn he karfe a-downe,
By-for his forther arsowne,
Lybeous stedys swyre.   1970
Lybeous was werreour slyȝe
K 2000 And smote evyn to his thiȝe:
He karfe bone and lyre;
Ne halpe hym not his armour,
His chawntementis ne his chambur: 1975
f. 103ᵛ Dow[n]e ffell that sory syre.

Lybeous of his hors alight
With Mabone for-to fight,
Jn ffelde bothe in feere.
Swyche strokys they dight   1980
That sparkelys sprongen downe right
K 2010 From shelde and helmes clere;
As they bothe to-geder smytte,
Her bothe swerdys mette:
As ye may se hem bere.   1985
Mabon, the more shreweos,
For-karffe the swerde of Sir Lybeous
Attweyne quyte and skere.

Tho was Lybeous asshamed
And in his harte sore agramed,   1990
For he had lorne his swerde,
K 2020 And his stede was lamed
And he shulde be defamed
To Arthur kynge his lorde.
To Yrayne swythe he ranne   1995
And hente his swerde vp thanne:
Was sharpe on eche a syde;
And ranne to Maboune right
And faste they gonne to fight:
Off love was ther no woorde!   2000

But euer fauȝt Maboun
As a wod lyoun
Lybeauus for-to slo;
But Lybeauus karf adoun   1930
Hys scheld wyth hys fachoun,
þat he tok Yrayn fro.
Wyth-out more tale teld
þe left arm wyth þe scheld
Well euene he smot of þo;   1935
þo spak Maboun hym tylle:
'Of þyne dentys ylle,
Gentyll knyȝt now ho!

And J woll yelde me,
Jn trewþe and lewte,   1940
At þyn owene wylle,
And þat lady fre
þat ys yn my pouste
J wyll þe take tylle.
For þoruȝ þat swordes dent   1945
Myn hond Y haue y-schent:
þat femyn wyll me spylle;
J femynede hem boþe,
Certayn wyth-oute[n] oþe,
Jn feld our fon to fylle.'   1950

f. 56ʳᵇ   Seyde Lybeauus, 'Be my þryfte,
J nell naȝt of þy ȝefte,
All þys world to wynne;
But ley on strokes swyfte:
Our on schall oþer lyfte   1955
þat hedde of be þe skynne!'
Maboun and Lybeauus
Faste to-gedere hewes
And stente for no synne;
Lybeauus was more of myȝt   1960
And karf hys helm bryȝt
And hys hedde a-twynne.

1949 wyth-outen oþe: *MS.* wᵗ oute noþe

But evyr faught Maboune
K 2030   As hit were a lyoune
Sir Lybeous for-to sloo;
But Lybeous karffe adowne
His shilde with his fawchon,   2005
That he toke Jrayne ffroo.
Jn the right tale y-tolde
The lyfte arme with the shelde
Aweye he smote alsoo;
f. 104ʳ   Than cryed Mabon hym tyll: 2010
'Thi strokys arne full ylle;
K 2040   Gentill knyght nowe hoo!

Ay will yelde me to the,
Jn love and grete laughte,
At thine owne wille,   2015
And that lady ffre
That is in my powste
Takyn Y will the tille.
For thorough the swerdis dynt
My honde Y haue j-tynte: 2020
The venym will me spille;
K 2050   J venymed hem bothe,
Certeyn with-outen othe,
Ther-with oure fone to felle.'

Quod Lybeous, 'Be my thryfte,   2025
J will nought of thi yefte,
For all this worlde to wynne;
But lay on strokys swyfte:
One of vs shall other lefte
The hede by the chynne!'   2030
Tho Mabon and Lybeous
K 2060   Faste to-geder hewes
And slaked not for no synne;
Lybeous was more of myght:
He clove his helme downe right   2035
And his hede atwynne.

2017 my: *followed by deleted letter*
subsequently   2031 Mabon: e *added*

þo Maboun was y-sclayn
He ran þer he lefte Yrayn
Wyth fachoun yn hys fest;   1965
For-to cleue hys brayn,
þer-of he was sertayn
And trewly was hys tryst.
And whanne he com þore,
Away he was y-bore: 1970
Whyder-ward he nyste.
He softe hym for þe nones
Wyde yn alle þe wones:
To fy3te more hym lyste.

And whanne he ne fond hym no3t   1975
He held hym-self be-cau3t
And gan to syke sare,
And seyde, yn word and þou3t,
'þys wyll be sore a-bou3t
þat he ys þus fram me y-fare!'   1980

On kne hym sette þat gentyll kny3t
And prayde to Marie bry3t
Keuere hym of hys care.

As he prayde þus yn halle,
Out of þe ston walle   1985
A wyndow doun fyll þare,
And a greet wonder wyth-all
Jn hys herte gan fall
As he sat and be-held:
A warm come out apace   1990
Wyth a womannes face,
Was 3ong and noþyng eld;
Hyr body and hyr wyngys
Schynede yn all þynges,
As gold gaylyche y-gyld were.   1995

f. 56va

Tho Mabon was slayne
He ranne ther was Yrayne
With a fawchoune in his fiste;
For-to cleue his brayne: 2040
J tell you for certayne,
K 2070 To fight more hym lyste!
f. 104ᵛ But whan he come there,
Away he was y-bore:
Jn-to whate stede he nuste. 2045
Tho sought he hym for the nonys
Wyde in all the wonys:
Jn trewthe well he truste.

And whan he fonde him noughte
He helde him-selfe be-kaughte 2050
And by-ganne to syke sore,
K 2080 And seide, in worde and thought,
'This will be dere bought
That he is fro me fare!
He will with sorcerye 2055
Do me tormentrye:
That is my moste care.'
Sore he sate and sighte,
He nuste whate do he myght,
He was of blysse all bare. 2060

As he sate thus in halle,
K 2090 Oute at a stone walle
A wyndowe fayre vnfelde;
Grete wondyr with-all
Jn his herte ganne falle 2065
And he sate and be-helde.
A worme ther ganne oute-pas
With a womanes face:
'Yonge Y am and nothinge olde.'
Hir body and hir wyngis 2070
Shone in all [þ]ynchis,
K 2100 As amell gaye and gilte.

2071 þynchis: *MS.* pynchis

Her tayle was myche vn-mete,
Hyr pawes grymly grete,
As ye may lyþe and lere.
Lybeauus be-gan to swete
þer he satte yn hys sete,   2000
Maad as he were;
So sore hym gan agryse
þat he ne myȝte aryse
þauȝ hyt hadde y-bene all a-fere!
And er Lybeauus hyt wyste,   2005
þe warm wyth mouþ hym kyste
All aboute hys swyre.

And after þat kyssynge
þe warmys tayle and wynge
Anon hyt fell fro hyre: 2010
So fayr, yn all þyng,
Woman, wyth-out lesyng,
Ne saw he neuer er þo;
But sche stod be-fore hym naked
And all her body quaked: 2015
þer-fore was Lybeauus wo.
Sche seyde, 'Knyȝt gentyle,
God yelde þe dy whyle
þat my fon þou woldest slo!

þou hast y-slawe nouþe   2020
Two clerkes kouþe:
To deeþ þey wold me haue y-do.

f. 56vb   Be est, norþ and sowþe,
Be wordes of har mouþe,
Well many man kouþ þey schend.   2025
Wyth hare chauntement
To warm me hadde þey y-went,
Jn wo to welde and wende,
Tyll Y hadde kyste Gaweyn,
Eyþer som oþer knyȝt, sertayn,   2030
þat wer of hys kende.

Hir tayle was mekyll vnnethe,
f. 105ʳ   Hir peynis gryme and grete,
As ye may listen and lere.   2075
Syr Lybeous swelt for swete
There he sate in his sete,
As alle had ben in fyre;
So sore he was agaste
Hym thought his herte to-braste   2080
As she neyhid hym nere.
K 2110   And ere that Lybeous wiste,
The worme with mouth him kyste
And clypped aboute the swyre.

And aftyr this kyssynge   2085
Off the worme tayle and wynge
Swyftly fell hir froo:
So fayre, of all thinke,
Woman, with-oute lesynge,
Sawe he neuer ere thoo;   2090
But she was moder naked,
K 2120   As God had hir maked:
The[r]for was Lybeous woo.
She sayde, 'Knyght gentyll,
God yelde the thi wille   2095
My foon thou woldest sloo!

Thowe haste slayne nowthe
Two clerkys kowthe,
That wroughten by the fende.
Este, west, northe and sowthe,   2100
With maystres of her mouthe,
K 2130   Many man con they shende.
Thorowe ther chauntement
To a worme they had me went,
Jn wo to leven and lende,   2105
f. 105ᵛ   Tyll [J] had kyssed Gaweyne,
That is doughti knyght, certayne,
Or some of his kynde.

2073 *followed by catchword* hyr peynis   2093 Therfor: *caret after* e;
r *above line*   2106 J: *above line*; *caret after* Tyll   2108 Or: *over erasure*

And for þou sauyst my lyf,
Casteles ten and fyf
J ȝeue þe wyth-outen ende,
And Y to be þy wyf,   2035
Ay wyth-out stryf,
Ȝyf hyt ys Artours wylle.'
Lybeauus was glad and blyþe
And lepte to horse swyþe
And lefte þat lady stylle;   2040
But euer he dradde Yrayn,
For he was naȝt y-slayn:
Wyth speche he wold hym spylle.

To þe castell gate he rod
And houede and abod,   2045
To Jhesu he bad wyth good wylle
Sende hym tydyngys glad
Of ham þat long hadde
þat lady do vylanye.
Lybeauus Lambard tolde   2050
And oþre knyȝtes bolde
How hym þer gan a-gye,
And how Maboun was y-slayn
And wondede was Yrayn,
þoruȝ grace of Seynt Marie.   2055

And how þat lady bryȝt
To a warm was dyȝt,
þoruȝ kraft of chaunterye,
f. 57ra   And how þoruȝ kus of a knyȝt
Woman sche was aplyȝt   2060
And a semyly creature:
'But sche stod me be-fore,
Nakeþ as sche was y-bore,
And seyde, "Now Y am sure

2039 horse: *preceded by expuncted and deleted* ha   2047 glad: *preceded by expuncted and deleted* good   2051 bolde: *loop (of another* l?) *above* o

Syr, for thou savyst my lyfe,
Castellys fyfty and fyve   2110
Take Y will the till,
K 2140   And my-sylfe to be thy wyfe,
Styll withe-oute any st[r]yfe,
And hit [be] Arthures will.'
Lybeous was glad and blythe   2115
And lepte to hors als swythe
And that lady stille;
But sore [he] dradded Jrayne
For he was nought j-slayne,
With speche lyste he do him spylle.   2120

To the castell Lybeous rode,
K 2150   Ther-for the folke abode
And be-ganne to crye.

Syr Lybeous to Lambard tolde
And to oþer knyghtis bolde   2125
Howe he hem thre ganne gye,
And how Mabon was slayne
And wounded was Jrayne,
K 2160   Thorowe myght of Marye.

And howe her lady bright   2130
To a dragon was y-dight,
Thorowe her chawnterye,
And thorow the c[o]sse of a knyght
Woman she was aplight,
A comly creature: 2135
'But she stode be-fore,
As naked as she was bore,
f. 106ʳ   And sayde, "Nowe am Y sure

2113 stryfe: r *above line; caret after* t   2114 be: *above line, caret after*
hit   2118 he: *above line; caret after* sore   2130 her: *followed by*
deleted ha   2133 cosse: v *over original* o

My fomen beþ y-slayn,   2065
Maboun and Yrayn:
Jn pes now may we dure."'

Whan Syr Lybeauus, knyȝt of prys,
Hadde y-tolde þe styward, y-wys,
All þys aventure,   2070
A robe of purpure bys,
Y-peluryd wyth puryd grys,
Anon he lette forþ brynge;
Calles and keuerchefs ryche
He sente her pryuylyche,   2075
Anon wyth-out dwellynge,
And whan sche was redy dyȝt
Sche rod wyth mayn and myȝt
And wyth her anoþer kyng.

And all þe peple of þe toune   2080
Wyth a fayr processyoun
þyder þey gonne þrynge.
Whan þe lady was come to towne,
Of gold and ryche stones a krowne
Vp-on her heed was sette,   2085
And weren glad and blyþe
And þonkede God fele syde
þat her bales bette.
Alle þe lordes of dygnyte
Dede her omage and feawte,   2090
As hyt was due dette.
þus Lybeauus, wys and wyȝt,
Wan þat ylke lady bryȝt
Out of þe deueles nette.

f. 57rb   Seuenyȝt þey made soiour   2095
Wyth Lambard yn þe tour
And all the peple yn same,
And þo wente þey wyth honour
To þe noble kyng Artour
Wyth moche gle and game,   2100

2067 we: *preceded by expuncted and deleted* w *and blotted* e

K 2170   My fone thou haste slayne,
          Mabon and Yrayne: 2140
          Jn pees thou dost me brynge."'

          When Lybeous Disconyous
          Had tolde the stywarde thus,
          Bothe worde and endeng,
          A robe of purpyll riche,   2145
          Pillured with pure grice,
          He sent hir on hyenge;
          Kerchewes and garlandis ryche
K 2180   He sent hir preveliche,
          A byrd hit ganne hir bringe;   2150
          Whan she was redy dight
          She went with many a knyght
          To hir owne wonnynge.

          All the folke of Synadowne
          With a well fayre procession   2155
          Her lady conne home brynge.
          When she was comen to towne,
          Off gold and stonys a crowne
K 2190   Vpon hir hede was sett,
          And were gladde and blythe   2160
          And thanked God fele sythe
          That hir balys were bett.
          Than all the lordis of dignite
          Did hir homage and fewte,
          As hit was dewe dette.   2165
          And euche lord in his degre
          Gave hir yeftis grete plente,
          When they with hir mett.

f. 106ᵛ   Sevyn dayes they dide soioure
          With Sir Lambert in the towre   2170
          And all the peeple in same;
K 2200   Tho went thei with honour
          Taward Kynge Arthoure
          With mekyll gle and game;

And þonkede Godes myȝtes,
Artour and hys knyȝtes,
þat he ne hadde no schame.
Artour yaf her also blyue
Lybeauus to be hys wyfe,   2105
þat was so gentyll a dame.

þe joye of þat bredale
Nys not told yn tale
Ne rekened yn no gest:
Barons and lordynges fale   2110
Come to þat semyly sale
And ladyes well honeste.
þer was ryche seruyse
Of all þat men kouþ deuyse
To lest and ek to mest;   2115
þe menstrales yn bour and halle
Hadde ryche yftes wyth-alle,
And þey þat weryn vn-wrest.

Fourty dayes þey dwellede
And har feste helde   2120
Wyth Artour þe kyng.
As þe Frenssch tale teld,
Artour wyth knyȝtes beld
At hom gan hem brynge.
Fele ȝer þey leuede yn same   2125
Wyth moche gle and game,
Lybeauus and þat swete þyng.
Jhesu Cryst our Sauyour
And hys moder, þat swete flour,
Graunte vs alle good endynge.   2130
        Amen
Explicit Libeauus Desconus

2113 seruyse: *second* se *over* st   2121 kyng: *preceded by expuncted and
deleted* kny   2128 Cryst: *preceded by deleted downstroke of* r

They thanked God with al his myghtis,   2175
Arthur and all his knyghtis,
That he hade no shame.
Arthur gave als blyve
Lybeous that lady to wyfe,
That was so gentill a dame.   2180

The myrrour of that brydale
K 2210 No man myght tell with tale,
Jn ryme nor in geste:
Jn that semely saale
Were lordys many and fale   2185
And ladies full honeste.
There was riche service
Bothe to lorde and ladyes
To leste and eke to moste;
Thare were gevyn riche giftis   2190
Euche mynstrale her thriftis,
K 2220 And some that were vnbrest.

Fourty dayes thei dwelden
And ther here feste helden
With Arthur the kynge.   2195
As the Frensshe tale vs tolde,
Arthur kyng with his knyghtis bolde
Home he gonne hem brynge.
Sevyn yere they levid same
With mekyll joye and game,   2200
He and that swete thynge.
f. 107ʳ K 2230 Nowe Jhesu Criste oure Savioure
And his moder, that swete floure,
Grawnte vs gode endynge.   Amen.

Explicit Lybious Disconyas

COMMENTARY

1–3 The invocation of Our Lord and Lady here and in the last three lines of the romance owes something to the opening formula of *Arthour and Merlin* (AM):

> Jesu Crist, heuen king,
> Al ous graunt gode ending,
> & seynt Marie, þat swete þing,
> So be at our bigining
> & help ous at our nede.

5 *Wys of wytte* is hardly borne out by some of the references to Lybeaus made in the stanzas which follow: *full savage* (L 19), (*full*) *nys* (22, 51) and *wytles and wylde* (176). But this uncouth side to his nature is only rarely stressed in these early pages; his polite approach to Arthur in 85–90 contrasts strongly with Perceval's behaviour at the same point in his story (SP 485–528) and does nothing to justify the maiden's insult in 176. Only his outburst in 182–9 could really be interpreted as a sign of lack of breeding (see the note to these lines). This mixture of attributes suggests that Chestre was familiar with both versions of the *enfances* of the Fair Unknown, as defined by Philipot (see above, p. 49 and n. 2), no less than that he was likely to repeat convenient phrases where they were not always wholly apt: Lybeaus may greet Arthur and his knights *wyth honour* in 39 because Elene does the same in 147. By omitting lines corresponding to L 16–21 the redactor of *C simplified matters to some extent (see above, p. 9 and n. 3), but in *ANP the ambivalence became still more marked, since the mention of the hero's *fayr vyys* at 19 and 60 gave way to lines in which he was presented as *feyr and wyse*.

7 BD alone among the cognates names the hero Guinglain, and then only after he has achieved his mission (3233, etc.). The early disclosure of his identity here and in 13 is clumsy, but not untypical of Chestre's methods: a very similar piece of anticipation can be found in 82. Certainly the present line cannot give any support to Kaluza's theory (p. lx) that the first three and a half stanzas of the texts that have survived were not Chestre's work but the interpolation of a later scribe; see also the note to 182–9, below.

L 13–24 Neither in C nor L is this stanza completely satisfactory, since in the first it is defective and in the second it is clumsy, with lines 16–18 looking like an anticipation of 22–24. Since, however, C omits a number of whole and half-stanzas that are unquestionably genuine it is unlikely that the gap here should go back to the archetype and have later been made good in L or its source. Moreover, the content of the passage missing from C is traditional enough, since the motif of homicide is also found in *Papegau*, where it has been detached from the hero of the romance and associated with the significantly named *Jaiant sans Nom*, the foolish and gigantic son of a dwarf (p. 81).

17 The omission in C of lines which correspond to L 16–21 suggests a different interpretation of *wykkede loos* in this text; the phrase now relates more naturally to the mother than to the son, and the 'evil reputation' would most probably be for adultery rather than for homicide. The mother's shame can be paralleled in some of the more remote cognates of LD, most clearly in lines 153–72 of the Auchinleck *Sir Degarre*, which describe the lady's grief at finding herself pregnant, but also in Zatzikhoven's *Lanzelet*, where the hero's foster-mother refuses to tell him his name, because of her *schamen und . . . manecvalt nôt* (322).

21 Kaluza made much of the fact that those lines of LD which are preserved without variation in all surviving texts contain three main stresses (pp. lviii f. and lx). But this need not mean that all lines in Chestre's original had followed the three-beat pattern; it could equally well be argued that such clean-cut lines as 21 were those most likely to be preserved intact whatever the nature of the transmission. The other lines that have survived unscathed in all texts are 55, 68, 69, 73, 133, 151, 165, 176, 204, 205, 428, 447, 456, 468, 496, 498, 591, 609, 633, 756, 786, 933, 974, 996, 1023, 1062, 1098, 1169, 1210, 1283, 1337, 1431, 1561, 1580, 1610, 1683, 1694, 1745, 1788, 1814, 1880, 1938, 1943, 1988, 1991, 2006. To these may be added 1522 and 1539 of which very slightly corrupt versions (which leave the metrical basis unaltered) are offered by one text only.

28–30 Only in the corresponding lines of P (note especially *That soone he made ffull tame*) is it suggested that Lybeaus has to kill a knight in order to provide himself with arms, after the manner of Sir Perceval (SP 741–8). The account given in CL is more closely paralleled in Malory's story of *La Cote Mal Tayle*, where the hero finds his father murdered and swears to wear his badly hacked surcoat until he finds an opportunity of avenging him (ed. Vinaver, ii. 459).

35 Arthur's court is also located at Glastonbury in SL 149 f., but in very few other Arthurian romances; *Durmart* alone consistently associates the king with *Glastingebiere* (9321, 9366, 9380, 9383; variants *Glatingebieres* 6004 and *Gla(n)dingesbieres* 5330 and 5415).

L 48 Both here and in the second of the doggerel passages which serve to patch up the defective version of *L (for which see above, p. 13) the redactor seems to have had in mind a version of the story in which the hero or his family had suffered at the hands of powerful enemies: in the present line he says that he will make his *mone* to Arthur; in L 91 he refers to *my fomen*, not the king's.

82–4 In fact, Lybeaus never receives any such training in arms, since
the messengers from Synadoun arrive very shortly after he has been
committed to Gawain's care. But in some of the cognate romances he
is thoroughly instructed in knightly accomplishments before he sets
out on his mission: see particularly W 1593–1603 and 3018 f., where
his tutor is likewise said to be Gawain.

85–90 In BD the hero does not define the boon for which he asks in
84–6; in *Papegau* he is identified with the young king Arthur and so
is able to grant the first adventure to himself (p. 2).

117 The precise meaning of *blaunner* (*blawndenere* L) has been discussed at most length by Kaluza (pp. 136 f.), who used a quotation
from *Richard Cœuer de Lion* (RCL) to support his claim that the word
was originally a compound of OF. *blanc* and *ner* and so alluded to a kind
of ermine. However, Brunner, in his later edition of RCL, does not
record the form quoted by Kaluza (*blaun and nere*) among the variants
of 6592: *bla(u)ndener(e)*, *blaundynnere*, *blaundemere*, *blaunner*.

120 The messenger's horse is described as a *palfray* in 254 and the
present, unlikely, allusion to a *destrere* seems a mere convenience for
the sake of rhyme. The two are carefully differentiated in BD 5062 f.:

> Sor lor palefrois, sans destriers;
> Escus ne armes ne portoient.

121–32 A striking parallel to this description occurs in the Auchinleck
Sir Degarre (SD):

> þer com a dwerw into þe halle.
> Four fet of lengthe was in him;
> His visage was stout and grim;
> Boþe his berd and his fax
> Was crisp an ȝhalew as wax;
> Grete sscholdres and quarre;
> Riȝt stoutliche loked he;
> Mochele were hise fet and honde
> Ase þe meste man of þe londe;
> He was iclothed wel ariȝt,
> His sschon icouped as a kniȝt;
> He hadde on a sorcot ouert,
> Iforred wiȝ blaundeuer apert.
>   (780–92)

The account given in LD is the more self-consistent, since it is free
from the rather grotesque implications of SD 785 and 787 f., and at
the same time corresponds more closely with the dignified picture that
is given of Tidogolain in BD 157–66; furthermore, in *plex* it offers
a much less commonplace reading than the *fax* of SD 783. These
facts would suggest that SD had borrowed the passage from LD, but

this is put out of the question by the relative chronology of the two works (see Introduction, pp. 66–8 for the date of composition of the latter), no less than by other material which they have in common, in which SD is fairly clearly the source: see especially the note to 947–51. We have therefore to assume that Chestre took from the SD passage only those details of the dwarf that would harmonize with the picture which his primary source had given of that character.

126 In spite of the unusual phrasing the reference here must be to the *surcot ouvert* which was an important article of both male and female dress in the thirteenth to fifteenth centuries: see Joan Evans, *Dress in Mediaeval France*, Oxford, 1952, pp. 17, 31 f. and 43 f., frontispiece, and fig. 67.

128 Kaluza did not incorporate *plex* (*plax* N) into his edited text, presumably because Ritson's gloss of 'shield' was inadequate. But in his note to the line he guesses correctly that the word must refer to the dwarf's hair (*OED*. derives it tentatively from Latin *plex-us* ('plaiting') and glosses it 'plait or braid (of hair)'). No cognate romance describes the dwarf's hair in this way, but it is worth remarking that the phantom king of W is said to have *zöpfe alsam ein wîp* (4629), since although this character is never actually said to be a dwarf, he is yet named Belnain in *Papegau*, and in both of these closely related romances he—like Teondeleyn—guides the hero to the enchanted palace.

136–41 The dwarf's skill in music is also stressed in W 1727–31, but for a parallel to Teondeleyn's skill as a narrator or story-teller (*dysour*) we must turn to *Papegau*, where the parrot that has taken over the most distinctive attributes of its dwarf guardian (see above, p. 46 and n. 1) figures in both capacities (*Papegau*, pp. 11 and 22 f.).

151 For the identification of Synadoun see the note to 800.

L 189 *That ben abled* could well derive from an antecedent * *That be noblee* corresponding to N's *That bene price*. The doubling of final -e can be paralleled in *sawee* L 917 and *owee* L 1075.

L 192 At this point MS. P reads *And said sir verament*. This variant does not occur in any other text of LD, and it is therefore of some interest to find it preserved in the highly compressed account of the opening scenes of LD that is found in Copland's text of *The Squyr of Lowe Degre* (c. 1555–60):

> 'Thus my love, syr, may ye wynne,
> Yf ye have grace of victory,
> As ever had Syr Lybyus, or Syr Guy,
> Whan the dwarfe and mayde Ely
> Came to Arthoure kyng so fre,
> As a kyng of great renowne,
> That wan the lady of Synadowne,

Lybius was graunted the batayle tho,
Therfore the dwarfe was full wo,
And sayd, 'Arthur, thou arte to blame.
To bydde this chylde go sucke his dame
Better hym semeth, so mote I thryve,
Than for to do these batayles fyve
At the chapell of Salebraunce.'
These wordes began great distaunce;
The[y] sawe they had the victory,
They kneled downe and cryed mercy;
And afterward, syr, verament,
They called hym knyght absolent:
Emperours, dukes, knyghtes, and quene,
At his commaundement for to bene.'

(612–32)

These lines form part of a most awkward interpolation into the second
of the scenes between the squire and his lady, and lines 612–4 may
well be a displaced answer to a complaint made by the squire in the
course of their earlier conversation:

'Wolde God that I were a kynges sonne,
That ladyes love that I myght wonne!
Or els so bolde in eche fyght,
As Syr Lybius that gentell knyght,
Or els so bolde in chyvalry,
As Syr Gawayne, or Syr Guy.'

(75–80)

(For a discussion of this matter, see pp. lxxxiv f. of W. E. Mead's
Introduction to his edition of the romance.) As far as LD is concerned,
these passages make it clear that (1) the *Squyr* can hardly have provided
Chaucer with the familiarity which he displays with the story of
Lybeaus in *Sir Thopas* (they contain no hint of an elf-queen (la Dame
d'Amore) or her gigantic champion (Maugys)), and (2) they were
derived from an earlier form of MS. P. Line 622 in the first passage
can also be paralleled in that text (as, this time, in HAN)—it forms
part of the stanza which follows L 216 (see Appendix (*b*))—while the
reference to *batayles fyve* may derive from the *battells five or thre* that
is peculiar to P and N (see the note which follows). When we further
reflect that the variant of L 192 that appears in the *Squyr* is not only
unique in itself, but also helps to define a spurious eighteen-line
stanza (= L 175–92) that is found in no other text, it seems un-
deniable that some of the most characteristic readings of P had
already been developed by the sixteenth century.

L 197 In N and P the number of combats is given as *five othir thre*;
in A, as *two or thre*. Of the fights in which Lybeaus is involved before
he rescues the queen of Synadoun, Elene is able to warn him of four

(259–70, 719–38, 1238–54, and 1480–1506). It is the dwarf who identifies Otes (although he cannot foresee that Lybeaus will have to fight with him (1005–14)), and Lambard who gives him information about the enchanters (1687–1728).

L 200 The evocative motif of the Adventurous Chapel is not developed in LD nor is it mentioned in any of the close cognates. For the *Poynte Perilowse* of L 199 see the note to 282.

182–9 These lines of violent boasting are susceptible of more than one explanation. If, as Kaluza supposed, the introduction to LD had originally been quite different from that which has been preserved (op. cit., p. lx), it might have said enough about the youthful exploits of Lybeaus to give literal point to the present lines (L 19–21 are surely too laconic and too dissimilar in their implications to justify them). But it seems more likely that 182–9 were introduced for the sole purpose of bringing out the uncouth side of the hero's character—which is heavily stressed in SP and *Carduino*, but only intermittently touched upon in LD (most notably in lines 785–9, L 849–54, 915, 1060–8 and 1747–52 (for which see the relevant notes below)). In phrasing, the lines rather oddly parallel part of a speech which Nereja, the female messenger of W, makes at roughly the same point in the story:

> 'wer vehten welle, der hebe sich dar!
> des vindet er dâ vil guot stat.
> er wirt sîn âne zwîvel sat,
> wan dâ ist manger tôt gelegen.'
>
> (1765–8)

L 208–13 Although obviously spurious, these lines amplify the 'genuine' 187–9 in the heroic vein of much of Chestre's own writing. With L 212, for example, we may compare AM 5577–80, which tell how those of the king's vassals who had failed to help him in battle were to be seized as traitors and *hing bi þe winde*.

203 As Kaluza points out, this use of *y-layd* is rather surprising, since lines of this kind more commonly imply the beginning than the end of a meal in the ME. romances. He therefore favoured the *vnleide* of N, although he admitted that he could find no other examples of the word. Certainly a confusion of *y-* and *vn-* is reflected at at least one other point in our texts (L 1512 *j-steke* for the *vn-steke* preserved in C), but the total lack of agreement of the manuscripts at this point (*þeo cloþ weore laid* H, *tabul was vnleide* N, *bord was vpbrayd* A, *vncouered the table* P) suggests an archetypal reading that was felt to stand in need of rationalization, and this the reading of C could well have provided.

205–10 At this point in BD the hero simply reassumes the armour he had been wearing on his arrival at court (261–8); in LD, however, he is never said to have removed the arms with which he was furnished in 31–3 and 76–81. Chestre's lack of precision in this matter is further discussed in the note to 1280.

213 It is curious that MSS. C and H should coincide in spoiling the sequence of tail-rhymes by reading *hestes* at this point. Since there are hardly any other errors peculiar to these two texts this coincidence may be further proof that the archetype of all extant copies was itself corrupt. *hestes* would then have been corrected back to the *hiȝtis* of Chestre's original in the source of ANP, and the correction taken over into *L from a text in that tradition (see the note to L 896). The archetypal error suggests the use of ȝ for [s] as well as for [ç] and [θ]: cf. 222 *Frenȝsch*.

218–21 Passages of enumeration such as this are extremely common in AM; see, for example, 8266–70.

220 Although the first letter of *Eweyn* is not the scribe's usual form of capital *e* it can hardly be the *G* suggested by Bliss (*Launfal*, p. 83) as the characteristic vertical stroke is not present. If we were to take it strictly at face-value, indeed, we should have to read *Sweyn* here.

224 *Gypell* does not seem to be recorded outside the C-text of LD (in which it is also found at 1176 and 1383); presumably it is a variant form of the *gypoun* that is implied by the readings of HAN (*griffown*, *ryppon*, *gippon*), a short tunic that could have been worn beneath armour as well as over it.

232 As we have seen (pp. 18 f.), the manuscript variants of this line afford conclusive proof that the archetype of the six texts was already corrupt. Possibly the substitution of Lancelot for Agravain arose from a confused memory of SL 13–18 with its catalogue of Round Table knights; not only are all five of the knights mentioned in the variants of LD 229–40 found here, but the two who have become confused are set next to each other:

> Sere Perseuall and Syr Gawayn,
> Syr Gyheryes and Syr Agrafrayn,
> And Launcelet du Lake;
> Syr Kay and Syr Ewayn,
> þat well couþe fyȝte yn playn,
> Bateles forto take.

Influence by the SL passage is made still more plausible by the fact that the text of *Launfal* may have immediately preceded that of *Lybeaus* in the original manuscript: see *MÆ* xxxi (1962), 109.

265 In BD the guardian of the passage is named Blioblieris, and Willaume de Salebrant is one of the three companions who try to avenge his humiliation (529). In their fight with Descouneus, Salebrant is the first to attack (1064) and the only one of the three to be killed (1109).

267 A comparison with 952 f. suggests that the variant of L is to be preferred at this point, and that in Chestre's original the rhyme had been of *wyt and *ryt. Since *wyth* 267 is in any case an adjective [ON. *vigt*] it could only have rhymed on the *ryȝtte* of 270 if (1) the front palatal spirant had been effaced in *wiȝt, or (2) the verb had represented not OE. *rīdan* but ME. *riȝten*. G. V. Smithers (ii. 116) has suggested that such a verb, in the sense of 'charge' and broadly cognate with MDu. *rechten*, may be implied by the 3 sg. pr. *riȝth* that is found within the line in verses 3900 and 3905 of *Kyng Alisaunder*. Other possible examples of this verb are to be found in the texts of LD: within the line we have *ryȝt* in 403 and *reyȝt* in N at L 1833 (where it is a corruption of *knyȝt); in rhyme, *oute-right* in L 1659 (: *wytte* (n.)) and *riȝt* in N at L 315 (: *fiȝt* (v.)). But whichever of these explanations is adopted, the 'rhyme' of 267 and 270 is unlikely to have been present in Chestre's original: the shift of [içt] > [i(:)t], while implied by some of the spellings of C can hardly have taken place when LD was composed (see above, pp. 29 f. and 38); on the other hand a rhyme upon [içt] would have the effect of splitting the stanza into two halves.

278 Such cordiality is hardly likely at this point in the story, and it would thus seem preferable to adopt the variant of L. All the same, 278 by conflating two tags that are fairly common in SL and SO (*Wyth merthe and mochell honour* (SL 264) and *With ioye and greet solemnyte* (SO 1187)) has its own kind of authenticity, although it need not on that account have formed part of Chestre's original. Like the corruption of 232 it could be the work of a scribe who was thoroughly familiar with the two texts standing before LD in his copy.

282 It is not easy to decide between the variants of C and L here. No cognate romance mentions anything like the *Vale Perylous* of C, although in both BD 279 and *Carduino*, ii. 8, the companions pass through an unspecified valley early on in their travels. The *Poynte Perylous* of L roughly corresponds to *le Gué Perilleus* of the same episode in BD (323), but the OF. romance makes no mention of the *cause* with which the *Poynte* is presumably identified in L 301. For this feature we must go to the much later encounter with Malgiers (Maugys LD) in BD 1952–4:

> Et une caucie i ravoit
> Del pavillon dusques au pont
> Por les iaugues qui defors sont.

284 This type of heraldic device is a favourite with Chestre: see also 857, L 1337, 1539, 1568, SL 328 f., and SO 953 f. and 1473 f.

314–15 This detail and much of 325–36 closely parallel *Sir Tristrem* 1035–6 and 1057–62.

340 Since there is a clear example of the insertion of excrescent *r* in 1376 *strout*, it is possible that *drynge* here corresponds to the *dynge* of

LAN, but it seems rather more likely to represent the *þrynge* that is found in the virtually identical 1150 *So harde þey gonne þrynge.*

344 *Lonche* seems to have been introduced solely to fill out the rhyme. Strictly speaking, the verb should mean that Selebraunche here pierced his opponent's shield with his sword, but if this was so he could hardly have cut off part of that shield at the same time, especially when we remember that his weapon (a falchion) was calculated to do more damage with its edge than with its point. The verb is thus doubly inappropriate here and may be contrasted with the *cleft* that is used, out of rhyme, in SO 1114 in a passage describing an almost identical moment of fighting:

> Þe geaunt smot to hym well snell
> With a scharp fachoun of stell;
> Of Florentys scheld a kantell
>   He cleft þon ry3t.

348 The other four texts make it clear that this line must have read **In (his) herte was agast* in *LHANP. The authenticity of this reading is suggested by a further episode from the fight between Florent and Guymerraunt, quoted above:

> He smot eft and be þe hylt
> Hys swerd tobrast.
> Þo, forsode, to be yspylt
>   He was agast.
>   (1101–4)

360 This detail is unexpected as we are not told elsewhere that there had been any onlookers apart from Elene and Teondeleyn (contrast BD 331 ff. and W 1972 ff., in both of which the knight of this first encounter is attended by servants of his own). The phrasing suggests *Amis* 867 *Þat mani man schuld it sen.*

361–6 William's reminder that it would be dishonourable to kill an unarmed knight is not found in the corresponding fight with Blioblieris in BD; it may derive from the sequel to this, in which Helie begs the three *conpaignons* of this knight not to fight with Descouneus before he has had a chance of arming himself (BD 1015–30).

397 At this point P quite sensibly emends the archetypal **em William* to *Cozen Will*, so making the line agree with the earlier substitution of *emes sonis* for *susteres sones* (391) in the source of HANP.

404 Descouneus is accompanied by *un escuier* (BD 270–8) who, helped by the dwarf, attends to the needs of Helie and himself (BD 930–51). In LD both Teondeleyn and his doublet Gyfflet are described as squires of the hero (404 and 451, 1456–8): see also the note to 481–3.

405 With the substitution of *wy3t* for the *berne* demanded by rhyme we may compare a number of points in the Caligula text of the *Seege of Jerusalem* where the synonyms for 'man' that are typical of the alliterative school are replaced by the less distinctive *manne, prince, kynge*, or *kny3t*.

407 The *a*-rhymes make it plain that *swore* must be a past participle and not an infinitive (contrast L 430 *swere*). Kaluza (p. 157) cites an approximate parallel from *Otuel* 47 f.:

> And alle þei were togidere sworn,
> þat cristendom scholde be lorn.

424–5 An odd rhyme that it is very difficult to accept at face-value. There can be little doubt that the second rhyme-word is OE. *rōd*, and this might at first suggest that the final consonant of $\bar{\varrho}þ$ (acc. sg.) had shifted from [θ] > [d]. But this is put out of the question by the fact that the vowel which immediately precedes this consonant is fully stressed, and it seems best to look upon the 'rhyme' as an attempt to rationalize an earlier scribal error by which the reading preserved in L had been rendered **And þau3 þe traytour be roþe*; this attempt was to some degree conditioned by the interchange of the symbols þ and *d* that is so distinctive a feature of the C-tradition of copying.

424–9 This passage and 436–44 parallel the later description of the preliminaries to the fight with Otes and his men: (1) both bodies of supporters threaten Lybeaus as a *traytour* (425–9 and 1089–92), (2) the arming of both groups is described (436–41 and 1093–8), and (3) the unsuspecting hero keeps riding quietly on (442–4 and 1099–1101). Of the cognates only E offers any significant parallels; see especially E 3522 ff. and *Romania*, lxxxvii (1966), 37 f.

430–41 Although this stanza does little to advance the action its authenticity is put beyond doubt by the way in which it corresponds to BD 583–91, and its use of a narrative device (in 430–2) that was a particular favourite of Chestre's; see the note to 1219–21.

445–7 A curious passage, since the phrasing suggests that Lybeaus and Elene slept together (see Introduction, p. 58). No cognate makes explicit mention of such a liaison at this point, although Renaut gives a very detailed account of the reconciliation of hero and guide (BD 829–59; compare LD 448–50). In E, however, the two related motifs appear much further on in the story, where they still serve to mark the end of the estrangement of hero and heroine (E 4879 ff. and 5199 ff.). LD 445–7 may have produced the suggestion, peculiar to L 1481, that in becoming the lover of the Dame d'Amore, Lybeaus was unfaithful to Elene.

451–3 These lines correspond to a much more extensive and differently placed passage in BD. There the fight with the giants (LD 559–687) is inserted between those with Blioblieris and his three avengers; it ends with the discovery of the giants' hoard of provisions and an elaborate feast contrived by the hero's squire, Robert (BD 901–51).

454–65 The scribe of C or *C may have altered the rhyme-scheme in the second couplet because he substituted for *jornay* the alternative form *jorne* (cf. 431). The version of C in 460–5 seems more authentic than the corresponding part of L since (1) the Cambridge University text of *Bevis* that offers parallels with other parts of LD (see the notes to 1123–8 and 1153–8) contains two lines that strikingly resemble 460 f.:

> Well armyd yn-to the tethe
> And all sweryn Befyse dethe;
> (f. 108ᵛᵇ)

(2) *roun(e)*, whether as noun or verb, was a favourite word with Chestre, and was used in a variety of contexts and senses. It often acquired unexpectedly violent force; see the notes to 972 and 1159.

457–9 Since Arthur's court is often located at Caerleon in the romances, these lines suggest that Chestre had known of a version of the story of the Fair Unknown in which the would-be avengers were knights of the Round Table. In *Carduino* a group of such knights— Agueriesse (Gaheriet), Mordarette (Mordred), Calvano (Gawain), and a fourth, unnamed, brother—had been responsible for the murder of the hero's father; Carduino fights with the first of these not long after leaving Arthur's court (compare the Selebraunche episode in LD), but does not encounter the other three until the very end of the story, when he is reconciled with them. The *Prose Tristan*, which has preserved the same story in a much weakened form, names Agravain as the last of the brothers. For a discussion of the relation of this text to *Carduino* see R. S. Loomis, *Arthurian Tradition and Chrétien de Troyes*, pp. 399–402.

L 474–6 MSS. ANP agree with L in the general arrangement of the stanza containing these lines, but have substituted for them three in which Elene is directly menaced:

> And that maide briȝt
> That is so feire of siȝt
> Lede we wolle to toune.

The threatened abduction of the hero's companion formed a traditional part of one version of the story of the Fair Unknown (it is present in *Carduino*, ii. 22 and E 2941–2) but it need not on that account have been present in Chestre's original: see *MÆ* xxxii (1963), 19.

471 This is a good example of a favourite type of adverbial phrase in which two antonyms are linked to give intensive force to the verb: cf. W 8795 *beidiu mit ernste und mit spil*. Such phrases usually defy literal translation and this particular instance so perplexed the redactor of *LHANP that he substituted the more straightforward **In ernest and nouȝt in game*. The same phrase appears to have been eliminated in *HANP in the stanza which follows L 216 (and *Y rede þe in game* substituted) but restored in *P.

481–3 At one point in the joust between Launfal and Sir Valentyne:

> Gyfre kedde he was good at nede
> And lepte vpon hys maystrys stede.   (SL 580 f.)

For the resemblances between Gyfre and Gyfflet—the character in LD who later replaces the dwarf as the hero's squire—see the notes to 1456–8 and 1513–87.

490 Kaluza derived *ȝ-erne* from OE. *ge-eornian* (v.) and not *georn* (adv.). The parallel with SO 965 *Vpon a stede he gan yerne* shows that he was right, and even though *ȝ* is nowhere else confused with *y* in SO, SL, or LD it occasionally alternates with *þ* in these texts: see the note to 1139.

493 Compare SL 513 *Hym þoȝte he brente bryȝte*, which Trounce regarded as a weaker version of, and therefore a borrowing from, the line in LD (*MÆ* ii (1933), 196). For the interpretation of parallels between LD and SO or SL, see *MÆ* xxxi (1962), 104–7.

508–10 The picture which C gives of the whole fight is confused. The absence of L 502–13 makes it appear that only two of the brothers have made separate attacks upon the hero, and of these Sir Gower seems unlikely to give any further trouble after 478–83. Taken in isolation, 509–10 could thus be regarded as a cry of triumph and not as the complaint suggested by 508, but this impression is immediately contradicted by the lines which follow in which Lybeaus is again fighting with two opponents, even though there has been no mention of Gower's recovery or of any attack made by the youngest of the three nephews. The three lines must originally have read:

> 'Allas,' he seyde þo,
> 'Oon aȝenes two,
> To fyȝte þat ys nouȝt good.'

L 538 For the rhyme with L 541 (*He þreow him in luytel space* H), see *Richard Cœur de Lion* (RCL) 6179 f.:

> And soone after in a lytyl spase
> þorwȝ þe help of Goddes grace.

559 This detail seems at odds with the dignified picture given of Teondeleyn in 121–5, but LD is not the only version of the story to make him subject to lapses into cowardice. Such cowardice is presented very vividly in *Papegau*, pp. 14–15; more elegantly in BD 823 f.:

> Li nains fu en la forest long,
> De l'aprocier n'avoit pas soig.

However, the actual phrasing of 559 may owe something to the description given of the besieged Saracens in RCL 3989: *For drede þey begunne to quake.*

559–91 The most striking analogue to this part of the romance is offered by Wace's *Brut*, in the episode in which Arthur, Kei, Bedoer, and their squires visit the Mont St. Michel. There they see a fire (11337–8) and hear great lamentation (11357–8), at which Bedoer quakes with fear (11359). A giant is found to have violated Eleine, a young maiden (11407–12) and to be preparing a meal at a fire (11481–4). In LD and BD the rape of the young girl is only a threatened, not an accomplished fact (LD 577 f. and BD 713–16). Also of interest is the warning that Bedoer is given against meeting with the giant (11382–8), since this can be paralleled in Helie's attempt to dissuade Descouneus from attempting the adventure (BD 731–44).

563 Compare the more explicit *to lepe to horse þo was he dyȝt* of RCL 5684.

565 Although it is not usual for *bost* to be used without overtones of roughness or deliberate ostentation, it seems more likely to refer here to the outcry set up by the maiden Vyolette than to that of the giants who have captured her. Compare BD 631–4:

> En la forest oï un brait
> Lonc a quatre arcies de trait.
> Molt est doce la vois qui crie;
> Ce sanble mestier ait d'aïe.

Chestre gives a more detailed description of the girl's lamentation in 584–91.

596 The point of this line must be that the manly action of Lybeaus belied his years. Compare 966 and 1038 of the 'Northern' *Octavian* (MS. C), where the narrator, in the course of describing the fight between Florent and the Saracen giant, comments *there was no chyldys play*.

600 This contains a rare phrase that is also found in SO 81 *To daunce wente be ryght asyse*.

616–18 The giant in Wace does not strike Arthur with the *char de porc* that he had been roasting at the fire, but one detail in the fight which ensues certainly brings the spitted boar of LD to mind:

> Dunc veïssiez geiant dever!
> Cume sengler parmi l'espied,
> Quant li chien l'unt lunges chacied,
> S'embat cuntre le veneür.   (11518–21)

L 657 ANP here insert a stanza which describes the fierce blows struck by the giant: see Appendix (*c*). The hot fat which falls from the boar adds to the hero's difficulties, and recalls a passage in the *First Continuation* of *Perceval* (the 'short' redaction, ed. W. Roach, Philadelphia, 1949). Here a very large knight strikes at Kay with a bird that has been roasting over a fire and

> Li sains del paon li coula
> Si come il parti et creva,
> Parmi les mailles del hauberc.   (9373–5)

This bird had earlier been described as *molt bien lardez* (9276).

632 It is interesting to note that although the phrase *yn saȝt* is found in rhyme at 1030, the negative adj. *unsaht* has twice been replaced by other rhyme-words in C: at 1331 by *vn-syȝt* (discussed in the note to 1327–31), and by *vp-sawȝt* here. This word is presumably to be equated with *upsoht* (pp.), and must therefore exemplify the same shift of *ouht > auht* that is found in 1978 ff. (see Introduction, p. 30). The meaning seems most likely to be 'risen up': compare the example from the *Wars of Alexander* (*he sleȝly vp soȝt & his sete leuys*) given in *OED*. under 'Seek' v. 14.

643–4 The variants which the manuscript copies offer of these lines are more than usually tangled. Each one yokes together an 'informative' verse (*Hym þat he yaf er wounde* C(L); *To þat oþir he wende* H(ANP), and a tag (*Jn þat ylke stounde* C; *Jn Frensshe as it is j-ffounde* L(HANP)). In the second group the reading of C appears the less authentic in that it could be a simple reminiscence of 641 (*Lybeaus, þat ylke stounde*), but the same cliché is also found, in rhyme, in the ANP variant of the 'informative' line (*To þat oþer he went þat stound*). However, this coincidence need not imply that we have here—as in the superficially comparable case noted at 1616—any valid pointer to the archetypal form of the line; it seems much more likely that the redactor of *ANP independently drew upon the tag found in the first couplet of the stanza to create an acceptable rhyme out of the impossible *founde*: *wende* preserved in H. It will be noted that by suggesting that the Black Giant had previously been no more than wounded, CL contradict 601–3, which make it quite plain that he has been killed, but this can hardly be used to prove the superior authenticity of the HANP version of the 'informative' line, since other parts of LD show Chestre to have been quite unconcerned to accommodate statements made in one part of his work with those found at another; see Introduction, pp. 56 f., for an even more striking ambiguity about the fate of one of a pair of the hero's opponents.

660 The name of this character recalls the Antore who in AM 9751 meets his death at the hands of giants, but in his function he more closely resembles the aged father of Enide (E 375 *et passim*). The corresponding figure in BD is not characterized at all (see 892), but in Platin's *Giglan* he is described as *ancien* ([l. iv^v]), and it seems possible that the name in LD may have arisen from a contracted form of the adjective *anci(e)nor* (? *anciōr*) in the OF. source. But whatever the provenance of the name it was sufficiently unfamiliar to be replaced by that of Arthur in two of the less reliable texts of LD (at 660 in P and 768 in AP). This king is also associated with the scene in the version given of it in the *Didot Perceval*, since the giant there waits for the girl's father to set out for Arthur's court, before abducting her (MS. E 285 ff.); in W the influence of the story of Guenievre's abduction has brought the Round Table into the very centre of the scene, since the giants there

> hêten si gezücket
> dem milten künige Artûs
> ze Karidôl vor sînem hûs,
>
> (2080–2)

and by doing so quite put that court to shame:

> die edeln rîter enwessen wâ
> si hin wâren gekêret;
> des was ir herze gesêret
> und ouch der hof gunêret.
>
> (2084–7)

661–6 In BD the girl makes no mention of any past siege of her father's home:

> Li jaians me pris ciés mon pere:
> Et un vergier hui main entrai
> Et por moi deduire i alai;
> Li jaians ert desous l'entree,
> Trova la porte desfremee,
> Iluec me prist, si m'en porta;
> Ici son conpaignon trova.
>
> (892–8)

Chestre's account seems to have been influenced by the later scene at the Île d'Or, in which he tells how another black giant (Maugys) besieges a city to gain possession of a lady (1243–51): this modification makes it seem strange that Vyolette should wander about, so freely and unsuspectingly, on her own. BD 893, it may be noted, gives support to the variant which C offers of 664 (and which Kaluza had rejected as implausible): *ʒesterday yn þe mornynge*.

668 Renaut mentions that the giants had kept their plunder *desos la cave* (BD 902).

688–99 This, the second stanza in C that is not preserved in any other text, is shown to be genuine by its content no less than its rhyme-scheme. The offer of Violette to Lybeaus corresponds to the point in the episode of the hawk in E where the hero tells his host that he wishes to marry his daughter, Enide, and offers two castles to him (E 1311 ff.). That the *vavasor* is here the recipient and not the would-be donor of the castles results from the way in which he is represented as a poor man in Chrétien's romance. A possible hint for this special development may be preserved in LD 659.

715 The hero's '*Oo*' may be a miscopying of *Qd in *C. As Kaluza pointed out (pp. xl f.), the use of *þan seyde* throughout C to introduce passages of direct speech seems less authentic than the *quod* of L.

L 750–3 Only in Chestre's version of the story is the contest for the bird represented as so forbidding an undertaking. In fact, however, the motif of decapitation does not properly belong to the adventure at all, but has been transferred to it from the episode at the Île d'Or, where Malgiers, defender and suitor of the lady of the castle, is accustomed to behead all the knights that he defeats at the passage (BD 1993–2000). The shift may owe something to Chestre's familiarity with the story of Lanval, in which there is likewise a contest of beauty that may prove fatal to the hero: compare SL 802 f.:

> yf he myȝte not brynge hys lef,
> He schud be hongede as a þef.

736–8 In his version of the encounter with the beheading knight, Renaut seems to have kept closer to a primitive form of the episode in that the heads of defeated knights are there set on the stakes of a palisade and not on battlements as in LD (BD 1956–60). Compare the description of the double row of spears which encircles Schaffilun's tent in W 3309 f.

752–3 If we take *be-gyle* at face-value these lines must mean 'makes a habit of overcoming his opponents by trickery'; this was clearly the view which the redactor of P took of them (he renames the hero's opponent Giffron la Fraudeus at L 768 and speaks of his *subtulle wile* at L 776), but it is not really borne out by anything that Gyffroun does in the fight which follows. What is stressed by the onlookers is the fact that he has always won in the past, and this suggests that Chestre had intended the lines to carry no meaning more sinister than 'is accustomed (because of his skill or experience) to defeat his opponents'. But it is hard to find a comparable use of *be-gyle* elsewhere in ME., and the appearance of this word and of *vs* in the present lines seems to have been dictated by the needs of rhyme rather than by any other consideration. For another accusation of underhand behaviour (*gyle*) that seems to be undeserved, see the note to 1061.

L 792 In W 2900 ff. the hero is told by Hojir (Gyffroun LD) to be ready to fight after he has attended mass.

785–9 In spite of the bloodthirsty custom with which he has been associated Gyffroun is in himself one of the most polite and reasonable of all the hero's antagonists: see the note to 796–8. The present lines may reflect Chestre's wish to make his hero's character consistent with his rough woodland upbringing; there may also be a reminiscence of SL 763–5 where Arthur blusters:

> 'þat þy lemmannes lodlokest mayde
> Was fayrer þan my wyf, þou seyde:
> þat was a fowll lesynge!'

792 This suggests that Elene may have to depend upon the splendour of her dress rather than her beauty if she is to carry off the prize. Certainly the description of her in 832–43 says nothing about her personal charms (as that of her rival does in 880–91), and this omission

does something to prepare us for her subsequent defeat, which completely reverses what happens in the same episode in BD. Here the
plainness of the discomfited rival is not relative but absolute:

> Molt estoit et laide et frencie.
> N'i a celui cui ne dessie
> Qu'il le maintint por le plus bele.
>
> (1727-9)

See also the note to 901-3.

796-8 Gyffroun's seeming uncertainty about the rules of the competition is also reflected in ANP, and is hard to reconcile with 724-9.
The hero's answer recalls the passage in SL in which the knights
appointed to give judgement upon Launfal decide that:

> yf he myȝte hys lemman brynge
> þat he made of swych ȝelpynge,
>   Oþer þe maydenes were
> Bryȝtere þan þe quene of hewe,
> Launfal schuld be holde trewe
>   Of þat, yn all manere.
>
> (796-801)

800 It is usual to identify Cardueil with modern Carlisle (see, for
example, W. A. Nitze's note in *University of California Publications
in Modern Philology*, xxxviii (1955), 268 f.). But in AM at least a more
southerly location for the town must be assumed since (1) Gawain and
his supporters pass through it on their way from London to Bedingham (7703-6) and (2) this same Bedingham is said to lie between
Schorham and *Arundel in Cornwaile* (7683-5). Chestre's irresponsible
approach to geography elsewhere (see the note to 1222-4) makes it
impossible to be sure that he did not have Carlisle in mind at this
point, but the city would undeniably form an unlikely stage in a
journey made from Glastonbury to Segontium (for this identification
of Synadoun see *Speculum*, xxii (1947), 520-33), and when we also
take into account the variant forms of 813 and 990 *Karlof* and *Cardelof*,
and the ease with which Launfal journeys from *Kardeuyle* in SL 8 to
Karlyoun in SL 88, it seems rather more likely that he equated the
city with Cardiff.

L 849-54 These lines give clear expression to the more uncouth side
of the hero's character. The stanza containing them is not found in C,
but this may well be a deliberate omission: see above, pp. 9 f.
Certainly the rhyme-scheme is 'correct' and the phonetic developments implied by the rhymes *seid*:*dede* and *wende*:*mankynde* typical
of the language of the archetype but not of what we can infer of the
more Northern source of LHANP.

844-91 Many of the details in this passage can be paralleled in the
description of Launfal's *amie* in SL 925-48.

856–61 That Gyffroun was traditionally a Red Knight and so cognate with the villain of SP has been quite obscured in LD but emerges clearly in W where the corresponding figure of Hojir is said to have red hair and a red beard no less than red armour (2577 f., 2841 f., 2935 f., and 2997). BD, on the other hand, is not much more precise in this respect than LD: the only lines which could be attenuated survivals of the motif are 1711–13:

> Ses escus a argent estoit,
> Roses vermelles i avoit,
> De sinople les roses sont.

As has already been suggested (p.16), Chestre's original may well have contained a more recognizable derivative of the *roses* of BD, in a line absent from the archetype but restored in *HANP.

862–3 Neither C nor L has preserved the original rhyme at this point; this must have been the **ryd: *myd* that is implied by the *rood: myd* of H and is also found in L 1638 f.

L 896 Since L is basically the least corrupt representative of its manuscript group it is surprising to find that it offers a few corruptions which appear connected with some found in A or AN. Thus L 896 can be related to *the two ladys waygewr* of A, and L 903 *ryght ffyne* to the *ruffyne* of N and the *reyfyen* of A (both presumably descended from **rofyne* for **rosyne* in their common source). At L 1275 f. the rhyme *wene: grene* looks like an effort to make phonetic sense of the impossible *June: grene* (for **June: *toun*) of AN, but since H is defective here it is equally likely that the rhyme of AN may go back to the source of LHANP, and that the anomaly is resolved in different ways in L and in P.

894 At this point CLHN agree in reading *dyscryue* [OF. *descrivre*] instead of the *dyscrye* [OF. *descrier*] that is demanded by rhyme. That AP should offer the correct reading suggests that we have here a further example of the way in which *ANP might correct an archetypal reading that was self-evidently corrupt (with the corruption restored in *N under the influence of a text in the C-tradition): see Introduction, pp. 18 f. and 23–5, and the note to 232.

901–3 We can rule out the possibility that *lauendere* was meant in the sense of 'harlot' here (for which see G. P. Krapp, *MLN* xvii (1902), 204), but it is curious that Elene should be quite so contemptuously treated by the mob, and that her inferiority to her rival should be expressed in terms of rank and demeanour rather than of beauty. It is, however, possible that in a more primitive version of the scene an ugly but gorgeously dressed mistress of the aggressive knight had been opposed to a lady (championed by the hero of the romance) who was beautiful but shabby—BD 1727–35 and *Papegau*, p. 7 stress the ugliness of the first, and E 402–10 the wretched dress of the

second—and that from these elements Chestre contrived a synthesis
of his own, perhaps under the influence of the final scene of SL, in
which Launfal's mistress, when she at last appears, makes all the ladies
at court seem *also donne/As ys þe mone ayen þe sonne* (SL 988 f.). It
may also be noted that in the OF. *Durmart*—a romance that has
a number of features in common with LD—the hero is insulted *parmi
le marchie* (703; cf. LD 803 and 850 f.) because of his previous un-
princely behaviour, with the taunt that he would govern the country
assi cum une chamberiere (711).

911 The reading of C while obviously corrupt is not nonsensical,
since the scribe could have understood *fawkoun* to mean 'sword' rather
than 'falcon'. This suggestion is developed in P where the line reads
Take my head on thy ffawchyon.

915 *Hore* contradicts the general impression that is given of Gyffroun
as a man in the prime of life and may be no more than a convenient
rhyme-word, the use of which could have been prompted by the fact
that, in the corresponding scene of SD, the hero's opponent was his
grandfather. But it is also possible that the very unsuitability of 915
to describe Gyffroun was deliberate, it being meant as a further
example of the boorishness which Lybeaus displays throughout this
episode and the one which follows.

916 Compare in the corresponding episode in W *was touc nu mêr dâ
von geseit?* (2764).

919 *Coronal*, a lance-head with spreading points, seems to have been
a word of restricted distribution in ME., being otherwise mentioned
only in RCL 6283 and SD 568 and 1023.

928–39 In the combat with Gyffroun, as in that with Lambard
(1630–8), Lybeaus accomplishes more by his firmness in the saddle
than by any particular skill in jousting (see also 955–63). In this he
follows Degarre, whose lack of sophistication in this respect is deliberately underlined by the narrator:

> Ac Degarré was so strong
> þat in þe sadel stille he set,
> And in þe stiropes held his fet;
> For soþe i seie, wiʒoute lesing,
> He ne couþe nammore of iusting.
>   (SD 514–18)

947–51 This passage corresponds closely to SD 549–54.

> Þat alle þe lordings þat þer ben
> Þat þe iusting miʒte sen
> Seiden hi ne seʒe neuer wiʒ egʒe
> Man þat mighte so longe dreghʒe,
> In wraþþe for noþing,
> Sitten a strok of here king.

Chestre's familiarity with this romance, in which so much of the action springs from the king's custom of defending his daughter against all her suitors, may explain why LD represents the contest for the hawk as a recurring and not as an isolated event: a comparison of LD 724–9 with SD 29–33 and 436–42 will show that Gyffroun's personal responsibility for arranging the terms of jousting very closely parallels the king's practice. Verbal echoes of SD are also very noticeable in two other episodes of LD in which a knight maintains a custom of fighting with all comers: the encounters with Selebraunche (LD 319–24: SD 933–7) and Lambard (LD 1600 f.: SD 509 f.; LD L 1678: SD 569; LD L 1689: SD 542; LD 1639: SD 578).

952–3 These lines must originally have read:

> *Gyffroun hys cours out-ryt
> And was wode out of wyt.

L 1659 f. is very similar in phrasing, and both couplets derive from SD 537 f.:

> And Degarré his cours out ritte,
> And was agramed out of his witte.

The author of SD was accustomed to use present verbal forms in passages describing past events (see 508, 510, 523, 547 f., 566, etc.), and Schleich is certainly right in taking the *out ritte* of SD 537 as a present form (*Sire Degarre*, pp. 35–6); Chestre, on the other hand, does not usually mix his tenses in this way and almost certainly intended *out-ryt* as a preterite in spite of the fact that no such form, whether strong (with the vowel from the plural *riden*) or weak (on the model of such verbs as OE. *cīdan* and *hȳdan*) is recorded elsewhere in ME.: see K. Brunner, *Die englische Sprache*, ii. 193 and K. D. Bülbring, *Geschichte des Ablauts*, pp. 31 f. and 116 f. It seems, indeed, that in taking over a handy couplet intact, Chestre has been compelled to use one of the rhyme-words in a way that is quite opposed to his normal practice; compare the very free treatment of the semantics of words and phrases in rhyme-position that is discussed in the notes to 120, 344, 360, 565, 643–4, 752–3, 915, 985–90, 1061, 1586, and 1844.

972 *Roun* must here be glossed either 'lamentation' or 'cries of pain'. Both senses are unusual but we find an equally strained use of the word in SO 461, 941, and 1693. Further possible examples of Chestre's use of *roun(e)* are discussed in the notes to 454–65 and 1159.

974 The name of this emissary varies from one text to another (see the Names of Places and Persons), but all the forms could be derived from an archetypal *Claudas*.

976 One would have expected Claudas, like the other messengers to Arthur, to have related the adventure by word of mouth; it could then have been committed to writing in accordance with the custom of the court (cf. *Giglan* (a. iiᵛ) *et les faisoit mettre en escript le roy Artus par* *quattre clerc3 qui a ce estoyent ordonne3*). The association of a written account with this particular episode is obliquely reflected in stanza 5 of *Bruto di Brettagna* (based upon a story told by Capellanus in his *De Amore*). In this the hero is told how he is to win for his mistress

un nobile sparviere
che sta legato ad una stanga d'oro.
Appresso quell'uccel, ch'e si maniere,
due bracchi stan che vaglion un tesoro,
la carta de le regole d'amore,
dove son scritte'n dorato colore.

A rather similar combination of motifs is found in the scene in *Papegau* in which la Dame aux Cheveux Blons receives the hero in a room which contains a falcon carved out of precious stone, at the feet of which is a tablet exhorting strict obedience to her commands (p. 29).

981 From this point the hero's name is almost always written *Lybeauus* in C.

985-90 Arthur's gift of treasure at this point is not paralleled in any of the cognates, but it corresponds broadly to his offer of *greet spendyng* to Launfal in SL 79-81. Kaluza (p. 180) implies that Kölbing's gloss of *honest* as 'noble' (*Amis*, p. 232) would serve here, but the phrase as a whole remains awkward, and the use of the word seems prompted by the exigencies of rhyme rather than by any real aptness.

990-1008 The disruption of the original pattern of tail-rhymes probably took place in *C and was initiated by the writing of *þan* for **to[u]n* at 990 (the interchange of *þ*/*th* and *t* is not common in MS. Caligula, but we find *thold* and *smerþe* in SO 634 and SO 853, while the C-scribe occasionally writes *doun* (adv.) as *don*, with a horizontal stroke above the two minims: see the Frontispiece). A return to the correct definition of the stanzas was achieved by padding out the twelve lines of L 1029-40 to fifteen. In the Naples text the line corresponding to L 1031 has also been made to rhyme on [u:n] by the substitution of *reboun(d)* for the correct *gale* preserved in H. Since other evidence shows *C and *N to have been closely related, it seems likely that (1) in *C this line had already been corrupted to **And houndes grete of roun* (see the note to 1159); (2) this was taken over into *N as *And houndis make reboun*, but was expanded to a couplet in 1003-4, and (3) a new line (1002) was inserted to provide the rhyme on [u:n] necessary to complete the pattern of the previous stanza, and another (1006) to fill out 1003-14 to the requisite length.

1009 In BD 1486 the huntsman knight is given the name of Orguillous de la Lande. His name in LD may derive from the treacherous duke Otus in *Guy*; Otus regards Guy as a *treytour* (A 1298) and demands of his vassals:

'His bodi oliue ȝe schul me bring
And slen his feren eld and ȝing.
Y schal him in mi prisoun do;
Out no comeþ he neuer mo.'

(A 1307–10)

Oblivious of the threat, Guy rides on at a leisurely pace (A 1329 f.).
The same episode has also left its mark on SL 505–10.

1010–14 This relationship is also implied by L 1245–7 but is not
mentioned in any cognate version of the episode. In *Papegau*, however,
we find in count Andois a vassal of the oppressed queen (Flor de Mont)
who had failed to help her against her enemy, here because of a grudge
which he bore her father (p. 55). For the Wirral as a refuge for outlaws,
see *Sir Gawain and the Green Knight*, ed. J. R. R. Tolkien and E. V.
Gordon, 2nd edn., rev. N. Davis, Oxford, 1967, p. 98.

1021–3 Compare the multi-coloured Peticrewe (*He rede, was grene
and blewe*) in *Sir Tristrem* 2404.

L 1067 MS. H also reads *freo* at this point while AN have the correct
fere. Possibly the corruption was already present in *LHANP but
corrected in *ANP.

1045–7 Compare:

Florent let þe trumpettys blowe,
Þat yn þe cyte men schulde knowe,
Þat hy were all sount.

(SO 1250–2)

1060–8 As Kaluza noted (p. cxlix), the wording of this exchange
owes much to Bevis's rejection of the advances of Josian. This dialogue
is most economically presented in the text of MS. Chetham 8009,
f. 135ʳ:

'Go forthe, carle, out of my fare,
Mahoun geve the sorowe and care!'
'Damysell,' said Beues, 'I am no carle
My fader was bothe knyght and erle!'

But in no text of *Bevis* does the hero mention his mother, as Otes
does in 1067 f.; Chestre may therefore also have had in mind the
passage in AM in which the *iustise* replies to Merlin's unflattering
account of his conception by saying:

'Þou gabbest, conioun:
Mi fader was an heiȝe baroun,
Mi moder is a leuedi fre,
Oliue ȝete þou miȝt hir se.'

(1071–4)

1061 None of the chief senses of *gyle* in ME. ('cunning', 'treachery',
'deceit', or 'trick') seems justified by anything that Otes has said or
done up to this point. It is possible that Chestre was here thinking

less of his present than of his future behaviour—his act of leading a small army against Lybeaus is certainly unsporting—or even that he was influenced by memories of the huntsman's treacherous namesake in *Guy* (for whom see the note to 1009). But it is even more likely that *gyle* occurs here because it formed part of a convenient sequence of rhyme-words that had already been used at 558 ff. (*gyle*: *myle*: *peryle*: *Gyle*), three of which were taken over bodily into the present context. In the earlier stanza, the mention of *gyle* was perfectly apt, as the word had been associated with the practices of horse-thieves.

1081–98 Renaut tells us that the servants of the huntsman helped to get him ready for the fight with the hero:

> 'Alés,' fait il, 'mi escuier,
> Amenés moi mon bon destrier.'
>   (BD 1379 f.)

But neither in this text nor in W do they give him active support against Lybeaus; the only significant parallel to this feature is offered by E, in the description of the expedition which Guivret leads in pursuit of Erec (E 4928 ff.; see *Romania* lxxxvii (1966), 42–5).

1120–2 Detail of this kind is common in the heroic romances: compare *Bevis* A 882–4 and AM 4959–62.

1123–8 The second line of this passage exactly parallels one in the Cambridge University Library text of *Bevis* (f. 127ra), which tells how the giant Ascopard *bare downe hors and man* in his onslaught. The giant had earlier been described as *a fende stale fro helle* (f. 126va: compare 1127). It is common enough for the heroes of romance to regard their Saracen opponents as devils because of their colour and size (see, for example, LD 1289 and stanzas 95 and 255 of the Auchinleck *Guy*); almost equally common for the Saracens to look upon the Christians as such because of their superhuman prowess (AM 6191–4) or ferocity (RCL 3484 f.).

1132–3 The same image is found at two points in the Fillingham *Otuel and Roland* (ed. M. I. O'Sullivan (E.E.T.S. 198), London, 1935):

> Wel sone the cristen were by-set,
> As der that beȝth with-inne the net,
> With ten thousand and mo,
>   (2152–4)

and

> Tho Turpyn was by-set,
> As a der in the net,
> Ther a-mong the paynemes.
>   (2637–9)

1135–43 The distinction made between two groups of opponents (the *knytes and squyeres* of 1096–8 and Otes and his vassals in 1135–43) recalls the separate bodies of foresters and knights who attack *Bevis* in A 841–3. MS. Auchinleck gives the number of the first group as ten; the Cambridge University Library text, as twelve.

1139 A recurring feature in this part of the Caligula text is the representation of OE. *þūhte* (3 sg. pt.) and *þōhton* (3 pl. pt.) by *þouȝ*: see the Frontispiece and also 1430, 1448, and 1586. This seems less likely to result from carelessness than to depend upon some peculiarities of the spelling-system of C and its antecedents: (1) the use of ȝ in place of *þ* or *th*: LD 624 *þoȝ* (*doþ) and the inverted *dorþ* (*þorȝ) of SL 1021; (2) of ȝd for *þ*: SO 111 *couȝde* and 119 *haȝd*, and (3) of ȝt for *þ* or *th*: LD 226 *syȝt* (adv.), 292 *rydyȝt*, 1445 *lyȝt* (3 sg. pr.) and SO 975 *worȝt* and the inverted LD 267 *wyth* (a.), 885 *strath* and SL 265 *wrouth*. These would have confronted any scribe working in the later stages of the transmission with the possibility of interchanging ȝ and *þ*, and *þ* and ȝt and so might have suggested to him that ȝ and ȝt were themselves interchangeable. That these last two symbols were used indiscriminately in C is confirmed by the *Bra(u)ndyȝt* ('Brindisi') of SO 497 and 1838, which can only be explained in terms of an antecedent **Bra(u)ndyȝ*, in which ȝ stood for final *s* (see the note to 213), and would thus be identical with the *Braundys* of RCL 623 and 1434.

1153–8 The huntsman's sons are not mentioned in any of the cognates, but this passage stands very close to one found on f. 109rb of the Cambridge University Library *Bevis*:

> Two ffosters he smote adowne
> Wyth þe dynte of hys tronchon
> vj he slewe at dyntys thre
> And odur vj away can flee.

1159 At first sight *ronne* appears to be the 3 pl. pt. of OE. *rinnan* in the sense of 'moved rapidly' or, perhaps, 'were struck'. However, the only other example of this form in C is at 1003 (*And houndes ronne greet and smale*), which is governed by the *herde* of 1001 and would thus more properly refer to sound than to movement, and it is in fact possible to derive both examples of the word from OE. *rūnian* in the unusual senses of 'bay' and 'resound', especially when it is remembered that Chestre has elsewhere used *roun(e)* in contexts that force an extension of its normal semantic range in ME.: see *MÆ* xxxi (1962), 100. It is true that the context of 1159 demands a 3 pl. pt. and not an inf. form, but the characteristic interchange of *þ* and *d* in *C makes it possible that *ronne þo* in this line represents an earlier *rounede. This interpretation is supported by the *rounde* of L 1174 (and also by the corresponding line in P (*And round the(y) stroakes he gan fflinge*)), which could easily be an anticipation of 1159 with the rhyme-word altered to fit the new pattern of tail-rhymes and the unfamiliar preterite form taken over as an adjective (= 'swingeing', 'severe'). Since 1003 cannot have formed part of Chestre's original its *ronne* is less certainly derived from earlier *roune (here an infinitive), but the presence of the latter word in *C would do much to explain the diversely corrupt versions of C and N at this point (see the note to 990–1008). In any case, the scribal tradition of *C was sufficiently conservative for the range of some of Chestre's idiosyncrasies to have been extended: see the note to 278.

1163–4 Such prodigal shedding of blood is extremely common in the heroic romances: see, for example, AM 5295 f. and 8089 f. and RCL 5105 f.

L 1188–9 A curious rhyme which implies an earlier *dryve:*skyye (*sky3e). Since the present *dryve*:*skythe* at least provides an assonance (and so may be compared with *lepe* L 957: *breke*; *freke* L 960: *sete*, and *vnnethe* L 2073: *grete*) the representation of *y or **3* by *th* may not have been wholly accidental.

1165–7 Compare with this passage and 1180–2, SO 1101–6:

> He smot eft and be þe hylt
> Hys swerd tobrast.
> þo, forsode, to be yspylt
> He was agast.
> An ax he hente of metall broun,
> þat heng on hys formest arsoun.

1189–94 The submission of one character to another under a (chestnut) tree occurs in a number of romances. Sometimes the dominating character possesses supernatural powers, as in *Sir Gowther*, st. 20, where a fiend begets a child on a lady; sometimes both characters are human, as in *Le Bone Florence* 1505, where the villainous Miles attempts (but fails) to seduce the heroine. In LD we have a still less primitive version of the motif, in which all traces of the supernatural have vanished and both characters are male. As such it may be compared with *Erl of Tolous* 1124 f., which treat of the discomfiture of the earl's opponent, and the (more interesting) lines in MS. A of *Bevis* which tell that during the hero's flight from Brademond,

> He reinede his hors to a chesteine
> And felle aslepe vpon þe pleine;
> And alse a slep, in is sweuene
> Him þou3te, Brademond and kinges seuen
> Stod ouer him wiþ swerdes drawe,
> Al slepande him wolde han slawe.
> (1699–1704)

The more primitive form of the motif is discussed by Bliss in his introduction to *Sir Orfeo*, pp. xxxv–xxxvii.

1207–18 This stanza very closely resembles the account given to Lambard in 1663–74. The later passage is broadly paralleled in BD

2711–24 but nothing in any of the cognates corresponds to the present stanza.

L 1245–68 Although these stanzas are not preserved in C they are correctly rhymed and at least one motif which they contain is particularly apt to the story of Lybeaus. For a close study of the character of Otes shows him to correspond in some vital respects to Guivret, the dwarf king who is at first violently hostile towards Erec but who later shows him great courtesy (see the note to 1081–98). The healing of the hero's wounds by Otes at this point is paralleled in Guivret's actions in E 5151 ff.

L 1247 *Free*, which is obviously corrupt, turns up at the same point in MS. P (where it has been assimilated into the tail-rhyme scheme by the alteration of *lende* (L 1250) to *bee*). This common error is important as it shows that the combined authority of L and the second half of P need not automatically weigh down that of A and N, and so allows us to accept the reading of AN against that of LP at L 1311 f.: see the note to these lines. A third point at which A and N present a reading that is superior to those of L and P is in the line *Howe aventours kny3t yonge* (: *kyng*). This was clumsily altered to *Howe suche a knyght in ffyghtyng* in L 1261, and this version was fused with one resembling that of AN to produce in P *how a knight younge/In ffighting had him woone.*

1219–21 These lines imply that we are to hear more of Otes, but in fact he never reappears. They offer a pointless example of a narrative device that is also found at 430–2, and is thoroughly characteristic of SO, where it is justified by the frequent shifts of attention from the adventures of Floraunce and her son Octavian to those of her other son Florent; see, for example, SO 661–4:

> Now reste we her a lytyll wy3t,
> And forþer telle, as hyt ys ry3t,
> How þat oder chyld was dy3t,
> That dwellede yn Fraunce.

1222–4 The mention of Ireland implies a very devious journey from Glastonbury to Segontium, and is best explained (as Schofield suggested on p. 233 of his *Studies on the Libeaus Desconus*) as a misunderstanding of a passage that in content stood close to W 3286–91:

> Mit vreuden riten si dô dan.
> der getwerge einez in began
> sagen schœniu mære,
> wer sîn herre wære
> der ez dar hêt gesant,
> und wiez stüende in Îrlant.

1225–30 To these lines are found the most striking of all the verbal parallels between LD and AM:

> Mirie it is in time of June,
> When fenel hongeþ abrod in toun;
> Violet & rose flour
> Woneþ þan in maidens bour.
> þe sonne is hot, þe day is long,
> Foules make miri song.

(3059–64; see also 4675 f. and 4679 f.) This is the only passage in
LD that reproduces the type of seasonal headpiece defined by G. V.
Smithers in *Kyng Alisaunder*, ii. 35–40. By occurring in conjunction
with the formula discussed in the note to 1219–21 it punctuates the
narrative in a way that is very common (and usually functional) in
AM: see especially AM 1706 ff., 4195 ff., 5347 ff., 6591 ff., 7614 ff.

1234 *Palys* here corresponds to the *lices . . . molt bien faites de pels
agus* of BD 1956 f. In LD the palisade is no longer crowned with the
heads of defeated knights, as this motif has been transferred to the
episode of the falcon: see the notes to L 750–3 and 736–8.

1243–8 In BD the corresponding figure of Malgiers li Gris undertook
the defence of a causeway for seven years in order to win the love of
the lady of the Île d'Or (2009–12). Other versions of the same
character are found in *La Vengeance Raguidel* and the *Livre d'Artus*
and between them suggest that in Chestre's source the knight had
been represented as a very tall knight bearing black arms: *Vengeance*
633, *Livre*, p. 62. This figure appears to have been confused in the
author's mind with the typical Saracen giant of the heroic romances
on which he drew so extensively, to produce the gigantic black
oppressor of this episode. In the process, the original situation by
which Malgiers defended a passage in order to give proof of his
desirability as a husband was replaced by one in which he was a
rejected suitor determined to win the lady by force: compare *King of
Tars*, V. 142, *Sir Gowther*, sts. 32–3, and *Eglamour* 532–7.

L 1311–12 This couplet is also found in P; N (supported by a more
corrupt A) reads:

> Eche here of his browyn
> Is liche the here of a swyn,

lines which recall part of the description of the giant Guymerraunt in
SO 931 f.:

> A greet fot was betwex hys bryn,
> Hys browys, as brystelys of a swyn,

and thus seem nearer to Chestre's original. For the possible superiority
of readings in AN to variants in LP see the note to L 1247.

L 1316 AN here interpolate a stanza which amplifies the grotesque
description contained in L 1305–16: see Appendix (*c*).

1264–5 In AM 6339 f. King Ban says that he will fight with the giant Saphiran in place of the young Arthur:

> 'For þou art to ȝong & ek to lite,
> Oȝain swiche a deuel to smite!'

1280 Before setting out from Glastonbury, Lybeaus had been presented with *a gypell as whyte as melk*, but 223–8 make it plain that this was worn under the hauberk, not on top of it, and Lybeaus had in any case subsequently received fresh clothes and arms from earl Antore. Since these last are described as *bryȝt* in 702 it is conceivable that the *whyt* of the present reference could be glossed as 'shining', but it is also possible that 1280—like 1538, which describes his armour as *rose reed* in colour—is a weak reminiscence of what in the OF. *Octavian* had been an ironical reference to Florent's arms, made, like LD 1280, by a Saracen giant:

> 'Durement sont enruilies.
> [Di] qui les t'a ore enblanchies?'
>
> (2333–4)

1291–3 The description of Maugys's size in L 1305–16 makes his fighting on horseback unexpected. But Chestre was not wholly consistent in remodelling Malgiers on the lines of a Saracen giant (see the note to 1243–8) and he allowed 1291–3 and 1321–6 to survive from the original combat between two knights, instead of replacing them by passages in the style of the earlier encounter with the Red and Black Giants (see especially 616–21). The discrepancy was largely eliminated in *ANP: see *MÆ* xxxii (1963), 13 f.

1295 In his note to this line, Kaluza remarked that none of the extant readings was completely satisfactory and he therefore emended the variant that seemed to him to make best sense (P *Lay on pount tornere* > *Leyn out in pount tournis*). This seems reasonable, but the reading is not supported by BD, where the lady and her maidens watch the fight from the safer vantage points of the *estres* and *fenestres* of the castle (2116–21), while all the surviving manuscripts other than P or H (which is defective here) either state or imply an original which had stated that the spectators watched from the towers of the castle: *tour(e)s* CL, *korvelle* N, *curryculys* A—the last two, presumably, from a *tourelles* with a superscript *r* that was wrongly inserted in transcription, and an initial *t* that was misread as *c/k*. When we further remember the rationalizing of incongruous detail that is found at other points in P, it seems more likely that *pount tornere* should derive from a phrase very like *pomet tours*, than the other way round. Neither *OED.* nor Godefroy records anything like this phrase, but it is clear that OF. *pomet* could duplicate many of the senses of *pomel*, and the latter is used to describe the ornamental top of a tower in *Didot Perceval* E 460 f. In 1295, therefore, we may have an attributive use of *pomet* to convey the idea that would in OF. have been rendered by the participial adjective *pometé*. If the reading of C is authentic, *tour[i]s* must have rhymed upon [iː], but there is nothing unlikely in this: [i] is found in syllables not under the main stress in SO: *croked* 1045: *beloked*:*bytok hyt*:*forsok hyt*, while rhymes of [i] and [iː] occur elsewhere in LD: see above, p. 29.

1327–31 It seems likely that this sequence, like 1975 ff., had originally rhymed upon [ɑuχt] throughout, although it may not still have done so in the archetype. However, *vn-syȝt* may be more than a ghost word, since it might have developed from an earlier **unseht* by the phonetic change that is implied by rhymes of *eiȝtte* (num.) with *kniȝtte* or *riȝt* in *Kyng Alisaunder* and AM (thus Smithers, ii. 48 f.; Liedholm (p. 110) is more sceptical about such rhymes).

1333–62 This passage offers further proof of Chestre's familiarity with the heroic romances. As Kaluza recognized (pp. cl–cliii), it owes a great deal to a passage in the fight between Guy and the giant Amoraunt. Here the giant becomes thirsty and asks Guy's permission to drink, points out the dishonour of overcoming an enemy by letting him die of thirst, and promises to let him drink in turn whenever he wishes to do so. Guy agrees and Amoraunt quenches his thirst, but later denies Guy permission to do the same unless he discloses his identity to him. But even when he has done this, Amoraunt refuses to let him go, and he has to make a dash for the river. While he is drinking he is knocked into it by the giant, but he quickly recovers, curses the giant for his treachery, and says that although 'baptized' by Amoraunt, he does not owe his name to him. In the Auchinleck MS. this scene extends from stanza 113 to 129, but does not contain the vital reference to the hero's 'baptism' that is found in the Anglo-Norman *Gui* 8824–6 and the texts found in MSS. Caius 107 (8514–17) and Cambridge University Library ff. ii. 38 (8265–8): Auchinleck cannot therefore have been the sole text of *Guy* that was known to Chestre. It will be noted that some details of the original account have been reshuffled in LD and some of their significance lost; certainly the 'baptism' has now much less point.

1363–5 Compare AM 9221–2:

> þo bigan bataile newe,
> Ich on oþer wiþ swerd hewe.

1369–74 This passage also reproduces an incident in *Guy*. In the fight with Colbrond, the heathen giant, Guy loses both his sword and his shield, and asks his opponent to lend him some of the many weapons which he carries about him (Auchinleck, st. 266). Colbrond refuses but is not quick enough to prevent Guy from snatching an axe from his collection and killing him with it.

1379–80 Guy and Amoraunt also fight until nightfall (Auchinleck, st. 131).

1384–94 These lines closely parallel the end of the fight with Guymerraunt in SO. Florent strikes the giant such a violent blow that

> Hys scholderbon awey forþ fleȝ
> And hys ryȝt arm;
>
> (1139–40)

the left arm soon follows it and then

> To fle þe geaunt haþ yment;
> But Florent yaf hym swych a dent,
> As he forþ fleȝ,
> þat þe geaunt to grounde ys went.
>
> (1148–51)

Florent then cuts off his head.

1425 *Wycches* C is supported by H as well as N. This allusion completes the degradation of the lady of the Île d'Or; perhaps her association with the Saracen Maugys brought to mind such dangerously seductive beauties as the daughter of Angys (Hengest) who in AM 477 ff. causes Fortiger to forget his Christianity.

1426–34 These lines suggest that the lady's beauty may have been an illusion created by her magic; if so they might correspond to the point in BD at which Giflet's hideous mistress is said to appear beautiful to him. Renaut comments:

> Mais nus hom ne se puet garder
> K'Amors nel face bestorner;
> La laide fait biele sanbler,
> Tant set de guille et d'encanter.
>
> (1732–5)

In the corresponding scene in *Papegau*, music of the kind mentioned in LD 1426–8 accompanies the arrival of the hideous lady (p. 7).

1434 This malediction is typical of the harsh treatment which Chestre alone accords the lady. For the phrasing, see the '*Wel iuel mot sche þriue*' directed at the unnatural wife in *Amis* 1752.

1438–40 The accusation of treachery to Arthur is peculiar to LD; compare the more sharply defined moment in SL 683 f. where Launfal rejects Guinevere's advances, maintaining that he will never be a traitor to his king.

1453 This detail is unexpected as we had not been told that the horse killed in 1318 was ever replaced. Possibly in an earlier form of the story of Lybeaus, the Dame d'Amore (not yet an unsympathetic character) had presented the hero with a steed: see R. S. Loomis, *Arthurian Tradition and Chrétien de Troyes*, pp. 87–91.

1456–8 The variants of H (*Hire styward fer and neor*) and P (*And the steward stout in ffere*) imply an original **Her styward stout and fer*

[OF. *f(i)er*]. The steward Gyfflet corresponds in some important respects to Gyfre, the personal servant of Launfal, and both are to be related to Guivret, the helpful dwarf king who in *Erec* performs many of the functions assumed by Teondeleyn in LD.

L 1530–68 This passage has been much revised in AN: see Appendix (*c*). The effect of these changes is to heighten the sinister aspects of Lambard (for which see the notes to 1487 and 1525–39), since (1) there is now no mention of the unpleasant treatment which the people of Synadoun are ready to mete out to Lybeaus if he should be defeated; (2) the steward is said to inhabit a castle that really belongs to the oppressed queen, and (3) he is characterized as *a gyant felle*. At this point in AN, indeed, the situation which confronts Lybeaus at Synadoun has been made to sound very like that which had faced him at the Îlle d'Or, but the reviser soon gave up all idea of turning Lambard into a completely unsympathetic character, and reverted to Chestre's view of him.

1487 Other characters of roughly similar name in the Arthurian romances (Lampades AM) do not correspond in any vital respect to Lambard (Lanpart BD). In the Anglo-Norman *Gui*, however, we find a Lambert who is a vassal of Otes (Otus *Guy*) and who equals him in villainy (*Gui* 1193, etc.). In LD, Lambard is essentially a 'good' character, but his habit of fighting with all visitors to the castle, including those who had come to rescue his lady, could easily have raised doubts about his real nature and caused the author of the OF. *Lybeaus* to bestow upon him a name with associations of treachery. Doubts about his true character may be implied by the hero's remark in LD 1511 that he will *make þe lady quyt* by overcoming Lambard, since this suggests that he regards the steward as the villain of the piece (he does not in fact learn that the queen is the victim of enchanters, and not of any knight, until 1681–98). See the preceding note for the development of this idea in ANP.

1513–87 During the whole of the actual combat with Lambard, Gyfflet replaces Teondeleyn as the personal servant of Lybeaus (the absence of the dwarf from the scene is explained in AN in the stanza which immediately precedes L 1569). When he rides with his master to the steward's castle he is presumably carrying the *fayre schaftes fyfe* as a squire ought, but when they ask for lodging it is for *aunterous knyʒtes* in the plural, both acknowledge Arthur as their lord, both are described by the porter as *knyʒtes bolde*, are told to get their armour ready for the coming battle, and await Lambard in the field. In C the difference in status of the two characters is still further obscured, since the *rose reed armure* is said to be common to both (only Lybeaus wears it in L 1599 f.) and Lambard declares himself ready to joust *wyth hem* (*with hym* L 1604). After all this it comes as a surprise to find that Gyfflet plays no part whatever in the combat. He does not fight

at his master's side as a knight, nor does he—as a squire—keep him
supplied with fresh weapons when he has need of them (after 1593 and
1611): contrast Robert, the squire of Descouneus, who is prompt to
supply a fresh lance in BD 2662–6, and Gyfre who in SL 580–8 and
592–4 replaces Launfal's helmet and shield after they have been
struck down by Sir Valentyne. Gyfflet simply vanishes from the scene,
only reappearing at 1748, where he once more wishes to accompany
Lybeaus on a dangerous mission, but is not this time permitted to
do so. We can only suppose that Chestre had at first conceived of
Gyfflet, like Gyfre, as an especially powerful 'helper' of the hero, but
quietly dropped the idea (as he was not obliged to do in SL) when he
found that to realize it would entail a more thorough recasting of the
story than he was prepared to undertake.

1525–39 Lambard's readiness to kill or turn away the knight who has
come to rescue his queen is made more strange by this scene with the
porter, which makes it clear that the help sought at Arthur's court has
arrived. BD 2597–612, on the other hand, show that the OF. Lanpart
was not aware of the hero's identity until after the combat.

1547–8 This simile is not very happy as it suggests cowardice or
weakness in Lybeaus and makes the porter seem too aggressive.
Compare:

> þe soudan drof hem yn the feld,
> As hond doþ þe hare,
> (SO 1529–30)

and

> And that Rycharde with theyr folke fares
> As grehoundes do with hares.
> (RCL 5109–10)

L 1629–36 These lines present, more diffusely, details given in SO
967–70 of the arms of one of the Christian knights:

> Hys scheld was gold and asur fyn,
> A lyoun rampant was þer yn,
> Wyth border of ermyn
> Scheld and trappur.

1585 *OED.* defines *grate* in this line as 'a collision (of weapons)'. This
is not at all convincing; much more attractive is Kaluza's suggestion
that the whole phrase relates to the act of placing the lance handle
under the arm or in the saddle rest, before attacking an opponent
(p. 202). Lines 744–6 of *The Seege of Jerusalem* may contain another
example of the word:

> A brynye, browded þicke with a brest-plate,
> þe grate was of gray steel ;' & of gold riche ;
> þer-ouer he casteþ a cote;' colourede of his armys.

The editors of the E.E.T.S. text suggest that *grate* here designates a lance-rest fixed to the breastplate. 'Possibly it was so called because the lance pressed or rubbed against it' (p. 99).

1586 Compare *almost he com(e) to late* in RCL 4864 and 6986, and LD 1182 where a line identical with 1586 describes the hero's recovery from a swoon. The words are less apt in their present context since the joust is Lambard's own idea and conducted on his own terms; he is not therefore likely to have been taken unawares by his opponents' readiness for combat.

1606–8 The violence of these lines is peculiar to LD; in BD and W the combat is much less serious and ends immediately the hero has demonstrated his superiority (BD 2695–8; W 3949–54).

1616 This detail is not paralleled at the same point in either BD or W but is found in SD 569 (*He smot þe kyng in þe lainer*), and at one point in Renaut's description of the combat with Malgiers:

> A un entrejet qu'il jeta
> Les las del elme li trencha;
> Li elmes chaï en la place,
> Desarmee remest la face.
> (BD 2177–80)

It is difficult to reconstruct the archetypal form of the line. L is certainly smoother than C, but it is odd that both A and N should agree with the latter in mentioning the steward's name: N *And Libeous smote Lambert*; A *Syr smote Lamberte*. Possibly all descend from an original *Lybeaus hyt Lambard yn þe layner, and the last word was corrupted to *launcer* in C but was lost (with the two preceding) in the source of AN. The failure of rhyme that resulted was allowed to stand in N (*Lambert:power*) but was eliminated in A (*Lamberte:herd*).

L 1700 AN follow this line with three which suggest that the joust with the steward was as much a test of the stranger's fitness to undertake the principal adventure as a necessary preliminary to getting a night's lodging. See Appendix (*c*).

1646 This line anticipates the statement of 2029–31 and BD 3356–62 that only a kinsman of Gawain could release the captive queen: see the note to 7.

L 1712 This line is followed in AN by a stanza in which Lybeaus asks Lambard if it is he who has been persecuting the captive queen, and is assured that it is not. See Appendix (*c*).

1700–1 *of our toun* suggests that the *palys* was outside the city: see *OED.* 'Of' prep. I. 4. *Palys* could be OF. *palais* and so correspond to the *palais molt grant et marbrin* of BD 2813 and the *palagio di marmo luciente* of *Carduino*, ii. 56, but the spelling suggests the meaning 'palisade', as do 1759–61. Furthermore, in the same adventure in W, E, and *Gereint* the hero rides to his objective through some kind of encircling barrier: a belt of (black) mist in *Gereint* (WB, col. 449) and W 6725–9, of air in E 5689–92.

1711–16 The same motifs occur in conjunction in W 4309–15, but in much modified form. There the victims of the enchanter (the rightful king and the vassals that died with him) must suffer purgatorial torments in the castle of Korntin:

> man hœret dâ niwan wê! wê!
> schrîen die langen naht;
> des tages ist ez âne braht
> und alles schalles lære.
> ez ist uns ein swære
> daz wir des niht mugen gesehen
> wâ von od wie ez sî geschehen.

1747–52 The cognates of LD make it plain that no one could go with the hero on this adventure and escape with his life: see BD 2797–800, E 5825–7, and *Carduino*, ii. 50. Chestre, however, perhaps with 757 in mind, made the threat to Gyfflet proceed from Lybeaus himself; an odd mistake that is preserved in LHAN but softened in P (*Sayd he shold backe againe/And att home abyde*), and recast in C so that the threat came to be directed against the enchanters.

1753–8 For the corruptions which have been introduced into this passage, see the note to 2044–9.

1763 A later statement in CLANP that Lybeaus seats himself *an þat deys* (1801) implies that the noun should be glossed 'raised platform'; only in the variant of H (*at þeo deys*) must it mean '(high) table'. In BD 2920 Renaut mentions *une grant table* (*table dormant* (3095)), on which Descouneus finally goes to sleep. See also pp. 55 f. above.

1768 C's version of this line is the less commonplace, and there is other evidence for supposing it to stand closer to the archetype than the variant offered by LHANP. (1) This variant (*ferther in he yede*) might be a partial anticipation of the *jnner-more he ȝede* preserved in 1786; (2) *ner þe dore he ȝede* could be an isolated detail preserved from the complex set out in BD 2953 ff. (*plus tost que pot vers l'uis se trait*), which describe the flight of the first enchanter into an inner room, and the hero's pursuit of him as far as, but not across, the threshold of it.

1770 This detail recalls such helpful mounts as Bevis's Arondel (A 4447–50) and the sultan's horse in SO 1419 f. In SL 484–6, Launfal's horse unseats a number of his opponents, very much as that of Lybeaus had done in an earlier episode (1123–5).

1789–1800 These lines serve to relate the enchanted hall to stock descriptions of Otherworld palaces in medieval literature (for which, see H. R. Patch, *The Other World, passim*). In W, both Korntin, the purgatory of the dead king, and Glois, the stronghold of the enchanter, are of surpassing splendour (W 4594–608, 7060–89), but in both BD and *Carduino* the elaborately wrought palace of the enchanter is set in the middle of a partially devastated city (BD 2801–16 and 2857–79; *Carduino*, ii. 40–2 and 46). For Chestre's knowledge of this last motif, see Introduction, p. 64.

1804–6 The minstrels never return and the torches are never afterwards said to have been relighted. In BD each minstrel has before him *un cierge espris* (2884); these are extinguished immediately after the fight with Evrain, relighted in 2972–5, and finally carried off by the minstrels after the defeat of Mabon (3081–4). The whole palace is lighted up once more when the serpent enters (3128–34), but relapses into darkness when it leaves (3200–2). Descouneus then falls asleep until it is day.

1807–18 In BD a comparable upheaval occurs both when the enchanters first devastate the city, and when they are finally defeated (BD 3073–100 and 3324–36).

1821–4 Renaut makes no mention of the noise made by the enchanters' horses, but offers an oblique parallel with these lines in his comment on the hero's recovery of his own horse after temporarily losing it in the darkness that follows the flight of the first enchanter: *liés fut quant il ot son ceval* (BD 2988). Here the context makes it plain that the verb must be a preterite form of *avoir* and not a present of *oïr*, but Chestre's freedom in rendering OF. material at other points makes it quite possible that he should here have confused the two forms. Such a confusion might have been helped by his familiarity with the motif embodied in 1821—a familiarity proved by his use of it in SL 1024–6, where it derives from *Graelent* 745–50. It is interesting that Wirnt, as part of the massive amplification of the hero's journey from Roimunt (Synadoun LD) to the enchanter's castle of Glois, should tell how the neighing of his horse saves Wigalois from what looks like certain death, by frightening his opponent away (W 6422 ff.). In the passages noted, both BD and W therefore make the horse the property of the hero and not—as in LD—of his enemy, and the superior authenticity of this variant is further suggested by a later scene in which Wigalois is suddenly cheered up by finding a horse to replace the one he had lost on his way to fight with the enchanter (W 8425–7; see the note to LD 2038–40).

1825–7 At first sight these lines seem the result of quite haphazard borrowing from *Amis*:

> þan þai loked in to þe feld
> & seiȝe a kniȝt wiþ spere & scheld
> Com prikeand þer wiþ pride.
>
> (1219–21)

But in fact the open-air setting of this climactic adventure is insisted upon in other versions of the story; Erec fights with Mabonagrain in an orchard (E 5689 ff.; cf. *Mab.*, p. 272; WB, col. 449), while Carduino

is careful to remain in the open throughout his fight with the enchanter
(ii. 46–8). The present lines may have prompted the even more curious
passage which P inserts after L 2057, to describe the hero's search for
Yrayn in open country: see Appendix (g).

1844 *Skyll* must mean 'leap' or 'mount' here; in SO 326 and 559,
'leap' and 'move rapidly'. None of these senses is found elsewhere
in ME.

1901 The rhyme-word must originally have been the *charmure that
is preserved in AN, and the couplet of which it forms part would
closely have resembled one found in the thirteenth-century *Roman
de la Poire*, 376 f.:

> ja nel garra armeüre
> Ni enchantemenz, ne charmeüre.

The same word must also have occurred in the original of 2058;
see above, p. 19.

1939–50 No offer of this kind is made by the enchanter in any of the
cognates of LD, and the second part of the speech is especially curious,
since it contradicts 1934 f., where we were told that the whole of
Maboun's left arm had been struck off. But the detail of the poisoned
sword, at least, may not be wholly fortuitous (borrowed, for example,
from RCL 7132–5, which tell how Richard was wounded in the arm
by a poisoned weapon), since in the Second Branch of the *Mabinogion*,
Bran—who is undeniably cognate with Maboun in some respects—
is injured by a venomous spear (*Mab.*, p. 37; WB, col. 56).

1963–74 Some of the detail in this stanza can be paralleled in Renaut's
account of the death of Mabon. Descouneus splits the enchanter's
skull, foul smoke issues from his mouth, and then:

> Tos fu devenus claire pure,
> Qui molt estoit et laide et sure.
> Isi li canja sa figure,
> Molt estoit de male nature.
>
> (BD 3067–70)

Chestre might have misunderstood such a passage to mean that the
enchanter had simply vanished, and transferred this detail to Yrayn,
whose fate in the combat was traditionally left vague (see Introduction,
pp. 56 f.). Rôaz, the enchanter of W, also disappears after his death:

> Rôaz der wart verstolen dan
> zehant von der tievel schar
> daz sîn dâ nieman wart gewar
> unz daz man in ûz solde tragen.
>
> (8136–9)

L 2049–57 Descouneus gives way to equally pessimistic thoughts
after he has allowed the serpent to kiss him (BD 3203–11). In MS. P,
L 2057 is followed by a passage that describes the hero's search for

and killing of Yrayn, and his initial failure to find the captive queen. The first part thus settles a point that was never cleared up in the archetype; the second provides a neat transition to the encounter with the serpent.

1981–3 The substitution of these three lines for the half-stanza preserved in L 2055–60 caused the redefinition of the limits of subsequent stanzas (by altering their tail-lines) as far as 2058, at which point the archetypal corruption of **charmure* to *chaunterye* made further changes unnecessary.

1991 This detail is not found in any of the cognates; in BD 3134 f. and 3139 f. the serpent's face is said to be as repulsive as the rest of her body. The detail in LD may reflect the kind of representation of the serpent in Genesis that is implied in Chaucer's *Man of Law's Tale* (B 360): see T. Ehrenstein, *Das Alte Testament im Bilde*, Vienna, 1923, ch. ii, nos. 52, 54, 61, 69, and 70.

L 2076–8 In *Papegau* the beast into which the deposed king has been transformed is said to be *si vermeille qu'il sembloit qu'elle fust embrasee* (p. 64).

2002–4 The reading of C may be supported by RCL 3029 f.:

> He my3te hym nou3t of hys bed stere,
> þou3 his pauyloune hadde be on ffere.

2029–31 In BD 3216–42 Descouneus is informed about his parentage by the voice of the lady of the Ìlle d'Or; in W 5822–5 he suddenly realizes his true identity after recovering from the fight with the serpent Pfetan.

2035–7 The lady's determination to submit to Arthur's wishes is rather unexpected, but in BD 3405 the same condition (*se Artus le me velt loer*) serves to give the hero time to remember his desertion of the lady of the Ìlle d'Or (BD 3676–736), to whom he had promised to return after achieving the adventure at the enchanted city (3117–24). No causal connexion is established in this romance between his procrastination and his return to his former love, but one such may have existed in an earlier version of the story. For the problems raised by the second visit to the Ìlle d'Or, see Introduction, pp. 51 ff.

2038–40 This departure on a horse seemingly killed in 1894–6 is unexpected, and it is not surprising that P should here have substituted a passage in which Lybeaus announces his intention of finding clothes for the transformed lady—a detail not given in C until 2071–6. No parallel to this sudden departure is offered by BD, but Wirnt, in the passage discussed at 1821–4, speaks of a sudden raising of his hero's spirits after he has ridden about rapidly on a newly acquired steed:

> dô er ûf daz ros gesaz,
> sîns jâmers er ein teil vergaz
> und vie ze vreuden niuwen muot.
>   (W 8425–7)

L 2120 AN follow this line with a stanza in which the hero goes back into the castle to search for Yrayn, finds him in a private room (*chambour*), and cuts off his head (see Appendix (*c*)). In itself this removes all doubts about the fate of the second enchanter, but these are allowed to reappear in the stanza which follows, since the statement that Yrayn was only wounded (while Maboun had been killed) stands unaltered at L 2128.

2043 This line may mean 'he might destroy him with his spells'. The phrasing is that of *Amis* 641, where Amis, worried by Belisaunt's threat of denouncing him, fears that '*Wiþ hir speche sche wil me spille*'.

2044–9 The importance of these lines to the textual status of P₂ has already been discussed; it remains to comment on their relation to 1753–8. Both these half-stanzas of C resemble each other more closely in that text than in any other, and at the same time seem to varying degrees inferior to their counterparts in L. The tail-lines of 1753–8 do not rhyme with those of the first half of the stanza, the couplets of 2044–9 present a rather unconvincing-looking set of *a*-rhymes, and both passages, by substituting a single speaker for a group of people (at 1756 and 2046) credit his with actions more proper to other characters. In fact, each passage has endowed the other with some incongruous feature: an anticipation of the couplet following 2044–9 prompted the discrepant tail-rhymes of 1755–8, while 1756 f., which are perfectly apt in rhyme, have been carried over to 2047 f., where they may not have been. Cross influence of this kind is only likely to have occurred in a transmission that depended, to some degree at least, upon memory, and it presumably took place in an early form of *C; see above, pp. 10 f.

2056–67 This stanza is omitted in P, a logical step in view of the fact that Yrayn's death had been described in the passage inserted in that text after L 2057: see the note to L 2049–57. 2058 *chaunterye* was correctly emended to *charmure* by Kaluza: see the note to 1901.

2107–9 There is no description of the wedding celebrations in BD, where the ending is deliberately left open. See above, p. 43.

L 2192 With *vnbrest* should be compared the *vnprest* of H. None of the senses elsewhere attested for these words will give satisfaction in this context; in spite of the late date of LD it is very tempting to suppose an initial miscopying of **vnprest* (*vn-wrest* C) as *vnprest*, and a further corruption of the form to *vnbrest* in L; compare the corruption in AN of 1131 *slep* to *slew*. Immediately after L 2192 three stanzas are interpolated in AN (the second and third of which are also present in H) which reintroduce characters and motifs from the beginning of the story. In the first of these stanzas, the mother of Lybeaus turns up at the feast, recognizes her son, and reveals his identity to Gawain; in the second, Gawain communicates the news to the queen of Synadoun, and a general reunion takes place; in the third, Lybeaus asks for and obtains his father's blessing before setting out once more for Synadoun (cf. 241–9) and Gawain orders all those present to call the hero Gengelayne in future (cf. 67–72). See above, pp. 16–18 and sections (b) and (c) of the Appendix.

GLOSSARY

THE glossary is primarily a record of the words and forms of C, which of all the texts reflects in its spellings the dialect closest to that implied by the rhymes of LD. Words of very common occurrence and obvious meaning have usually been omitted or represented by only one example. Significant words not found in C but offered by one or more of the remaining copies are also listed. References to the Caligula text are given without prefix, those to any of the other texts are preceded by the relevant symbols. On the (relatively rare) occasions when reference is made to any of H, A, N, or P, the symbol for the text(s) in question is followed in brackets by a line-reference to L. Thus *besemyth* which occurs in HANP in the second line of a stanza that immediately follows L 216 (a stanza given in full in the Appendix, section (*b*)) carries the reference HANP (L 216ᵇ).

The order of the glossary is alphabetical, but *i* and *y* are glossed together under *i*, *3* after *g*, *þ* after *t*, and *v* for [v] after *v* for [u]. Words which involve the substitution of initial *d* for *þ* or vice versa are given under the more usual form of the word concerned in ME.: *þo* ('do') under *d*; *denkeþ* ('intend') under *þ*. On occasion, words with initial *k* have been glossed under *c*, words with initial *y*, under *3*. Dialectal variants of a single ME. word have usually been grouped together: for example, *eld*, *old(e)*; *leste*, *lyste*; *pall(e)*, *pell*, and *sare*, *sore*.

abyde *v.* tarry 313, 819; wait for 1116, 1752; 2 *sg. pr. sb.* 1059; 3 *sg. pt.* *abod* 1754, 2045, *abode* 851, 1189, *aboþe* 1118; 3 *pl. pt.* *abode* L 2122, *abyde* 1562, 1584.

abled *pp.* excellent L 189.

abood *n.* delay 778.

aboue *adv.* above 1816; *aboune* up A (L 495).

a-bou3t *pp.* paid for 1979.

aboute, abowte *adv.* around 505, 582, 720; on all sides 714, 963; prep. 230, 840, 2007.

acketoun *n.* padded jacket worn under mail 1175.

a-dy3t *pp.* fashioned 227; appointed 711; *euell a.* in poor condition 1353.

adoun, adowun *adv.* down 324, 373, 480.

afeng *3 sg. pt.* received 1401.

aferde *pp. a.* afraid 182.

a-fere *adv.* on fire 2004.

a-for *prep.* before L 352.

a-fote *adv.* on foot 332, 1327, 1904.

after, aftyr *prep.* after 692, 1130, 2008; behind 868; for 1083; in pursuit of 1190; *adv.* 440, 1390.

aftyr-ward *adv.* subsequently 1415.

agayn(e), a3en, ayen *adv.* back 464, 955, 1105, 1375; again 1090, 1282, 1627.

agayn, a3ens, ayens *prep.* against 270, 415, 421; towards 779, 1398, 1440.

agast *a.* terrified 1853.

a-gye *v.* get along 2052.

a-go *pp.* gone away 331.

agramede *pp.* angered 1916.

agreued *pp.* enraged 502.

agryse *v.* be terrified 2002; 3 *sg. pt.* *agros* 1884.

ay *adv.* ever 693, 2036; *a. wyth-outen ende* in perpetuity 531.

ayder *a.* each 883; pron. each one 1606, 1631.

alday *adv.* the whole day 1138.

algate *adv.* all the way N (L 1578), P (L 1815).

aly3te *3 sg. pt.* dismounted 1761.

all(e) *a.* all 38, 100; *adv.* 108, 202, 312; entirely 15, 692; *n.* all 62, 67, 385; *a. and some* everyone 1088.

al(l)mest *adv.* almost 1182, 1586.

almy3t *a.* almighty 1362.

alowte *v.* yield humbly 1254.

also, als, as *adv.* also 234, 703; then 332; *a. blyue* at once 688, 2104, *a. 3erne* 494, *a. sket* 484, 1895, *a. snell* 739, 808, 817, *a. swythe* L 1603, *a. tyte* 784, 832; correl. with *as* (127), 224, 1273.

alwey *adv.* all the time 257.

alweldand *prp.* omnipotent HAN (L 2192ᵃᵃ).

amall *n.* enamel 879.

amydde(s), amydward *prep.* in the middle of 803, 827, 852, 1765.

amys *adv.* wrongly 1479.

a-morn, a-morow *adv.* next morning 454, 763, 1738.

amounteþ *3 sg. pr.* means 1476.

an *prep.* on 374, 462, 1172; in 1277.

ano(o)n *adv.* at once 32, 44, 86, 245; *a. ry3t(es)* at once 73, 193, 210, 327.

apace *adv.* quickly 1990.

apayd *pp.* pleased ANP (L 1712ʰ).

aply3t *adv.* truly 45, 645, 799, 2060.

apryse *n.* undertaking 594.

arafte *3 sg. pt.* struck 1129.

arayde *pp.* adorned 837; *arrayed* equipped P (L 1545).

arblaste *n.* cross-bow 1120.

ary3t *adv.* correctly 1143.

aryse *v.* get up 603, 2003; imp. *arys* 562; 3 sg. pt. *aros* 685, 773, 1881.

aryved *pp.* ? edged L 866.

arme, army *v.* arm 210, 217; 3 sg. pt. *armede* 766; 3 pl. pt. *armede* 436; pp. *armed* 1537, *armede* 1581, *y-armed* 460, *j-armeþ* 281.

armes, armys *n. pl.* arms 29, 76, 1900; *dy3te hem to a.* armed 1093.

armur(e) *n.* armour 33, 767, 1538, 1828.

a-rowe *adv.* all together 70.

arsoun *n.* saddle-bow 321, 1172, 1181, 1322; saddle 483, 623, 1614.

artes *n. pl.* magic arts 1695.

as *conj.* as 18, 25, 78, 101; as if 1161.

asayle *v.* attack 426, 1866; *to-gydere a.* attack each other 1377.

aschamed *pp. a.* mortified 1597, 1639, 1915.

a-see *v.* see L 762.

asyse *n.* manner 600.

askeþ *3 sg. pr.* demands 90; imp. *axede* request 1490; 3 sg. pt. *axede* asked 23, 1237, 1474; 3 pl. pt. 1520.

askyng *n.* request 92.

askrye *v.* proclaim H (L 956).

asonder *v.* split 1818; *adv.* in pieces 922, 1303.

assente *3 sg. pt.* agreed L 1224.

asure *n.* blue L 1629.

a-swogh *adv.* unconscious 1171.

at *prep.* at 52, 105, 810; to 1742, 2124; in 3; of 24; *at ones* together 1144.

atyre *n.* equipment 1566; *of ryche a.* splendidly ornamented 238.

a-tweyn, a-twynne, a-two *adv.* in two 359, 630, 1392, 1914, 1962.

a-þre *adv.* in three 635.

avaunt *n.* pride HANP (L 1762).

avauntors *n. pl.* boasters L 1145.

auentayle *n.* chain-mail protecting the neck 1618.

au3te *1 sg. pt. sb.* owned 1027.

aunterous *a.* perilous 279; bold 1119, 1521; rash 1833.

avow *n.* solemn promise 1287.

away, awey(e) *adv.* away 325, 1188; *wer a.* had gone 1806; *aweywerd* adv. ANP (L 1214).

awake *v.* be stirred up 1095.

awe *n.* threatening 183.

aw3t *n.* anything 96.

aw(y)ede *v.* go mad 395, 618, 957.

awreke *v.* avenge 1421; pp. 419.

bay *n.: to b.* at bay 1563.

bay(e) *a.* bay coloured 462, 1044, 1461.

bak *n.* back 1392; *b. and syde* from all sides 872; adv. 1288.

bales *n. pl.* sorrow 2088.

bandwon *n.* disposal 529.

baptys(t)e *n.* baptism 212, 1360.

barbe *n.* part of helmet protecting the chin L 372.

bare *a.* bereft L 2060.

barme *n.* lap 577.

basnet *n.* light helmet 500, 1169.

batayle *n.* combat 1395; adventure which involves fighting 93, 190; pl. *batayles* L 197; *holde b.* fight 423; *jn b. and yn fyȝt* in fighting of all kinds 705.

be *v.* be 58; 1 sg. pr. *am* 51; 2 sg. pr. *art* 94, *artow* 1058; 3 sg. pr. *ys* 50; 1 pl. pr. *beþ* 299; 3 pl. pr. 597; 1 sg. pr. sb. *be* 591; 2 sg. pr. sb. 829; 3 sg. pr. sb. 93; 1 sg. pt. *was* 46; 2 sg. pt. *wer* 654; 3 sg. pt. *was* 7, *wes* 946; 3 pl. pt. *wer* 29, *wher* 392, *weren* 393, *wore* 1275; 1 sg. pt. sb. *wer* 1069; 2 sg. pt. sb. 563, *wher* 260, *werst* 1503; 3 sg. pt. sb. *wer* 189, *were* 15, *wore* 404; pp. *be* 659, *y-be* 1307, *ben* 670, *y-bene* 2004.

be, by *prep.* by 9, 1494.

beau *a.* fair: *b. frer* fair sir 291; *bewfere* good companion L 314; *bewpere* reverend sir ANP (L 314).

be-cauȝt *pp. a.* cheated 1976.

bede *v.* offer 1493; 3 sg. pt. commanded A (L 403).

beer *g. pl.* bears' L 1630.

be-fell(e) *3 sg. pt.* happened 25, 1225; pp. *be-falle* 1834.

be-for(e) *prep.* before 329, 350; in front of 1278, 1763; in the presence of 38, 47, 62; adv. ahead 262; *b. and ek be-hynde* completely 122.

be-gan *3 sg. pt.* began 1813; *seþe he ferst b.* since he first set out 984; did (preterite auxiliary) 258, 388, 769; 3 pl. pt. 1363.

be-gyle *v.* trick, overcome 753.

be-gyn(n)ynge *n.* beginning: *shall be his b.* will be his first adventure L 201; *tolde him the b.* told him the whole story L 1260.

be-hynde, by-hynde *adv.* behind 122; after 1042.

be-holde *v.* view L 1846, L 1864; 3 sg. pt. *be-held* saw 1105; looked 1989.

be-yete *n.* advantage L 1700.

be-yete *pp.* begotten 8.

beld, bold(e) bold, valiant 1536, 1558, 2123; fierce 1272.

be-leyde *pp.* besieged 1248.

be-leueþ *3 sg. pt.* remained 1393.

bemes *n. pl.* trumpets 1497.

bename *pp.*? slain A (L 33).

bende *n.* imprisonment 252.

bere *v.* bear 415; *b. to* thrust at 472 f.; *b. awey* carry off L 511; 1 sg. pr. *b. record* testify 165; 3 sg. pr. *berreth* has L 1311, *bereth* L 1765; 1 sg. pr. sb. *bere doun* overthrow 913; 2 sg. pr. (sb.) *berest d.* 910; 3 sg. pr. (sb.) *beryþ d.* 1495; 3 sg. pt. *bar* carried 856, 865, 1868; *b. doun* 1124, 1856; 3 pl. pt. *bore* carried 967; pp. *y-bore* 971, 1478; born 46, 654, 1642.

berne *n.* warrior L 428.

berne *v.* burn 583; be consumed 493; prp. *brennynge* blazing 1785; 3 sg. pt. *brende* 1767; 3 pl. pt. 1804; pp. *y-brent* 1569.

besemyth *3 sg. pr.* is fitting HANP (L 216ᵇ).

be-sette *3 pl. pt.* kept watch on 662; pp. trapped, brought to bay 1132.

be-syde *prep.* by the side of 255, 770, 1056.

best *n.* animal 1563.

best(e) *a.* best 207; *wyth þe b.* the very best 989.

be-sterede *3 sg. pt.* exerted 1183.

be-swette *pp. a.* covered in sweat 108.

bet *adv.*? further H (L 1818).

be-take *v.*: *b. aweye* remove L 587; 3 sg. pt. *be-tok* placed in the charge of 82.

bete *3 sg. pr. sb.* relieve 1492; 3 sg. pt. *bette* 2088; pp. *bett* L 2162.

bete *pp. a.* ornamented L 135.

beten *3 pl. pt.* slammed 1808.

be-tyde *v.* happen 1053; 3 sg. pr. sb. 274, *be-tyt* 1341.

be-tokeneth *3 sg. pr.* means L 1538.

be-trayde *pp. a.* trapped 1820.

bette *adv.* better 1822.

be-thynke *imp.* take care L 1308.

byddest *2 sg. pr.* request 1340; 3 sg. pt. *bad* 86; told 1543; prayed 1755, 2046.

bide *v.* endure: *b. bataile* engage in fighting N (L 446); 1 sg. pt. *bode þys day* lived to see this day 587.

by-dene *adv.* together 1210, L 638, L 1728.

byged *3 pl. pt.* provided with shelter A (L 581).

biggyng *n.* building ANP (L 1892[1]).

byker(e) *n.* fight 1059, 1116.

byrd(e) *n.* maiden L 275, L 2150; pl. *birdes* L 1058.

bys *a.* dark 2071.

blame *v.* reproach 401.

blaunner *n.* white fur 117.

blaw *n.* blow A (L 207).

ble *n.* appearance 281, 458.

blerede *3 sg. pt.*: *b. hys yȝe* deceived him 1433.

blynne *v.* leave off ANP (L 834).

blysse *n.* joy L 2060.

blyþe *a.* merry 649, 1216, 1672.

blyue *adv.* quickly 688, 1515, 2104.

blosme *n.* blossom 579.

body *n.* body 14; *boþ b. and fasoun* every part 828.

boȝte, bouȝt *3 sg. pt.* redeemed 195, 675.

bond *n.* serf: *boþe b. and fre* everyone 804.

bond *n.* circlet ANP (L 906).

bone *n.* boon 86, 1340.

boneyre *a.* complaisant 1726.

boon *a.* fair: *b. frere* fair sir H (L 314).

boote *n.* use P (L 1391).

boourdour *n.* jester L 148.

borde *n.* entertainment ANP (L 1997).

bordure *n.* surrounding band 858.

borgays *n.* citizen 1626; pl. *burgeyses* L 1800.

bost *n.* outcry 565.

bot(e), but *conj.* but 52; unless 494, 532, 1072, *b. ȝef* unless 370; adv. *(ne) b.* merely, only 902, 1033.

boun *pp. a.* ready 763, 1174, 1496, *redy b.* 622, 865; *make b.* prepare 822; *off bowne* on the point of falling off ANP (L 1676).

bour *n.* private room 1206; *b. and halle* all the apartments 2116.

bowe *n.* longbow 1120; pl. *bowes turkoys* Turkish bows P (L 1147).

brace *v.* take hold of, grapple with L 539.

braide *n.* moment ANP (L 1381).

brayn(e) *n.* brain 1317, 1966; *se hare b.* dash their brains out 1751.

bredale *n.* wedding feast 2107.

brede *n.* breadth 735, 884, 963.

brederen *n. pl.* brothers 523.

bregge *n.* bridge 1252, 1271.

breke *v.* break 929; 3 sg. pt. *brak* 476, 630, 1615; 3 pl. pt. 1873, *breke* 922, *breeke* 1303.

brere *n.* briar 579.

brest *v.* break L 508; 3 sg. pt. *brast* 359, 1166; 3 pl. pt. *brosten* L 951, *borsten* L 1947.

bryȝt *a.* fair 14, 110, 161, *b. and schene* 1032, 1413; shining 76, 226, *b. of ble* 281, 458, *b. and broune* 552; adv. brightly 583, 882, 1767.

brym *n.* brink 1378.

bryng(e) *v.* bring 795, 892; escort 1744, 2124; *forþ b.* bring out 2073; *b. out of* deliver from 252; 3 sg. pr. *bryngeþ* 727; imp. *breng* 929; 3 sg. pt. *broȝt* 232, 235, *broȝte* 1742; 3 pl. pt. *brouȝt* 669, 1658; pp. 1628, *broȝt* 152.

brystillus *n. pl.* bristles L 1312.

brond *n.* piece of burning wood 1569; sword 505.

broun(e), browne *a.* brown 462, 1461; shining 552; unattractive 805.

browe *n.* eyebrow 883; pl. *browyn* ANP (L 1311).

bugle *n.* hunting horn 1045.

buske *v.* get ready 822.

butte *n.* end N (L 657[b]).

calles *n. pl.* head-dresses 2074.

can, kan *1 sg. pr.* am able 96; 3 sg. pr. knows: *werry k.* knows how to fight 981; *of sorcery k.* has skill in magic 1442; *k. craft* is experienced 1601; 3 sg. pt. *kowþe* 1424, *coupe* 136; 3 pl. pt. *kouþ* 2025, 2114.

care, kar *n.* worry 755; lamentation 972; sorrow 1983.

karfull *a.* sorrowful 1110.

cas, kas *n.* situation 148, 388, 1341; plight 1110.

caste, kaste *3 sg. pt.* considered 348; put on 840; offered 1412; *doun c.* overthrew 959; 3 pl. pt. put on 223; pp. *y-kast* thrown 1472.

castell *n.* castle 279, 663, 710; *c. halle and bour* all his property 1197; pl. *kasteles* 691, *casteles* 2033; *castelles* towers 1235.

catelle *n.* wealth, property ANP (L 2014).

cause *n.* causeway L 301.

certayn(e) *adv.* certainly 164, 1718, 1733.

certe *n.: say yn c.* swear 129.

certes *adv.* indeed 1068.

chalaunge *v.* lay claim to 742.

chambre *n.* inner room 1405.

champyo(u)n *n.* defender 214; *chose for c.* supreme in battle 489.

charmys *n. pl.* spells 1901.

charmour *n.* ? enchantment ANP (L 1975).

chauntement *n.* enchantment 1901, 2026.

chaunterye *n.* enchantment 2058.

chefferon *n.* chevron L 254.

cheyers *n. pl.* chairs L 922.

chepyng *n.* market-place 893.

chere *n.* appearance 576; behaviour 1675.

cherll *n.* churl, fellow 1062, 1065.

chesteyn *n.* chestnut 1191.

chyde *v.* reproach 169, 258; 2 sg. pr. sb. complain 1062.

chyld(e) *n.* boy 18, 31, 49; daughter 681.

chyldhede *n.* childish behaviour ANP (L 853).

chyualrye *n.* knighthood 1529.

chosyn *3 sg. pt.* declared L 1266; pp. *chose* excellent 489.

clave *3 sg. pt.* remained L 525.

clene *a.* pure L 1055.

clepeþ *imp. pl.* call 67; 3 pl. pr. 661, 1240, 1269; 3 sg. pt. *clepede* 20, 54, 65; pp. *clepede* 109, *y-clepede* 379.

cler(e) *a.* beautiful 898; shining 1137, 1152, 1908.

clerkes *n. pl.* magicians 1690, 1694, 2021.

cleue *v.* cut through 1966; 3 sg. pt. *cleuede* 506, *clove* L 2035.

clypped *3 sg. pt.* coiled L 2084; pp. *y-clepte* embraced 578.

clyue *n.* rock 1163.

clodede *3 sg. pt.* dressed 1407; pp. *clodeþ* 115, 121, 870, *y-clodeþ* 1776, *j-clodeþ* 1043.

clos *n.: yn c.* well guarded 16; well covered 1890.

coyfe *n.* hood of mail P (L 372).

colled *3 sg. pt.* embraced P (L 2084).

coltre *n.* (iron blade in front of) ploughshare ANP (L 657[b]).

come *v.* come 549; 1 sg. pr. *come* 410; 2 sg. pr. *comyst* 782; 3 sg. pr. *comeþ* 848; 3 sg. pr. sb. *come* 1259; 3 sg. pt. *com* 106; 3 pl. pt. *come* 2111; pp. *com* 1646, *come* 1536.

commande *3 sg. pt.* told 820; *comaunded* ordered L 230.

coniurment *n.* incantations A (L 2103).

conquerour *n.* champion 4.

consente *3 sg. pt.* agreed 1198.

constable *n.* chief officer of the household 1488, 1532, 1660.

cor *n.* filth L 1533.

cor(o)nall *n.* lance-head ending in spreading points 930, 1577, 1604; pl. *coronals* 919.

corneres *n. pl.* nooks 1789.

covere, keuere *v.* recover L 1248; relieve 1983; 3 sg. pt. *keuerede state* recovered confidence 1179.

cours *n.* coursing 1040; joust L 980; *take c.* ride against 310, 598.

courser, cursere *n.* horse 620, 1187.

craft(e), kraft *n.* power 2058; skill: *of c.* skilful 311, 599; *kan c.* has skill, is experienced 1601.

crye *v.* cry out 361, 1102, 1711; proclaim 726; *c. mercy* beg for pardon 448; 3 sg. pt. *cryde* 584, 780, *kryde* 466; 3 pl. pt. *cryde* 463, 519.

croun *n.* crown of head 240, 501.

croupe, kroupe *n.* hind-quarters 323, 938.

croupoun, crowpoun *n.* hind-quarters ANP (L 1198, L 1384).

crouþe *n.* instrument of the viol family 138.

curryculys *n. pl.* chariots A (L 1357).

day, þay *n.* day 75, 256, 1462; *vp-on a d.* one day 25; *d. oþer nyȝt* at any time 292, 722, 747; *d. ne nyȝt* at no time 411; pl. *dayes* 992, 2119; *be d. and be nyȝt* at all times 1716.

dame *n.* mother 24, 65, 1068; lady 652, 2106.

dar *1 sg. pr.* dare 129; 3 sg. pt. *dorst* 1689, *dorste* 1744, *þorste* 1704; 3 pl. pt. *þorst* 1155.

dede *n.* deed 6, 34, 704; pl. *dede* 1251, 1506, *dedes* 983, 1211.

deed *a.* dead 621, 1318.

deeþ *n.* death 2022; g. sg. *dedys wounde* mortal wound 1607.

defamed *pp. a.* dishonoured 1919.

defens *n.* protection N (L 769); *stode d. aȝayne* stood at bay ANP (L 1451).

degre *n.* rank L 2166.

deys *n.* dais, high table 1763, 1801, 1813.

dele, dely *v.* strike 177, 287, 1578; 3 sg. pt. *delede* 1365.

delyte *n.* desire 785.

delyte *n.* delay ANP (L 1409).

dell *n.* part 1352.

demeaning *n.* (usual) way P (L 695).

dent(e) *n.* blow 168, 177, 1371, 1578; pl. *dentes* 923, 1304, 1365, *dentys* 1257, 1937.

departede *3 pl. pt.* went their ways 385, 538.

de-ray *n.* outcry 396.

dere, þeer *n.* wild animal(s) 27, 1133.

dere *a.* noble 18; adv. dearly 195, *þere* 1158.

deriþ *3 pl. pr.* torment H (L 1778); 3 sg. pt. *dered* harmed HANP (L 1733).

derkede *3 sg. pt.* grew dark 1379.

descouerours *n. pl.* judges at a tournament 926.

descrye *v.* proclaim 927.

descryue, dyscryue *v.* describe 1330, 1428; make known 894.

despyte, dyspyt *n.* insult 787; scorn 1279; opposition 1347; humiliation 1508.

destrer(e) *n.* (war-)horse 120, 569, 1044; pl. *destrerys* 1097.

dette *n.* service due 2091.

device *n.: att d.* perfectly well P (L 122).

deuyse *v.* think of 2114.

dyȝnyte *n.* high rank 2089.

dyȝte *v.* strike 1906; *d. to deþe* kill 1719; 3 pl. pt. built 550; *d. to armes* armed 1093; pp. *dyȝt* dressed 792; turned 2057; *redy d.* ready 2077; *d. to synne* brought into sin 1728; *y-dyȝt* adorned 130; *to horse þat þou wer y.* you should be mounted 563.

dym *a.* dark 1379.

dynge *v.* strike (blows) 1147, 1311.

dynte *n.* blow L 177, L 1433, L 1640; pl. *dyntis* L 952, *dyntys* L 1316, *dyntes* L 1427.

dysmayde, þysmayd *pp. a.* daunted 202; terrified 1819.

dysour *n.* story-teller 139; pl. *dissoures* L 955.

dysseyved *pp. a.* betrayed L 1894.

do, þo *v.* do 532, 1721; undertake 160; cause 365; *for-to done* to achieve 95; 2 sg. pr. *doost* 1443; 3 sg. pr. *doþ* 723, *þoȝ* 624; 3 pl. pr. *don* 1479; *doþ turmentrye* torture 1714; 3 sg. pr. sb. *do* 1266; imp. *þo* 309, *do* 424; *do come* bring 1600; 1 sg. pt. *þede* 1008; 3 sg. pt. *dede* 1416; *d. of* took off 31, 1406; 3 pl. pt. *dede* 2090; pp. *do* 34, *don* 398, *y-do* 1692.

doftyr *n.* daughter 689.

dolour *n.* sorrow 150, 1446, 1656.

dore *n.* door(way) 1768; pl. *dores* 1807, *þores* 1795.

do(u)ȝty, þo(u)ȝty *a.* valiant 6, 177, 704, 1578, 1851; comp. *þoȝtyer* 1091.

doun(e), down *adv.* down 202, 382, 1318; *d. ryȝt* straight down 353; at once 1184.

doune *n.* hill 1002.

dou(u)te, dowte *n.* fear 17, 183, 564; (fear of) danger 717, 1245.

dradde *3 sg. pt.* feared 2041.

drauȝt, drawȝte *n.* blow, attack, 629, 1130.

drawe *2 pl. pr. sb.* withdraw 1111; *3 sg. pt. drouȝ* drew 1922; *3 pl. pt. drouȝ* 1309, *þrouȝ* 1874.

dreche *3 pl. pr.* torment L 1778.

drede *n.* fear 187, 559, 1698.

dreyȝ *v.* survive 950.

þrest *3 sg. pt.* dressed 1738.

dryue *v.* go 1512; *doun d.* force down 1162; *d. dyntys* strike blows L 1316; pp. *driue* made P (L 1871).

due *a.* proper 2091.

dure *v.* live 2067; *durye* endure L 979.

dwelle *v.* remain 529; *3 sg. pt. dwellede* 1156; *3 pl. pt.* 553, 762, 1418.

dwellyng(e) *n.* delay 44, 245, 438, 2076.

dwerk(e) *n.* dwarf 107, 121, 204, 255.

ech *a.* every 84, 180, 263; *e. a* 737, 1352, 1772.

eem *n.* uncle 397, 424; *emes sonis* cousins HANP (L 412).

eft(e) *adv.* again 637; afterwards 477.

egge *n.* edge: *of e. and ord* at all points 1923.

egre *a.* fierce 237, 492, 625; *wyth e. mode* fiercely 504, 1787.

eye *n.* eye 1712, 1800, *yȝe* 1433; pl. *eyen* 886.

eyr *n.* heir 1724.

eyþer, eyder *pron.* each (of two) 920, 1332, 1364, 1877.

eyþer *conj.* or 2030.

ek *adv.* also 122, 405, 1817.

eld, old(e), hold *a.* old 658, 1992; *o. and y(e)nge* everyone 895, 1018.

ende *n.* end 384, 634; *wyth-outen e.* perpetually 531, 2034.

endentyd *pp.* inlaid ANP (L 871), *ydentid, dynt* ANP (L 1630).

endynge *n.* end 2130.

enpyre *n.* land 843.

entent *n.* will L 642.

enuye *n.* hostility 921.

er, yer *conj.* before 304, 428, 637; *er þan* 371, 534.

erbere *n.* flower-garden 899.

erynde *n.* mission 143.

ernest *n.* earnest: *jn e. and yn game* as hard as possible 471.

errour *n.* fury 1081.

erþe *n.* ground 1814.

estate *n.* rank P (L 1205).

euell *n.* harm 666; *a. euele* painful 939; *adv. euell* badly 1353, 1434.

euen(e) *adv.* just 1517; completely 1935.

euer *adv.* ever 587, 651; always 288, 477; incessantly 258; still 2041; *e. fauȝt* went on fighting 628; *e. ryden* went on riding 544.

euerych *a.* every 236; *pron.* each one 461.

euer-mare *adv.* eternally 1131.

eues *n.* edge (of a wood) P (L 580).

euesong *n.: e. tyme* sunset 1334.

ex *n.* axe 1180.

extente *n.* agreement 1195.

fable *n.* falsehood: *wyth-out(e) f.* truly 1534, 1682.

fa(w)choun, fawkoun *n.* curved sword 234, 374, 408, 911; pl. *fauchouns* 338.

fay *n.* faith 524, 1439, 1650.

fayle *n.* fail: *wyth-out f.* certainly 420; *saunȝ f.* 1386, 1860.

fayn *a.* glad 217, 1395, 1540; *fawe* willing 1114.

fayr(e), feyr *a.* fair 13, 707, 1723; comp. *fayryr* 727, *fayrer* 798; *adv. fayre* courteously 997; (*boþe*) *f. and well* very courteously 1491, 1522; quite honestly 1215; *f. and bryȝt* very brightly 1785.

fayrye *n.* magic 1432, 1706.

fale *a.* many 1007, 2110, *fele* 650, 1007, 1217, 1670.

fall *n.*: *euele f.* mishap 939.

fall(e) *v.* fall 1262, 1811; *as kas hyt be-gan f.* as it happened 388; *jn hys herte gan f.* came into his heart 1988; 3 sg. pr. *falleþ* is fitting 987; 3 sg. pt. *fyll* fell 1385, *fell* 324; happened 1435; *of Lybeauus how hyt f.* what happened to L. 1212; 3 pl. pt. *fell* 1592; pp. *y-falle* 148.

fame *n.* renown 687.

fantasme *n.* illusion 1432.

fare *v.* go 1514, 1544; 2 sg. pr. *faryst* behave L 853; pp. *y-fare* escaped 1980.

farward, forward *n.* agreement 384, 815, 912; *jn f. þat* on condition that 1199; *al f.* very promptly; *in þat f.* as he had promised HANP (L 2142).

fasoun, fass(y)oune *n.* face, form 486, 555, 791, 828, 1467.

faste *adv.* firmly 319, 958; vigorously 339, 511, 1121; hard 1459.

faunnplate *n.* (lance-)guard 1554.

fauusere *n.* arched roof 1817.

feawte *n.* fealty 2090.

fekyll *a.* untrustworthy L 1753.

felaw *n.* fellow 1280; pl. *ffellaves in fere* fellow men L 21.

feld *n.* field (of combat) 917, 945, 1106; *yn f.* in combat 413, 1950; *yn-to þe f.* to the ground 1314, 1386, 1611.

feld-ward *adv.* towards the field (of combat) 1582.

fele *1 sg. pr.* am conscious of L 596; 3 sg. pt. *feld* felt 503.

fell *n.* skin 1899.

fell(e), fylle *v.* strike down 1530, 1847, 1950; *f. (a)doun* 495, 1146; 3 sg. pt. *felde adowun* 480.

fell *a.* terrible 1404; fierce 1608; keen 234, 498; adv. fiercely 339.

feloun *a.* deadly 318; terrible 1855, 1892; *of male felon* treacherous N (L 1966).

femyn *n.* poison 1947.

femynede *1 sg. pt.* envenomed 1948.

fen *n.* ordure 1471, 1500.

fend *n.* devil 1127; pl. *fendes* 588; g. pl. 1357.

fenell *n.* fennel 1226.

fense *v.* fight, defend oneself ANP (L 1451).

fer(e), feer, fyer *n.* fire 560, 571, 583, 1766; sparks 341.

fer *a.* fierce 568.

fer *adv.* far 299; from afar 566; *f. and ner* in all ways 452; *f. and wyde* from all parts 871.

ferd, ferþe *3 pl. pt.*: *f. as* resembled 923, 1304.

fere *n.* companion 1041, 1357; *yn f.* together 118, 204, 300.

ffere *v.* parallel P (L 123).

ferly *a.* marvellous 931; adv. wonderfully 435, 1007.

ferst(e) *a.* first 89; n. 218; adv. 685, 984.

ferþde *n.* fourth 221.

ferþer *adv.* further 1744.

fest *n.* fist 1965; pl. *fystis* L 1315.

fet(te) *pp.* escorted 1209, 1664.

fyȝt(e) *n.* adventure involving fighting 89, 160; onslaught 266; encounter 648; *take f.* fight 293; *yn fyȝt(es)* 1146, 1302, 1530, 1770; *wyth f.* by force of arms 1260.

fyȝt(e), fe(y)ȝte *v.* fight 184, 263, 516, 633, 1071; imp. sg. *fyȝt* 464; 1 pl. pr. sb. *fyȝte* 332; 3 sg. pt. *fauȝt* 626, 628, 1161; 3 pl. pt. *foȝte* 339, *faȝt* 1031.

fyȝtyng(e), feȝtynge *n.* combat 95, 272, 435, 1806.

fyle *a.* degrading 1064; unpleasant 1223; horrible 1300.

fyn *a.* refined 1567; pure 1792.

fynde *v.* find 125; 1 sg. pt. *fond* 47, 330; 3 sg. pt. 28; 3 pl. pt. *fownden* L 1806; pp. *founde* 209; *well f.* well met 1660.

fyȝtyng(e) see above.

ffitt *n.* bout (of fighting) P (L 296).

flat *a.* prostrate 480.

fle *v.* flee 1154, 1188; hasten 1390; 3 sg. pr. *fleþ* 187; 3 sg. pt. *flawe* 604, 1013, *flauȝ* 1389.

fle *v.* fly 353.

flynge *v.* fly 1314; prp. *flyngynge* rushing 1016.

flome *n.* river 212.

florysseþ *pp. a.* decorated 1797.

flour(e), flowr *n.* flower (of women) 2, 2129; (of knighthood) 1529; profit L 1012; pl. *flours* flowers 1022; *flowres* ornamentation 860.

flowr *n.* flour 1399.

fo *n.* foe 516; pl. *fon* 1530, 1690.

folk *n.* people 871, 1398; vassals 1046.

fomen *n. pl.* foes 1174, 2065.

fonde *1 sg. pr.* make trial of strength HANP (L 2192ᶜᶜ).

fone *v.* ? acquire A (L 269).

fonge *v.* pick 1374.

for(e) *prep.* for, on account of 17, 69, 478, 1257; as the result of 648; as (a) 1503; conj. because 46, 63, 312, 565; so that 557, 1046.

for-fare *v.* destroy 1128; pp. *forfard* lost, worn out (by a journey) 1484.

for-gate *3 sg. pt.* forgot L 1481; pp. *for-ȝette* abandoned 591.

for-ȝaf *3 sg. pt.* forgave 450.

for-karf *3 sg. pt.* cut through 1325, 1370.

forlang *n.* furlong 306.

for-lore *pp.* lost 906, 965.

for-sake *v.* desist 191.

for-soþ(e) *adv.* truly 78, 420, 708, 896.

for-to *prep.* to 83, 95, 246, 298.

forþ *adv.* on 277, 424, 444, 678; prep. *forþ wyth* together with 1384.

forþer *a.* front 1894.

forthy *adv.* to that P (L 849).

fous *a.* eager 288.

fowles *g. pl.* birds' 1229.

fram, from *prep.* from 299, 681.

fre *a.* noble 63, 87, 392, 434.

frede *3 sg. pt.* felt N (L 527).

frek *n.* man 931.

frely *a.* noble L 1034; adv. *ffrely* extremely L 362.

ffrened *3 sg. pt.* sought favour P (L 1473).

fressch *a.* eager 1740, 1841, 1864.

fro *prep.* from 593, 639, 944.

fulfelde *pp. a.* crowded 1106.

full *a.* full 119; adv. quite 30, 290, 663; exceedingly 22, 336, 419.

full *a.* foul 1471.

ffurthermore *adv.* further in ANP (L 1845).

fusoun *n.* plenty 100.

gaderede *3 pl. pt.* collected 1473.

gay *a.* lively 253; gallant 393; bright 29, 838; handsome 1020; fine 848, 1463, 1830.

gaylych(e) *adv.* brightly 1276, 1995.

gale *n.* barking HANP (L 1031).

game *n.* game 596; sport 27, 53; (sexual) 447; music 136; g. *and play* 542.

gan *3 sg. pt.* began 169, 559, 928; did 32, 241, 344, 556; 3 pl. pt. *gon* 280, 440, 517, *gonn* 338, *gonne* 314, 337, 340.

garlaundys *n. pl.* ornamental wreaths 1830.

garssoun *n.* young man 1499.

gate *n.* way 1516.

gate, yate *n.* gate 1489, 1517; pl. *gates* 1236.

gent *adv.* tastefully 1575.

gentyl(e), gentyll *a.* noble 652, 687, 749; well proportioned 14, 110, 873.

gentylman *n.* nobleman 1366; pl. *gentyll-men* 1208.

gerdell *n.* girdle 128.

gere *n.* equipment ANP (L 1316ⁱ); *geere* clothes P (L 2115ⁱ).

gerfaucoun, gerfawcoun, gerfawkoun *n.* large falcon 793, 806, 831, 966, *jerfaukon* 728, *jerfawucon* 742.

gertte *3 sg. pt.* girded 77.

gest *n.* story 2109.

gete *imp.* get 197; 2 sg. pr. *getest* 194; 3 sg. pr. *geteþ* 1485; 1 sg. pt. *gat* HANP (L 2192ᑫ).

gye *v.* deal with L 2126.

gyle *n.* cunning 1061; treachery 558, 1012; *gile* craft L 1031.

gyn(ne) *n.* skill 1571, 1701, 1837.

gynnyng(e) *n.* beginning: *at þe ferst g.* at the outset 1308; *fram her ferst g.* in all their lives 1019.

gypell *n.* short tunic 224, 1176, 1383.

gysarmes *n. pl.* battle axes (with pointed blade) 1094.

gyse *n.* fashion H (L 309).

glad *a.* glad 88; *g. and blyþe* completely happy 649, 1216, 1672.

gle *n.* music L 1853; *g. and game* rejoicing 684, 1677, 2100; joy 2126.

glede *n.* live coal 624.

go *v.* go 536; 1 pl. pr. *goþ* 371; 2 sg. pr. sb. *go* 304; imp. *go* 197; 3 sg. pt. *ȝede* went 35, 1768; fell 621; 3 pl. pt. *yede* 99; 3 sg. pt. *wente* 26, 431; 3 pl. pt. 455, 968; 3 sg. pt. sb. 1199; *y-gon* in the past 1050.

gome *n.* man 1091.

gore *n.* filth 1471.

gorgere *n.* armour for the throat 1618.

gouernowre *n.* ruler 1525.

goules *n.* red 856.

gray *a.* grey 886; *n.* grey fur 839.

grame *n.* harm HANP (L 418).

grate *n.* lance-rest 1585.

graunte *v.* grant 1339; 1 sg. pr. *grante* 92; *graunte* agree 809; 3 sg. pr. sb. *grante* 166, *graunte* 250, 1720; imp. 41; 3 sg. pt. *grauntede* 1345; agreed 1204, 1411.

gre *n.* honour HANP (L 216[l]).

grece *n.* fat ANP (L 657[h]).

grede *v.* proclaim 726.

gre(e)tte *3 sg. pt.* greeted 39, 147.

grehond *n.* (grey)hound 1547; pl. *grehoundes* 1037.

grette *3 pl. pt.* cried out 1004.

greuely *a.* deadly N (L 1160).

greues *n. pl.* groves 551, 610.

greuyþ *3 sg. pr.* grieves 406.

gryffoun *n.* (painted) griffin 81, 231.

grylle *a.* fierce 1875.

grym(me) *a.* fierce, terrible 512, 597, 1376, 1875; comp. *grymmer* more fearsome L 1117; adv. *grym* terribly 1884.

grymly *a.* terrible 1134; adv. terribly 1632.

grynned *3 sg. pt.* grimaced A NP (L 1660).

grys *n.* grey fur 2072; *g. and gray* 839.

gryse *a.* fearsome 597.

grysly *a.* fearsome 576; adv. A (L 729).

grome *n.* man L 1117.

ȝef, ȝyf, yef, yf *conj.* 89, 162, 910, 1601; *all ȝ.* even if 15; *but ȝ.* unless 370.

ȝefte *n.* offer 1952; pl. *yftes* gifts 2117.

ȝelde, yeld(e) *v.* yield 412, 530, 1939; 3 sg. pr. sb. *ȝelde* repay 673, *yelde* 2018; 3 sg. pr. sb. *yeld* yielded 1193.

ȝer, yere(s) *n. pl.* years 1007, 1050, 2125.

ȝerne, yerne *adv.* fast 399, 494; hard 584.

ȝ-erne, y-erne *v.* gallop 440, 490.

ȝet, ȝyt, yet *adv.* yet 696; in the past 182; before 949; conj. nevertheless 1265, 1824.

ȝeue, yeue *v.* give 61, 939; 1 sg. pr. *ȝeue* 2034, *yeue* 1061; 3 sg. pr. sb. *ȝef* 303; imp. sg. *ȝef* 244; 1 sg. pt. *yaf* 1055; 3 sg. pt. 76, 638.

ȝyng, yenge, ȝong, yong(e) *a.* young 94, 157, 441, 562, 1992; *n.* *yenge* 895, *ynge* 1018.

ȝore *adv.* for a long time past 663.

haylsed *3 sg. pt.* embraced HANP (L 2192[u]).

hales *n. pl.* nooks, secret places 1773.

ham, hem *pron.* them 3, 39, 289, 547, 918.

hame *n.* home 52; adv. *hom* back 818, 971, 1082.

hangeþ *3 sg. pr. intr.* hangs 1226; 3 sg. pt. *heng* 1322; 3 pl. pt. *henge* 128; 3 sg. pt. tr. *heng* 230, *henge* 79.

happid *3 sg. pt.* happened ANP (L 1386).

hard(e) *a.* hard 1483; bold 1703; adv. fiercely, vigorously 340, 499, 513, 1150.

har(e), her, hyr *a.* their 3, 342, 384, 995, 1695.

harkeneþ *3 pl. pr.* listen 4; imp. 434.

harme *n.* danger L 696.

harnesse *n.* equipment P (L 317, L 1982).

hastely *adv.*: *h. and blyue* as quickly as possible 1515.

hauberke, hawberk *n.* coat of mail 226, 352, 1863, 1871.

haue *v.* have 729; possess 693; *h. hys game* hunt 27; 1 sg. pr. *haue* 185; 2 sg. pr. *hast* 369, *haste* 178; 3 sg. pr. *haþ* 398; 1 pl. pr. *haueþ* 298, *haue* 1713; 3 pl. pr. *haueþ* 1692, *haue* 1700, *han* 1263; imp. sg. *haue* 699; 3 sg. pt. *hadde* 34; 3 pl. pt. 102, *had* 1757, *hadden* 540; 1 sg. pt. sb. *had* 89, *hadde* 2029, *hedde* 670; 3 sg. pt. sb. *hadde* 671.

he *pron.* she 1012, 2103.

hede *n.* lance-head L 509.

hey3, hye3, hy3e *a.* tall 1099, 1235, 1763; *an he3* on the top 354.

helen *v.* heal L 1251.

hell *n.* hill 1099.

helm *n.* helmet 238, 354, 497; pl. *helmes* 342, 1152, 1908.

helpe *v.* help 614; 3 sg. pr. sb. *helpe* 3; imp. sg. *help* 589; *what h. mo tales telld?* what is the point of saying more? 916; 3 sg. pt. *holpe* L 552; 3 pl. pt. *halp* 1900.

hende, hendy *a.* gracious, courteous 142, 243, 333, 698.

hent(e) *3 sg. pt.* seized 570, 1180, 1321; took 609.

her *n.* hair 881.

her *v.* hear 1147; 1 sg. pr. *here* 565; 1 pl. pr. *hereþ* 1711; 3 sg. pt. *herd* 1447, *herde* 979; 2 pl. pt. 12; 3 pl. pt. 962.

her(e) *adv.* here 292, 294, 312; from here 306, at this point 1219; *h. abowte* hereabouts 720; *h. before* in front 403; ahead 657; until now 1643.

herawdes *n. pl.* heralds 926.

herborow *n.* lodging ANP (L 1532^k).

herye *v.* praise 1625.

hernest *pp. a.* adorned ANP (L 128).

her-of *adv.* of this 442.

hes *a.* his 1349.

heste *n.* command 1653; pl. *hestes* vows 213.

hete *n.* heat 108; passion 199.

heuene *g. pl.* of the heavens 605, 823.

hewen *v.* cut off L 1795; 3 pl. pt. *hewe* struck blows 1879; *hewes* 1958.

hy *pron. fem. sg.* she 448, 449; pl. they 338.

hyder *adv.* here 171, 378, 528.

hyenge *n.* haste L 2147.

hi3e *n.* haste L 800.

hy3t *3 sg. pr. intr.* is called 59, 708; *hatte* 72, 1696; 3 sg. pt. *hy3t* 24, 974, *hy3te* 1400, 1580; tr. *hette* ordered 206, *hat* 383; pp. *hatte* called 1246; *hy3t* promised 417.

hym-self *pron. emph.* 22, 1142; refl. 1820, 1823, 1854.

hynde *n.* hind 1036, 1040.

hynder *a.* rear 321, 1172, 1181.

hyt(te) *3 sg. pt.* struck 506, 1612, 1616; pp. *y-hytte* wounded 273.

ho *pron. interr.* who 398, 1525; rel. *ho þat* whoever 292, 721, 727.

ho *interj.* stop! 1938.

hod *n.* hood 1624.

holde *v.* keep 213; *h. batayle* fight 423; *h. vp* maintain 167, 216; 3 sg. pr. *halt* 1684; 3 sg. pt. *held* held 577; considered 1820, 1854, 1976; 3 pl. pt. *held* 814, *helde* 2120; pp. *holde* 1758.

hole *a.* whole 208.

honche *n.* haunch 268.

hond *n.* hound 1020; pl. *houndes* 1003.

hond(e) *n.* hand 247; *yn h.* in his hand 631, *an h.* 1277; pl. *handes* 1054, 1368.

honest(e) *a.* honourable 2112; *an hundred pound h.* fully a hundred pounds 988.

honour *n.* good reputation 1505; *wyth h.* respectfully 39, 147; creditably 156; magnificently 986, 2098; *Y am to þyne h.* I greet you humbly 1203.

hontes *n. pl.* hunters 1004.

hore *n.* filth 1477.

hore *a.* grey 658, 915.

hors(e) *n.* horse 952; *to h.* on horseback 241, 563, 677, 2039; g. sg. *horses* 323; pl. *hors* 558.

houeþ *3 sg. pr.* is 1056; *3 sg. pt.
houede* waited: *h. and abod(e)* 851,
1754, 2045; *3 pl. pt. houede* 1039;
h. and abyde 1562.
hous *n.* dwelling 775.
how *adv.* how 873; *pron. rel.* 276,
680, 1031; *interr.* 797; *h. þat* 978.

yare *a.* ready 1513, 1543.
ychastid *pp.* punished, reproved
N (L 1476).
y-ǵeld, y-ǵyld *pp. a.* gilded 1276,
1995.
y-ǵrounde *pp. a.* ground 1604.
y-lyke *a.* similar (to) 1037.
ylke *a.* same 329, 347, 641, 644.
ylle *n.* evil 782; *a.* deadly 1257,
1937; *adv.* badly: *lykede y.* dis-
pleased 1872.
y-mene *adv.* together 608, 1666.
yn, jn *n.* lodging 761, 1490.
ynde *n.* blue cloth 121, 1043; *a. jnde*
blue 1828.
y-nome *pp.* stolen 1087.
y-nowȝ *n.* enough 102.
yonder *adv.:* *y. be-forne* ahead
L 687.
y-payd *pp.* pleased 1822.
y-paynted *pp. a.* decorated with
paintings 1798.
yre(n) *n.* iron 239, 437.
yre *n.* anger 1893.
y-rest *pp.* been resting 1138.
y-same *adv.* together 468; in company 1455.
y-tynt *pp.* lost 261.
y-wys *adv.* indeed 23, 1473, 2069.

j-bent *pp. a.* curved L 913.
jepowne *n.* short tunic L 1445.
j-karneled *pp. a.* embattled 714.
jmaǵerye *n.* paintings 1797.
jnner, jnner-more *adv.* further in
1771, 1786.
jolelye *adv.* merrily L 1035.
jornay, jorne *n.* journey 431, 455,
1460.
j-powderd *pp. a.* flecked L 904.
j-pured *pp. a.* trimmed L 126.
juell *n.* precious object 1025.
juste, justy *v.* joust 909, 951,
1542.

justes *n. pl.* encounters: *j. he wyll
þe bede* he will joust with you 1493.

kaȝte, kauȝt *3 sg. pt.* took hold of
631, 1028.
kaytyf *n.* wretch 259.
kalle *v.* cry out 1832.
kantell *n.* corner 346.
karf *3 sg. pt.* cut 1961; *k. adoun*
struck down 1895, 1930.
karnell *n.* battlement 737; *pl.
cornyllus* L 732.
kempys *n. pl.* champions A (L
1057).
kende *n.* people 124; family 381,
2031.
kende *3 sg. pt.* guided 1080.
kende *pp. a.* recognized 599.
kene *a.* valiant 1211, 1596, 1667.
kenne, kynne *n.* kindred 1646,
1710, 1725.
kepeþ *3 sg. pr.* guards 262; *3 sg. pt.
kepte* 16, 1890.
keþ *n.* friends 381.
keuerchefs, keuerchers *n. pl.*
kerchieves 836, 2074.
kinde *n.* nature: *as the k. of his
estate* as was natural to him P
(L 1205).
kynde *a.* noble L 192, L 272.
kyssynǵe *n.* kiss 2008.
kyste *3 sg. pt.* kissed 2006; *pp.* 2029.
kythe *v.* make known L 1805; *refl.*
HANP (L 2192ᵛ); *pp. y-kidde*
famed (as) N (L 688).
knele *imp.* kneel 373; *3 sg. pt.
knelede* 37, 145; *prp. kneoland*
HANP (L 2192ᶻ).
knowe *v.* know 1008; recognize
1046; *3 sg. pt. knew* realized 1882;
pp. knowe 1503.
kopeþ *pp. a.* slashed 131.
kouþe *a.* notorious 2021.
krest *n.* plume (ornament) on
helmet 352.

labour *n.* undertaking L 194.
lay *n.* open country P (L 34).
lay(e) *n.* faith 328, L 1501.
laynore *n.* strap (of helmet) L 1678.
lamed *pp.* disabled 1918.
lappe *n.* skirt (of garment) L 1686.

lardes *n. pl.* lords 1294.

large *a.* generous: *l. of pay* ANP (L 1640ᵇ).

lasse *n.* less: *l. and more* everyone 968.

last *n.* last: *aftyr-ward at l.* in the long run 1415.

lauendere *n.* washerwoman 902.

lauendrye *n.* (profession of) washing N (L 932).

laughte *3 sg. pt.* pulled L 662; 3 pl. pt. received L 1392.

launche, lonche *v.* cut, wound 269, 344.

lawe *n.* custom 192.

lede *v.* bring 862, 977; conduct 1405; *l. away* abduct 1689; 3 sg. pt. *ledde* 1206, *ladde* 610, 1769.

lefe *a.* willing N (L 167).

lefte *3 sg. pt.* remained L 1182.

legge *v.* lay down 1253; imp. *ley on* strike 1954; pp. *leyd* put down 867; *y-layd* put away 203.

leyn *n.* concealment ANP (L 2192ʰ), *layine* P (L 554).

leyn *3 pl. pr.* or *pt.*: *l. out* ? lean(ed) out, look(ed) out 1295.

lemman *n.* mistress 724, 744, 789, 805.

lende *v.* stay L 1250; remain L 2105.

lengell, lyngell, *n.* straps (of horse's harness) 286, 861, 1274, 1574, 1829.

lengþe *n.* length: *yn l. and brede* from all sides 735; completely 884; everywhere 963.

lepe *v.* jump up and down L 957; 3 sg. pt. *lep* leaped 254, 483, *lepte* 569, 623, 2039; 3 pl. pt. 1097, *leptede* 439.

lere *v.* learn 1911, 1998; pp. *y-lerde* 185.

leren *v.* learn: *nys noþinge to l.* is not in need of any instruction L 425.

les *n.* falsehood: *wyth-oute l.* truly 765, 947.

lese *v.* lose 1505; pp. *lorne* L 504, L 854, *y-lore* 1917.

lesyng(e) *n.* falsehood: *wyth-oute l.* truly 341, 667, 896, 1745.

lest *n.* most humble: *l. and mest* everyone 2115.

leste *3 sg. pt.* lasted 992.

leste, lyste *3 sg. pt.* pleased 1736, 1974.

let(te) *imp. sg.* let 297, 363, 1338; imp. 1 pl. *lete* 430; imp. 2 pl. *leteþ* 1051, *late* desist 1551; 3 sg. pt. *lette* had 2073; *l. yn* 1523; *l. stylle* let alone 1869.

lettyng *n.* delay ANP (L 1257).

leue *n.* leave 997.

leue *v.* leave 294; imp. sg. *leve* L 473; 2 sg. pr. sb. *leue* 1072; 3 sg. pt. *lefte* 1964, 2040.

leuede *3 sg. pt.* believed 1301.

leven *v.* live L 2105; 3 pl. pt. *leuede* 2125.

levyr *adv.* rather L 859.

lewte *n.* faith 1940, *laughte* L 2014.

lybard *n.* leopard 1583.

lyf, lyue *n.* life 692, 2032; *of l. hast þou no grace* you will not be allowed to live 369; g. sg. *lyues* 1501; pl. 1158.

lyfte *v.* lift: *l. of* cut off 1955.

lyȝt *3 sg. pr.* lies 1445; 3 sg. pt. *lay* 28, 326, 1373, *ley* 1348; dwelled 36. See also 3 pl. pr. or pt. *leyn* 1295.

lyȝt *a.* eager 155, 158, 336; swift 1187, 1583; pp. a. blazing 1767; adv. *lightlye* P (L 1610).

lykede *3 sg. pt.* pleased 1872.

lykynge *n.* enjoyment 1736; pl. *lykynges* L 1810; a. pleasing 1026, 1560.

lyme *n.* mortar 713.

lynde *n.* lime tree 1039.

lynne *v.* leave off ANP (L 834).

lyre *n.* flesh 1325, 1899.

lyte *a.* small 1264.

lyþe *v.* listen, hear 1911, 1998; *listen and lithe* L 1802.

lithelye *adv.* quickly P (L 1995).

logen *v.* lodge L 726.

logge *n.* arbour 550, 611.

lo(u)ȝ *3 sg. pt.* laughed 487, 718; 3 pl. pt. 946.

loke *v.* see 276; *l. on* look at 804; imp. pl. *lokeþ* 1552; 3 sg. pt. *lokede* 1790, 1825.

lond *n.* land(s) 693, 1196; g. sg. *londis* of the country L 216.

long *a.* long 889; adv. 2048, *longe* 326; comp. *leng* 819, *lenger* 1189, *lengere* 313.

longe *n.* lungs 602.

lo(o)s(e) *n.* reputation 17; fame 686, 1887; praise L 932.

lordynges *n. pl.* sirs 434; men of high rank 2110.

lorell *n.* worthless fellow 259.

loþlych *a.* horrible 574.

loue *n.* love 296; *for l. of* on account of 19; for the sake of 69, 296, 362, 590.

louede *2 sg. pt. sb.* valued: *yef þow l. þy prow* if you knew what was good for you 1284.

lo(w)de, lowþe *adv.* loudly 1148; *boþe l. and styll(e)* in all ways 1205, 1298.

lowe *n.* hill 1000.

lowe *adv.* humbly 723.

lowte *v.* bow down 723; 3 sg. pt. *lowted* P (L 1197).

ma(a)d *a.* frenzied 2001; *m. of mode* confounded 1167.

macched *pp.*: *m. with* set against L 1309.

madd-hede *n.* madness L 853.

may *n.* maiden 539, 690, 845, *mayde* 106, 109, 142, *meyde* 300, *mayden* 647; pl. *maydenes* 1499.

may *1 sg. pr.* am able to, can 696; 2 sg. pr. *mayst* 736, *myʒt* 302; 3 sg. pr. *may* 266; 1 pl. pr. 2067; 2 pl. pr. 70; 3 pl. pr. 1459; 3 sg. pt. *myʒt* 891, *myʒte* 114; 3 pl. pt. *myʒt* 549, *myʒte* 209; 3 sg. pt. sb. 494.

mayl(e), mayll *n.* mail-armour 429, 1176, 1383; pl. *mayles* iron rings 228.

mayn(e) *n.* strength 479, 1389; *of m.* powerful 77, 659, 1960; *wyth m. and myʒt* mightily 1865; hard 2078.

mayne *n.* retinue 855, 1774.

maystrye *n.* great power 1693; pl. *maystres of mouthe* powerful spells L 2101.

make *v.* make: *m. boun* get ready 822; *m. redy* 1290; *m. yare* 1543; *m. quyt* free 1511; imp. *make* 1513; 1 sg. pt. *made* 1287; 3 sg. pt. 74; 3 pl. pt. *made* 396, *maden* 1779; pp. *make* 560, *y-makeþ* 1706, *made* 30, *j-made* 85.

mammettes *n. pl.* idols 1275.

man *n.* man 6; one 1022; g. sg. *mannys* 183; pl. *men* 186; one: *m. clepeþ* am called 661; *m. gon bryng* were brought 892; *me(n) clepeþ* is called 1240, 1269, 1464.

maner(e) *n.* kind 100, 1427; way L 18, L 1406.

mangerre *n.* feast ANP (L 2192[b]).

manhod *n.* (reputation for) valour 174.

mankende *n.* mankind 522, 1128.

mantyll *n.* cloak 838, 874.

margarett *n.* pearl(s) P (L 907).

market *n.* market-place 803, 850.

masterye *n.* victory P (L 781).

mate *a.* exhausted 1173.

maugre *prep.* in spite of 915.

mede *n.* reward 627, 729.

meete *a.* adequate P (L 1691).

meke *a*, submissive 1726.

mekyll *a.* great L 714, L 1133, L 2200.

melk *n.* milk 224, 887.

melle *v.* fight N (L 1309).

melodye *n.* music 1426, 1781.

mene *1 sg. pr.* speak 1038.

menstracy *n.* music 1427.

menstrale *n.* minstrel 1783; pl. *menstrales* 1776, 1802, 1806.

mercy *n.* mercy 519; forgiveness 448.

mery *a.* pleasing 1229, 1778; *m. man of mouþe* skilful singer, raconteur 141; *with thi m. mouthe* cheerfully L 53.

merte *n.* marten's fur A (L 138).

merþe *n.* joy 278.

mete *n.* meal: *to m.* to table 99.

mett(e) *3 sg. pt.* met 390, 1436; placed P (L 402); 3 pl. pt. *metten* came together 1638; *mette to-gydere* 1630, 1849, 1910.

mych(e) *a.* much 136, 1812; adv. extremely 1996.

mydde *prep.* ? straight over 323.

myddell, medyllest *a.* eldest but one 490, L 502.

myde *prep.* with L 1639.

mydsomer *n.* midsummer 1023.

myȝt(e)(s) *n.* strength 166, 1623; power 1713; *of m.* powerful, mighty 77, 659, 1328, 1527; *wyth m. and mayn(e)* vigorously 479; at full speed 1389.

mylde *a.* gentle 589; *wyth m. chere* courteously 1675.

mynstrye *n.* ? special skill L 1755.

myrrour *n.* account L 2181.

mo, mor(e), mare *a.* more, greater 198, 916, 1241, 1880; *m. ne lasse* of any kind 1774; *adv.* 51, 1974.

moch(e), mochell *a.* great 684, 1677, 2100; *n. m. of* a great deal about 1424.

mode *n.* heart, mind 504, 1167.

moder, modyr *n.* mother 2, 2129; *m. naked* stark naked L 2091.

mok *n.* dung H (L 1539).

mold *n.* earth P (L 136).

molde *n.* head 841, 877.

mone *n.* complaint L 48.

most(e) *a.* greatest L 2057; *m. of myȝte(s)* of greatest strength, authority 1527, 1590; *n. mest* most powerful men 2115.

mot *1 sg. pr.* must 412, 830; *2 sg. pr. most* 1836; *3 sg. pr. mot* 293, 731, 1253; *3 sg. pr. sb.* may 1434.

motis *n. pl.* notes L 1035.

mou(u)ntance *n.* distance 1034; time (taken to ride) 104.

na(u)ȝt, noȝt *adv.* not 23, 59, 326, 696.

nay *interj.* no! 520, 908, 1641.

naye *v.* neigh 1821.

naked, nakeþ *a.* naked 2014, 2063.

name *n.* name 7; renown 134, 264, 656.

ne *conj.* nor 112, 200, 1483.

nede *n.* wants 1492; *at n.* in (time of) need 3, 236; *all þat n. was* all that was necessary 453.

neydyr *conj.* neither 200.

neyȝ *adv.* almost 1162, 1165, 1861; *prep.* close to 357;

nell *1 sg. pr.* will not 1952; *3 sg. pr.* 308, 929; *3 sg. pt. nold* 1546, *nolde* 200; *3 pl. pt.* 313.

ner(e) *adv.* nearer 1768; *nyȝhe n.* draw nearer 1155; *nyȝede n.* 572.

nessche *a.* soft: *for n. ne hard* for any consideration 1483.

nete *n.* bull ANP (L 1316ᶠ).

nette *n.* snare 1133, 2094.

neuer-more *adv.* never at any time 409.

newe *a.* fresh 1363.

nygremansye, nygremauncye *n.* magic 1694, 1705.

nyȝhe *v.* approach 1155; *3 sg. pt. nyȝede* 572.

nys *3 sg. pr.* is not 422, 1247, 1702; *3 sg. pt. nas* 112, 908, 1571.

nys *a.* foolish 22, 51.

noble *a.* noble 350; excellent 139, 703.

noye *n.* annoyance N (L 223).

noyse *n.* (loud) sound L 1852.

nones : *for þe n.* (meaningless) 1972.

norserye *n.* breeding 903.

norþ *n.*: *be n. and be souþe* everywhere 135.

not *1 sg. pr.* do not know 50, 1654; *3 sg. pt. nyste* 1971; *3 pl. pt. nyste* 547.

note *n.* music 1778; *pl. notes* songs 1230.

noþer *conj.* neither 416.

noþyng *n.* nothing 1319; *for n.* for no consideration 1125, 1551; *adv.* not at all 1992, *nodyng* 116.

nouþe *adv.* now 144; just now 2020.

now *adv.* now 261; henceforth 67, 173.

now(h)er *adv.* nowhere 1247, 1250.

no wyȝt *adv.* not at all 442.

o *num.* one 406.

of *prep.* of 4; by 8, 414; from 459, 812; in 704, 903; outside 1700.

of *adv.* off 31, 642, 733.

of-bras *v.* force off N (L 451).

of-sente *3 sg. pt.* sent for 1564.

of-sprynge *v.* fly out L 1367.

okes *n. pl.* oak trees 1261.

omage *n.* homage 2090.

(o)on *pron.* one 191, 509, 574; *our o.* one of us 1955.

on *prep.* on, upon 79, 83, 113; in 26, 665.

ones *adv.* once: *at o.* at the same time 1144.

ony *a.* any 90, 127, 438.

oo *ind. art.* a 1278.

oo *interj.* oh! 715.

ord *n.* point 1923.

ore *n.* grace, favour 1337.

orgenes *n. pl.* (portable) organs 1778.

ostell *n.* lodging 1485, 1520.

oþ(e) *n.* oath 370; *certayn wyth-outen o.* truly 164, 1949; *do þyn o.* perform what you have sworn 424.

oþer, oþyr, oþre *a.* other 21, 194, 2051; second L 539; pron. the other 920; second 219; *oþres* of the other 1332; *hyt nell non o. be* there is no other course 308.

oþer *conj.* or 268, 292, 294, 722.

ouer *prep.* over 938; upon 1811; *o. all* everywhere in L 1560.

ouer-come *pp. a.* defeated 377, 413, 527, 1202.

ouer-geld *pp. a.* covered with gilding 80.

ouerhand *n.* supremacy P (L 275^b).

ouert *a.* open 126.

ouer-twert *prep.* across 1017.

oughte *a.* valiant L 1804.

oules *n. pl.* owls 857.

our *n.* hour 1333.

out-barred *pp.* ? shut out H (L 1546).

out-braste *3 sg. pt.* flew out 342.

out-breke *v.* escape 1420, 1451.

out-flyng *v.* draw (violently) 338.

oute-pas *v.* come out L 2067.

oute-rage *n.* grievous harm L 20.

out-ryt *3 sg. pt.* rode out 952.

out-scape *v.* escape P (L 1482).

out-sprynge *v.* fly out 1151, 1305.

owe(ne) *a.* own 229, 414, 1049.

owee *v.* own L 1075; 3 sg. pr. *owyþ* 719.

owher *adv.* anywhere 1242.

pace, passe *v.* go 1771; proceed 297; *alyue p.* escape with one's life 363; 1 sg. pr. *pace* 758; 3 sg. pr. *passeþ* crosses 1252; 3 sg. pr. sb. *passe* traverse 428.

pay *n.* liking 1644; *lykynge (vn-)to my p.* 1026, 1560.

paynture *n.* (style of) painting 1573.

paytrell, paytrill *n.* breast armour of horse P (L 1336, L 1636).

palfray *n.* (small) saddle-horse 254, 844.

palys *n.* palace, palisade 771, 1234, 1466, 1701.

palysed *pp. a.* enclosed with palisade L 1528.

pall(e), pell *n.* rich cloth 389, 870, 1407, 1776.

par amour *adv. phr.* as a favour 42.

pardye *adv. phr.* certainly A (L 1316^c).

pare *v.* shave ANP (L 1712^f); *p. of* A (L 1201).

parfyte *a.* blameless L 1406.

park *n.* enclosed tract of land 709.

partye *n.* ? distinction, strife 897; body of supporters 918.

pas *n.* step: *p. be p.* at a comfortable pace 444, 1101.

pase *n.* passage 262.

pauillyons *n. pl.* (large) tents P (L 1284, L 1528).

peces *n. pl.* pieces 1305, 1592.

peynis *n. pl.* wings L 2074.

pelured, y-peluryd *pp. a.* trimmed (with fur) 117, 839, 875, 2072.

peple *n.* inhabitants 2080, 2097; body of men 1107, 1126.

per(e) *n.* equal 114, 1247.

perce *v.* pierce 1175.

peryle *n.* danger 564, 1058; dangerous course of action 750; fear (of danger) 1013.

perische *v.* pierce, destroy ANP (L 1201).

person *n.* man L 397; pl. *persones* L 1239; *of persoune* in myself L 557.

pert *a.* smart 123; adv. *pertely* plainly ANP (L 2126).

pes(e) *n.* peace 762, 2067; *yn p.* silent 1802.

pych *n.* pitch 575, 1249, 1273.

pight *pp.* stuck L 510.

pylte *n.* rush: *in a p.* hastily A (C 79).

pysane *n.* armour protecting neck and upper chest 1618.

place *n.* place: *yn p.* here (in the field) 366; *ech a p.* every part 1772; *jn p. ther* where L 510; *in that p.* there and then L 541.

play *n.* sport 26, 84, 542.

play(e) *v.* joust 1557; have sport 1824; 2 sg. pr. *pleyyst: p. a wonder wylde game* will be involved in a very dangerous sport 1073–4.

playn *n.* field (of battle) 83, 1326.

playnge *n.* recreation 665.

plate *n.* plate armour 1176, 1383.

plente *n.* great number 1236.

plex *n. pl.* plaits 128.

ply3t *v.* pledge 524; 3 pl. pt. 537.

poynt *n.* point 355; perfection N (C 84).

pomely *a.* dappled 844.

pomet *a.* provided with spherical ornaments 1295.

posterne *n.* private door 1450.

pouert *n.* poverty 132.

pound *n. pl.* pounds (weight) 988.

pount tornere *n.* drawbridge P (L 1357).

pouste *n.* power 1943.

power(e) *n.* strength 198; force 1615.

pray *1 sg. pr.* entreat 42; 3 sg. pr. *prayd* 154; 3 sg. pt. *prayde* 1982; 3 pl. pt. 613, 1297.

precyous *a.* costly 285; dear 1839.

prede, pryde *n.* honour 173, 261; *yn p.* splendid 469, 777, 816, 1119.

present *n.* present 683; pl. *presentes* 1213.

prest(e) *a.* ready 312, 1135; adv. phr. *also p.* at once 1075.

prestabelle *a.* willing N (L 1593).

preue *v.* determine: *p. þys sy3t* reach a decision about what we see 797; 3 sg. pt. *prouede* strove 1606; *preuede hys my3t* tried his hardest 1877.

prykede 3 *sg. pt.* spurred 469; prp. *prykynde* galloping 777.

pryme *n.* six a.m. 1333.

pryns *n.* prince 469; pl. *prynces* 816.

prys *n.* excellence: *of p.* excellent 1243, 1292, 2068.

prys *a.* excellent 180.

pryso(u)n(e) *n.* prison, imprisonment 152, 1445, 1684; prisoner 377, 1202, *prysoner* 412; pl. *prysouns* 527.

pryuylyche *adv.* privately 2075.

processioun, processyoun *n.* procession 1397, 2081.

prof(e)rede 3 *sg. pt.* offered 689; proposed to 1408.

profyt(e) *n.* good 1283; benefit 1344; *þo p.* do honour to 835; exalt the reputation of 1510.

profytable *a.* worthy 10, 1531.

proud, prowd(e) *a.* proud, splendid, excellent 285, 771; *p. yn pryde* 816, 869, 1234, 1466; *p. of prys* of supreme excellence 1292; *p. yn palle* splendidly dressed 389, 1835.

prow *n.* advantage 1284.

pullede 3 *sg. pt.* plucked 1178.

pured *pp. a.* trimmed L 1902.

purfild *pp. a.* bordered L 868.

purpel *a.* purple 870.

purpur *a.* purple 1828; n. *purpure* purple cloth 2071.

quake *v.* tremble 559, 1814; 3 sg. pt. *quaked* 2015.

quede *a.* evil 1315.

queynte *a.* skilful 351; cunning 1315; *q. of gyn(ne)* curiously contrived 1571, 1701; extremely skilful 1837.

quelþe *pp.* killed 1192.

quenchede 3 *pl. pt.* went out 1805.

quyk *adv.* quickly 1846.

quyt *a.* free: *make q.* free 1511; adv.: *q. and skere* completely 1914.

quyte *v.* requite 1361; *q. mede* settle accounts with 627.

rach, rech *n.* hunting dog 1016, 1038, 1049, 1072.

rayne *n.* rein(s) 482.

raysed *pp.* taken up L 227.

rappes *n. pl.* blows 287, 1159.

rau3ht 3 *sg. pt.* gave ANP (L 668).

raundoun *n.* great speed 315, 942.
reall *a.* royal 876; adv. *ryally* magnificently 711.
rebound *n.* noise N (L 1031).
record *n.* witness 165.
rede *n.* advice: *do be r.* take advice L 852.
rede *v.* tell 12, 979, 1143, 1695; 1 sg. pr. advise 1111.
redy *a.* ready 467, 1290; prepared 1070, 1644; *r. boun* 622, 865.
regge *n.* back 961.
rekened *pp.* told 2109.
rende *v.* tear (to pieces) L 475.
renynge *prp.* running L 1042; 3 sg. pt. *ran* 325; charged 1123; 3 pl. pt. *ronne* ? coursed 1003, ? were given 1159: see Commentary.
renoun *n.* fame 764; *of r.* famous 101, 376, 993, 1201, *of renounnes* 526.
rente *n.* revenue 1196.
resoun(ne) *n.* speech 97, 760; *be ryȝt r.* in the correct way 1605.
resseyued *3 sg. pt.* greeted L 1463.
reste *n.* rest 548; (eternal) repose 303.
reste *1 pl. pr. sb.* let us stop 1219.
resting *n.* dwelling-place ANP (L 1892ᶠ).
reue *2 sg. pr. sb.* take away P (L 1098); pp. *raft (of)* removed 733.
ryche *a.* costly, splendid 33, 80, 238, 876; noble 656; comp. *rychere* 1794, 1799; adv. *rychely* splendidly 227.
ryde *v.* ride 106; 3 sg. pr. *ryȝt* 403, *ryȝtte* 270 (see Commentary), *rydyȝt* 292; prp. *rydynge* L 470; imp. pl. *ryde* 1489, *rydeþ* 1555; 3 sg. pt. *rod* 242, *rode* 850, *rood* 1582, *ryde* 1605; 3 pl. pt. *ryde* 542, *ryden* 277, *rode* 1117; pp. *ryde* 1033.
ryȝt(e) *n.* rights 167, 1722; pl. *ryȝtes* 216; *wyth r.* as is proper 795; *at all r.* at all points 1581.
ryȝt(e) *a.* right 639; proper, correct 600, 1605; direct, straight 387, 885, 995; adv. straight, directly 290, 463, 1885, 1924; due 1078; to the full 1743; very 88, 357, 1361; just 372, 800, 1080.

ryme *n.* poem 1143.
rynge *v.* resound 1148.
ryse *n.* branch 1244.
ryue *a.* numerous 1159.
ro *n.* peace H (L 1809).
robe *n.* robe 833; gown 2071.
rode *n.* complexion 880, 1244.
rof *n.* roof 1816.
ros *3 sg. pt.* got up 765.
rosyne *a.* rose-coloured 874.
rost *n.* roast meat 566.
rote *n.* instrument of viol family 1777.
roþe *n.* cross 425.
roun *n.* lamentation 972.
rounde, rownd(e) *a.* round 11; (in section) 1603; full L 125; severe L 1174.
roune *v.* speak 465.
rout *n.* company P (L 405).
rowme *a.* full 116.
rufull *a.* sorrowful 972.

sadly *adv.* forcefully ANP (L 1174).
saȝt *n.:* *yn s.* peacefully 1030.
say *n.* silk 81.
say *v.* make trial of L 92.
say, sey *v.* say 129, 743; 1 sg. pr. *say* 78; 2 sg. pr. *seyst* 787; 3 sg. pr. *seyþ* 222; imp. *seye* 1201, *say* 1280; 3 sg. pt. *sede* 980, 1319, *seyd* 271, 1840, *seyde* 40, 43, *sayd* 1823, *sayde* 1024; 3 pl. pt. *seyde* 397.
saket *n.* lance-head 1554.
sale *n.* hall 225, 1011, 2111; pl. *sales* 1227.
same *adv.:* *yn s.* together 62, 137, 595, 678.
samyte *n.* silk (interwoven with gold) 833.
sare, sore *a.* painful 1134; adv. grievously, bitterly 406, 1177, 1597, 1977, 1979; severely 619; intensely, extremely 1336, 1853.
savage *a.* wild L 19, L 850.
saue *v.* save 593; 2 sg. pr. *sauyst* 2032; 3 sg. pr. sb. *saue* L 46.
saue *prep.* except for 1748.
saunȝ *prep.* without 1386, 1860.
sautrye, sawtrye *n.* stringed instrument resembling dulcimer 137, 1780.

saw *n.* warning ANP (L 204).

schaft(e) *n.* lance 310, 598, 929; pl. *schaftes* 864, 1518, *saftes* 922.

schall *1 sg. pr.* shall 160; 2 sg. pr. *schalt* 175; 3 sg. pr. *schall* 172; 1 pl. pr. *schull* 426, *scholl* 797; 3 pl. pr. *schull* 524; 1 sg. pt. *schold* 1256, *shulde* 1115; 3 sg. pt. *schold* 125, *scholde* 1788, *schuld* 557, *schulde* 1388.

schalmuses *n. pl.* players upon wind instruments 1762.

scham(e) *n.* shame 1449; dishonour 593, 681, 1342; *don þys s.* dishonoured in this way 398.

schame *v.* put to shame 1733.

schamelych *adv.* shamefully 1086.

scharp *a.* sharp 1604, 1923.

schauede *3 sg. pt.* shaved off 356.

schawe *n.* thicket 1112.

sched *3 sg. pt.* spilled out A (L 1379).

schend(e) *v.* disgrace 1086; destroy 2025; 3 sg. pt. *shende* damaged L 530; pp. *y-schent* put to shame 174, 615, 670, 1854; ? lost the use of 1946.

schene *a.* fair, bright 110, 284, 604, 1593; n. beautiful woman N (L 428).

scherte *n.* shirt 223.

schewy *v.* show 746.

schylle *a.* sonorous 781.

schyneþ *3 sg. pr.* shines 882, 3 sg. pt. *schon* 881; 3 pl. pt. *schynede* 1994.

schon *n. pl.* shoes 130.

schop *3 sg. pt.* created 522.

schote *3 pl. pt.* shot 1121.

schour *n.* combat 1156.

schrede *v.* dress 32.

schrewe *n.* wicked person 1880, 1912; pl. *schrewys* 1670.

s(c)leȝ *a.* expert 351, 1897.

se *v.* see, look at 96, 735, *y-se* 280; *sene* 113; 1 sg. pr. *se* 307; 3 sg. pr. *ses* L 793; 3 sg. pr. sb. *see* watch over L 46; 1 sg. pt. *sawe* 1025, *saw* 1359, *syȝ* 1643; 3 sg. pt. *saw* 573, *sawe* 560, *seyȝ* 360; 3 pl. pt. *saw* 457, *sawe* 394, *seyȝ* 949, *syȝ* 853, *sygh* 888, *syȝe* 1100; pp. *seye* 1800, *y-seyn* 1261.

selcouþ *a.* wonderful 1791.

sely *a.* strange 1296.

selk *n.* silk 223.

selken *a.* silken 883.

selue *a.* same 75, 390, 767, 859.

semely, semyly, semelych *a.* stately, fair 113, 225, 849, 1011; superl. *semelekest* 821.

semeþ *3 sg. pr.* looks like 902; 3 sg. pt. *semede* 132.

sende *v.* send 154; 3 sg. pr. sb. grant 1258; 3 sg. pt. *sende* 1083, *sente* 606; pp. *y-sent* 171, *sent* 982.

sene *a.* manifest 1602.

ser *n.* sir 1057.

sercle *n.* coronet, diadem 841, 877.

sertayn(e), serteyn *a.* fixed, definite 1195, 1541, 1750; determined 1967; adv. *sertayn* truly, 2030.

sertente *n.: in s.* truly L 138.

sertes *adv.* truly 72, 533.

seruede *3 sg. pt.* attended upon 452; treated 645; was the vassal of 1010; pp. *served* ? wounded P (L 526).

seruyse *n.* (performance of) ceremony 1361; serving 2113.

set(te) *3 sg. pt.* dealt 499, 619, 1168; placed 240, 845; refl. 1801; 3 pl. pt. 1850; *to-gedere s.* attacked each other 1909; pp. placed 734, 802, 2085.

seþe(n) *conj.* since 46, 984, 1642.

seuenyȝt *n.* week 2095.

shape *n.* ? dimensions P (L 1647).

shoved *3 sg. pt.* thrust L 1696.

syde *n.* side 107; edge 9.

syde *n. pl.* times 650, 1217, 1673, 2087.

syȝt(e) *n.* sight 289, 1186, 1296; appearance 13, 48, 1791; *yn s.* before him 352, 1764; *wyth s.* 888, 1359, 1587.

syȝt *adv.* then 226.

syke *v.* sigh 1977; 3 sg. pt. *sighte* L 2058.

sykyr *a.* firm 1650; adv. *sykyrly* truly 1651.

synne *n.* sin: *for no s.* for no consideration 1959.

syre *n.* father 229; lord 1902.

sytole *n.* stringed instrument 137, 1780.

sytte, sette *v.* sit 588, 1613; 3 sg. pr. *sytteth* L 961; 3 sg. pr. sb. *sytte* 276; 3 sg. pt. *sat* 319, *satte* 202, *set* 485, *sette* 1981; 3 pl. pt. *sete* 1676, *setten* 1635; pp. *sete* 103, *y-sete* 105.

skapy *v.* escape 302.

skars *a.* close-fitting 116.

skere *adv.* unharmed 297; completely 1914.

sket *adv.* quickly 484, 1895.

skyll *v.* leap 1844.

skythe *n.* cloud L 1189.

skolle *n.* skull L 1196.

slaked 3 *pl. pt.* weakened L 2033.

sle, slo *v.* kill 441, 533, 1140, 1929; 3 sg. pt. *slouȝ* 1153; pp. *sclayn* 1861, *y-sclayn* 1963, *j-sclayne* 30, *y-slayn* 2042, *slawe* 1115, *y-slawe* 186, *j-slawe* 1388.

slep 3 *sg. pt.* slept 1131.

slowe *a.* ignoble 1506.

smale, small *a.* small 228; slender 873, 889.

smert *adv.* vigorously 601, *smertly* L 1412.

smerte *v.* feel pain 1177.

smyte *v.* strike 1265; 3 sg. pt. *smot* 317, *smote* 1585, *smyt* 497; *s. a strok* 1323, 1382; 3 pl. pt. *smyte* 511.

snell *adv.* quickly 739, 808, 817, 1354.

socour *n.* help 606, 671, 1403; *do s.* 1659.

soffte *adv.* quietly L 1056.

softe 3 *sg. pt.* looked for 1972.

soiour *n.* stay: *made s.* stayed 2095.

soiourne *v.* delay 411.

solas *n.* delight 447.

sole *n.* mire P (L 605).

solempnyte *n.* ceremony 278.

somdell *adv.* to some extent 185.

somerys *g. sg.* summer's 1228.

som-whyle *adv.* at one time 1010.

sone *adv.* immediately 1132.

sopere *n.* supper 1676.

sorcery *n.* witchcraft 1424, 1442.

sorow *n.* grief 1449.

sotil *a.* curious H (L 309).

soþ *a.* true 163; adv. truly 1006; n. *sothe* L 754.

souk *imp.* suck HANP (L 216ᵏ).

sounde *a.* undamaged 208.

souped 3 *pl. pt.* took supper L 1799.

space *n.* time 251; moment L 542.

spare *v.* stop 1125; hesitate 1546; 3 sg. pt. *spared* desisted 1671.

sparkylles *n. pl.* sparks L 1176.

speche *n.* spell(s) 2043.

spede *n.* success 251.

spede *v.* be successful 732; get the upper hand 954; 3 sg. pr. sb. prosper L 3.

speke *v.* speak, say 41, 928, 1447; 3 sg. pt. *spak* said 142, 1936; spoke 1558.

spendy *v.* spend 986.

sper(e) *n.* spear, lance 184, 232, 269, 318, 734; pl. *sperys* 518.

spylle *v.* destroy 1947, 2043; kill 1260, 1878; pp. *y-spylt* 1165.

spyte *n.* spit 582, 630; (metal) tip of spit ANP (L 657ᵃ).

splente *n.* (overlapping) metal plate N (L 1445).

spryng(e) *v.* leap 241, 668, 677; rush 337; spread 172; pp. *spronge* 264.

square *a.* square (in section) 1589.

stark *a.* strong 710; fierce 1766.

state *n.* (normal) bearing 1179.

staunch *v.* ? withstand 266.

stede *n.* horse 235, 325; g. sg. *stedes* 1316; pl. 439, 462, 1292.

stede *n.* place 1047, 1502.

stef *a.* unyielding 919, 1577; adv. *styfly* stoutly L 537.

steked 3 *sg. pt.* fixed L 509; pp. *steke* 932; *j-steke* fastened L 1512.

stel(e) *n.* steel 239, 437.

stelde *pp. a.* tipped with steel 919.

ster(r)yd 3 *sg. pt.* roused L 1205, L 1209.

sterne *a.* fierce, formidable 402, 439, 491, 580, 1391.

stert 3 *sg. pt.* leaped ANP (L 1918).

styll(e) *adv.* still 1263; quietly 1205, 1298; alone 1869, 2040; *s. yn pese* in peace 762.

stynte *v.* delay L 434; 3 pl. pt. *stente* desisted 1959.

styropes *n. pl.* stirrups 320.
stythe *a.* strong L 1808.
styward *n.* steward 1456, 1486, 1579.
ston(e) *n.* stone 713; pl. *stones* 1810; precious stones 842, 878, 2084.
stonde *v.* stand 1764; 3 sg. pr. *stant* 737; 3 sg. pt. *stod* 1783; *stode* remained 1170, went H (L 1860); pp. *stonde* 1263.
store *a.* fierce 1766; formidable L 728.
stounde *n.* (moment of) time 205, 347, 641, 644.
stoupe *v.* fall 322, 937.
stoure *n.* fight L 1182; ? time P (L 112).
stout(e) *a.* proud, haughty, splendid 29, 123, 253, 1566, 1647; valiant 393, 402, 1251; strong, formidable 710, 1376; comp. *stouter* 10.
strath *a.* straight 885.
stre *n.* straw 422.
strete *n.* highway 188.
stryde *v.* bestride 769.
stryf *n.* contention 2036.
stryke *v.* dash 1036.
strok *n.* blow 499, 638; pl. *strokes* 512, 619.
strong *a.* strong 152; powerful 1365; comp. *stranger* 1600.
sturdy *a.* fine ANP (L 1877).
surcote *n.*: *s. ouert* open surcoat 126.
sure *a.* reliable 864; certain 2064; adv. securely 766, 1537.
susteres sones *n. pl.* nephews 391.
sute *n.*: *of s.* in one livery 1141; matching L 309.
swayn *n.* serving man 1748.
swart *n.* black 575.
swelt *3 sg. pt.* was (on the point of) dying L 2076.
swer *imp.* swear 374; 2 sg. pr. sb. *swere* 370; 3 sg. pt. *swor* 383, 1750, *swore* 1541; *s. hys þeþ* swore to kill him 461; 3 pl. pt. *sweren* 535; pp. *swor* 1718; pp. a. *swore* 407.
swerd(e), sword(e) *n.* sword 77, 168, 184, 1913; g. sg. *swordes* 1945; pl. *swerdes* 1094, *swordes* 552.

swere, swyre *n.* neck 230, 840, 889, 1324, 1896.
swete *n.* sweat L 2076.
swete *v.* sweat 1999.
swete *a.* sweet 2, 296.
sw(h)ych(e), *a.* such 272, 908, 1213.
swyfte *a.* rapid 1954; adv. *swyftly* L 2087.
swyn *n.* pig ANP (L 1312).
swynġ *v.* fly A (L 1376).
swyþe, swyde *adv.* very 1114; greatly 134; immediately 2039; *swythe* promptly L 1603, L 1995.
swounynġe *n.* faint L 1197.

taborus *n. pl.* players on the tabor 925.
take(n) *v.* take 548; steal 557; undertake 190; *t. fyȝt* fight 293; 3 pl. pr. *takeþ* gather 1477; imp. *take* 310; 3 sg. pr. sb. *tak* 911; 3 sg. pt. *tok* took 387; received 212; *toke* gave L 1055; 3 pl. pt. *tok* 761, *toke* 1735, *token* 995; pp. *take* captured 1012, 1089.
tale *n.* tale 222; pl. *tales: oþer t.* other matters 1221; *mo(re) t. tel(l)d* further speech 916, 1933.
talent *n.* will 612; intention 1848.
talkynġe *n.* speech 970.
talkynġe *prp.* conversing 1015; 3 pl. pt. *talkede* spoke 1680.
tame *a.* harmless 30.
tars *n.* rich cloth (of Tarsia) 115.
teche *v.* instruct 83.
tee *v.* follow L 1452.
telle *v.* tell, relate, say 143, 890; 1 sg. pr. *telle* 1239; imp. *tell* 45; 1 pl. pr. sb. *telle* 1221; 1 sg. pt. *teld* 815; 3 sg. pt. 1595, *tolde* 679; 3 pl. pt. *tolde* 1031; pp. *teld* 1933, *telld* 916, *told* 2108, *y-told* 1559, *y-tolde* 2069.
tene *n.* harm 1416.
tente *3 sg. pt.* was alight L 1841; pp. *j-tende* L 1859.
ter *n.* tar P (L 1335).
terne, turne *v.* turn 581, 1288; imp. *turne* 464, *torne* 1282; 3 pl. pt. *turnede* 1747.
tyde *n.* time 170, 316, 774, 810.

tydynge *n.* news 679, 1756; pl. *tydyngys* 2047.

tyght *3 pl. pt.* intended L 726; pp. *ty3t* 540.

tyll(e) *prep.* until 256, 541; to 1720, 1936; at 1364, 1846; conj. until 203, 410, 1334.

tyre *v.* dress 834.

tyt(e), tyd *adv.* quickly 784, 832, 955, 1282, 1507; *titely* L 1920.

to *prep.* to 26; against 1588; as 683, 867; adv. too 94, 1182.

to-brak *3 sg. pt.* broke (violently) 961, 1859.

to-brast(e) *3 sg. pt.* broke in pieces 1633, 1852; was bursting L 2080; 3 pl. pt. burst open 320.

tochede *3 sg. pt.* grazed 501.

to-drawe *pp.* torn asunder 189.

to-gedere, to-gydere *adv.* together 314, 337, 446, 941.

to-karf *3 sg. pt.* cut (to pieces) 1913.

to-rasshe *v.* tear to pieces L 451.

torne *pp.* torn (to pieces) L 860.

to-tar *3 sg. pt.* tore 1871.

toun(e), towne *n.* town, city 530, 761, 2083; *yn t.* among men 1226; by the people 1470; *to t.* to any habitation 549.

tour *n.* castle 530, 1082, 2096; keep 1437; *t. and toun* everything possessed 530; pl. *tours* towers 1295.

toward *prep.* in the direction of 456, 546, 571; on the way to 432; a. *towerd* impending, in existence ANP (L 157).

to-wawe *pp.* blown about L 212.

traye *n.* affliction L 1478.

trappes *n.* horse-cloths 286.

trappur(e) *n.* horse-cloths 861, 1274, 1574, 1829.

trawayle *n.* difficult undertaking HANP (L 723).

tre *n.* tree 1191; tree trunk, club 631, 634, 637; *of t.* wooden 1271.

tresour *n.* treasure 985, 1196.

trespas *n.* offence 450, 1104.

trewe *a.* trustworthy 162; adv. *trewly* certainly 1968.

trewes *n. pl.* peace 537.

trewþe *n.* good faith 1940.

trye *a.* excellent 1803.

tryst *n.* hope 1968.

tryste *a.* trusty L 1877.

trompes, trompys *n. pl.* trumpeters 1496, 1762.

trompours *n. pl.* trumpeters 925.

tronchon *n.* staff L 662.

turmentrye *n.* torture 1714.

turnement *n.* tournament 180.

twayne, tweye *a.* two 523, 1827.

two *n.* two 305; a. 573; adv. twice 1356, *to* 744.

þay, day, þey, dey *pron.* they 102, 538, 967, 1309.

þan(n)(e), *adv.* then, thereupon 43, 55, 70, 169.

þankede, þonkede, þonkeþ *3 sg. pt.* thanked 605, 650, 1217, 1402, 1673; 3 pl. pt. *þonkede* 2087, 2101.

þannes *adv.* from there 561.

þar(e), dar, þore, þer *adv. dem.* there 86, 1418, 1588; then, on that occasion 616, 754, 1870.

þat *a.* that, the 2, 31, 33; *þ. on* 574, 1142, 1831; adv. *þat so* soever 66, 93; pron. dem. that 510, 736; rel. that, which, who(m) 4, 29, 58, 114; conj. that 308, 320; so that 359, 360, 1170.

þau3, þou3, þey *conj.* even if, although 260, 429, 934, 1062, 1264.

þe, de *pron.* thee 42, 673.

þe, de *def. art.* the 11, 451.

þef *n.* thief, scoundrel 464, 557; pl. *theeues* evil doers P (L 1297).

þe(y)3 *n.* thigh 476, 1898.

þen *conj.* than 1425.

denkeþ *1 pl. pr.* intend 465; 1 sg. pt. *þou3te* suspected 666; 3 sg. pt. *þou3t* resolved 1627, 1865; 3 pl pt. *þou3* 1139, *þo3te* 1145.

þer-ate *adv.* there 1490.

þer-fore *adv.* as a result 620; (and) so 699, 793, 1289, 1727; on that account 909, 1884.

þer-ynne, þer-jnne *adv.* in it 553, 1708; into it 1704; upon it 1275, 1568.

þer-of *adv.* about that 755, 1540, 1967; *þ. þo þy best* try your hardest to do that 1076.

þer-on *adv.* upon it 1577.

þer-out *adv.* outside it 1118.

þer-to *adv.* to (do) that 165, 336, 1713, 1848.

þer-vnþer *prep.* at the bottom of 1002.

ther-with *adv.* with that L 2024.

þy, dy *a.* thy 168, 309, 2018; *þyn* 45, *þyne* 1203.

þyder *adv.* thither, to that place 1514, 2082.

dydyr-ward *adv.* on the way there 1668.

þykke, dykke *a.* closely-set 228, 429.

þyng *n.* thing 406; person 2127; *yn all þyng(es)* in all respects 1994, 2011.

þyngeþ, þyngyþ *3 sg. pr.* seems 94, 196, 1479; 3 sg. pt. *þoȝte* 493, *þouȝt* 1812, *þouȝte* 1182, *þouȝ* 1430, 1448, 1586.

þyrd(d)e, þyrþe *a.* third 256, 541, 1462; *n.* 220.

þys *pron.* this 56; *a.* 172; pl. *þese* 433.

þo *adv.* then, thereupon 74, 301, 334, 358; *pron.* those 201, 1594; *conj.* when 979.

þonder, þunder, donder *n.* thunder 923, 1304, 1809.

þor(u)ȝ, þrouȝ *prep.* through 268, 500, 1169; as a result of 1506, 1945.

þor(u)ȝ-out *prep.* right through 345; throughout 1498.

þou, þow *pron.* thou 94, 1284; obl. *þe* 42, *de* 673.

þrede *n.* thread 883.

þrest *3 sg. pt.* thrust 1738.

þryfte *n.* prosperity 1951; pl. *thriftis* earnings L 2191.

þrynge, drynge *v.* strive 340, 1150; throng 2082.

þryue *v.* prosper 1434.

þro *a.* eager 1335.

þrowe, drowe *n.* time: *þat þ.* at once 1005, 1048.

þrowe *v.* throw 1500; 3 sg. pt. *threwe* L 541.

durste *n.* thirst 1343.

durstede *3 sg. pt.* thirsted 1336.

þus *adv.* so, thus 385, 417, 538; in this way 780, 1433, 1533.

vncouered *pp.* removed the cloth from P (L 227).

vn-crystenede *pp. a.* unbaptized 1358.

vnder, vnþer *adv.* below 1815; defeated 1307; *prep.* beneath 1039, 1191.

vnderne *n.* late morning 810.

vnderstond *1 sg. pr.* believe ANP (L 1712ᵏ).

vnfelde *3 sg. pt.* opened L 2063.

vnheld *v.* open P (L 2063).

vnkowthe *a.* strange L 49.

vnlace *v.* cut through (and remove). ANP (L 451).

vn-lek *3 sg. pt.* flew asunder 1816.

vn-mete *a.* huge 1629, 1996.

vnnethe *a.* ? frightening L 2073.

vnneþe *adv.* with difficulty 1613.

vn-syȝt *a.* hostile 1331, *vnsawght* L 661.

vn-steke *pp. a.* unlocked 1450.

vn-wrest *a.* poor 2118.

vp-ȝelde *v.* surrender 517.

vp-haf *3 sg. pt.* lifted up 247, 637.

vp-on *prep.* upon 408; on 841; against 257; *v. a day* one day 25.

vp-ryȝt *adv.* erect 738, 1614; ? supine 1620.

vp-sawȝt *pp.* risen up 632.

vp-start *3 sg. pt.* leaped up 157, 1354; *start vp* 327, 1320.

v(u)s *n.* practice, custom 752, 773, 908, 1469; *yn v.* habitually, always 67, 379; *swych v.* of such a kind 272.

vale *a.* valley 1004.

valour *n.* worth 140, 153; profit 982.

veluwet *n.* velvet 838.

verament *adv.* truly P (L 192).

veretye *n.* truth P (L 138).

vylany(e) *n.* disgrace 364; *spak v.* insulted 449; *do(þ) v.* treat(s) shamefully 1655, 1715, 2049.

vy(y)s *n.* face 19, 60.

vyous *a.* eager L 311.

voys *n.* voice 781; sound 1809.

volatyle *n.* wild fowl L 109.

way *n.* way, path 387, 995, 1078; *be w. or strete* anywhere 188.

wajour *n.* prize 867.

wake *v.* keep watch 556.

wall(e) *n.* wall 933, 1810; *wyth-yn w.* anywhere 149, 1782.

war *a.* conscious 1867.

warm *n.* serpent, dragon 1990, 2006, 2027, 2057; *g. sg. warmys* 2009.

wast *n.* refuse 1471.

wawe *n.* wall, barrier P (L 1138).

w(h)ate *adv.* quickly 1548, 1741.

wax *3 sg. pt.* became L 526.

wede *n.* armour 31, 701, 1406, 1454.

weet *a.* wet 1353.

welde *v.* rule, possess L 1787; endure 2028; *on liue weelde* go on living P (L 383).

wel(l) *adv.* very 134, 285, 405.

wellaway *interj.* alas! 586.

welle *n.* spring 1528.

wende *v.* journey, go 246, 298, 375, 525; imp. sg. *wend* 424; 2 sg. pr. sb. *wende* 1502; 1 pl. pr. sb. *wende* L 855; 1 sg. pt. *wente* 665; 3 sg. pt. *wende* ? brandished L 529; pp. *y-went* transformed 2027.

wene *n.* doubt 1481.

wene *v.* suppose 1599; 1 sg. pr. 1109; 2 sg. pt. *wendest* 1357.

wepene-les *a.* without weapons 366.

were *v.* defend 233.

werk *n.* building 1467.

werre *n.* battle 233, 1095.

werry *v.* fight 981.

werrour *n.* warrior 5, 267, 351.

wete, wyte *v.* know 70; learn 1787; *wit* be aware of L 615; *to w. and naȝt to wene* without any doubt at all 1599; 3 sg. pr. *wat* 59; 3 sg. pt. *wyste* 442, 2005.

wete *v.* protect 585.

weuede *3 sg. pt.* brandished 505.

wham *pron.* whom 1698; whomsoever 1129.

whan(n)(e), *conj.* when 34, 58, 394, 1579.

whar, wher *conj.* where 28, 197, 654.

wherfore *adv.* for what reason 1654.

whesch *3 pl. pt.* washed 99.

whett *a.* whatsoever 1502.

whyder-ward *adv.* to what place 1971.

whyle *n.* (short) time 103, 1033, 1219; time spent, trouble 2018; adv. once 1066; conj. when 52.

whyt(e) *a.* fair 788; shining 857; n. 1280.

wyde *a.* broad 1122, 1235; adv. far and wide 172, 264; *fer and w.* 871; *w. wher* L 143; *w. yn alle þe wones* in every part of the building 1973.

wyȝt *n.* person 405.

w(h)yȝt, wyth *a.* strong, valiant 5, 196, 267, 330.

wykkede *a.* evil 17; foul 1104.

wyld(e) *a.* wild 176, 507; desolate 545, 1079; dangerous 1074.

wile *n.* guile P (L 776).

wyll(e) *n.* will, wish 246, 1204, 1266, 1345, 1843; disposal, command 1194, 1941.

wyll *I sg. pr.* will 61, *well* 909, *woll* 757; 2 sg. pr. *wyltow* 1640; 3 sg. pr. *wyll* 263; 1 pl. pr. *wylleþ* 304, *wyllyþ* 1514; 2 pl. pr. *wyllen* 532; 3 pl. pr. *wyll* 1719; 1 sg. pt. *wolde* 188; 2 sg. pt. *woldest* 2019; 3 sg. pt. *wold* 493, *wolde* 58; 1 pl. pt. *wolde* 1071; 3 pl. pt. *wold* 395, *wolde* 536; 3 sg. pt. sb. *wold* grant 1027.

wynd *n.* rush (of air) HANP (L 216ᵉ); *wyne* wind L 212; pl. *wyndes* blasts L 1324.

wynne *n.* joy L 1787.

wynne *v.* win 806, 831; gain 764, 1953; capture 1707; rescue 156, 161, 1731; 3 sg. pt. *wan* 680, 978, 1215, 2093; made way ANP (L 2192ᵛ); *wanne* caught ANP (L 2120ᶠ); pp. *wonne* L 735.

wys *a.* skilful 349, 2092; *w. of wytte* 5.

wyt(te) *n.* intelligence, senses 5; *out of w.* beside himself 496, 953, L 290, L 1660.

wyth-all(e) *adv.* in addition, moreover 1576, 2117; at the same time 1987.

wyth-yn, wyth-jnne *prep.* in 1645; inside 149, 1437, 1782; adv. 1734.

wyth-out(e)(n) *prep.* without 44, 164; outside 1545; adv. *boþe w. and wyth-jnne* in all ways 1734.

wytles *a.* foolish 176.

wytterly, wittirly *adv.* truly ANP (L 1316ᵇ, L 1712¹).

wyue *v.* marry 696.

wo *n.* sorrow 681, 2028; a. sorrowful 636, 2016.

wod(e) *a.* mad 953, 1161; ferocious 507, 1928.

wode *n.* forest 26, 1112, 1117.

wokis *g. pl.* weeks' L 1023.

won *n.* dwelling 716; pl. *wones* 1973.

wonde *v.* refrain 1256.

wondede *pp.* wounded 2054.

wonder, wonþer *n.* marvel 1812; astonishment 1987; *hadde w.* was astonished 1306, 1469; a. marvellous 56; adv. exceedingly 1074.

wone *n.* abundance ANP (L 2188).

woneþ *3 sg. pr.* lives 657.

wonnynge *n.* dwelling L 2153.

wont *pp. a.* accustomed 1770.

word *n.* word 41; speech 162, 1408; report 172; boast HANP (L 216ᵈ); *w. and ende* in every detail 384, *worde and endeng* L 2144; *yn w. and þou3t* in all ways 1978; pl. *wordes* 1064; incantations 2024.

wordly *a.* excellent 716.

worþ *a.* worth 422; *w. swych fyfe* five times as strong 260.

wowe *n.* hostility ANP (L 1340).

wrake *v.* avenge P (L 1483).

wrapp *v.* envelop P (L 2105).

wreake *n.* vindictiveness P (L 1967).

wreþþe *n.* anger 199.

wryten *pp.* set down in writing 976.

wrong *3 pl. pt.* wrung 1368.

wroþe *a.* angry 1310, 1889.

wrou3t *3 sg. pt.* created 672; 3 pl. pt. *wroughten* worked L 2099; pp. *j-wro3t* devised 1575; *wrought* done L 1803.

NAMES OF PERSONS AND PLACES

AGRAFRAYN Agravain 221, ANP (L 258); *Agfayne* L, *Egrefayn* H, *Griffayn* N, *Geffreyn, Gefferen* A, *Agrauaine* P.

ALYSANDER Alexander 935.

ANTORE father of Vyolette 660; g. *Antores* 768; *A(u)nctour(s)* L, *Arthore* P, *Arthors* AP.

ARTOUR Arthur 11, 36, 40; g. *Artours* 192, *Artourys* 1085.

BEAU-FY3, BEWFYS Guinglain 20, 54; *Beuys* A.

BEDLEM Bethlehem L 857.

CARDELOF, KARLOF, CAR-DEUYLE, KARDEUYLE ? Cardiff 708, 800, 813, 990; *Cordile, Kardill* L, *Karlille* N, *Cardigan* P.

CHAPELL OF AWNTROUS Adventurous Chapel L 200; *of Antrus* A.

(LA) DAME D'AMORE enchantress of the Yle d'Or 1400; *Diamour* N, *Denamowre* A(H), *Madam de Armoroure* P.

(S.) DENYS 57.

(S.) EDWARD 1674; *Leonarde* L.

ELENE messenger from Synadowne 109, 169, 607.

EWEYN, OWEYN Yvain 220, 235; *Jwayne* L.

FAYRE VN-KNOWE Guinglain 71.

GAWEYN Gawain 8, 82, 179; g. *Gawenys* 1646.

G(E)YNLEYN Guinglain 7, 13; *Gyngelayn(e)* L.

GYFFLET(TE), GYLET Guinglain's squire 1458, 1513, 1748; *Gyrflete, Jurflete, Jerflete* L, *Jeff(e)lot* HN(P), *Gesloke* A.

GYFFROUN LE FLOWDOUS, ~ FLUDOUS knight competing for the falcon 751, 772, 904, *Gyfroun* 731, 808; g. *Gyffrouns* 824; ~ *le Froudous* H(A), ~ *le Froundes, Freudys* L(A), ~ *le Freudous* L(A), ~ *le Fred(ie)us, Frediens* N, ~ *la Fraudeus* P.

(S.) GYLE 567, 756, 1060.

GLASTYNGBERY Glastonbury 35.

GLUDAS emissary to Arthur's court 974; *Clewdas* N, *Claudas* P, *Caudas* H, *Cadas* L, *Lucas* A.

GOWER nephew of William Salebraunche 474; *Gawer* N, *Baner* P, *Banerer* A.

YL(L)E D'OR(E) besieged by Maugis 1240, 1269; *Jle Dolour* L.

YRAYN, JRAYN enchanter 1697, 1699, 1717, 1732; *Jro(w)n(e)* P.

YRLAND Ireland 1224; *Cornewale* AN, *England* P.

(S.) JAME 49, 64, 400, 592.

JHESU(S) 296, 335, 1755, 2046; *J. Cryst* 1, 2128.

(S.) JON 715, 1688.

JORDAN PN (L 235).

KARLYLE, KARLELL Carlisle 1067, 1572; *Carlehille* L(A).

KARLOWNE Caerleon 459; *Carboun* L, *Skarlyoun* A.

KENT 1572.

LAMBARD steward at Synadowne 1487, 1540, 1580, 1597; g. *Lambardys* 1633; *Lanward, Lancharde* L.

LAUNCELET Lancelot 179, 232, 936, *L. du Lake* 1092; *Launselake* N, *Lanslate* A.

LYBEAU(S) DESCONUS, ~ DES-CONOUS Guinglain 68, 181, 271, 334, 694, *Lybeauus* 981, 991, 994, 1028, *Lybeawe* 1913.

MABOUN enchanter 1696, 1699, 1717, 1732; g. *Mabouunys* 1721.

(S.) MARIE 2055.

MAU(U)GYS, MAUUGEYS giant 1246, 1270, 1291, 1315; g. *Maugys* 1324; *Ma(u)gus* AN, *Mangus* N.

(S.) MERTYNE AN (L 1074).

(S.) MYCHELL 740, 811, 1218, 1355.

OTES DE LYLE huntsman knight 1009, 1057, 1063; *de la Byle* A.

PERCEUAL(E) Perceval 179, 219, 240, 936.

POYNTE PERYLOUS, ~PERILOWSE Perilous Passage L 199, L 305.

(S.) QUINTIN P (L 840).

SATAN 1127.

(S.) SAUOUR 1662.

SYNADOUN, SYNADOWNE Segontium 151, 215, 456, 546, 996.

TEONDELEYN,   TEANDELAYN dwarf guide 133, 481; *Theodoleyn* L, *Teodline*, *Teddelyne* P, *Deodelyne* N, *Wyndeleyn* A.

TERMAGAUNT heathen god 1301.

VALE PERYLOUS Perilous Valley 282.

VYOLETTE maiden abducted by giants 661, 690.

WALES 1224.

WYLLEAM   CELEBRONCHE,   ~ SELEBRAUNCHE knight of the passage 265, 343, *Wyllyam* 386, 394, *Wylyam* 430; ~ *Delaraunche* L, ~ *Delabrawunche* H(AP).

WYRHALE Wirral 1014; *Worrall* P.

APPENDIX

(a) READINGS IN MSS. H OR A THAT SUPPORT VARIANTS IN C

7 callyd Gyngeleyn A; 17 doute A; 22 And hymselue A; 31 He dyd off A; 33 rych armour A; 48 so feyre of A; 49 The chyld A; 87 so fre A; 89 J had A; 106 Ther camme A; 111 A lady as A; 125 Syche one A; 132 Ther semyd A; 161 lady bryght A; 178 of mayn A; 183 mannys saw A; 192 Arthor law A; 213 hestes H; 231 a griffown HA; 246 forto wende H; 249 hende H; 262 þis pas H; 264 His name HA; 287 To dele men H; 291 boon frere H; 303 gode rest HA; 304 f. go:two AH; 337 spryng A; 342 Oute of þer helmys AH; 350 as a kny3t H; 377 prisoun HA; 381 kyth and kynde H; 389 þreo knytis HA; 400 He said HA; 401 On þat is HA; 418 thre A; 419 wele A; 421 He one A; 452 fer and nere A; 502 Than was A; 506 cleuyd A; 509 One A; 511 Fast þei A; 517 gan vp3eld A; 527 prisoun HA; 532 doon so HA; 535 sworen him þoo H; 544 riden euer west H; 557 no theof HA; 564 doute A; 565 gret bost HA; 577 f. barme: arme H; 585 hire H; 601 he smot smert HA; 603 neuer myght he A; 619 strok he sette H; 623 leop of H; 630 His spyte H; 634 þe ende A; 637 hit eft vp haf H; 655 Iame HA; 657 her beforne A; 666 Non euel HA; 675 blod HA; 710 stout H; 717 doute H; 719 þis owiþ HA; 722 Beo hit H; 723 He doth hym A; 742 þeo gyrfawcon H; 760 resoun A; 777 as prynce in pryde A; 778 mor abode A; 780 f. cryd: hyde A; 800 ryght A; 815 forwerd A; 837 Areyd A; 840 Sche cast A; 845 sett þat mey A; 861 lyngell H; 865 bar HA; 867 þat layd was to wayoure H; 874 rosyn H; 875 Pelowred H; 896 Forsoþe HA; 899 rose in erber H; 903 norisserye HA; 912 beforn A; 916 tellyd A; 928 speke HA; 930 wiþ one cronal H; 932 steke H; 934 as wy3t werryour H; 944 feol him fro HA; 950 dry3e HA; 952 his cours owt ryd H; 959 doun he H; 1007 3eres ferly fale H; 1009 f. de lyle: somwhyle H; 1016 flyng H; 1027 Wold God A; 1029 And 3af him maide Eleyne HA; 1030 al sau3t HA; 1040 To seo HA; 1049 was myn owne H; 1079 wyld A; 1100 þei A; 1136 foreste A; 1168 hym sette A; 1186 þat syght A; 1225 þe moneth of Jone A; 1260 schall hym spylle A; 1282 also tyte A; 1297 God of his wyll A; 1298 Both lowd and styll A; 1344 profyte A; 1401 wel (: feol) H; 1405 lede (: wede) AH; 1419 And also A; 1425 [w]yches fyue H; 1432 fantume H; 1448 wold breke HA; 1466 And paleys H; 1477 hore H; 1487 men clepen H; 1508 grete A; 1514 fare A; 1568 borys hedys A; 1581 at all A; 1611 Jnto þeo feld adoun HA; 1645 By þeo þou3t myn heorte is yn H; 1649 kny3t H; 1663 Anon HA; 1691 Fals of HA; 1693 maystry HA; 1750 his oth certayn H; 1762 schalmes A; 1803 so

god entray H; 1820 bytrayed HA; 1821 Stedes HA; 1830 garlond gay HA; 1835 prowd in paule A; 1851 dou3ty dynte A; 1856 bare hym downe A; 1868 And A; 1877 my3ht A; 1884 Therfore A; 1910 Ther suerdys togeþer mette A; 1911 As 3e may lysten and lere A; 1996 vnmete A; 2028 wende A; 2046 To Jhesu A; 2071 purpre bys H; 2078 wiþ mayn and my3t H; 2116 f. all: halle A; 2126 gleo H.

(b) READINGS DERIVED FROM THE COMMON SOURCE OF MSS. H, A, N, AND P

(Note: only six fragments of H have survived; these comprise L 216^d–425, L 541–764, L 879–1097, L 1434–1550, L 1668–1907, and L 2136–2204.)

After L 216:   [The meyd ansuerd full snelle
That besemyth þe ryght wele
Whoso loky3ht on the AN(P)]
þow dorstest nou3t for al þy word
Abyde þeo wynd of a sweord
By ou3t þat Y can seo
þanne þeo dwery seyde in þat stounde
þeo dede men in [þe] grounde
Of þe aferd may beo
Y rede þe in game
Go hom and souk þy dame
And wynne þer þy gre
                    (216^{a–1}) H(AN(P));

L 233 to (at AN) ry3tes HAN; L 255 riche entyre HA; L 292 Sone (Swithe P) wol he HAP; C 298 han fer HAPN; C 305 bytweone ows to HA(P); L 347 Jnto þe feld adoun HAP;

L 354 f.   Now my stede is away
Fy3t on fote J þe pray   AHP;

L 361 on to dyng HA; L 362 ferly HA; C 348 was agast HANP; L 369 all wyth myght ANHP; L 371 wy3t and HAP; L 389 no space HAP;

L 390 f.   Bot if þou suere to me anone
Or þat thou hens gon A(P)(H);

L 394 sweord broun HANP; L 412 emes sonis HAP; L 418 do þe thys grame AH; L 543 fel him fro HANP; L 552 bou3t monkuynde HAP(N); L 569 Wenten HAN; L 573 *and* L 584 burde HAN; L 596 sauowr of rost HAP; L 602 Whan he com to þeo fuyre (there N) HAN; L 606 Fowle HPAN; L 609 rose HANP; L 624 gret prys HAP; L 674 To þat oþir he wende H(ANP); L 676 hedes twaye (: þat may) HAN; L 678 þat he wan in fy3t HNAP; L 723 Jn trawayle HANP; L 726 þider þay hadyn ty3t HANP; L 732 Wiþ towres

HANP; L 744 And worthyest in wede HAP; L 763 brynge þe HANP;
L 889 Dyȝt al wiþ (oþer AN) floures HPAN; L 891 Tway skwyeres
HAN; L 934 By þe loue of Jhesus HAN; L 945 Nomore tale þay
tolde HAN; L 949 Eyþir aȝeyns oþir heold HNA; L 954 Munstrals
and HAN; L 960 Seo now (So N) þis HAN; L 972 Jeffron þo HN;
L 1031 And houndes grete of gale HA; L 1034 For ȝeres ferly fale HN;
L 1039 for dowt of peryle HAN; L 1041 stode talkyng HA; L 1043
Ryȝt into þeo HA; L 1044 þay saide wiþowte lesyng HAN; L 1051
Y saw neuer non so wel H(ANP);

L 1053 f.   God leue hit weore myn
                  Libeus him tok wiþ hondis twayn H(A);

L 1060 þeo space HANP; L 1076 Not fully gon a ȝere AN(H); L 1085
By Peter and HN; L 1090 Sertys AH;
L 1437 f.   Fast he (And Libeus AN) ran to him aȝeyn
                  And smot [to N] him wiþ mayn HAN;

L 1442 þeo knyȝtis heold bataile HAN; L 1471 Euer to beon HNA;
L 1480 Sho made him dwelle thore NHA; L 1511-13 lacking HAN;
L 1514 For þat HAN; L 1516 oþir wede HAN; L 1670 Egre as any
HAN; L 1671 Libeus smot Lambard þo (so A) HNA; L 1675 þat
he myȝt nouȝt HAN; L 1677 His scheld HAN; L 1681 helm in fere
HANP; L 1687 Fast gon þey HN; L 1690 þer was HAN; L1695-7
lacking HAN;
L 1701 f.

      Syr Lambert was aschamyd (sore agramed H)
      Syr [Libeus HN] seyd be not agramyd (agreuyd N, aschamed H)
      ANH;

L 1705 knyȝt biforne (tofore H) NAH; L 1707 By þeo þouȝt (faith P)
myn heorte is (that J am PA) yn HNAP; L 1730 þat þay hadde
HAN; L 1733 And him dered (greuyd AN) noþyng HAN; C 1682 To
sir Lambard þeo constable HAN; L 1760 For heom HANP; L 1762
Maden an hows of gret avaunt (name N, ston A) HNA; L 1763 A place
HAN; L 1772 of kynges kynne HN; L 1777 alle maner HN; L 1806
They fonde (fedde N) þem at soper AHN; L 1817 þat stod vp HAN;
L 1829 faste þay cried HAN; L 1849 He syȝh nouȝt in þat place (in
þe face A) HNA; L 1851 Harpe pype HAN; L 1865 weore so faire
of HAN; L 1878 þat ware bryȝt HANP; L 1879 went out HAN;
L 1902 Jn riȝt good armour NHA;

L 2142 f.   Whan Libeus al (in þat AN) forward
                  Had told to sir Lambard HAN;

L 2144 word and ende HAN; L 2164 Sente HAN; L 2166-8 lacking
HANP;
before L 2171:   Whan þay hadde doun
                  þay toke leue at vchon H(AN);

after L 2192 *and the extra stanza found in* AN (L 2192ᵃ⁻ˡ):

Sir Gawayn kny3t of renoun
Saide to þeo lady of Synaydoun
Madame treowely
He þat weddid (wanne N) þe wiþ pruyde
Y gat (wanne N) him by a forest syde
On a gentil lady
þanne þat lady blyþe was
And ful ofte kyssed his fas
And haylse[d] (kyssed AN) him sykyrly
Sir Libeus þan wolde kyþe
He wente to his fader swyþe
And kyssed him tymes monye

He [fell on kneys AN] þat stounde
And saide (sate N) kneoland on grounde
For Godis loue alweldand
þat made þeo world so round
Fayre fadir or Y fonde
Blesse me wiþ þyn hond (3our blyssyng A)
þat hynde kny3t Gawayn
Blessyd þeo child (his son AN) wiþ mayn
And made him seoþþe vp stande
He comaundyd kny3t and sweyn
To clepe Libeus Gengelayne
þat was lord of lond   (L 2192ᵐ⁻ˡˡ)   H(AN);

L 2196 As þeo gest HA.

(c) READINGS DERIVED FROM THE COMMON SOURCE OF MSS. A, N, AND P

L 13 feyr and bry3ht ANP; L 20 lyghtly AP; L 25 so feyr and wyse
AP; L 32 Gyngeleyn AP; C 38 Jmonge lordys and ladys alle AP;
C 41 Sofer me AP;

L 52 f.   x (14 P) 3ere olde J ame
                Off werres wele J canne AP;

L 54 a (my P) ryght AP; L 56 wythoute lesynge AN; C 48 No chyld
so AP; L 70 That þou woldyst AP; L 71 þou hyght AP; L 72 And
art soe ffaire and wise PA; L 79 alle thus NP;

L 82 f.   Loke 3e calle hym jn same (this name P)
                Jn ernys and in game AP;

C 81 gryffyn gay AP; C 84 euery prynsys AP; L 109 Of wild ffoule
(dere A) and venison PNA; L 112 Nad thei ysate NAP; L 113 Bot
(Well P) þe space AP;

L 124 f.   The may þat was so schen
                      Sche was clothyd in gren AP;

L 126 And furred AP; L 128 And wele hernest (bordered P) wyth
sylke AP; L 136 ȝalow as floure A(P); L 144 Est west northe and
southe AP; L 148 He was a gode gestoure AP; L 152 To tell þe tale
bedene (: J wene A, Hellen P) AP; L 155 Amonge þe lordys (and
lordlingis N, and ladyes P) alle ANP;

L 157 ff.   A case þer is now towerd
                      Was þer neuer non so herd
                      Nor of so grete dolour AP;

L 167 Jn herte he was full lyght AP; L 168 my lord Arthour NP;
L 176 To wyn þat lady bryght ANP; L 189 Full wyse in AP; L 191
Sterte to AN; L 197 Bataile v (two A) othir thre NPA; L 204 of
mannys saw AN; L 205 To pley wyth a swerd AP; L 208 for a threte
AP; L 216 For sych is ANP; L 216^d (HANP) all þe werld AN; L 223
styll sate A(P); L 233 þe child ANP; L 235 fflome Jordan PN;
L 237 And becomme ANP; L 241 Sir Percevale and sir Gawayn NAP;
L 242 In that semely sale NA; L 251 nayles AP; L 258 Sir Agrauaine
P(N)(A); L 259 That was gode in euery were (euerywhere P) AP;
L 266 my lord wyth crowne A(P); L 268 lettyng (lesing A) NPA;
L 281 gan þei AP; L 285 This wey AP; L 289 warre AP;

L 309 f.   Wele was armyd þat knyȝht
                      Forsoth at all ryght A(P);

L 311 As it was (Euer hath bene N) his vse APN; L 314 bewpere
AN; L 332 Go forth and do AP; L 361 suerdys AP; L 370 anon ryght
ANP; L 372 doun ryȝht (: wyth myght) ANP; L 399 calys þus AP;
L 401 Vnknawyn knyght and hend AP; L 404 And forth he gan
wende ANP;

L 411 f.   The thre knyȝhtys in fere
                      Were his emys sones dere AP;

L 428 The[y] rydyn forth full ȝerne AP; L 431 suerd (bronde N)
APN; L 433 Tyll J com to Arthor AP; L 437 Be power of ANP;
C 419 avengyd AP; L 445 a fle AP; L 447 Go furthe NPA; L 451
vnlace AP; L 452 double maile (nayle A) PA; L 453 wyst not þat
wyght AP (: jentyll knyght ANP); L 466 þer wey AP; L 471 anon
ryght ANP;

L 474 ff.   And that maide briȝt
                      That is so feire of siȝt
                      Lede we wolle to toune NA(P);

L 481 sted þat tyde AN(P); L 484 than bere NP;

L 487 ff.   Sir Lybius rode att him anon PAN
                      And brake in tow his thigh (rigge N) bone PN
                      And lett him lye there lame PN(A)
                      The knyȝt merci gan crye NPA
                      Syr Libeus sykerly ANP;

L 496 He rode þan wyth that ANP; L 497 To þe mey ther sche sate
ANP; L 501 Js a gode champyoun AP; L 508–10 *lacking* ANP;

L 514 ff.   The yongist brothir gan furth ride
                        And preke his stede that tide
                        Egir as lioun wiȝt NA(P);

L 517–19 *lacking* ANP;

after L 519:   He seyd to syr Libeus anon
                        Syr knyght be seynt John
                        Thou arte a fell champyoun (and liȝt N)
                        Be God þat dyȝed on tre
                        Just J wyll wyth þe
                        J trow to bere þe doune AN(P);

L 521 On Libeus gan he hytte ANP; L 525 He kerfe ANP; L 528 of
egyr AN; L 532 Than seide Libious tho (so A) NPA; L 539 He smote
þe mydlyst (eldest P) in þat place ANP; L 541 He feld (fledde N) AN;
L 543 His ryght arme fell hym fro ANP; L 569 way NP; L 576
(*transposed with* L 579) And ther they (he A) liȝte adoun NPA;
L 578 For nede þei must rest ANP; L 591 Fro hym (them P) not
(but P) ANP; L 593 we wer AP;

L 598 f.   Syr Lybeus was stowt and gay
                        And lepe on his palfrey ANP;

L 601 f.   As he went (And rode P) forth (ffull P) fast
                        Two gyantys he fond at þe last ANP;

L 640 They went ANP; L 641 And lodged them vnder (leyd them
in A) the leaues PA; L 648 As wolfe þat wer full wode (: ȝode) AP;

L 652 f.   Syr Lybeus than full smerte (with ffeirce hart P)
                        Oute of his sadyll (swythe he P) sterte ANP;

L. 656 his suerd brouune AN;

after L 657:   T[he] gyant spyte sykerlye
                        Was mor than a coltre
                        That he had (rosted P) on þe bore
                        He leyd on Libeus faste
                        While þe sper (spit NP) wold last
                        Euer more and mor
                        The bore was full hote þan
                        The grece on Lybeus ran
                        [Swithe fast thore NP]
                        The gyant was styff and strong
                        And xv fote he was long
                        [And smote Libeous sore NP] (L 657^{a-l}) (A)(N)P;

L 658 f.   And euer þe gyant smote
                        To Libeus wele J wote ANP;

L 660 Tyll ANP;

L 667 f.   Or he his schaft vpcauȝh[t]
                    Libeus a stroke hym rauȝht AP;

L 674 To þat oþer he went þat stound ANP; L 689 That is a man AN;
L 700 hym ANP; L 704 That on þe rode AP; L 715 in Arthors ANP;
L 725 þer wey AP; L 728 styff and ANP; L 740 Be he baron or knyght
ANP; L 746 joly faucoun (*also at* L 759, L 810, L 823, L 848, and
L 895) AP; L 748 not so feyre of syght AN; L 755 aryght (ffull right P)
AP; L 763 Forsothe J AN; L 775 Or þat J passe thys place AP; L 782
Sertys ANP; L 785 Kyng Arthors AP; L 798 shrill PA; L 806 As
thyn be dey or nyght ANP; L 814 Where NAP; aplyȝht AN; L 821
on them so fre AP; L 832 That foreward forto holde NP(A) (: vp
thay yolde NP); L 834 Sir Libeous er he wolde blynne (lynne A)
(:his jnne) NPA; L 838 That bryght was and schen ANP; L 839
Loke þou make þe bowne APN; L 841 Y wene (will winn P) NAP;
L 850 herdy dede A(P); L 852 doyst be no mans redde ANP; L 853
chyldhede ANP;

L 855 ff.   Therfor J the praye
                   Wend (Wandir N) we forth owre (on thy P) wey
                   That we comm not hym beforn ANP;

L 861 f.   The meyd feyr and fre
                   Hyȝed hyr sykerly (certeyne to be N) APN;

L 867 vyolet mantyll AP; L 868 soth to sey AP; L 870 The stonys
aboute APN; L 871 Wer presyows endentyd (and sett with P) wyth
gold ANP; L 872 þat schyre AP; L 877 a full feyr mey AP;

L 885 f.   He bore a scheld of grene
                   That wele was dyȝht J wene AN(P);

L 890 Was geyer þan any trumpour AN; L 892 bare be hys syde
APN; L 898 full of AN; L 900 full wyde AN; L 903 ruffyne N, reyfyen
A; L 904 Furred wele ANP; L 906 The bond AN; L 917 (*transposed
with* L 914) Sche was full feyre in syght AN; L 921 Than sho made to
brynge NA; L 923 discry AP; L 928 As bryght as (euer was any P)
rose on brere AP; L 939 fell me AN; L 941 couenaunt NA; L 944
Thoff þou be wroth þerforn AN; L 948 Wyth strokys styff on scheld
AN; L 955 Harpours and gestours NA; L 959 A schefte good withalle
NA; L 971 renoune NP; L 980 A stroke of AN;

L 981 f.   Geffron rode to him swithe
                   Forsothe fele sithe NA;

L 987 smote NP; L 995 joly faucoun AN; L 1001 Wyth many a bold
baroun AN; L 1002 jentyll faucoun AN; L 1005 The knyȝt him
furthe (forsooth he A) yede NA;

L 1008 f.   To Arthor he hym bare
                   Than (That N) þe kyng he swere AN;

L 1027 Rode on ANP; L 1045 Sith NA; L 1050 full (alsoe P) sone
(: neuer none) ANP; L 1068 Than came theraftir bihynde (þe hynde
A) NA;

L 1074 ff.   He seyd be seynt Mertyne
                  That ilke rache was myne
                  Not fully gon a ȝere AN(P);

L 1087 thi while NP; L 1091 Carle was J neuer none (:dame) AN; L 1101 do þi beste AN; L 1108 Rode home in þat stowre (schour N) AN;

L 1116 f.   Thei seid he schulde be honge
                  Thouȝ he were also stronge NA;

L 1119 f.   They dyȝht þem full wele
                  Jn jrene and in stele AN;

L 1125 Fer on NA; L 1129 schall abyȝe (abide N) AN; L 1131 stode and bihilde NA; L 1138 Vnder (Yonder into P) ANP; L 1140 The soth (Forsothe N) forto seyn AN; L 1142 Them all J schall abyde AN; L 1156 He slew (cleuith N) wyth his drauȝht AN; L 1157 And slew for euermor AN; L 1159 As fisch is NAP; L 1160 With (grymly A) groomes PA; L 1165 And abode in NA; L 1167 Jn armour AN; L 1172 sle hym AN;

L 1173 f.   Ther myȝht men here (se N) ryȝht
                  Strokys sadly lyght (pliȝt N) AN;

L 1177 Forsoþe ANP; L 1178 Throuȝht helme and basnet þer AN; L 1181 com hym ANP; L 1182 lord fauȝht AN; L 1185 Thei (Syr Libeus A) leide on strokis ryue NA(P);

L 1188 f.   Togyder gan þei dryue
                  As beys about an hyue AN;

L 1198 Ouer hys hors crowpoun AN; L 1201 To perische NP; L 1202 Thorow helme basne[t] and plate AN; L 1204 plukyd vp ANP; L 1214 Aweywerd AN;

L 1233 ff.   The duerfe and meyd Elyn
                  Went wyth Libeus J wene
                  Vnto syr Otys castell AN;

L 1243 f.   And thanked God often sithe
                  And alsoe saint Michall P(A);

L 1246 f.   Schuld wynne in fyght
                  Hys lady feyre and hend AN;

L 1249 Furti daies with the knyȝt NA; L 1253 By the 6 weekes (xl deys A) end PNA; L 1257 wythoute lettyng AN;

L 1260 f.   He told vnto þe kyng
                  How suche a (aventours N) knyght ȝeng AN(P);

L 1264 And hys knyȝhtys in same AN; L 1273 Jn aventour and peryle AN; L 1274 Jn Cornewale and in Wales AN;

L 1276 f.   When þe leuys (and buski[s] N) wex grene
                  And floures in sembly sales AN;

L 1279 f.   Mery is thanne the songe
                   Of the ny3tingale[s] NA;

L 1297 Hys pere not fownd is AN; L 1306 And (Forsothe A) also
swithe stronge (: longe) NA; L 1307 fyfty AN; L 1310 For he is full
grymly (wondir grisly N) AN;

L 1311 ff.   Eche here of his browyn (berd gryme A)
                   Is liche the [brystelles A] of a swyn
                   [Forsoth A] wyttirly
                   His armys (bonys A) bith wondir long
                   And himsilue also strong
                   He sleith al that comyth him by NA;

after L 1316:   Forsoth (And so N) he is as grymly
                   As J telle the vereley (wittirly N)
                   [He is also grete N]
                   As any ox or cow
                   Forsoth a[s] J sey 3ow
                   A[n] asse or any nete
                   Wyth carte styffe and gode
                   Vneth be þe rode
                   Mey hym and hys gere lede
                   He is styff and sture (stronge N)
                   Ther may no man hys dyntys dore
                   So than (Forsothe so N) are þei grete (L 1316^{a-1}) (A)(N);

L 1336 Lybeus saw neuer non syche AN; L 1337 Fowre AN;

L 1338 ff.   For no while he stode
                   But to Libeous 3ode
                   And seid to him with wowe N(A);

L 1341–3 and 1344–6 transposed;

L 1341 f.   When he saw Libeus wyth syght
                   He seyd to hym anon ryght AN;

L 1347 apli3t NA;

L 1353 ff.   Magus on fote forth 3ede
                   And Lybeus rode to hym on stede
                   Forsoth þan full ryght AN;

L 1358 To behold þat fyght AN; L 1362 And gyff grace þat þe gyant
AN; L 1374 Magus þo ANP; L 1375 hys suerd AN;

L 1380 ff.   Libeous nothing saide
                   But stert vp [in A] a braide
                   Ri3t ful sone ayaine NA;

L 1383 An ax he hente full sone (: croupoun A, [n]ekke bone N) AN;

L 1386 ff.   That a pese of (happid to N) his scheld
                   [Hit flye fro him N] in þe feld
                   And fell doune on (ri3t into N) þe pleyn (A)N;

L 1392 Depe wondys þei rauȝht (caught P) ANP; L 1397 Jn fyght wer
þei tho (there N) AN(P); L 1404 it were for the (þe to : slo A) NA;
L 1409 Wythouten (With N) more delyte AN; L 1421 To þe my
trouȝht J plyȝht AN; L 1422 for thi AN;

L 1451 ff.   He stode defens (to fense A) aȝayne
                       Sir Libeous so to him smote
                       That at the secunde stroke NA;

L 1463 fulle welle (sone A) NA; L 1468 And changyd þer AN; L 1469
Jn paule sche clothyd hym welle AN; L 1479 Fully thre wekys and
mor AN; L 1481 And also maide Elyne NA; L 1484 The lady of
Synadowne AP;

L 1518 f.   The ladys stewerd hend
                      He made wyth hym to wend AN;

after L 1520:   Thei rode furthe talkyng
                      And also fast syngyng
                      Lauȝe and made good game NA;

L 1521 f.   Sir Libeous and that may
                      Rode furthe on hare iornay NA;

L 1530 ff.   Syr Lybeus askyd þat mey
                      Whos was þat castell gey
                      That stode þer in þat towne AN;

L 1533-68 replaced by:
                      And sche hym tolyd anon
                      Syr sche seyd by seynt John
                      Jt is my ladys fre
                      Jn ȝon feyre castell
                      Wonnys a gyant felle
                      Forsothe wytterly
                      Hys name is callyd Lamberte
                      Of all þys lond stewerte
                      Scrtys as J tell þe
                      And whoso comys into þat gate
                      To aske herborow þerate
                      Just wyth hym wyll he;

                      Quod Lybeus be my lewte
                      That wold J blythly se
                      For ouȝht þat may betyde
                      Thof he be neuer so stoute
                      Forsoth J schall make hym to lowte
                      So schall J to hym ryde
                      Therfor meyden Elyn
                      Ȝe and þe duerfe bedene
                      Jn þe towne ȝe mey me byd
                      Forth than þe meyd rode

The due[r]fe not abode
He rode nyȝe be hyr syde (L 1532^{a-x}) AN;

L 1569 to Jeffelot (Gesloke A) tite NA; L 1570 To me it were NA;
L 1571 To lete for man on lyue NA; L 1573 And wynne that lady
white (bryȝht A) NA; L 1576 Wyth me forto fare AN; L 1578 furthe
algate (all hate A) NA; L 1583 For two of Arthorus knyȝhtys AN;
L 1585 Lete þem into þe castelle AN; L 1590 Kyng of all curtasy
AN(P); L 1597 Ther (Thei N) be AN; L 1598 Two knyȝhtys fers
(faire N) and bold AN; L 1600 Jn full rych (With rich and royall P)
armour ANP; L 1616 Othir els your dethe is gete NA; L 1621 Thys
be wordys wele told AN(P); L 1625 Went þei not awey AN; L 1627
oþer wede AN; L 1629 A scheld he bere full fyne AN; L 1630 iii
boris hedis ydentid (wer dynt A) therjnne NA; L 1633 Saw he neuer
so AN; L 1634–6 *lacking* AN; L 1637 Jn lond APN;

L 1638 f.   Two squyars rode bi his side
              iii scheftis thei bare that tide NA;

after L 1640:   He was wonder gay
              And also large of pay
              Jn werre and in tournament AN;

L 1645 Prowde as any lyberd (Lombard N) AN; L 1646 To abyde
AN;

L 1647 f.   He sey Lybeus þat tyde
              And fast (first N) to hym gan ryde AN;

L 1650 He than to hym bare AN; L 1655 Wyth ther strokys bedene
AN; L 1660 As man that (And grynned as he A) were wode (: out-
rode) NA; L 1661 full of tene AN; L 1666 Wyth hedys AN; L 1668
They prykyd in þat AN; L 1676 Off hys hors (Of this N) he was bowne
AN; L 1678 And Libeous smote Lambert NA; L 1692 *lacking* AN;

after L 1700:   Syr Lambert suore full sone
              By hym þat made (schope N) son and mone
              He schall my lady gete AN;

L 1706 So strong be þys dey AN;

after L 1712·   Arte þou he seyd Lybeus tho
              That hath don so mykyll wo
              To þe quen of Synadoun
              Tell þou me or we hens gon
              Or J suere (the telle N) be seynt Jhon
              That J schall pare thy croune
              The stewerd ansuerd and seyd
              Syr be not yll apayd
              For sche is my lady
              Sche is quen of all þys lond
              And J hyr stewerd J vnderstond
              Forsoth wytterly (sicurly N) (L 1712^{a-l}) AN;

L 1719–21 *lacking* AN; L 1731 And told how AN; L 1736 Jhesus
heuyn kyng AN; L 1757 Sertys ry3ht to rede AN; L 1776–8 *lacking*
AP;

L 1803 ff.   Howe that proude steward
                    That men clepith sir Lambert
                    With Libeous his craft (case A) gan kithe NA;

L 1807 And made þem nobull cher A(N);

L 1809 ff.   Ther than gan þei duell
                    Jn that ilke castell
                    All [þe] long nyght AN;

L 1816 Ry3ht vnto AP; L 1823 fayne wolde NA; L 1827 a3en he rode
ANP; L 1831 Of hym AN; L 1832 Thyder sou3ht full wyde AN;
L 1836 Trumpys pypus AN; L 1840 He saw a fyre AN; L 1845 forth
gan (ffurthermore P) ANP; L 1846 Forth into þe plas AN; L 1847
Ther þe fyre was in haule AN; L 1848 Neþer (Somme N) of mor AN;
L 1852 Orgeynus mery of AN; L 1854 Wyth fydell and AP; L 1856
Was wyth (wrete N) jn þe AN; L 1863 He wente abowte in þe halle
(: pyllers alle) AN; L 1867 Were þei wrou3ht all AN; L 1877 That
were so sturdy AN;

L 1890 f.   The haule roffe also
                    Hym thou3ht wold cleue in two AN;

after L 1892 *comes the following stanza, now preserved only in* N *but
which the* NA *variant of* L 1893 *shows must have originated in* *ANP·

                    Sir Libeous therof had mervaile
                    And seide withouten faile
                    This is a wondur [thing]
                    Y trowe the devill of helle
                    Be in this castelle
                    And hath here his resting
                    Thou3 the devil and his dame
                    Come with his brothir in same
                    To dethe Y schalle him dynge
                    Y schalle neuer enis fle
                    Er that Y se what he be
                    Aboute [in] this biggyng (L 1892^{a-l}) N;

L 1893 As he sate thus and saide NA; L 1894 Him thou3t NA; L 1906
And loude he gan AN; L 1916 leue (loue N) of AN; L 1917 Sir
Libeous with good hert (: stert) NAP; L 1920 smertly AN; L 1924 On
þer scheldys þei hytte AN;

L 1932 f.   That hors he bore to grownd
                    And Mabon fell þat stound AN;

L 1939 Syr Libeus AN; L 1940 Thou3ht hym AN; L 1958 hys herte
aros AN; L 1969 Wyth hys suerd broune (: cleft down) AN;

L 1975 f.   Acaton noþer his charmour (: armour)
                 So he quitte hym his hyre AN;

L 1986 f.
        Mabon smote to Lybeus full swythe (blyþe N)
        And brake Lybeus suerd þat was stythe (ful swithe N) AN;

L 1997 (*transposed with* L 2000) As gestours tellys at bord (in borde N)
AN; L 2006 hys broþer fro AN; L 2008 ryght arme AN; L 2014
With bodi and catelle (castellus A) fre NA; L 2015 (*transposed with*
L 2018) Schall be at þi wyll AN;

L 2022–4 *replaced by*:
                 Therfore thowe sauy my life
                 And euer withouten strife
                 Y schal be at thi wille NA;

L 2028 ff.   Turne þe thefe and fyght (yef thowe myght N)
                 For J schall as J hyght
                 Hew thy hede off þi chyn AN;

L 2033 let not (left it N) APN; L 2036 And smot it (his hede N) off
by þe chyn AN; L 2039 Wyth his swerd in (drawne to P) fyght (fist N)
(: ffull right P) APN; L 2040 Forto se AN;

L 2049 f.   And when he my3ht not fynd Jram
                 He 3ede a3ene serteyn AN;

L 2052 in dede and thou3ht AN;

L 2058 f.   He satte full styll (fast N) and thou3ht
                 What he best do mought AN;

L 2072 As it wer gleterring (betyn N) gold AN; L 2076 suette for hete
ANP; L 2084 And hynge NA; L 2092 As þe clerkys AN; L 2097
sleyn forsothe (: þat well couthe) AN; L 2105 Euer in wo to wende
AN; L 2108 hys kynne ANP; L 2114 3our wyll APN; L 2119 þat
he had hym not AN; L 2120 With spere (spyte A) he thou3t him
spille NA;

after L 2120:   Syr Lybeus þe kny3ht gode
                  Jnto þe castell (sadil he N) 3ode
                  To seke (loke N) after Jram
                  He lokyd into þe chambour
                  Ther he (That N) was in (an hie N) towre
                  [And þer sone he hym wanne
                  He went into þe towre
                  And in þat jlke chambour A *only*]
                  [And ther N] He saw Jram [þat man A]
                  He drew hys suerd wyth my3ht
                  And smote off hys hede wyth ry3ht (ari3t N)
                  Forsoth of Jram than (L 2120ᵃ⁻ˡ) AN;

L 2126 Hys tale full pertely AN; L 2132 my3ht off sorcery AN;
L 2141 Therfore God ioy the send NA; L 2145 of purpur pryce AN;

L 2146 Furred ANP; L 2147 to bigynnyng NA; L 2163 knyȝhtys
douȝty (thrytte N) AN; L 2165 As it was law in londus AN, *followed
directly in* A *by* L 2169;

after L 2170 (HANP):   All men bowyd to hyr hondys
And when þei had þus don
They toke leue and went son A;

in N, L 2170[b-c] *precede* L 2170[a] *and the passage is placed between*
L 2168 *and* L 2169; L 2175 of his myȝt NA; L 2185 Were lordis
(brydys A) gret and smalle NA;

L 2187 ff.   Ther was wel sertayne (many a man A)
Servise fulle good wone
Bothe [to A] most and lest NA;

L 2190 ff.   Forsothe the mynstrals alle
That were in the halle
Had ȝiftis at that fest (of þe beste A) NA;

after L 2192:   Syr Lybeus moder so fre
Come (ȝede N) to þat mangerre
Hyr rudd was rede as ryse
Sche knew Lybeus wele be syȝht
And wyst wele anon ryȝht
That he was of mych pryse
Sche went to Syr Gawen
And seyd wythouten leyn (delayne N)
Thys is owre chyld so fre
Than was he glad and blyth
And kyssed hym (hur N) many a sythe
And seyd þat lykes me (L 2192[a-l]) AN;

L 2192[s-t] (HANP)   Than þat lady was blyth
And thankyd hym many a syth AN;

L 2192[v-x] (HANP)   Than Lybeus to hym wan (ranne N)
And þer he kyssed þat man
Forsoth treuly AN;

L 2192[cc] (HANP) Feyr fader wele be ȝe fownd AN; L 2199 x ȝere
AN; L 2204 To heuen blys vs bryng AN.

(d) READINGS PECULIAR TO MS. H

L 227 þeo cloþ weore laid (: sore amaied); L 247 A griffown; L 249
þat oþir an; L 259 to beore; L 289 wraþþe; L 295 Y sweore by swete
Ihesus; L 296 þat he was neuer ȝet; L 309 Wiþ sotil gyse of trappes;
L 311 was irows; L 314 boon frere; L 320 passe sure; L 360 flyng;
L 363 lette þey slyng; L 391 Apon my sweord broun (: anon); L 412
Williams emes sonis weoren heo; L 541 in luytel space (: place);

L 577 f.   Nyȝt on heom com fast
Jn þat wilde forest;

L 581 þay logged heom; L 594 of any gyle; L 598 frech(s) (: destres); L 601 As he com heom neore; L 616 alas þis daye; L 632 þoruȝ þeo breost into þeo hert; L 636 God had hir; L 646 sore; L 650 tofore; L 656 a tronchoun; L 664 Wiþ þat tronchoun of treo; L 693 þeo castel al abowte; L 698 leues gonne flyng; L 735 To whom þat hit ouȝt (: stowte); L 753 To schewe; L 880 þer fully abood; L 892 bar him myd (: rood); L 897 þer as þey conne ryde; L 941 was ȝore; L 944 berd hore; L 956 askrye; L 958 Tak me oon þat; C 952 cours owt ryd; L 982 Him greued owt; L 1072 For sir Otes; L 1076 Nouȝt ago ful ȝore; L 1087 þy peryle; L 1094 [S]yr; L 1097 playe; L 1451 He feol; L 1501 þow fals knyȝt in þy lay; L 1518 Hire styward fer and neor; L 1522 On þat old jornay; L 1528 preoued in pryde; L 1539 mok and hore; L 1546 beo out barred; L 1693 Eyþir on oþir schaftes set; L 1712 Siker and in good fay; L 1727 To come to; L 1732 Mette wiþ mony; L 1736 seynt Jame; L 1757 Hire han forto; L 1778 And deriþ hire; L 1807 Many mon and faire (: soper); L 1809 ro and rest; L 1818 þay dorst him nouȝt bet bryng; L 1832 And heom þat dude þe dede (: cried); L 1836–8 *lacking*; L 1848 Of lyue; L 1852 Orgoyns vois; L 1856 wyȝht in wold; L 1857 Tofore; L 1859 And made muche lyȝt; L 1860 firþer stode; L 1866 of coralle; L 1877 so god entray; L 1882 þay clapped; L 1893 seet amayed; L 2141 Yn reste we may ende; *after* L 2170 þat weore heore byȝete; L 2188 Boþe to fool and wyse; L 2191 Vche mynstral aryȝhtis (: ȝifthes); L 2192 weore vnprest; L 2199 Twenty ȝer; L 2204 Spede vs at oure nede.

(e) READINGS PECULIAR TO MS. A

L 5 Wytty knyght and gode weryour; L 14 of face and body ryght; L 24 worthy; L 33 To se wyld dere bename; L 86 Lete make; C 79 He caste on hym in a pylte (: ouergylte); L 95 Full sone þe kyng a; L 106 Ryght wythouten resoun; L 118 hendy Elyn; C 126 He was so stoute in herte; L 136 His sercote; L 137 and wythin of anoþer colour; L 138 Wele furryd aboute wyth merte; L 147 Herpe fidyll þan wele he couthe; L 153 it is forsothe (: mouthe); L 183 thy lordys; L 186 mannes dynte; L 192 konyng kyng; L 207 And hath had many a blaw; L 226 euyll payd (: bord was vp brayd); L 247 A ryppon; L 248 Emong þem chosyn som fayle; L 252 awne fere (: swer); L 258 Gefferen; L 269 My wyll is gode to fone; L 275 Thorow þat lady hend; L 280 Sone vpon þe knyght; L 293 All þat he may hytte; L 295 That wey wyll we aventour vs; L 296 Jff we may hym mete; L 307 gold J wene; C 311 man of; L 341 spere so longe; L 343 his sper; L 344 Be God and be seynt Jhon; L 359 Therto þan wyll J lyȝht; L 393 Fast þou knele; L 403 hym bede; L 406 Home to; L 415 Thei comme to hym wyth dred; L 448 þe thefe; L 462 hys squyre; L 464 þat myster was; L 488 *lacking*; L 493 mayster Wyndeleyn; L 495 in þe sadyll aboune; L 529 he heuyd; L 531 vnwyse and; L 540 arme so; L 556 So ȝe schall sey; L 560 And be at ʒour renoun; L 565 swore it schuld be so; L 581 They byged them wyth leuys; L 630 And rode both ryʒht and wyse; L 636 Sych grace sche had hir; L 648 As wolfe þat wer full wode (: ʒode); L 657¹ (ANP) And þat greuyd hym sore; L 657¹ (ANP) He smote fast wyth þe bore; L 688 and wyde knaw knyght; L 693 That was of so grete power; L 710 he sauyd; L 715 dyd rys (: was of pryce); L 717 And of worthy fame; L 729 That grysly; L 731 saw J; L 746 as fome; L 816 wyth all my myʒht; L 826 Hold þe grant J wyll; L 832 That forwerd to be fullfyllyd (: held); L 845 Both togeder jn fassyoun; L 863 That sche were atyred; L 896 The two ladys waygewr; L 900 was gederyd; L 908 rych jewell; L 920 Forsotht no man myght; L 931 Wer worthy to be; L 953 of þe eyre; L 966 Thoffe he wer wyghter (: Arthor); L 974 anone (: rawundon);

L 984 ff.   He rode aʒens hym a[s] gode
He leyd at hym as he wer wode
As man þat had grete nede;

L 1012 Off dyuerse batels; L 1029 onne þe row; L 1034 To sey wythouten feyle; L 1035 Syr Otys it blew so wele (: somewhile); L 1038 wyth wyle; L 1040 West into þe vayle; L 1052 So mekyll;

L 1053 f.   Wold God sche seyd þat he myn wer
Syr Libeus toke þe hunde þer;

L 1057 kempys fauʒht; L 1068 Than comme after þe hynde; L 1073 they were; L 1081 J toke hym þe meyd to; L 1082 That stondys; L 1085 Sertys and; L 1089 Quod syr Otys in þat while; L 1092 An erle my fader was welle; L 1102 Jn hast yff þou lyste (: do þi beste); L 1111 Off Arthors halle is a knyʒht; L 1113 refte hym; L 1127 Ridyng forth hys pase; L 1129 thou schall abyʒe; L 1136 Here comys a sory; L 1145 As prynce; L 1154 Oure kynd he wyll forfare; L 1169 Jn romans; L 1172 in þat tyde; L 1179 and þe knyʒhtys thre; L 1184 To helpe them in fere; L 1193 mad of rede; L 1196 That to þe flesch it bode; L 1201 To pare of hys crowne; L 1207 He smote þe knyght doun be þe kne (: þat hong hym ne); L 1208 Thorow habergoun and plate; L 1210 iij knyghtys;

L 1215 ff.   Syr Libeus no le[n]ger abode
Faste as he wer wode
After hym rode he
Vnder a cheston tre he had hym quellyd;
Had he not to hym aʒelde;

L 1221 entent; L 1239 prysoneres fowre; L 1243 (ANP) a C sythe; L 1245 herdy; L 1255 redy wey; L 1294 Hyr rudde is reder þan þe ryse; L 1300–1 Jn all þys lond is non so stoute;

L 1308 f.   Syr Lybeus thinke on thy suete
That þou not wyth hym mete;

L 1316ᶜ (ANP) And also pardye; L 1326 lacking; L 1327 J sett no[t] by hym a myte; L 1339 (ANP) To Lybeus sone he rode; L 1340

(ANP) He was blake as any bere; L 1351 For þe thow fend; L 1357
Rode in þer curryculys; L 1364 be sleyn; L 1367 The sperkyllus;
L 1369 Ne þat syr Lybeus was smyte in two (: wounder þo); L 1375
flyȝe hym; L 1376 And fro hym it gan swyng; L 1377 Syr Magus dyde
quyte him th[o] (: stede so); L 1379 That he sched hys breyn; L 1387
(ANP) Fell dounne; L 1389 Togyder; L 1394 Ayther oþer to slo;
L 1406 full lytell profyte; L 1418 to þe lyȝht; L 1433 armys strong;
L 1454 hys arme; L 1455 he leuyd; L 1475–6 *lacking*; L 1488 Off
many a dyuerse melody; L 1489 Sche mad hym; L 1490 That myght
no man; L 1501 take hede to þi ley; L 1516 Hys armour; L 1601 thre
loxus; L 1605–7 *lacking*;

L 1608–12 *replaced by*:
    The porter went aȝen ryȝht
    And seyd to þe gentyll knyght;

L 1632 broþeres; L 1651 A scheld þat was square; L 1669 To dele
depe wond; L 1677 Hys scheld he smote so herd (: Lamberte); L 1680
Peyȝen wynteyn; L 1682 And Lambert flew vpryght; L 1683–8
lacking; L 1691 *lacking*; L 1700 Wythowtyn any lete; L 1708 ȝyff
þou wer of; L 1710–12 *lacking*;

L 1713–18 *replaced by*:
    Syr Lybeus ansuerd tho
    J wold feyne wyte who
    Hath brouȝht hyr in dolour;

L 1722 ff.   Syr Lambert seyd tho
      They ben clerkys two
      That do þat dyshonour;

L 1728 duerff J wene (: dedys bedene); L 1746–8 *lacking*; L 1767–9
lacking; L 1772 Ther wythin is dyȝht; L 1775 no syght; L 1783 To
do all þer wyll; L 1788–90 *lacking*; L 1794–6 *lacking*; L 1799 suppyd
þan belyue; L 1800 Baronus and burges fele in fay (: sembly say);
L 1844 That was full gode in; L 1858 A torch brynand þer stode
(: mynst[r]ell gode); L 1882 They hytt into; L 1903 Was legud wyth
trapor; L 1921 forto kylle; L 1929 spere feloun; L 1955 Than full
sone he ros; L 1963 *lacking*; L 1983 togyder streke; L 1988–96 *lacking*;
L 2005 swerd browne; L 2009 He bare awey; L 2021 That well nyȝe;
L 2035 his hed;

L 2046 f.   Than he swet for þe nons
      Both in flesch and in bonus;

L 2099 Off sorcery be; L 2103 coniurment; L 2104 had me schent;
L 2118 And seyd he dred; L 2121 Fro þe; L 2129 of God and of;
L 2134 sche was pyght; L 2152 men of myȝht;

after L 2204:
    Here endys þe lyfe
    J tell ȝow wythouten stryfe
    Off gentyll Libeus Disconeus

For his saule now byd ȝe
A pater noster and an aue
For þe loue off Jhesus
That he of hys sawle haue pyte
And off owrys iff hys wyll be
When we schall wend þerto
And ȝe þat haue herd þys talkyng
ȝe schall haue þe blyssing
Of Jhesu Cryst all so
    Amen quod Rate.

(f) READINGS PECULIAR TO MS. N

L 5 That was wis witty and; L 12 Hurd neuer yet man rede; L 14 and feire of siȝt; L 20 blitheli wolde do outrage; C 31 drowe of; C 37 As he sate; L 60 None so feire a wight; L 64 But whan Y was tame at home; L 83 The feire on thatte Y knowe; C 80 With gresons ouergilde; C 81 Jpeyntid of lengthe ful gay;

C 82 f.   Aftur him taught Gaweyn
                      With strenghe in the pleyn;

C 84 Poynt of; L 102 Whate bone; L 123 Ther myght none be; L 138 Forsothe to se with sight; L 146 Sotil swithe in; L 148–50 *lacking*; L 152 Damesel telle me; L 154 kene in; L 159 Y note nouȝt suche of; L 166 Than stert vp a; L 167 In hert that was lefe and wight; L 192 thou gentil; L 201 Ther schalle he bigynne; L 205 Bothe with spere and with schild; L 223 for noye and; L 225 For alle that thei myȝt do; L 226 downe as careful maide (: was vnleide); L 232 To army him hole; L 236 That he schulde haue myght; L 258 A griffon he brouȝt with him; L 282 thou wrecche thou caitife L 283 were so stife; L 293 ayens him mete; L 297 Tide so whate; L 315 Whate man that he[r] furth riȝt; L 331 no betir; L 338 grete renowne; L 352 Bi this ilke day;

L 360 f.   Swerdis thei drowe bothe
                      As men that were wrothe;

L 362 furthe fast; L 372 Vesour and; L 377 to nye; L 381 mercy to cry; L 389 Thou getist of me; L 397 J am come to your prisoun;

C 391 f.   His sustir sones he mette there
                      Feire knyȝtis and fre;

L 401 kynde and kithe; L 415 As wolfe that; L 428 wel faire schene; L 429 me more; L 446 To bide bataile; L 451 hauberk of bras; L 502 stode and bihilde; L 527 he frede; L 530 Al that him toke; L 552 that bouȝt vs bothe; L 554 sicour me; *between* L 556 *and* L 557 To yelde you towre and toune; L 561 To oure lyuys ende; L 563 sle you two (: so); L 570 yheȝt; L 575 grene forest; L 587–9 *lacking*; L 611–12 On a spitte a bore gan turne; L 613–14 *lacking*; L 657 To ȝelde;

L 657ᵃ⁻ᵇ (ANP) The giaunt with the spit ȝaue a stroke
                But the butte of a yong oke;

L 688 An erle ykidde a noble knyȝt; L 690 is furre ytolde; L 699 his
fere; L 729 wondir wel; L 769 he hath defens (: Frediens); L 775 hens
pace; L 776 this stede; L 778 Thei leftin; L 788 place; L 815–17
lacking; L 845 Faire of facioune; L 850 Nowe is this a wondir dede;
L 863 Fast to hur atyre; L 887 border(s)ryng flour; L 892 iij speris;
L 893 That good were and sure; L 932 In hur lauendrye; L 942 fille
downe; L 976 And seide bothe more and las (: was); L 983 And ȝit;
L 992 Fer of; L 1002 ybore was; L 1021 furtenyȝt; L 1031 And
houndis make rebound; L 1047 colours gay; L 1048 *lacking*; L 1062
come rennyng (: hir folowyng); L 1064 bigan to mene; C 1041 and
sho in fere; L 1097 Forsothe we; L 1102 Here Y am alle prest; L 1103
schall with vs wynde than (: game); L 1123 hare palfrais; L 1128 ride
(: abide); L 1145 Sir Libeous rode in pride; L 1153 Here comyth
the; L 1154 That makith wilde fire fare; L 1160 greuely; L 1179
lacking; L 1196 That at the skulle withstode; L 1206 And hent that
was him nye; L 1242–4 *lacking*; L 1245 douȝti; L 1253 Bi that day six
wokis; L 1300 Jn al this worlde is him none liche; L 1305 furti fote;
L 1309 With suche one to melle; L 1316ᶠ (ANP) Or as grete as eny;
L 1325 Jn litille stounde fulle stille; L 1334 Lokid as; L 1356 and
ladies briȝt; L 1357 in hare korvelle; L 1376 Without eny lesyng;
L 1377 cowthe moche quede; L 1390 No man bitwene ham myȝt;
L 1407 graunt it welle (: fille); L 1410 the wateris; L 1432 Claue atwo;
L 1440 was done; L 1441 A[nd] fer passid euensonge; L 1445 sple[n]te
plate; L 1461 *lacking*; L 1476 Alas that sho nad be ychastid (: latist);
L 1578 furthe algate; L 1584 portelle; L 1591 Chief of; L 1593 porter
prestabelle; L 1610 Ayen he toke the gate; L 1612 One is come to the
auentours knyȝt; L 1646 the fiȝtis; L 1649 with jee; L 1667 renoune;
L 1674 haue and hit; L 1689 fond to fiȝt;

L 1710–12 (*where* A *is defective*):

                Thou art ful stoute in fiȝt
                And also stronge a knyȝt
                Ful sikir bi my fay;

L 1713 answerid in hast (: lady chast); L 1715 As Y hight;

after L 1715:   No man schal make me agast
                  The while the life on me may last
                  To wynne hur with honour;

L 1724 By God oure sauiour; L 1732 many aventours (: Libeous);
L 1785 lond; L 1787 To wynne alle with wille (: meke and stille);
L 1799 But singith and; L 1807 And bade ham be blithe of chere;
L 1825 That he schulde Jeffelot slayne; L 1833 Sir Libeous reyȝt
his corcis; L 1842 And furthe in; L 1848 Somme of more; L 1859 Thei
were yliȝtid; L 1873 In this worlde a feirer nas; L 1874 That euer
man sawe; L 1885 On his hede; L 1887 The doris; L 1903 Was
couerid with colour; L 1911 Y holde the man of kyn; L 1929 And with

his sterk fauchon (: Mabon doun); L 1931 Vndir; L 1945 That hare; L 1966 a stroke of male felon; L 1971 wondir sliȝe; L 1973 *lacking*; L 1977 of hert was liȝt; L 1984 Hare strokis; L 1989 Libeous ful wo; L 1990 *lacking*;

L 1991 *replaced* by:

> For he had lorne so
> Forsothe his good swerde there;

L 1993 He had wende to haue come with schame; L 2004 claue; L 2021 That wounde; L 2027 to wilde; L 2051 And souȝt; L 2078 As he had be in werre; L 2094 gentille knyȝt (: thi fiȝt); L 2100 Bi northe and bi sowthe; L 2103-4 *lacking*; L 2110 lx and fyue; L 2136 him stode; L 2148 Suche riches; L 2184 halle; L 2192ʳ (HANP) And gate him of a giantis lady; L 2193 dwellid there (: hilde yfere); L 2196 As in romaunce it is tolde;

after L 2204:

> Qui scripcit carmen sit benedict[u]s Amen
> Hic explicit Libeus Disconyus
>
> He that louyth welle to fare
> Eu[i]r to spend and neuer spare
> But he haue the more good
> His here wol grow throw his hood
> quod More
> Hic pennam fixi penitet me si male scripsi

(g) READINGS PECULIAR TO MS. P

L 1 Jesus Christ christen kinge (: sweete thing);

L 4 f.

> That will listen to my tale
> Of a knight J will you tell;

L 10 without ffable; L 14 An hardye man and a wight;

L 17 f.

> For he shold not of noe armed knight
> Haue a sight in noe mannere;

L 24 hend child; L 28 was not soe wise; C 31 did on; L 33 Wild deere to hunt ffor game;

L 34 ff.

> And as he went ouer the lay
> He spyed a knight was stout and gay
> That soone he made ffull tame;

L 38 therin yeede; C 35 swithe hee; L 55 the king strong; L 56 To the child that was soe younge; C 45 Tell me what thou hight; L 63 vnwise; L 64 when J dwelled; L 73 giue thee; L 75 For thou art; L 77 Soe cleped thee neuer thy dame;

C 73 ff.

> King Arthur anon right
> With a sword ffaire and bright
> Trulye that same day
> Dubbed that child a knight
> And gaue him armes bright;

C 79 Hee gaue to him in that ilke (: ouergilte); L 94 made a knight (: asked right); L 106 When he had him thus told (: barons bold); L 112 sitten not a stoure (: of halfe an hower); L 114 Talking att their meate; L 115 a damsell at that tyde; L 119 Sent shee was vnto the king;

L 121 ff.   The maiden was ware and wise
                    And cold doe her message att device
                    Shee was not to ffere;

L 130 f.   The dwarfe was cladd with scarlett ffine
                    And ffured well with good ermine;

L 132 and keene; L 135 of greene;

L 136 ff.   His haire was yellow as fflower on mold
                    To his girdle hang shining as gold
                    The sooth to tell in veretye;

L 140 All as gay as any knight;

L 145–50 *replaced by*:
                    Much he cold of game and glee
                    Fiddle crowde and sowtrye
                    He was a merry man of mouth
                    Harpe ribble and sautrye
                    He cold much of minstrelsye
                    He was a good jestoure
                    There was none such in noe country
                    A jolly man fforsooth was hee
                    With ladyes in their bower;

L 153 And kneele before the king; L 156 my lord without leasing;

L 164 f.   Forto win her in ffight
                    With ioy and much honor;

L 166 Vp rose; L 169 My couenant is to haue that fight;

L 172 f.   The king said without othe
                    Thereof thou saiest soothe;

L 177 With sheeld and with speare dint; L 178 to say (: that ilke day); L 183 thy deeds; L 187 mickle maine; L 192 And said sir verament; L 199 bridge of perill (: aduenturous chappell); L 201 ffirst begining; L 204 For no mans threatninge; L 216c (HANP) on thee may know (: lawe); L 216d for thy berde; L 216h that lyen on; L 216j But betweene ernest and game; L 216k J counsell thee goe souke; L 219 that sitteth in Trinitye; L 221 another knight; L 223 ffor ire still did thinke (: eate nor drinke);

L 226 f.   Shee sate still without ffable
                    Till they had vncouered the table;

L 231 4 knights in ffere; L 233 ffull right; L 236 doe that he hight; L 242 And arrayed him like a knight; L 245 Them right fforto behold; L 248 That was worth 20 pound of golde; L 251 good and ffine; L 252 owne ffather(e) (: necke there); L 255 that was ffull rich;

L 256 In all the land there was none such; L 260 of a ffell ffashion;
L 266 lord of renowne; L 269 is fforth me to; L 270 vpp did lifft
(: to him gaue right);

L 273-5 *replaced by*:
        And said God that is of might
        And his mother Marry bright
        That is fflowre of all women
        Giue thee gracce fforto gone
        Forto gett the ouerhand of thy fone
        And speed thee in thy iourney Amen;

L 276 f.   Sir Lybius now rideth on his way
        And soe did that ffaire may;

L 279 Till itt beffell vpon; L 280 all the way; L 290 of great pride;
C 270 to him rides; L 295 J will not lett this nor thus; L 296 To play
with him a ffitt; L 302 aduenturous chappell (: bridge of perrill);
L 310 As he shold goe to ffight; L 313 Anon he went to him arright;
L 314 to him there; L 315 Who passeth; L 317 his harnesse; C 305
Deale stroakes betweene; L 329 A litle here; L 332 Goe fforth and
doe; L 335 For J ame here; L 344 He leaned on his; L 345 Sir Lybius
made him; L 346 He smote him over; L 356 a knight worthye;
C 334 sir Lybius; L 359 Therto ffull ready J am;

L 360 f.   Then together they went as tyte
        And with their swords they gan smite;

L 362 wonderous longe (: helmes strong); L 363 lett fflinge (: out gan
springe); L 368 And smote on his sheild soe ffast; C 347 att that
sonde; L 372 Coyfe and; L 377 And touched him ffull nye; L 380
might see with eye; L 383 let mee weelde (: in the feeld); L 391 Or
thou out of the ffelld gone; L 397 J am in battell ouerthrowne;

L 402 f.   Sir William mett him on his knee
        And the othe there made hee;

L 405 all the rout (: Arthurs court); L 407 ready way; L 408 sorry
case; L 409 proud and tall; L 415 And alway hanged downe his head;
L 416 They rode to him with great array; L 417 cozen Will[iam];
L 419 soe long (: and a stronge); L 425 not ffarr to;

L 426 ff.   A dwarfe rydeth with him in fere
        As he was his squier
        They ride away ffull yarne;

L 437 his might; L 448 Though thou be neuer soe wroth; L 455 a well
good pace; L 459 Shee cryed him mercye (: villanye); L 461 Shee
prayed him to fforgiue her that tyde (: that they had need);

L 475 f. (ANP)   Wee will her lead att night
        Herby vnto a towne;

L 478 Forto ffight J am all readye (: gan crye); L 481 (ANP) He rode against them that tyde; L 483 With mirth sport and game; L 492 Had smitten him downe; L 502 The 2ᵈ; L 503 lay in the;

L 505 f.   He smote sir Lybius in that tyde
                   On the sheeld with much pride;

L 512 With his good speare;

L 515 f. (ANP)   And hitt sir Lybius in that tyde
                   As a man of much might;

L 519ᵈ (ANP) that sitteth in Trinitye; L 526 Sir Lybius was served in that stead (: head); L 528 That the sword had drawen blood; L 531 wight and good; L 541 Hee hitt him soe in; L 542 To see itt was a wonderous case; L 545 And thought hee had noe might; L 554 Plight your trothes without layine (: twayne); L 557 In battaill wee be ouercome; L 564 As J am true knight; L 572 The[y] ffell together; L 575 wyde fforrest; L 580 Amonge the greene eues (: with bower and leaues); L 603 (ANP) Strong and stout were; L 605 blacke as any sole (: red as ffyerye cole); L 606 bothe they were; L 616 alas and euer away; L 654 of fyer (: his hyer); L 662 For a trunchyon fforth he goth (: that was wrath); L 665 Sir Lybius sword in 3 he hitt (: that spitt); L 675 And serued him right soe (: heads thoe); L 676 heads then (: maiden); L 690 Arthor; L 693 For the castle ore; L 694 Tonight; L 695 my demeaning; L 703 Sir knight God yeeld; L 709 in euery thing; L 717 And a right good name; L 725 Tooke their leaue and rode their way; L 729 ffull maruelouslye; L 730 Wrought itt;

L 733 f.   Sir Lybius said soe haue J blis
                   Worthy dwelling here itt is;

L 735 To them that stood in doubt; C 719 here dwelleth; L 742 Soe well he loueth his; L 745 ffairer then; L 751 take (: stake); L 753 Trulye withouten dread; L 754 you may see and heere (: corner(e)); L 756 alsoe soone (: John); L 761 alsoe bright; L 771 and sware; L 776 For all his subt[i]lle wile; L 777 questyon; L 780 he made him readie (: winne him the masterye); L 784 sayd armor; L 793 Then he was ware of;

L 795 f.   Fast he rode into that place
                 Sir Jeffron maruailed att that case;

L 809 Forto see with sight; L 813 alsoe right; L 814 and L 817 see that sight; L 816 wee will ffull right; L 826 and L 828 transposed; L 827 att yonder tyde; L 828 J wold ffaine as any man (: alsoe then); C 823 by saint Quintin (: J will winn); L 845 And of you bothe the ffashyon; L 849 forthy (: deed hardye); L 859 with great grame; L 863 Her fforto attyre; L 864 Forto doe all his delight; L 866 With good gold; L 869 her lyer; L 886 Richelye itt was to be seene; L 888 with rich colours; L 890 Like as itt were an emperour; L 893 and stoure; L 894 bare his head vpon; L 898 Faire and bright of much

pryde (: did a lady ryde); L 901 To see that ladye in that tyde; L 903
of purple ffine;

L 906 f.   A sercotte sett about her necke soe sweete
            With dyamond and with margarett;

L 908 emerall; L 909 Her colour was as the rose red; L 912 were alsoe
silke spread; L 918 Her body gentle and; L 921 Unto the markett
men gan bring; L 922 fforto sitt in; L 935 Thy head; L 940 head on
thy ffawchyon; L 941 And home with thee itt lead (: head indeed);

L 945 ff.   What needeth vs more to chyde
            But into the saddle let vs glyde
            To proue our mastery
            Either smote on others sheeld the while
            With crownackles that were of steele;

L 964 Swithe ouer; L 970 swithe thoe; L 974 ffeeld againe; L 975
that was there (: without more);

L 978 f.   That the[y] saw neuer a knight
            Ne noe man abide might;

L 981 f.   Another course gan the[y] ryde
            Sir Geffron was aggreeued that tyde;

L 986 As a doughtye man of deed; C 959 soone he; L 989 Him and
his horsse adowne; L 990 backe bone he brake (: itt cracke); L 992
Lost was his renowne; L 993 said lesse and more; L 996 The people
came sir Lybius before; L 998 Anon into; L 1001 rueffull mone;
L 1004 To bring to Arthur with the crowne; L 1009 He said to his
knights in that stead; L 1017 ready prest; L 1018 to spend with;
L 1021 That lasted 40 dayes att least; L 1029 in a throwe; L 1031
And hoinds of great game (: Many yeeres agone); L 1037 hall;
L 1051 Soe faire a ratch J neuer saw none; L 1052 Nor pleasanter to;
L 1056 all rightes (: ffighting with knights); L 1062 hind sterke;
L 1065 The[y] hunted still; L 1067 Vnder the fforrest side;

after L 1067:   There beside dwelled that knight
                   That sir Otes de Lile hight
                   A man of much pride;

L 1068 f.   He was cladd all in Jnde
                   And ffast pursued after the hind;

L 1073 And know where he were;

after L 1073:   As he rode by that woode right
                   There he saw that younge knight
                   And alsoe that ffaire may
                   The(y) dwarffe rode by his side
                   Sir Otes bade they shold abyde
                   They ledd his ratch away
                   Freinds he said why doe you soe
                   Let my ratch ffrom you goe
                   Good for you itt were;

L 1074 ff. (ANP)   J say to you without lye
                   This ratch has beene my
                   All out this 7 yeere;

L 1077 ff.   Sir Lybius said anon tho
                   J tooke him with my hands 2
                   And with me shall he abyde
                   J gaue him to this maid hend
                   That with me dothe wend
                   Riding by my side;

L 1085 To be slaine if; L 1086 in that while; L 1092 J say to thee
without ffayle; L 1096 As well as; L 1098 Or thou my ratch ffrom me
reue; L 1100 strong game; L 1102 Goe fforth and doe; L 1104 They
rode on; L 1105 Througe a deepe fforrest; L 1107 in that stower;
L 1115 soone be tane (: Gawaine); L 1120 With gleaues; L 1121 As
they wold warr on take; L 1125 hill trulye (: can espye); L 1127 a well
good pace; L 1138 woods wawe; L 1140 For here vpon this plaine;
L 1142 The battell J will; L 1145 Of him what may betyde;

L 1146 f.   Then the[y] smote at him with crossebowes
                   With speare and with bowes turkoys;

L 1149 with his horsse; L 1153 That hee was; L 1156 His death
wound there he caught; L 1157 And smote them downe bydeene;
L 1160 With groomes ffell and keene; L 1161 knights verelye (: come
ryding redylye); L 1166 To see; L 1167 In a sweate; L 1173 Fast
together can the[y] ding; L 1174 And round the(y) stroakes he gan
fflinge; L 1178 and hernesse cleere; L 1182 abode in; L 1185 Then
they gaue stroakes riue; L 1187 as they; L 1188 him bring (: of
a spring;

L 1197 f.   Then in a swoone he lowted lowe
                   He leaned on his saddle bow;

L 1199 was nye slake; L 1200 4 sonnes; L 1202 Double maile; L 1205
As the ki[n]de of his estate;

L 1206 f.   And soone he hent in his ffist
                   An axe that hanged on his sadle crest;

L 1208 itt was; L 1209 he ffought as; L 1210 Their horsses ffell
downe right; L 1212 saw the ffight; L 1217 a chest of; L 1218 killed
(: yeelded); L 1221 And fforto yeeld him his stent; L 1223 and tower;
L 1224 consented therto (: that he wold goe);

L 1228 f.   In battell J am ouerthrowne
                   And sent thee to honor;

L 1230 theretill: L 1231 Forto doe all his will; L 1232 They went
home; L 1238 And how that itt; L 1239 That hee had;

L 1246 ff.   Schold ffor that ladye ffight
                       That was soe ffaire and free
                       In the towne dwelled a knight
                       Att the ffull ffortnight
                       Sir Lybyius there gan bee;

L 1255 Rode fforthe on their way;

L 1257 f.   And alsoe the lord of that tower
                       Went vnto king Arthur;

L 1260 f. (ANP)   And told how a knight younge
                       In ffighting had him woone;

L 1262 And ouercome; *between* L 1262 *and* L 1263:
                       And said lord of great renowne
                       J am in battell brought adowne
                       With a knight soe bolde;

L 1266–8 *lacking*; L 1274 In England; L 1277 in seemlye manner(e);
L 1280 of birds on bryar; L 1284 With pauillyons of much pride;

L 1291 f.   There hath beene slaine knights more
                       Then beene in this countrye;

L 1297 There is noe more such theeues; L 1298 That ladye hee lyeth
about; L 1299 is heathen as; L 1300 Now there be no more such;
L 1305 20 ffoote;

L 1309 f.   Hee is more grimmner fforto see
                       Then any one aliue;

L 1313 is great and stout; L 1316 fforto driue about; L 1318 On our
way wee will; L 1323–5 *lacking*; L 1327 sore smyte;

after L 1328   J beseech God almight
                       That J may soe with him ffight
                       That g[i]ant fforto kill;

L 1334 As grimm as; L 1336 His paytrill and his crouper (: as ter);
L 1338 The[y] were gaylye gilt with gold (: he did hold); L 1340 And
alsoe his sword in ffere; L 1342 And said ffellow J thee quite; L 1343
Now what thou art mee tell (: loue thyselfe well); L 1356 ladyes there
(: on pount tornere); L 1376 he gan itt ffling; L 1377 gan smite in that
stead; L 1378 Sir Lybius horse; L 1381 sayd nothing (: dyinge);
L 1383 hent anon; L 1387 long and liuer(e); L 1388 And quitt him
well againe;

L 1389 ff.   Descriue the stroakes cold no man
                       That were giuen betwene them then
                       To bedd peace was no boote thoe;

L 1393 both sore ffought; L 1397 (ANP) They ffought together thoe;
L 1402 What loue; L 1403 happe; L 1405 shold dye; L 1406 And to
thee litle pryde;

L 1413 ff.   That into the riuer he goes
                 But vp anon he rose
                 Wonderffull he was dight
                 With his armour euery deale;

L 1427 And stroakes gaue with might; L 1430 They prayed all ffor
the knight; L 1433 armes great (: itt gett); L 1440 itt waxed wonderous
dimm; L 1442 lasted that battell; L 1445 Through hawberke; L 1446
Hee smote of by the; L 1452 gan hye (: stroakes mightye); L 1455
Thus was the gyant dead; L 1457 was the people; L 1459 The[y]
mett him with; L 1462 Hight Madam de Armoroure (: the lyllye
fflower); L 1463 Receiued that gentle knight; L 1464 in that stoure;
L 1466 Against that ffeend to ffight;

L 1468 f.   And in purple and pall shee him cledd (: ledd)
                And in rich royall weede;

L 1470 with honor (: lord of towne and tower); L 1472 And her owne
selfe to meede; L 1473 Sir Lybius ffrened her; L 1480 tarryed; L 1481
And his mayden with renowne (: Sinadone); L 1482 outscape (: to
wrake); L 1496 With ffalse sorcerye; L 1499 Betwene the castel and
the tower; L 1504 That can soe much curtesye (: of that ladye);

L 1512 f.   Att a posterne there beside
                By night they gan out ryde;

L 1518 stout in ffere; L 1521 fforth on their way; L 1522 But lightly
on; L 1524 Till itt beffell vpon a day; L 1528 pauillyons; L 1530 Then
said sir Lybius; L 1531 J haue great; L 1533 They gathered dirt and
mire; L 1540 was cast out beffore; L 1543 without leasing;

L 1545 f.   There is no king soe well arrayed
                Tho he had before payd;

C 1492 he bidd thee; L 1559 beaugles; L 1560 all this towne; L 1562
But dirt; L 1563 And but thou thither;

L 1569 ff.   Sir Lybius sayd that were despite
                Thither J will goe ffull tyte
                If J be man on liue;

L 1572 Arthurs delight; L 1576 And lett vs now goe hastilye (: ready);
L 1577 Anon that wee were bowne; L 1579 Till they ca[m]e to;
L 1580 That was of great renowne; L 1590 To be a king he is worthye;
L 1593 went without ffable;

L 1609 f.   But euen anon went (: stent)
                To them lightlye att the yate;

L 1616 Sheild plate and basnett; L 1621 tale is well told; L 1622 And
pleasant; L 1625 In their best array;

L 1626 f.   Sir Lamberd armed ffull weele
                Both in jron and in steele;

L 1629 sure and; L 1636 Was his paytrell and his armoure; L 1639 by his sside; L 1643 Armed him ffull well and bright; L 1645 Feircely as any; L 1647 Him tooke a speare of great shape;

L 1650 f.   Soone he rode to him that stond
              With a speare that was round;

L 1655 Of theire speares long; L 1657 That younge knight is ffull bold; L 1658 To him with a speare he fflounge; L 1659 Sir Lamberd did stifflye ssitt; L 1660 He was wrath out of his witt; L 1663 For this knight is not to lere (: a speare); L 1667 And ffast together did run; L 1674 Sir Lamberd him soe hitt; L 1678 on the visor; L 1679 That of went his; L 1690 he made to ffett (: sitt bett); L 1691 shaft ffull meete; L 1693 on their helmes sett; L 1697 hee sett; L 1709 Thou art soe;

L 1710 ff.   If thou wilt ffight ffor my ladye
              Welcome thou art to mee
              By my troth J say;

L 1714 for my ladye; L 1715 J promised soe to; L 1720 Certes has brought; L 1724 Into my strong tower; L 1725 Then mayd Ellen anon rightes (: with 5 knights); L 1729 of 6 battells; L 1731 Lybius then (: with strong men); L 1733 And beene in stowers hardye; L 1736 That he were soe mightye; L 1737 They welcomed him with; L 1741 Of ancyents; L 1746 hath put in; L 1749 said soe mote J gone; C 1691 in body and in bone;

L 1756 ff.   Their artes fforto reade of sorcerye
              Mabam the hight one in deede
              And Jron hight the other verelye
              Cla[r]ckes of nigromancye;

L 1770 There they keepe in; L 1779 Jron trulye (: to death trulye); L 1787 That is soe much of might; L 1788 and soe ffaire; L 1790 For the dolour that shees in; L 1795 Smite of there anon (: Jron); L 1796 Theire heads in that stoure;

after L 1796:   And wine that lady bright
              And bring her to her right
              With ioy and much honor;

L 1798 In that strong castle (: tales to tell); L 1799 To supp and make good cheere (: and heare); L 1800 burgesse all (: hall); L 1803 How sir Lybius; L 1805 His talking forto harke (: starke); L 1809 And after they went to rest; C 1736 And tooke their;

L 1812 f.   On the morrow anon right
              Sir Lybius was armed bright;

L 1815 led him algate; L 1817 Open they were; L 1818 No man durst him neere bringe; L 1825 Sayd he shold backe againe; L 1826 And att home abyde; L 1827 Sir Gcfflett againe gan ryde (: fforto abyde); L 1836 and shaumes ywis; C 1763 He ffound; L 1841 Brening ffaire and; L 1847 All about the; L 1848 Of nothing; L 1849 He saw no body that there was; C 1777 and note; L 1854 And alsoe fiddle; L 1856 Ne say he neuer in; L 1860 euermore yode; L 1867 All was fflourished in the hall; L 1868 Itt was ffull ffaire and bright; L 1871 That ymagyrye itt was driue; L 1873 Noe ffairer in noe place; L1874 Maruelous fforto descriue; L 1877 That made the mirth soe gay; L 1885 About him downe; L 1889 That was him;

L 1890 f.　　　　　　The hall began forto breake
　　　　　　　　　　And soe did the wall eke;

L 1892 shold fall; L 1896 (*transposed with* L 1897) Now J am; L 1902 purple and pale; L 1903 Well harnished in that stoure; L 1904 With great; L 1913 That is in prison (: of Goddes sonne); L 1920 ffeircly; L 1921 fforto spill; L 1922 For that was his entent; L 1924 Either on others helme sett; L 1950 And stifflye gan to other flight; L 1955 Vp he rose againe; L 1958 Therof he was not ffaine; L 1961 And auenge him on his enemye (: himselfe manlye); L 1966 He ffought as a lyon (: Jron); L 1967 with wreake (: necke); L 1972 atwo his thye in that stoure (: worthy warryour); L 1973 Ski[n]e bone and blood;

L 1974 f.　　　　　　Then helped him not his clergye
　　　　　　　　　　Neither his ffalse sorcerye
　　　　　　　　　　But downe he ffell with sorry moode;

L 1980 they gaue with might (: sprang out ffull bright); L 1982 helme and harnesse; L 1983 As either ffast on other bett; L 1985 may now heare; L 1987 The sword of sir Lybius he did hew; L 1988 and cleare; L 1995 lithelye; L 1997 That sharpe edge had and hard; L 2000 And like a madman he ffared; L 2002 As he had beene a wyld man (: Mabam); L 2008 left hand; L 2019 shr[u]eed dint; L 2024 fforto kill; L 2029 shall cut the other blythe (: stroakes swythe); L 2032 Fought together ffast then (: and Mabam); L 2033 And lett ffor nothing againe (: in twayne); L 2034 That sir Lybius that good knight; L 2038 And to Jrom he went againe; L 2042 He went to him ffull right; L 2045 he list; L 2049–51 *lacking*; L 2052 As he stood and him bethought; L 2053 That itt wold; L 2054 was; L 2055 wold; L 2056 Doe much; L 2057 was much;

after L 2057:　　　He tooke his sword hastilye
　　　　　　　　　　And rode vpon a hill hye
　　　　　　　　　　And looked round about
　　　　　　　　　　Then he was ware of [a] valley
　　　　　　　　　　Thitherward he tooke the way
　　　　　　　　　　As a sterne knight and stout

　　　　　　　　　　As he rode by a riuer side
　　　　　　　　　　He was ware of him that tyde
　　　　　　　　　　Vpon the riuer brimm
　　　　　　　　　　He rode to him ffull hott
　　　　　　　　　　And of his head he smote
　　　　　　　　　　Fast by the chinn

And when he had him slaine
Fast hee tooke the way againe
Forto haue that lady gent
As soone as he did thither come
Of his horsse he light downe
And into the hall hee went

And sought that ladye ffaire and hend
But he cold her not find
Therfor he sighed ffull sore
Still he sate mourni[n]g
For that ladye ffaire and young
For her was all his care;

L 2058 (*transposed with* L 2059) But still he sate and sore he sight;

L 2062 f.   He heard a window in the wall
                 Faire itt gan vnheld;

L 2070 The wormes tayle; L 2072 And gay fforto beholde;

L 2073 ff.   Grislye great was her taile
                 The clawes large without ffayle
                 Lothelye was her bodye;

L 2078 beene a ffire him by; L 2079 Then was sir Lybius euill agast;
L 2084 And colled about his lyre; C 2011 She was; L 2090 Fairer he
saw; L 2092 As Christ had her shaped;

L 2094 f.   Shee sayd God that on the rood gan bleed
                 Sir knight quitt thee thy meede;

L 2097 now ffull right (: wicked of might); L 2104 had me meant;
L 2105 Ne woe to wrapp me in; L 2113 Right without; L 2116–17
lacking;

after L 2115:   And thanked God often sythe
                  That him that grace had sent
                  And sayd my lord faire and ffree
                  All my loue J leaue with thee
                  By God omnipotent

                  J will goe my ladye bright
                  To the castle gate ffull right
                  Thither fforto wend
                  Forto feitch your geere
                  That yee were wont to weare
                  And them J will you send

                  Alsoe if itt be your will
                  J pray you to abyde still
                  Till J co[m]e againe
                  Sir shee said J you pray
                  Wend fforth [on] your [w]ay
                  Therof J am ffaine;

L 2118–20 *lacking*; C 2049 Done them tormentrye;

L 2124 ff.　　Sir Lybius is to the castle come
　　　　　　　And to sir Lamberd he told anon
　　　　　　　And alsoe the barronye;

L 2128 And sir Jron both twayine; L 2130–41 *lacking*;

L 2142 ff.　　When that knight soe keene
　　　　　　　Had told how itt had beene
　　　　　　　To them all bydeene;

L 2145 A rich robe good and ffine (: good ermine); L 2147 that ladye
sheene; L 2150 That mayd he wold home bring; L 2152 Thither they
went anon right; L 2153 Both old and young; L 2156 home they ffett;
L 2157 they were; L 2162 That ffrom woe them had brought; L 2165
As of right they ought;

L 2169 f.　　They dwelled 7 dayes in the tower
　　　　　　　There sir Lamberd was gouernor;

L 2172 And then they rode; *the text ends at* L 2171 The knights all in
same　　Fins, *which is transposed with* L 2174 With mirth joy and game.

PRINTED IN GREAT BRITAIN
AT THE UNIVERSITY PRESS, OXFORD
BY VIVIAN RIDLER
PRINTER TO THE UNIVERSITY

EARLY ENGLISH TEXT SOCIETY

THE Subscription to the Society, which constitutes full membership for private members and libraries, is £3. 3s. (U.S. and Canadian members $9.00) a year for the annual publications, due in advance on the 1st of JANUARY, and should be paid by Cheque, Postal Order, or Money Order made out to 'The Early English Text Society', to Dr. A. M. Hudson, Executive Secretary, Early English Text Society, Lady Margaret Hall, Oxford.

The payment of the annual subscription is the only prerequisite of membership.

Private members of the Society (but not libraries) may select other volumes of the Society's publications instead of those for the current year. The value of texts allowed against one annual subscription is 100s. (U.S. members 110s.), and all such transactions must be made through the Executive Secretary.

Members of the Society (including institutional members) may also, through the Executive Secretary, purchase copies of past E.E.T.S. publications and reprints for their own use at a discount of 4d. in the shilling.

The Society's texts are also available to non-members at listed prices through any bookseller.

The Society's texts are published by the Oxford University Press.

The Early English Text Society was founded in 1864 by Frederick James Furnivall, with the help of Richard Morris, Walter Skeat, and others, to bring the mass of unprinted Early English literature within the reach of students and provide sound texts from which the New English Dictionary could quote. In 1867 an Extra Series was started of texts already printed but not in satisfactory or readily obtainable editions.

In 1921 the Extra Series was discontinued and all the publications of 1921 and subsequent years have since been listed and numbered as part of the Original Series. Since 1921 just over a hundred new volumes have been issued; and since 1957 alone more than a hundred and thirty volumes have been reprinted at a cost of £65,000.

In this prospectus the Original Series and Extra Series for the years 1867–1920 are amalgamated, so as to show all the publications of the Society in a single list.

From 1 April 1969, since many of the old prices had become uneconomic in modern publishing conditions, a new price structure was introduced and the new prices are shown in this list. From the same date the discount allowed to members was increased from 2d. in the shilling to 4d. in the shilling.

Original Series, 1864–1969. Extra Series, 1867–1920

O.S.
1. Early English Alliterative Poems, ed. R. Morris. (*Reprinted 1965.*) 54s.   1864
2. Arthur, ed. F. J. Furnivall. (*Reprinted 1965.*) 10s.   ,,
3. Lauder on the Dewtie of Kyngis, &c., 1556, ed. F. Hall. (*Reprinted 1965.*) 18s.   ,,
4. Sir Gawayne and the Green Knight, ed. R. Morris. (*Out of print, see O.S. 210.*)
5. Hume's Orthographie and Congruitie of the Britan Tongue, ed. H. B. Wheatley. (*Reprinted 1965.*) 18s.   1865
6. Lancelot of the Laik, ed. W. W. Skeat. (*Reprinted 1965.*) 42s.   ,,
7. Genesis & Exodus, ed. R. Morris. (*Out of print.*)   ,,
8. Morte Arthure, ed. E. Brock. (*Reprinted 1967.*) 25s.   ,,
9. Thynne on Speght's ed. of Chaucer, A.D. 1599, ed. G. Kingsley and F. J. Furnivall. (*Reprinted 1965.*) 55s.   ,,
10. Merlin, Part I, ed. H. B. Wheatley. (*Out of print.*)   ,,
11. Lyndesay's Monarche, &c., ed. J. Small. Part I. (*Out of print.*)   ,,
12. The Wright's Chaste Wife, ed. F. J. Furnivall. (*Reprinted 1965.*) 10s.   ,,
13. Seinte Marherete, ed. O. Cockayne. (*Out of print, see O.S. 193.*)   1866
14. King Horn, Floriz and Blauncheflur, &c., ed. J. R. Lumby, re-ed. G. H. McKnight. (*Reprinted 1962.*) 50s.   ,,
15. Political, Religious, and Love Poems, ed. F. J. Furnivall. (*Reprinted 1965.*) 63s.   ,,
16. The Book of Quinte Essence, ed. F. J. Furnivall. (*Reprinted 1965.*) 10s.   ,,
17. Parallel Extracts from 45 MSS. of Piers the Plowman, ed. W. W. Skeat. (*Out of print.*)   ,,
18. Hali Meidenhad, ed. O. Cockayne, re-ed. F. J. Furnivall. (*Out of print.*)   ,,
19. Lyndesay's Monarche, &c., ed. J. Small. Part II. (*Out of print.*)   ,,
20. Richard Rolle de Hampole, English Prose Treatises of, ed. G. G. Perry. (*Out of print.*)   ,,
21. Merlin, ed. H. B. Wheatley. Part II. (*Out of print.*)   ,,
22. Partenay or Lusignen, ed. W. W. Skeat. (*Out of print.*)   ,,
23. Dan Michel's Ayenbite of Inwyt, ed. R. Morris and P. Gradon. Vol. I, Text. (*Reissued 1965.*) 54s.   ,,
24. Hymns to the Virgin and Christ; The Parliament of Devils, &c., ed. F. J. Furnivall. (*Out of print.*)   1867
25. The Stacions of Rome, the Pilgrims' Sea-voyage, with Clene Maydenhod, ed. F. J. Furnivall. (*Out of print.*)   ,,
26. Religious Pieces in Prose and Verse, from R. Thornton's MS., ed. G. G. Perry. (*See under 1913.*) (*Out of print.*)   ,,
27. Levins' Manipulus Vocabulorum, a rhyming Dictionary, ed. H. B. Wheatley. (*Out of print.*)   ,,
28. William's Vision of Piers the Plowman, ed. W. W. Skeat. A–Text. (*Reprinted 1968.*) 35s.   ,,
29. Old English Homilies (1220–30), ed. R. Morris. Series I, Part I. (*Out of print.*)   ,,
30. Pierce the Ploughmans Crede, ed. W. W. Skeat. (*Out of print.*)   ,,

E.S.
1. William of Palerne or William and the Werwolf, re-ed. W. W. Skeat. (*Out of print.*)   ,,
2. Early English Pronunciation, by A. J. Ellis. Part I. (*Out of print.*)   ,,

O.S.
31. Myrc's Duties of a Parish Priest, in Verse, ed. E. Peacock. (*Out of print.*)   1868
32. Early English Meals and Manners: the Boke of Norture of John Russell, the Bokes of Keruynge, Curtasye, and Demeanor, the Babees Book, Urbanitatis, &c., ed. F. J. Furnivall. (*Out of print.*)   ,,
33. The Book of the Knight of La Tour-Landry, ed. T. Wright. (*Out of print.*)   ,,
34. Old English Homilies (before 1300), ed. R. Morris. Series I, Part II. (*Out of print.*)   ,,
35. Lyndesay's Works, Part III: The Historie and Testament of Squyer Meldrum, ed. F. Hall. (*Reprinted 1965.*) 18s.   ,,

E.S.
3. Caxton's Book of Curtesye, in Three Versions, ed. F. J. Furnivall. (*Out of print.*)   ,,
4. Havelok the Dane, re-ed. W. W. Skeat. (*Out of print.*)   ,,
5. Chaucer's Boethius, ed. R. Morris. (*Reprinted 1969.*) 40s.   ,,
6. Chevelere Assigne, re-ed. Lord Aldenham. (*Out of print.*)   ,,

O.S.
36. Merlin, ed. H. B. Wheatley. Part III. On Arthurian Localities, by J. S. Stuart Glennie. (*Out of print.*)   1869
37. Sir David Lyndesay's Works, Part IV, Ane Satyre of the thrie Estaits, ed. F. Hall. (*Out of print.*)   ,,
38. William's Vision of Piers the Plowman, ed. W. W. Skeat. Part II. Text B. (*Reprinted 1964.*) 42s.   ,,
39, 56. The Gest Hystoriale of the Destruction of Troy, ed. D. Donaldson and G. A. Panton. Parts I and II. (*Reprinted as one volume 1968.*) 110s.   ,,

E.S.
7. Early English Pronunciation, by A. J. Ellis. Part II. (*Out of print.*)
8. Queene Elizabethes Achademy, &c., ed. F. J. Furnivall. Essays on early Italian and German Books of Courtesy, by W. M. Rossetti and E. Oswald. (*Out of print.*)   ,,
9. Awdeley's Fraternitye of Vacabondes, Harman's Caveat, &c., ed. E. Viles and F. J. Furnivall. (*Out of print.*)   ,,

O.S.
40. English Gilds, their Statutes and Customs, A.D. 1389, ed. Toulmin Smith and Lucy T. Smith, with an Essay on Gilds and Trades-Unions, by L. Brentano. (*Reprinted 1963.*) 100s.   1870
41. William Lauder's Minor Poems, ed. F. J. Furnivall. (*Out of print.*)   ,,
42. Bernardus De Cura Rei Familiaris, Early Scottish Prophecies, &c., ed. J. R. Lumby. (*Reprinted 1965.*) 18s.   ,,
43. Ratis Raving, and other Moral and Religious Pieces, ed. J. R. Lumby. (*Out of print.*)   ,,

E.S.
10. Andrew Boorde's Introduction of Knowledge, 1547, Dyetary of Helth, 1542, Barnes in Defence of the Berde, 1542–3, ed. F. J. Furnivall. (*Out of print.*)   ,,
11, 55. Barbour's Bruce, ed. W. W. Skeat. Parts I and IV. (*Reprinted as Volume I 1968.*) 63s.   ,,

O.S.
44. The Alliterative Romance of Joseph of Arimathie, or The Holy Grail: from the Vernon MS.; with W. de Worde's and Pynson's Lives of Joseph: ed. W. W. Skeat. (*Out of print.*)   1871

2

O.S. 45. King Alfred's West-Saxon Version of Gregory's Pastoral Care, ed., with an English translation, by Henry Sweet. Part I. (*Reprinted* 1958.) 55s.   1871
  46. Legends of the Holy Rood, Symbols of the Passion and Cross Poems, ed. R. Morris. (*Out of print*.)   ,,
  47. Sir David Lyndesay's Works, ed. J. A. H. Murray. Part V. (*Out of print*.)   ,,
  48. The Times' Whistle, and other Poems, by R. C., 1616; ed. J. M. Cowper. (*Out of print*.)   ,,
E.S. 12. England in Henry VIII's Time: a Dialogue between Cardinal Pole and Lupset, by Thom. Starkey, Chaplain to Henry VIII, ed. J. M. Cowper. Part II. (*Out of print*, Part I is E.S. 32, 1878.)   ,,
  13. A Supplicacyon of the Beggers, by Simon Fish, A.D. 1528–9, ed. F. J. Furnivall, with A Supplication to our Moste Soueraigne Lorde, A Supplication of the Poore Commons, and The Decaye of England by the Great Multitude of Sheep, ed. J. M. Cowper. (*Out of print*.)   ,,
  14. Early English Pronunciation, by A. J. Ellis. Part III. (*Out of print*.)   ,,
O.S. 49. An Old English Miscellany, containing a Bestiary, Kentish Sermons, Proverbs of Alfred, and Religious Poems of the 13th cent., ed. R. Morris. (*Out of print*.)   1872
  50. King Alfred's West-Saxon Version of Gregory's Pastoral Care, ed. H. Sweet. Part II. (*Reprinted* 1958.) 50s.   ,,
  51. Þe Liflade of St. Juliana, 2 versions, with translations, ed. O. Cockayne and E. Brock. (*Reprinted* 1957.) 38s.   ,,
  52. Palladius on Husbondrie, englisht, ed. Barton Lodge. Part I. (*Out of print*.)   ,,
E.S. 15. Robert Crowley's Thirty-One Epigrams, Voyce of the Last Trumpet, Way to Wealth, &c., ed. J. M. Cowper. (*Out of print*.)   ,,
  16. Chaucer's Treatise on the Astrolabe, ed. W. W. Skeat. (*Reprinted* 1969.) 40s.   ,,
  17. The Complaynt of Scotlande, with 4 Tracts, ed. J. A. H. Murray. Part I. (*Out of print*.)   ,,
O.S. 53. Old-English Homilies, Series II, and three Hymns to the Virgin and God, 13th-century, with the music to two of them, in old and modern notation, ed. R. Morris. (*Out of print*.)   1873
  54. The Vision of Piers Plowman, ed. W. W. Skeat. Part III. Text C. (*Reprinted* 1959.) 55s.   ,,
  55. Generydes, a Romance, ed. W. Aldis Wright. Part I. (*Out of print*.)   ,,
E.S. 18. The Complaynt of Scotlande, ed. J. A. H. Murray. Part II. (*Out of print*.)   ,,
  19. The Myroure of oure Ladye, ed. J. H. Blunt. (*Out of print*.)   ,,
O.S. 56. The Gest Hystoriale of the Destruction of Troy, in alliterative verse, ed. D. Donaldson and G. A. Panton. Part II. (*See* O.S. 39.)   1874
  57. Cursor Mundi, in four Texts, ed. R. Morris. Part I. (*Reprinted* 1961.) 40s.   ,,
  58, 63, 73. The Blickling Homilies, ed. R. Morris. Parts I, II, and III. (*Reprinted as one volume* 1967.) 70s.   ,,
E.S. 20. Lovelich's History of the Holy Grail, ed. F. J. Furnivall. Part I. (*Out of print*.)   ,,
  21, 29. Barbour's Bruce, ed. W. W. Skeat. Parts II and III. (*Reprinted as Volume II* 1968.) 90s.   ,,
  22. Henry Brinklow's Complaynt of Roderyck Mors and The Lamentacyon of a Christen Agaynst the Cytye of London, made by Roderigo Mors, ed. J. M. Cowper. (*Out of print*.)   ,,
  23. Early English Pronunciation, by A. J. Ellis. Part IV. (*Out of print*.)   ,,
O.S. 59. Cursor Mundi, in four Texts, ed. R. Morris. Part II. (*Reprinted* 1966.) 50s. (*Out of print*.)   1875
  60. Meditacyuns on the Soper of our Lorde, by Robert of Brunne, ed. J. M. Cowper. (*Out of print*.)   ,,
  61. The Romance and Prophecies of Thomas of Erceldoune, ed. J. A. H. Murray. (*Out of print*.)   ,,
E.S. 24. Lovelich's History of the Holy Grail, ed. F. J. Furnivall. Part II. (*Out of print*.)   ,,
  25, 26. Guy of Warwick, 15th-century Version, ed. J. Zupitza. Pts. I and II. (*Reprinted as one volume* 1966.) 75s.   ,,
O.S. 62. Cursor Mundi, in four Texts, ed. R. Morris. Part III. (*Reprinted* 1966.) 40s.   1876
  63. The Blickling Homilies, ed. R. Morris. Part II. (*See* O.S. 58.)   ,,
  64. Francis Thynne's Embleames and Epigrams, ed. F. J. Furnivall. (*Out of print*.)   ,,
  65. Be Domes Dæge (Bede's *De Die Judicii*), &c., ed. J. R. Lumby. (*Reprinted* 1964.) 30s.   ,,
E.S. 26. Guy of Warwick, 15th-century Version, ed. J. Zupitza. Part II. (*See* E.S. 25)   ,,
  27. The English Works of John Fisher, ed. J. E. B. Mayor. Part I. (*Out of print*.)   ,,
O.S. 66. Cursor Mundi, in four Texts, ed. R. Morris. Part IV. (*Reprinted* 1966.) 40s.   1877
  67. Notes on Piers Plowman, by W. W. Skeat. Part I. (*Out of print*.)   ,,
E.S. 28. Lovelich's Holy Grail, ed. F. J. Furnivall. Part III. (*Out of print*.)   ,,
  29. Barbour's Bruce, ed. W. W. Skeat. Part III. (*See* E.S. 21.)   ,,
O.S. 68. Cursor Mundi, in 4 Texts, ed. R. Morris. Part V. (*Reprinted* 1966.) 40s.   1878
  69. Adam Davie's 5 Dreams about Edward II, &c., ed. F. J. Furnivall. 30s.   ,,
  70. Generydes, a Romance, ed. W. Aldis Wright. Part II. (*Out of print*.)   ,,
E.S. 30. Lovelich's Holy Grail, ed. F. J. Furnivall. Part IV. (*Out of print*.)   ,,
  31. The Alliterative Romance of Alexander and Dindimus, ed. W. W. Skeat. (*Out of print*.)   ,,
  32. Starkey's England in Henry VIII's Time. Part I. Starkey's Life and Letters, ed. S. J. Herrtage. (*Out of print*.)   ,,
O.S. 71. The Lay Folks Mass-Book, four texts, ed. T. F. Simmons. (*Reprinted* 1968.) 90s.   1879
  72. Palladius on Husbondrie, englisht, ed. S. J. Herrtage. Part II. 42s.   ,,
E.S. 33. Gesta Romanorum, ed. S. J. Herrtage. (*Reprinted* 1962.) 100s.   ,,
  34. The Charlemagne Romances: 1. Sir Ferumbras, from Ashm. MS. 33, ed. S. J. Herrtage. (*Reprinted* 1966.) 54s.   ,,
O.S. 73. The Blickling Homilies, ed. R. Morris. Part III. (*See* O.S. 58.)   1880
  74. English Works of Wyclif, hitherto unprinted, ed. F. D. Matthew. (*Out of print*.)   ,,
E.S. 35. Charlemagne Romances: 2. The Sege of Melayne, Sir Otuell, &c., ed. S. J. Herrtage. (*Out of print*.)   ,,
  36, 37. Charlemagne Romances: 3 and 4. Lyf of Charles the Grete, ed. S. J. Herrtage. Parts I and II. (*Reprinted as one volume* 1967.) 54s.   ,,
O.S. 75. Catholicon Anglicum, an English-Latin Wordbook, from Lord Monson's MS., A.D. 1483, ed., with Introduction and Notes, by S. J. Herrtage and Preface by H. B. Wheatley. (*Out of print*.)   1881
  76, 82. Ælfric's Lives of Saints, in MS. Cott. Jul. E VII, ed. W. W. Skeat. Parts I and II. (*Reprinted as Volume I* 1966.) 60s.   ,,

4

E.S. 126. Lydgate's Troy Book, ed. H. Bergen. Part IV. (*Out of print.*)   1920
O.S. 160. The Old English Heptateuch, MS. Cott. Claud. B. IV, ed. S. J. Crawford. (*Reprinted* 1969.) 75s.   1921
161. Three O.E. Prose Texts, MS. Cott. Vit. A. xv, ed. S. Rypins. (*Out of print.*)   ,,
162. Facsimile of MS. Cotton Nero A. x (Pearl, Cleanness, Patience and Sir Gawain), Introduction
    by I. Gollancz. (*Reprinted* 1955.) 200s.   1922
163. Book of the Foundation of St. Bartholomew's Church in London, ed. N. Moore. (*Out of print.*) 1923
164. Pecock's Folewer to the Donet, ed. Elsie V. Hitchcock. (*Out of print.*)   ,,
165. Middleton's Chinon of England, with Leland's Assertio Arturii and Robinson's translation, ed.
    W. E. Mead. (*Out of print.*)   ,,
166. Stanzaic Life of Christ, ed. Frances A. Foster. (*Out of print.*)   1924
167. Trevisa's Dialogus inter Militem et Clericum, Sermon by FitzRalph, and Bygynnyng of the
    World, ed. A. J. Perry. (*Out of print.*)   ,,
168. Caxton's Ordre of Chyualry, ed. A. T. P. Byles. (*Out of print.*)   1925
169. The Southern Passion, ed. Beatrice Brown. (*Out of print.*)   ,,
170. Walton's Boethius, ed. M. Science. (*Out of print.*)   ,,
171. Pecock's Reule of Cristen Religioun, ed. W. C. Greet. (*Out of print.*)   1926
172. The Seege or Batayle of Troye, ed. M. E. Barnicle. (*Out of print.*)   ,,
173. Hawes' Pastime of Pleasure, ed. W. E. Mead. (*Out of print.*)   1927
174. The Life of St. Anne, ed. R. E. Parker. (*Out of print.*)   ,,
175. Barclay's Eclogues, ed. Beatrice White. (*Reprinted* 1961.) 55s.   ,,
176. Caxton's Prologues and Epilogues, ed. W. J. B. Crotch. (*Reprinted* 1956.) 54s.   ,,
177. Byrhtferth's Manual, ed. S. J. Crawford. (*Reprinted* 1966.) 63s.   1928
178. The Revelations of St. Birgitta, ed. W. P. Cumming. (*Out of print.*)   ,,
179. The Castell of Pleasure, ed. B. Cornelius. (*Out of print.*)   ,,
180. The Apologye of Syr Thomas More, ed. A. I. Taft. (*Out of print.*)   1929
181. The Dance of Death, ed. F. Warren. (*Out of print.*)   ,,
182. Speculum Christiani, ed. G. Holmstedt. (*Out of print.*)   ,,
183. The Northern Passion (Supplement), ed. W. Heuser and Frances Foster. (*Out of print.*)   1930
184. The Poems of John Audelay, ed. Ella K. Whiting. (*Out of print.*)   ,,
185. Lovelich's Merlin, ed. E. A. Kock. Part III. (*Out of print.*)   ,,
186. Harpsfield's Life of More, ed. Elsie V. Hitchcock and R. W. Chambers. (*Reprinted* 1963.) 105s. 1931
187. Whittinton and Stanbridge's Vulgaria, ed. B. White. (*Out of print.*)   ,,
188. The Siege of Jerusalem, ed. E. Kölbing and Mabel Day. (*Out of print.*)   ,,
189. Caxton's Fayttes of Armes and of Chyualrye, ed. A. T. Byles. 63s.   1932
190. English Mediæval Lapidaries, ed. Joan Evans and Mary Serjeantson. (*Reprinted* 1960.) 50s. ,,
191. The Seven Sages, ed. K. Brunner. (*Out of print.*)   ,,
191A.On the Continuity of English Prose, by R. W. Chambers. (*Reprinted* 1966.) 25s.   ,,
192. Lydgate's Minor Poems, ed. H. N. MacCracken. Part II, Secular Poems. (*Reprinted* 1961.) 75s. 1933
193. Seinte Marherete, re-ed. Frances Mack. (*Reprinted* 1958.) 50s.   ,,
194. The Exeter Book, Part II, ed. W. S. Mackie. (*Reprinted* 1938.) 42s.   ,,
195. The Quatrefoil of Love, ed. I. Gollancz and M. Weale. (*Out of print.*)   1934
196. A Short English Metrical Chronicle, ed. E. Zettl. (*Out of print.*)   ,,
197. Roper's Life of More, ed. Elsie V. Hitchcock. (*Reprinted* 1958.) 35s.   ,,
198. Firumbras and Otuel and Roland, ed. Mary O'Sullivan. (*Out of print.*)   ,,
199. Mum and the Sothsegger, ed. Mabel Day and R. Steele. (*Out of print.*)   ,,
200. Speculum Sacerdotale, ed. E. H. Weatherly. (*Out of print.*)   1935
201. Knyghthode and Bataile, ed. R. Dyboski and Z. M. Arend. (*Out of print.*)   ,,
202. Palsgrave's Acolastus, ed. P. L. Carver. (*Out of print.*)   ,,
203. Amis and Amiloun, ed. McEdward Leach. (*Reprinted* 1960.) 50s.   ,,
204. Valentine and Orson, ed. Arthur Dickson. (*Out of print.*)   1936
205. Tales from the Decameron, ed. H. G. Wright. (*Out of print.*)   ,,
206. Bokenham's Lives of Holy Women (Lives of the Saints), ed. Mary S. Serjeantson. (*Out of print.*) ,,
207. Liber de Diversis Medicinis, ed. Margaret S. Ogden. (*Out of print.*)   ,,
208. The Parker Chronicle and Laws (facsimile), ed. R. Flower and A. H. Smith. (*Out of print.*) 1937
209. Middle English Sermons from MS. Roy. 18 B. xxiii, ed. W. O. Ross. (*Reprinted* 1960.) 75s. 1938
210. Sir Gawain and the Green Knight, ed. I. Gollancz. With Introductory essays by Mabel Day
    and M. S. Serjeantson. (*Reprinted* 1966.) 25s.   ,,
211. Dictes and Sayings of the Philosophers, ed. C. F. Bühler. (*Reprinted* 1961.) 75s.   1939
212. The Book of Margery Kempe, Part I, ed. S. B. Meech and Hope Emily Allen. (*Reprinted* 1961.)
    70s.   ,,
213. Ælfric's De Temporibus Anni, ed. H. Henel. (*Out of print.*)   1940
214. Morley's Translation of Boccaccio's De Claris Mulieribus, ed. H. G. Wright. (*Out of print.*) ,,
215. English Poems of Charles of Orleans, Part I, ed. R. Steele. (*Out of print.*)   1941
216. The Latin Text of the Ancrene Riwle, ed. Charlotte D'Evelyn. (*Reprinted* 1957.) 45s.   ,,
217. The Book of Vices and Virtues, ed. W. Nelson Francis. (*Reprinted* 1968.) 75s.   1942
218. The Cloud of Unknowing and the Book of Privy Counselling, ed. Phyllis Hodgson. (*Reprinted*
    1958.) 40s.   1943
219. The French Text of the Ancrene Riwle, B.M. Cotton MS. Vitellius. F. VII, ed. J. A. Herbert.
    (*Reprinted* 1967.) 55s.   ,,
220. English Poems of Charles of Orleans, Part II, ed. R. Steele and Mabel Day. (*Out of print.*) 1944
221. Sir Degrevant, ed. L. F. Casson. (*Out of print.*)   ,,
222. Ro. Ba.'s Life of Syr Thomas More, ed. Elsie V. Hitchcock and Mgr. P. E. Hallett. (*Reprinted*
    1957.) 63s.   1945
223. Tretyse of Loue, ed. J. H. Fisher. (*Out of print.*)   ,,
224. Athelston, ed. A. McI. Trounce. (*Reprinted* 1957.) 42s.   1946
225. The English Text of the Ancrene Riwle, B.M. Cotton MS. Nero A. XIV, ed. Mabel Day.
    (*Reprinted* 1957.) 50s.   ,,

226. Respublica, re-ed. W. W. Greg. (*Out of print.*) 1946
227. Kyng Alisaunder, ed. G. V. Smithers. Vol. I, Text. (*Reprinted* 1961.) 75s. 1947
228. The Metrical Life of St. Robert of Knaresborough, ed. J. Bazire. (*Reprinted* 1968.) 42s. „
229. The English Text of the Ancrene Riwle, Gonville and Caius College MS. 234/120, ed. R. M. Wilson. With Introduction by N. R. Ker. (*Reprinted* 1957.) 35s. 1948
230. The Life of St. George by Alexander Barclay, ed. W. Nelson. (*Reprinted* 1960.) 40s. „
231. Deonise Hid Diuinite, and other treatises related to *The Cloud of Unknowing*, ed. Phyllis Hodgson. (*Reprinted* 1958.) 50s. 1949
232. The English Text of the Ancrene Riwle, B.M. Royal MS. 8 C. 1, ed. A. C. Baugh. (*Reprinted* 1958.) 30s. „
233. The Bibliotheca Historica of Diodorus Siculus translated by John Skelton, ed. F. M. Salter and H. L. R. Edwards. Vol. I, Text. (*Reprinted* 1968.) 80s. 1950
234. Caxton : Paris and Vienne, ed. MacEdward Leach. (*Out of print.*) 1951
235. The South English Legendary, Corpus Christi College Cambridge MS. 145 and B.M. M.S. Harley 2277, &c., ed. Charlotte D'Evelyn and Anna J. Mill. Text, Vol. I. (*Reprinted* 1967.) 63s. „
236. The South English Legendary. Text, Vol. II. (*Reprinted* 1967.) 63s. 1952
[E.S. 87. Two Coventry Corpus Christi Plays, re-ed. H. Craig. Second Edition. (*Reprinted* 1967.) 30s.]
237. Kyng Alisaunder, ed. G. V. Smithers. Vol. II, Introduction, Commentary, and Glossary. 50s. 1953
238. The Phonetic Writings of Robert Robinson, ed. E. J. Dobson. (*Reprinted* 1968.) 30s. „
239. The Bibliotheca Historica of Diodorus Siculus translated by John Skelton, ed. F. M. Salter and H. L. R. Edwards. Vol. II. Introduction, Notes, and Glossary. 30s. 1954
240. The French Text of the Ancrene Riwle, Trinity College, Cambridge, MS. R. 14, 7, ed. W. H. Trethewey. 55s. „
241. Þe Wohunge of ure Lauerd, and other pieces, ed. W. Meredith Thompson. 45s. 1955
242. The Salisbury Psalter, ed. Celia Sisam and Kenneth Sisam. (*Reprinted* 1969.) 90s. 1955–56
243. George Cavendish : The Life and Death of Cardinal Wolsey, ed. Richard S. Sylvester. (*Reprinted* 1961.) 45s. 1957
244. The South English Legendary. Vol. III, Introduction and Glossary, ed. C. D'Evelyn. 30s. „
245. Beowulf (facsimile). With Transliteration by J. Zupitza, new collotype plates, and Introduction by N. Davis. (*Reprinted* 1967.) 100s. 1958
246. The Parlement of the Thre Ages, ed. M. Y. Offord. (*Reprinted* 1967.) 40s. 1959
247. Facsimile of MS. Bodley 34 (Katherine Group). With Introduction by N. R. Ker. 63s. „
248. Þe Liflade ant te Passiun of Seinte Iuliene, ed. S. R. T. O. d'Ardenne. 40s. 1960
249. Ancrene Wisse, Corpus Christi College, Cambridge, MS. 402, ed. J. R. R. Tolkien. With an Introduction by N. R. Ker. 50s. „
250. Laȝamon's Brut, ed. G. L. Brook and R. F. Leslie. Vol. I, Text (first part). 100s. 1961
251. Facsimile of the Cotton and Jesus Manuscripts of the Owl and the Nightingale. With Introduction by N. R. Ker. 50s. 1962
252. The English Text of the Ancrene Riwle, B.M. Cotton MS. Titus D. xviii, ed. Frances M. Mack, and Lanhydrock Fragment, ed. A. Zettersten. 50s. „
253. The Bodley Version of Mandeville's Travels, ed. M. C. Seymour. 50s. 1963
254. Ywain and Gawain, ed. Albert B. Friedman and Norman T. Harrington. 50s. „
255. Facsimile of B.M. MS. Harley 2253 (The Harley Lyrics). With Introduction by N. R. Ker. 100s. 1964
256. Sir Eglamour of Artois, ed. Frances E. Richardson. 50s. 1965
257. Sir Thomas Chaloner : The Praise of Folie, ed. Clarence H. Miller. 50s. „
258. The Orchard of Syon, ed. Phyllis Hodgson and Gabriel M. Liegey. Vol. I, Text. 100s. 1966
259. Homilies of Ælfric : A Supplementary Collection, ed. J. C. Pope. Vol. I. 100s. 1967
260. Homilies of Ælfric : A Supplementary Collection, ed. J. C. Pope. Vol. II. 100s. 1968
261. Lybeaus Desconus, ed. M. Mills. 50s. 1969
262. The Macro Plays, re-ed. Mark Eccles. 50s. „

Forthcoming volumes

263. Caxton's History of Reynard the Fox, ed. N. F. Blake. (*At press.*) 50s. 1970
264. Scrope's Epistle of Othea, ed. C. F. Bühler. (*At press.*) 50s. „
265. The Cyrurgie of Guy de Chauliac, ed. Margaret S. Ogden. Vol. I, Text. (*At Press.*) 100s. 1971
266. Wulfstan's Canons of Edgar, ed. R. G. Fowler. (*At press.*) 50s. 1972
267. The English Text of the Ancrene Riwle, B. M. Cotton MS. Cleopatra C. vi, ed. E. J. Dobson. (*At press.*) 50s. „

Other texts are in preparation.

Supplementary Texts

The Society proposes to issue some Supplementary Texts from time to time as funds allow. These will be sent to members as part of the normal issue and will also be available to non-members at listed prices. The first of these, Supplementary Text 1, expected to appear in 1970, will be *Non-Cycle Plays and Fragments*, ed. Norman Davis (about 50s.). This is a completely revised and re-set edition of the texts in Extra Series 104 with some additional pieces. Supplementary Text 2, expected to appear in 1971, will be *Caxton's Knight of La Tour Landry*, ed. M. Y. Offord (at press, about 50s.).

April 1969

Publisher: LONDON · THE OXFORD UNIVERSITY PRESS, ELY HOUSE, 37 DOVER ST., W. 1